THE BOOK OF LIFE

THE
BOOK OF LIFE

ARRANGED AND EDITED BY

Newton Marshall Hall, A.M., D.D.

PASTOR EMERITUS OF THE NORTH CHURCH, SPRINGFIELD, MASS.
AUTHOR OF CIVIC RIGHTEOUSNESS AND CIVIC PRIDE

AND

Irving Francis Wood, Ph.D., D.D.

PROFESSOR OF RELIGION AND BIBLICAL LITERATURE
SMITH COLLEGE, NORTHAMPTON, MASSACHUSETTS
AUTHOR OF THE SPIRIT OF GOD IN BIBLICAL LITERATURE

JOINT AUTHORS OF THE BIBLE STORY,
EARLY DAYS OF ISRAEL, DAYS OF THE KINGS OF ISRAEL,
ADULT CLASSES AND HOW TO
TEACH THEM

Volume Four

BIBLE PROPHETS, STATESMEN

JOHN RUDIN & COMPANY INC.
CHICAGO

* * *

TWELFTH EDITION
1945

PRINTED IN THE U. S. A.

NEW
VICTORY
EDITION

THE ENTRANCE OF THY WORD GIVETH LIGHT

TO

FROM

PREFACE

THE greatest literature of the world, the loftiest, the most inspired, is found in the sermons, messages, and poems of the great Hebrew prophets and statesmen. It is a portion of the Bible which has been greatly neglected except by keen-sighted, discerning men—leaders of the people, like Lincoln and Roosevelt in the North, Lee and Jackson in the South, Gladstone and John Bright in England. No man of exceptional power of the English-speaking race in any field of life has been without a knowledge of the great prophets of Israel. No part of the Bible is more rewarding, no part is more likely to furnish material for great ethical and spiritual awakening. The mightiest souls of the ages are speaking here the messages of God through his chosen and inspired servants. And yet there seems to be a barrier of difficulty for the modern reader. Every effort has been made in this volume to break this barrier down, to restore the background, to furnish by the introduction of explanatory matter, pictures, and notes the aid which will make the Biblical material live again in its old power and beauty.

6536

CONTENTS

Volume IV

THE PROPHETS AND THE EXILE

THE LOWER SLOPE OF OLIVET
FROM JERUSALEM

THE lower slopes of Mount Olivet as seen
from the eastern wall of Jerusalem.

The Prophets

FROM the days of Elisha to those of the earliest of the great prophets is a period of only forty years, but during this time great changes took place in the two kingdoms of Judah and Israel. Two great kings, Jeroboam II in the North and Uzziah in the South, began their long and prosperous reigns. The pressure from the mighty empires of Egypt and Assyria was temporarily relieved. The boundaries of the little kingdoms were enlarged until they came to be almost as wide as those of the empire of Solomon. A new civilization came into being. Up to this time, the people of the mountain kingdoms had lived very simple lives. Now the luxury of the days of Solomon came back. Commerce brought wealth and luxury. The city with all its evils was really born in this era. Heretofore, the palace was the residence of the king alone. Now rich merchants began to build palaces in the city and summer houses on the hills, houses furnished richly, with expensive woods inlaid with ivory.

It was not a time of the worship of heathen gods nor of laxness in religious observance. There were temples and altars and shrines in abundance, and sacrifices smoked on every altar. Tithes were paid with regularity. Religion was well patronized and supported. But there was no heart in it. The poor were oppressed, priests were so lacking in true religion that they robbed the worshipers. Faith was simply formal lip-service.

Into this period, to meet its needs, came prophets of a new kind. The usual understanding of the word "prophet" is "one who predicts future events." This was perhaps the smallest part of the work of the

Hebrew prophets. They did predict the judgment of God upon an evil and unrepentant people. They did promise a radiant future for Israel. They did tell of the coming of a king, a redeemer, the Messiah. Their work, however, was for the most part concerned with their own time. They were preachers of righteousness, a righteousness which extended through all the walks of life. The very modern idea prevailed that religion had nothing to do with politics, with business, or with private life. The prophets denounced this idea with the greatest vigor. No amount of formal religion, they said, would make up for moral laxity. The Lord, they said, would not be pleased with rivers of oil and thousands of beasts slain upon the altars. What God wished was not 'temple treading,' ostentatious sacrifices, but personal holiness, mercy, justice, righteousness, repentance: "He hath shewed thee, O man, what is good: and what doth the Lord require of thee but to do justly and love mercy and walk humbly with thy God?" Such passages might be called the gospel of the Old Testament, for the teaching of Jesus was along similar lines. The sins which the prophet denounced were those which are most marked in a high state of civilization: the abuse of wealth, the oppression of the poor, and, let it be noticed, the sin of drunkenness, about which almost every prophet speaks with the most severe condemnation.

The prophets were statesmen. They loved their country and they most ardently desired to save her from peril. The prophecy of Isaiah gives a striking picture of the corruption and weakness of the nation. Judah was rich. Nobles lived in luxury. From all ranks, king to commoner, the strength and virtue of the old days had departed. It was a time when every nerve should have been strained to prepare for the great invasion about to sweep down from the North.

Every wall in the kingdom should have been strengthened, every method of defense studied. It was a time for purification and prayer, a time for searching of hearts and strengthening of faith. Instead, money was spent for luxuries, strength was wasted in debaucheries, every kind of religion was fashionable, even the worship of Jehovah, but it was all outward form; there was no morality in it. Politically the attempt was made to substitute diplomacy for national virtue and strength, by making alliances rather than by the purging of the State from evil.

In reading the prophets, the political situation must always be borne in mind. These little kingdoms were always menaced by more powerful peoples. Palestine has been called the bridge between Asia and Africa. The most ancient caravan-routes are through its territory. It has been the battle-ground of the nations since the dawn of history. A constant tide of invasion has swept across the land, so that it has been, in Gladstone's expressive phrase, 'like the shingle on the seashore swept by the fierce tides of the sea." The danger of invasion is always the background of the prophets' messages. It must be remembered also that these messages were originally spoken, not written. They were gathered up and preserved, sometimes in a fragmentary condition, in later times. If they sometimes seem disjointed, difficult to follow and to understand, this is the reason. For this reason also they have not been read and studied as they deserve to be, for there is no more noble and inspiring literature in the world than this.

The prophets were statesmen and orators and social reformers, but they were more than these; they were the great religious teachers of the world. "No religious movement in the world was more important than prophecy. In the Hebrew and Christian religions it furnishes the religious basis for morals, for the worship of one God; for individual religion as over against national religion; for the conception of a personal relation between God and man. Every idea which later Judaism and Christianity cherished as essential came at least in germ from the prophets."

There is an element in the prophetical writings which we call "Messianic prophecy." The prophets were looking for a redeemed Israel, a glorified nation triumphant over its foes, a city on Mount Zion full of glory and beauty. This would come naturally through some great leader, and this "Messianic hope" reached its culmination in Isaiah 53, where the redeemer of Israel is pictured, not as a king, but as a suffering servant of God and of the nation: "He was wounded for our transgressions, he was bruised for our iniquities, the chastisement of our peace was upon him and with his stripes we are healed." When Jesus came and announced that he was the Messiah,—"I that speak unto thee am he"; "This day is the Scripture fulfilled in your sight,"—there were many who could not believe. Even his disciples found it difficult,—"We trusted that it had been he who should have redeemed Israel." When the Gospels and the Epistles were written, it was natural that the writers should have searched the prophets to discover proof and confirmation of their faith. They found many passages in which the germ of the gospel was lying like seed ready to spring up into full fruition, many passages in which the prophets, agonizing for Israel in those far-off days, but facing the light, believing in God, looking for the deliverance of the people, foretold the coming of a day of salvation. Even if they did not anticipate just what Jesus would be like, how broad would be the sweep of the gospel, to include in its redemption, not only little Israel on her rocky heights, but every nation in the whole earth,

these mighty souls would have been the first at Bethlehem and the last at the cross, the first to spread the
good news after the resurrection. The gospel is con-
tained in the prophetic books. There is no more use-
ful study than to find it and to compare it with the later
gospel in the Acts and the Epistles.

Amos

The Herdsman of Tekoa and His Message to Samaria

A Preacher of Social Righteousness

The city of Samaria, the capital of the Northern Kingdom, with its magnificent situation on a high hill almost impregnable against attack, had come to be a city of wealth and power. Its story is the familiar one of wealth without any sense of obligation, the hovel crowding the palace, some people overfed and some starving for want of food. It is a condition which may be found in any great city of the world to-day except for the fact that Christ had not then come to the world and there was no Christian pity. There were no hospitals, no agencies for relieving poverty and suffering, no consideration for the weak, no sympathy. We must admit that conditions are often very bad in modern civilization, but they were far worse in the days when Uzziah was king of Judah and Jeroboam II was king of Israel.

Into this city there came suddenly one day a shepherd from the hills of Judah. A shepherd in the streets of Samaria was nothing new, but this shepherd was different. He did not come just to sell wool or to buy supplies for his mountain home. He came with a message. Out there in the mountain pastures overlooking the Dead Sea, this shepherd, while he watched his sheep, had been thinking. Doubtless he had visited the great city before and what he saw he pondered during the long days and the nights full of stars. Like David, who kept his flocks in the same pastures, he meditated upon God in the night watches. He thought of God, but he also thought of men, the poor people in the slums of Samaria. His thought found expression, in burning, impassioned prose with an unstudied rhythm which often passes into poetry.

He went up to Samaria and he told people what he thought about them, — the priest, the rich man in the bazaar, the woman of fashion, the unjust judge, — in plain, straight-forward language of the hills. His message was like a strong wind from the hills in

9

that city of cruelty and oppression and gross immorality. He used homely illustrations, — a plumbline, a basket of summer fruit, a heavy wagon full of sheaves, the oaks, the cedars, the shepherd who rescues a bone or a bit of an ear from the lion which has ravaged the fold, the little bird in the snare, the man who, fleeing from a lion, is attacked by a bear, comes into the dark house, leans his hand upon the wall, and is bitten by a serpent. He spoke, too, of the rolling thunder when the storm marches upon the mountain tops, the unfailing stream, the constellations of Orion and the Pleiades.

He spoke of the simple justice demanded by Jehovah, of the old faith which had been turned into unrighteousness and immorality, of corrupt priests and conscienceless wealth. And he threatened doom — that doom which was already gathering in thunder clouds on the north — the coming of Assyria.

It was an astonished and outraged city which heard this strange message from the shepherd of the hills. Probably very few of the people paid any attention to it. The priests indignantly bade him be gone, and play the prophet in his own country. And he went back to his flocks and his herds.

He had spoken for Jehovah and his task was finished. He passed, but the spirit which he set in motion lives on forever. He was the first of a mighty line of prophets, the first voice crying from the wilderness, crying of righteousness and judgment, the first voice speaking for human rights, the first champion of the poor and the downtrodden. "He is," says a writer, "one of the most wonderful appearances in the history of the human spirit."

The Prophecy of Amos

The words of Amos, who was among the herdmen of Tekoa, which he saw concerning Israel in the days of Uzziah, King of Judah, and in the days of Jeroboam, the son of Joash, King of Israel, two years before the earthquake.

WARNINGS TO ALL THE STATES OF PALESTINE: AMOS CLEVERLY LEADS HIS HEARERS TO HIS CLIMAX

THE LORD will roar from Zion, and utter his voice from Jerusalem; and the habitations of the shepherds shall mourn, and the top of Carmel shall wither.

DAMASCUS

Thus saith the LORD: "For three transgressions of Damascus, and for four, I will not turn away the punishment thereof; because they have threshed Gilead with threshing instruments of iron: but I will send a fire into the House of Hazael, which shall devour the palaces of Ben-hadad. I will break also the bar of Damascus, and cut off the inhabitant from the plain of Aven, and him that holdeth the sceptre from the house of Eden: and the people of Syria shall go into captivity unto Kir," saith the LORD.

GAZA

Thus saith the LORD: "For three transgressions of Gaza, and for four, I will not turn away the punishment thereof; because they carried away captive the

TEKOA
Photograph by
The Reverend Doctor Charles W. Gilkey
This was the home of the Prophet Amos. On these rocky hills he kept his flocks.

A WRETCHED VILLAGE OF PALESTINE
Photograph by
Professor Lewis Bayles Paton

It was in such wretched mud huts as these that the poor people lived in the days of the prophets while the rich were living in "cut stone" houses with "ivory furniture."

"Forasmuch therefore as your treading is upon the poor, and ye take from him burdens of wheat: ye have built houses of hewn stone, but ye shall not dwell in them."—*Amos 5:11.*

whole captivity, to deliver them up to Edom: but I will send a fire on the wall of Gaza, which shall devour the palaces thereof: and I will cut off the inhabitant from Ashdod, and him that holdeth the sceptre from Ashkelon, and I will turn mine hand against Ekron: and the remnant of the Philistines shall perish," saith the Lord GOD.

TYRE

Thus saith the LORD: "For three transgressions of Tyrus, and for four, I will not turn away the punishment thereof; because they delivered up the whole captivity to Edom, and remembered not the brotherly covenant: but I will send a fire on the wall of Tyrus, which shall devour the palaces thereof."

EDOM

Thus saith the LORD: "For three transgressions of Edom, and for four, I will not turn away the punishment thereof; because he did pursue his brother with the sword, and did cast off all pity, and his anger did tear perpetually, and he kept his wrath forever: but I will send a fire upon Teman, which shall devour the palaces of Bozrah."

AMMON

Thus saith the LORD: "For three transgressions of the children of Ammon, and for four, I will not turn away the punishment thereof; because they have ripped up the women with child of Gilead, that they might enlarge their border: but I will kindle a fire in the wall of Rabbah, and it shall devour the palaces thereof, with shouting in the day of battle, with a tempest in the day of the whirlwind: and their king shall go into captivity, he and his princes together," saith the LORD.

MOAB

Thus saith the LORD: "For three transgressions of Moab, and for four, I will not turn away the punishment thereof; because he burned the bones of the king of Edom into lime: but I will send a fire upon Moab, and it shall devour the palaces of Kirioth: and Moab shall die with tumult, with shouting, and with the sound of the trumpet: and I will cut off the judge from the midst thereof, and will slay all the princes thereof with him," saith the LORD.

JUDAH

Thus saith the LORD: "For three transgressions of Judah, and for four, I will not turn away the punishment thereof; because they have despised the law of the LORD, and have not kept his commandments, and their lies caused them to err, after the which their fathers have walked: but I will send a fire upon Judah, and it shall devour the palaces of Jerusalem."

THE DOOM COMES HOME TO ISRAEL HERSELF

Thus saith the LORD: "For three transgressions of Israel, and for four, I will not turn away the punishment thereof; because they sold the righteous for silver, and the poor for a pair of shoes; that pant after the dust of the earth on the head of the poor, and turn aside the way of the meek: and a man and his father will go in unto the same maid, to profane my holy name: and they lay themselves down upon clothes laid to pledge by every altar, and they drink the wine of the condemned in the house of their god. Yet destroyed I the Amorite before them, whose height was like the height of the cedars, and he was strong as the oaks; yet I destroyed his fruit from above, and his roots from beneath. Also I brought you up from the land of Egypt, and led you forty years through the wilderness, to possess the land of the Amorite. And I raised up of your sons for prophets, and of your young men for Nazarites. Is it not even thus, O ye children of Israel?" saith the LORD. "But ye gave the Nazarites wine to drink; and commanded the prophets, saying, 'Prophesy not.' Behold, I am pressed under you, as a cart is pressed that is full of sheaves. Therefore the flight shall perish from the swift, and the strong shall not strengthen his force, neither shall the mighty deliver himself: neither shall he stand that handleth the bow; and he that is swift of foot shall not deliver himself: neither shall he that rideth the horse deliver himself. And he that is courageous among the mighty shall flee away naked in that day," saith the LORD.

— Amos 1;2.

ISRAEL'S CRIMES AND DOOM

"YOU ONLY HAVE I KNOWN OF ALL THE FAMILIES OF THE EARTH: THEREFORE I WILL PUNISH YOU"

Hear this word that the LORD hath spoken against you, O children of Israel, against the whole family which I brought up from the land of Egypt, saying, "You only have I known of all the families of the earth: therefore I will punish you for all your iniquities."

Can two walk together, except they be agreed? Will a lion roar in the forest, when he hath no prey? Will a young lion cry out of his den, if he have taken nothing? Can a bird fall in a snare upon the earth, where no gin is for him? Shall one take up a snare from the earth, and have taken nothing at all? Shall a trumpet be blown in the city, and the people not be afraid? Shall there be evil in a city, and the LORD hath not done it? Surely the Lord GOD will do nothing, but he revealeth his secret unto his servants, the prophets. The lion hath roared, who will not fear? The Lord GOD hath spoken, who can but prophesy?

PEASANTS BRINGING IN HAY FROM THE FIELDS

Photograph by W. A. Pottenger expressly for The Book of Life

There are no hay carts in Palestine. The hay is brought in on the backs of donkeys, or, as in the picture, on the heads of peasants. Amos speaks of the "king's mowings." Probably slaves brought the hay in for the royal stables in just this fashion.

Publish in the palaces at Ashdod, and in the palaces in the land of Egypt, and say, "Assemble yourselves upon the mountains of Samaria, and behold the great tumults in the midst thereof, and the oppressed in the midst thereof."

"For they know not to do right," saith the LORD, "who store up violence and robbery in their palaces."

Therefore thus saith the Lord GOD: "An adversary there shall be even round about the land; and he shall bring down thy strength from thee, and thy palaces shall be spoiled."

Thus saith the LORD: "As the shepherd taketh out of the mouth of the lion two legs, or a piece of an ear.; so shall the children of Israel be taken out that dwell in Samaria in the corner of a bed, and in Damascus in a couch. Hear ye, and testify in the house of Jacob," saith the Lord GOD, the God of hosts, "that in the day that I shall visit the transgressions of Israel upon him I will also visit the altars of Beth-el: and the horns of the altar shall be cut off, and fall to the ground. And I will smite the winter house with the summer house; and the houses of ivory shall perish, and the great houses shall have an end," saith the LORD.

THE DOOM OF THE IDLE AND HEARTLESS WOMEN OF ISRAEL

Hear this word, ye kine of Bashan, that are in the mountain of Samaria, which oppress the poor, which crush the needy, which say to their masters, "Bring, and let us drink." The Lord GOD hath sworn by his holiness, that, lo, the days shall come upon you, that he will take you away with hooks, and your posterity with fishhooks. "And ye shall go out at the breaches, every cow at that which is before her; and ye shall cast them into the palace"; saith the LORD.

THE PEOPLE MAY SACRIFICE BUT IT IS VAIN. THE LORD IS PUNISHING THEM

"Come to Beth-el, and transgress; at Gilgal multiply transgression; and bring your sacrifices every morning, and your tithes after three years: and offer a sacrifice of thanksgiving with leaven, and proclaim and publish the free offerings: for this liketh you, O ye children of Israel," saith the Lord GOD.

"And I also have given you cleanness of teeth in all your cities, and want of bread in all your places: yet have ye not returned unto me," saith the LORD. "And also I have withholden the rain from you, when there were yet three months to the harvest: and I caused it to rain upon one city, and caused it not to rain upon another city: one piece was rained upon, and the piece whereupon it rained not withered. So two or three cities wandered unto one city, to drink water; but they were not satisfied: yet have ye not returned unto me," saith the LORD. "I have smitten you with blasting and mildew: when your gardens and your vineyards and your fig-trees and your olive-trees increased, the palmerworm devoured them: yet have ye not returned unto me," saith the LORD. "I have sent among you the pestilence after the manner of Egypt: your young men have I slain with the sword, and have taken away your horses; and I have made the stink of your camps to come up unto your nostrils: yet have ye not returned unto me," saith the LORD. "I have overthrown some of you, as God overthrew Sodom and Gomorrah, and ye were as a firebrand plucked out of the burning: yet have ye not returned unto me," saith the LORD.

AN UNKNOWN DOOM YET AWAITS A REBELLIOUS PEOPLE

"HE THAT FORMETH THE MOUNTAINS, THE LORD, THE GOD OF HOSTS, IS HIS NAME"

"Therefore thus will I do unto thee, O Israel: and because I will do this unto thee, prepare to meet thy God, O Israel. For, lo, he that formeth the mountains, and createth the wind, and declareth unto man what is his thought, that maketh the morning darkness, and treadeth upon the high places of the earth, The LORD, The God of hosts, is his name."   — Amos 3;4.

SHEEP AT TEKOA

Photograph by
the Reverend Doctor Charles W. Gilkey

These sheep might have formed a part of the flock of Amos, the prophet, in the days when he pondered the great things of God while he pastured his flocks in this barren pasture land.

THE LAMENT OF THE PROPHET

"SEEK YE ME AND YE SHALL LIVE"

Hear ye this word which I take up against you, even a lamentation, O house of Israel. The virgin of Israel is fallen; she shall no more rise: she is forsaken upon her land; there is none to raise her up. For thus saith the Lord GOD: "The city that went out by a thousand shall leave an hundred, and that which went forth by an hundred shall leave ten, to the house of Israel."

For thus saith the LORD unto the house of Israel, "Seek ye me, and ye shall live: but seek not Beth-el, nor enter into Gilgal, and pass not to Beer-sheba: for Gilgal shall surely go into captivity, and Beth-el shall come to naught. Seek the LORD, and ye shall live; lest he break out like fire in the house of Joseph, and devour it, and there be none to quench it in Beth-el."

"SEEK HIM THAT MAKETH THE PLEIADES AND ORION AND TURNETH THE SHADOW OF DEATH INTO MORNING. THE LORD IS HIS NAME"

Ye who turn judgment to wormwood, and leave off righteousness in the earth, seek him that maketh the seven stars and Orion, and turneth the shadow of death into the morning, and maketh the day dark with night: that calleth for the waters of the sea, and poureth them out upon the face of the earth: the LORD is his name: that strengtheneth the spoiled against the strong, so that the spoiled shall come against the fortress. They hate him that rebuketh in the gate, and they abhor him that speaketh uprightly. Forasmuch therefore as your treading is upon the poor, and ye take from him burdens of wheat: ye have built houses of hewn stone, but ye shall not dwell in them; ye have planted pleasant vineyards, but ye shall not drink wine of them. For I know your manifold transgressions and your mighty sins: they afflict the just, they take a bribe, and they turn aside the poor in the gate from their right. Therefore the prudent shall keep silence in that time; for it is an evil time. Seek good, and not evil, that ye may live: and so the LORD, the God of hosts, shall be with you, as ye have spoken. Hate the evil, and love the good, and establish judgment in the gate: it may be that the LORD God of hosts will be gracious unto the remnant of Joseph.

Therefore the LORD, the God of hosts, the LORD, saith thus: "Wailing shall be in all streets; and they shall say in all the highways, 'Alas! alas!' and they shall call the husbandman to mourning, and such as are skilful of lamentation to wailing. And in all vineyards shall be wailing: for I will pass through thee," saith the LORD.   — Amos 5:1–17.

The Day of the Lord Must Come with Pain and Punishment

"Woe unto you that desire the day of the Lord! to what end is it for you? The day of the Lord is darkness, and not light. As if a man did flee from a lion, and a bear met him; or went into the house, and leaned his hand on the wall, and a serpent bit him. Shall not the day of the Lord be darkness, and not light? even very dark, and no brightness in it?"

"I hate your feasts and your solemn assemblies"

"I hate, I despise your feast days, and I will not smell in your solemn assemblies. Though ye offer me burnt offerings and your meat offerings, I will not accept them: neither will I regard the peace offerings of your fat beasts. Take thou away from me the noise of thy songs; for I will not hear the melody of thy viols. But let judgment run down as waters, and righteousness as a mighty stream. Have ye offered unto me sacrifices and offerings in the wilderness forty years, O house of Israel? But ye have borne the tabernacle of your Moloch and Chiun your images, the star of your god, which ye made to yourselves. Therefore will I cause you to go into captivity beyond Damascus," saith the Lord, whose name is The God of hosts. —Amos 5:18–27.

"Woe to Them That Are at Ease in Zion"

Woe to them that are at ease in Zion, and trust in the mountain of Samaria, which are named chief of the nations, to whom the house of Israel came! Pass ye unto Calneh, and see; and from thence go ye to Hamath the great: then go down to Gath of the Philistines: be they better than these kingdoms or their border greater than your border? Ye that put far away the evil day, and cause the seat of violence to come near; that lie upon beds of ivory, and stretch themselves upon their couches, and eat the lambs out of the flock, and the calves out of the midst of the stall; that chant to the sound of the viol, and invent to themselves instruments of music, like David; that drink wine in bowls, and anoint themselves with the chief ointments: but they are not grieved for the affliction of Joseph.

Therefore now shall they go captive with the first that go captive, and the banquet of them that stretched themselves shall be removed. The Lord GOD hath sworn by himself; saith the LORD the God of hosts, "I abhor the excellency of Jacob, and hate his palaces: therefore will I deliver up the city with all that is therein." And it shall come to pass, if there remain ten men in one house, that they shall die. And a man's uncle shall take him up, and he that burneth him, to bring out the bones out of the house, and shall say unto him that is by the sides of the house, "Is there yet any with thee?" and he shall say, "No." Then shall he say, "Hold thy tongue: for we may not make mention of the name of the LORD. For, behold, the LORD commandeth, and he will smite the great house with breaches, and the little house with clefts."

Shall horses run upon the rock? Will one plow there with oxen? For ye have turned judgment into gall, and the fruit of righteousness into hemlock: ye which rejoice in a thing of naught, which say, "Have we not taken to us horns by our own strength?"

"But, behold, I will raise up against you a nation, O house of Israel," saith the LORD, the God of hosts; "and they shall afflict you from the entering in of Hemath unto the river of the wilderness."　　--Amos 6.

Visions of Amos

THE GRASSHOPPERS WHICH CAME AFTER THE KING'S MOWINGS

Thus hath the Lord God shewed unto me; and, behold, he formed grasshoppers in the beginning of the shooting up of the latter growth; and, lo, it was the latter growth after the king's mowings. And it came to pass, that when they had made an end of eating the grass of the land, then I said, "O Lord God, forgive, I beseech thee: by whom shall Jacob arise, for he is small?"

The Lord repented for this: "It shall not be," saith the Lord.

DROUGHT

Thus hath the Lord God shewed unto me: and, behold, the Lord God called to contend by fire, and it devoured the great deep, and did eat up a part. Then said I, "O Lord God, cease, I beseech thee: by whom shall Jacob arise, for he is small?"

The Lord repented for this: "This also shall not be," saith the Lord God.

THE LESSON OF THE PLUMBLINE

Thus he showed me: and, behold, the Lord stood upon a wall made by a plumbline, with a plumbline in his hand. And the Lord said unto me, "Amos, what seest thou?"

And I said, "A plumbline."

Then said the Lord, "Behold, I will set a plumbline in the midst of my people Israel: I will not again pass by them any more: and the high places of Isaac shall be desolate, and the sanctuaries of Israel shall be laid waste; and I will rise against the house of Jeroboam with the sword."

— Amos 7:1-9.

How Amaziah, the Priest of Beth-el, Tried to Silence Amos, and the Prophet's Reply

Then Amaziah, the priest of Beth-el, sent to Jeroboam, King of Israel, saying, "Amos hath conspired against thee in the midst of the house of Israel: the land is not able to bear all his words. For thus Amos saith, 'Jeroboam shall die by the sword, and Israel shall surely be led away captive out of their own land.'"

Also Amaziah said unto Amos, "O thou seer, go, flee thee away into the land of Judah, and there eat bread, and prophesy there: but prophesy not again any more at Beth-el: for it is the king's chapel, and it is the king's court."

"I Was an Herdman, and a Gatherer of Sycamore Fruit"

Then answered Amos, and said to Amaziah, "I was no prophet, neither was I a prophet's son; but I was an herdman, and a gatherer of sycamore fruit: and the LORD took me as I followed the flock, and the LORD said unto me, 'Go, prophesy unto my people Israel.' Now therefore hear thou the word of the LORD. Thou sayest, 'Prophesy not against Israel, and drop not thy word against the house of Isaac.'

"Therefore thus saith the LORD: 'Thy wife shall be an harlot in the city, and thy sons and thy daughters shall fall by the sword, and thy land shall be divided by line; and thou shalt die in a polluted land: and Israel shall surely go into captivity forth of his land.'"

— Amos 7:10–17.

The Lesson of the Summer Fruit

Thus hath the Lord GOD shewed unto me: and behold a basket of summer fruit. And he said, "Amos, what seest thou?"

And I said, "A basket of summer fruit."

Then said the LORD unto me, "The end is come upon my people of Israel; I will not again pass by them any more. And the songs of the temple shall be howlings in that day," saith the Lord GOD: "there shall be many dead bodies in every place; they shall cast them forth with silence."

— Amos 8:1–3.

"WOE TO THEM THAT BUY THE POOR FOR SILVER AND THE NEEDY FOR A PAIR OF SHOES"

Hear this, O ye that swallow up the needy, even to make the poor of the land to fail, saying, "When will

WILDERNESS OF JUDEA

Photograph by W. A. Pottenger expressly for The Book of Life

"When you realize that this howling waste came within reach of nearly every Jewish child; when you climb the Mount of Olives, or any hill about Bethlehem, or the hill of Tekoa, and, looking east, see those fifteen miles of chaos, sinking to a stretch of the Dead Sea, you begin to understand the influence of the desert on Jewish imagination and literature. It gave the ancient natives of Judea, as it gives the mere visitor of to-day, the sense of living next door to doom; the sense of how narrow is the border between life and death; the awe of the power of God, who can make contiguous regions so opposite in character. *"He turneth rivers into a wilderness, and watersprings into thirsty ground."* The desert is always in the face of the prophets, and its howling of beasts and its dry sand blow mournfully across their pages the foreboding of judgment."—*George Adam Smith.*

This is the region in which both David and Amos pastured their sheep.

the new moon be gone, that we may sell corn? And the Sabbath, that we may set forth wheat, making the ephah small, and the shekel great, and falsifying the balances by deceit? That we may buy the poor for silver, and the needy for a pair of shoes; yea, and sell the refuse of the wheat?"

The LORD hath sworn by the excellency of Jacob, "Surely I will never forget any of their works. Shall not the land tremble for this, and every one mourn that dwelleth therein? And it shall rise up wholly as a flood; and it shall be cast out and drowned, as by the flood of Egypt.

"And it shall come to pass in that day," saith the Lord GOD, "that I will cause the sun to go down at noon, and I will darken the earth in the clear day: and I will turn your feasts into mourning, and all your songs into lamentation; and I will bring up sackcloth upon all loins, and baldness upon every head; and I will make it as the mourning of an only son, and the end thereof as a bitter day.

A FAMINE FOR THE WORD OF THE LORD SHALL COME UPON THE PEOPLE

"Behold, the days come," saith the Lord GOD, "that I will send a famine in the land, not a famine of bread, nor a thirst for water, but of hearing the words of the LORD: and they shall wander from sea to sea, and from the north even to the east, they shall run to and fro to seek the word of the LORD, and shall not find it. In that day shall the fair virgins and young men faint for thirst. They that swear by the sin of Samaria, and say, 'Thy god, O Dan, liveth'; and, 'The manner of Beer-sheba liveth'; even they shall fall, and never rise up again."   — Amos 8:4–14.

The Vision of the Lord Ready to Smite: the Power of God

I saw the Lord standing upon the altar: and he said, "Smite the lintel of the door, that the posts may shake: and cut them in the head, all of them; and I will slay the last of them with the sword: he that fleeth of them shall not flee away, and he that escapeth of them shall not be delivered. Though they dig into hell, thence shall mine hand take them; though they climb up to heaven, thence will I bring them down: and though they hide themselves in the top of Carmel, I will search and take them out thence; and though they be hid from my sight in the bottom of the sea, thence will I command the serpent, and he shall bite them: and though they go into captivity before their enemies, thence will I command the sword, and it shall slay them: and I will set mine eyes upon them for evil, and not for good.

"And the Lord God of hosts is he that toucheth the land, and it shall melt, and all that dwell therein shall mourn: and it shall rise up wholly like a flood; and shall be drowned, as by the flood of Egypt. It is he that buildeth his stories in the heaven, and hath founded his troop in the earth; he that calleth for the waters of the sea, and poureth them out upon the face of the earth: The Lord is his name. Are ye not as children of the Ethiopians unto me, O children of Israel?" saith the Lord. "Have not I brought up Israel out of the land of Egypt, and the Philistines from Caphtor, and the Syrians from Kir? Behold, the eyes of the Lord God are upon the sinful kingdom, and I will destroy it from off the face of the earth; saving that I will not utterly destroy the house of Jacob," saith the Lord. "For, lo, I will command, and I will sift the house of Israel among all nations, like as corn is sifted in a sieve, yet shall not the least grain fall upon the earth. All the sinners of my people shall die by the sword, which say, 'The evil shall not overtake nor prevent us.'"

— Amos 9:1–10.

A Prophecy of Hope: the Tabernacle of David Shall Be Raised Up

In later days, after the fall of Jerusalem, some one added to Amos' words of doom a promise of hope. This promise was not for North Israel, which had long ago been swept away, as Amos had threatened, but for Judah. Perhaps it was added to show that God is not only a God of punishment, as Amos had pictured him, but a God of mercy as well.

"In that day will I raise up the tabernacle of David that is fallen, and close up the breaches thereof; and I will raise up his ruins, and I will build it as in the days of old: that they may possess the remnant of Edom, and of all the heathen, which are called by my name," saith the Lord that doeth this.

"Behold, the days come," saith the Lord, "that the plowman shall overtake the reaper, and the treader of grapes him that soweth seed; and the mountains shall drop sweet wine, and all the hills shall melt. And I will bring again the captivity of my people of Israel, and they shall build the waste cities, and inhabit them; and they shall plant vineyards, and drink the wine thereof; they shall also make gardens, and eat the fruit of them. And I will plant them upon their land, and they shall no more be pulled up out of their land which I have given them," saith the Lord thy God.

— Amos 9:11–15.

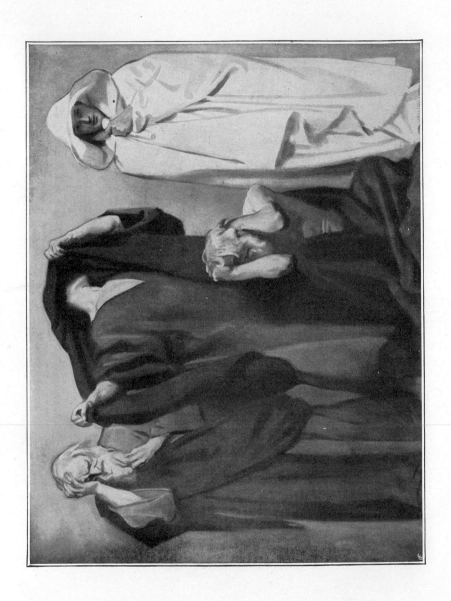

Hosea, the Evangelist of the Love of God

Hosea was a prophet of the Northern Kingdom who came a little later than Amos. Conditions were even worse than when Amos delivered his message. Evil had grown so rampant in Samaria that the house of worship was profaned by lewdness and blood, and bands of priests even robbed and murdered pilgrims on the way to the sanctuary. To this corrupt and degraded civilization, Hosea came, not simply as a prophet of doom, but as an evangelist, bringing a message of the undying love of God for his sinful people.

Hosea's message, intimate and tender, grew out of his own personal experience, his own agony of soul. It must have been very hard for Hosea to tell the story of his bitter shame, the tragedy of his wrecked home. His manner of telling it reveals the agony of his soul. He had, it seems, a wife who was unfaithful, who left his dishonored home. Later he found her in the market place, all her charm and attraction gone, a poor, sad thing, and he bought her, paying the price of a common household slave. He loved her still, forgave her, and hoped that she might, under the discipline of pain and sorrow, be worthy to be called his wife.

From his own experience, he turns to the nation which has sinned grievously, and gives his message that God loves Israel still. No matter how far the people have wandered, no matter how stained by sin, God is merciful and he will pardon. It is the first great message of forgiveness through repentance.

The style of the book is irregular and disjointed, like the broken words of a man under the stress of great grief. With attentive study it is possible to reconstruct a very delightful picture of this man. A lover of nature, even the beasts come within the wide scope of his love, — "and in that day, I will make a covenant for them with the beasts of the field and with the creeping things of the ground." "With Hosea, we feel all the seasons of the Syrian year: early rain and latter rain, the first flush of the young corn, the scent of the vine blossom, 'the first ripe fig of the fig-tree in her first season,' the bursting of the lily; the wild vine trailing on the hedge, the field of tares, the beauty of the full olive in sunshine and breeze; the mists and heavy dews of a summer morning in Ephraim, the night winds laden with the air of the mountains, 'the scent of Lebanon.' Or is it the dearer human sights in valley and field: the smoke from the hearth, the chaff from the threshing-floor, the doves startled to their towers, the fowler and his net; the breaking up of the fallow ground, the harrowing of the clods, the reapers, the heifer that treadeth out the corn; the team of draught oxen surmounting the steep road, and at the top the kindly driver feeding them. Where, I say, do we find anything like this, save in the parables of Jesus? For the love of Hosea was as the love of that greater Galilean; however high, however lonely it soared, it was yet rooted in the common life below, and fed with the unfailing grace of a thousand homely sources."

We have then the picture of a sweet-natured, kindly man, a poet, a gentleman, a man who loved God with all his heart, who took his own bitter grief and used it for the redemption of his people. This portrait is all the more notable because it stands against a background of lurid evil. We must not feel that the prophet altogether failed because the nation did not repent, but went on, heedless, to destruction. It may be that many a heart in Israel was touched by that message and brought to a knowledge of the redemptive love of God just as the message has lived and has always touched new hearts through all the ages. He put into Hebrew thought the idea of the tender love of God, and when we meet it in later song and prophecy, we may think of it as the fine flower from Hosea's suffering.

The Prophecy of Hosea

The word of the LORD that came unto Hosea, the son of Beeri, in the days of Uzziah, Jotham, Ahaz, and Hezekiah, Kings of Judah, and in the days of Jeroboam, the son of Joash, King of Israel. The beginning of the word of the LORD by Hosea.

HOSEA TAKES A WIFE

AND the LORD said to Hosea, "Go, take unto thee a wife of whoredoms and children of whoredoms: for the land hath committed great whoredom, departing from the LORD."

So he went and took Gomer, the daughter of Diblaim; which conceived, and bare him a son. And the LORD said unto him, "Call his name 'Jezreel'; for yet a little while, and I will avenge the blood of Jezreel upon the house of Jehu, and will cause to cease the kingdom of the house of Israel. And it shall come to pass at that day, that I will break the bow of Israel in the valley of Jezreel."

And she conceived again, and bare a daughter. And God said unto him, "Call her name 'Lo-ruhamah': for I will no more have mercy upon the house of Israel; but I will utterly take them away. But I will have mercy upon the house of Judah, and will save them by the LORD their God, and will not save them by bow, nor by sword, nor by battle, by horses, nor by horsemen."

Now when she had weaned Lo-ruhamah, she conceived, and bare a son. Then said God, "Call his name

'Lo-ammi': for ye are not my people, and I will not be your God. Yet the number of the children of Israel shall be as the sand of the sea, which cannot be measured nor numbered; and it shall come to pass, that in the place where it was said unto them, 'Ye are not my people,' there it shall be said unto them, 'Ye are the sons of the living God.' Then shall the children of Judah and the children of Israel be gathered together, and appoint themselves one head, and they shall come up out of the land: for great shall be the day of Jezreel.

— Hosea 1.

ISRAEL HAS FOLLOWED AFTER WICKEDNESS.
SHE MUST SUFFER

"Therefore, behold, I will hedge up thy way with thorns, and make a wall, that she shall not find her paths. And she shall follow after her lovers, but she shall not overtake them; and she shall seek them, but shall not find them: then shall she say, 'I will go and return to my first husband; for then was it better with me than now.' For she did not know that I gave her corn, and wine, and oil, and multiplied her silver and gold, which they prepared for Baal. Therefore will I return, and take away my corn in the time thereof, and my wine in the season thereof, and will recover my wool and my flax given to cover her nakedness. And now will I discover her lewdness in the sight of her lovers, and none shall deliver her out of mine hand. I will also cause all her mirth to cease, her feast days, her new moons, and her Sabbaths, and all her solemn feasts. And I will destroy her vines and her fig-trees, whereof she hath said, 'These are my rewards that my lovers have given me': and I will make them a forest, and the beasts of the field shall eat them. And I will visit upon her the days of Baalim, wherein she burned incense to

WOMAN AND CHILD

Photograph by
Professor Lewis Bayles Paton

This is an interesting group consisting of a peasant woman laden with
burdens and a little girl, with an ox in the background.

them, and she decked herself with her earrings and her
jewels, and she went after her lovers, and forgat me,"
saith the LORD.

A DOOR OF HOPE: THE LORD SETS HOSEA
AN EXAMPLE OF FORGIVENESS

"Therefore, behold, I will allure her, and bring her
into the wilderness, and speak comfortably unto her.
And I will give her her vineyards from thence, and the
valley of Achor for a door of hope: and she shall sing
there, as in the days of her youth, and as in the day
when she came up out of the land of Egypt. And it
shall be at that day," saith the LORD, "that thou shalt
call me 'Ishi'; and shalt call me no more 'Baali.' For I
will take away the names of Baalim out of her mouth,
and they shall no more be remembered by their name.

And in that day will I make a covenant for them with the beasts of the field, and with the fowls of heaven, and with the creeping things of the ground: and I will break the bow and the sword and the battle out of the earth, and will make them to lie down safely. And I will betroth thee unto me for ever; yea, I will betroth thee unto me in righteousness, and in judgment, and in lovingkindness, and in mercies. I will even betroth thee unto me in faithfulness: and thou shalt know the LORD. And it shall come to pass in that day, I will hear," saith the LORD, "I will hear the heavens, and they shall hear the earth; and the earth shall hear the corn, and the wine, and the oil; and they shall hear Jezreel. And I will sow her unto me in the earth; and I will have mercy upon her that had not obtained mercy; and I will say to them which were not my people, 'Thou art my people'; and they shall say, 'Thou art my God.'"

— Hosea 2:6-23.

THE WIFE IS BROUGHT BACK FROM HER SHAME— DIVINE FORGIVENESS HAS TAUGHT HUMAN FORGIVENESS

Then said the LORD unto me, "Go yet, love a woman beloved of her friend, yet an adulteress, according to the love of the LORD toward the children of Israel, who look to other gods, and love flagons of wine."

So I bought her to me for fifteen pieces of silver, and for an homer of barley, and an half homer of barley: and I said unto her, "Thou shalt abide for me many days; thou shalt not play the harlot, and thou shalt not be for another man: so will I also be for thee." For the children of Israel shall abide many days without a king, and without a prince, and without a sacrifice, and without an image, and without an ephod, and without teraphim : afterward shall the children of Israel return, and seek the LORD their God, and David, their king; and shall fear the LORD and his goodness in the latter days. — Hosea 3.

"THE LORD HATH A CONTROVERSY WITH HIS PEOPLE"

Hear the word of the LORD, ye children of Israel: for the LORD hath a controversy with the inhabitants of the land, because there is no truth, nor mercy, nor knowledge of God in the land. By swearing, and lying, and killing, and stealing, and committing adultery, they break out, and blood toucheth blood. Therefore shall the land mourn, and every one that dwelleth therein shall languish, with the beasts of the field, and with the fowls of heaven; yea, the fishes of the sea also shall be taken away. Yet let no man strive, nor reprove another: for thy people are as they that strive with the priest. Therefore shalt thou fall in the day, and the prophet also shall fall with thee in the night, and I will destroy thy mother. My people are destroyed for lack of knowledge: because thou hast rejected knowledge, I will also reject thee, that thou shalt be no priest to me: seeing thou hast forgotten the law of thy God, I will also forget thy children. As they were increased, so they sinned against me: therefore will I change their glory into shame. They eat up the sin of my people, and they set their heart on their iniquity. And there shall be, like people, like priest: and I will punish them for their ways, and reward them their doings.

"EPHRAIM IS JOINED TO IDOLS : LET HIM ALONE"

Ephraim is joined to idols: let him alone. Their drink is sour: they have committed whoredom continually. The wind hath bound her up in her wings, and they shall be ashamed because of their sacrifices.

PRIEST AND PROPHET STUMBLE

Hear ye this, O priests; and hearken, ye house of Israel; and give ye ear, O house of the king; for judgment is toward you, because ye have been a snare on Mizpah, and a net spread upon Tabor. And the revolters are profound to make slaughter, though I have been a rebuker of them all. I know Ephraim, and Israel is not hid from me: for now, O Ephraim, thou committest whoredom, and Israel is defiled. They will not frame their doings to turn unto their God: for the spirit of whoredoms is in the midst of them, and they have not known the LORD. And the pride of Israel doth testify to his face: therefore shall Israel and Ephraim fall in their iniquity; Judah also shall fall with them. They shall go with their flocks and with their herds to seek the LORD; but they shall not find him; he hath withdrawn himself from them. They have dealt treacherously against the LORD: for they have begotten strange children: now shall a month devour them with their portions. Blow ye the cornet in Gibeah, and the trumpet in Ramah: cry aloud at Beth-aven, after thee, O Benjamin. Ephraim shall be desolate in the day of rebuke: among the tribes of Israel have I made known that which shall surely be. The princes of Judah were like them that remove the bound: therefore I will pour out my wrath upon them like water. Ephraim is oppressed and broken in judgment, because he willingly walked after the commandment. Therefore will I be unto Ephraim as a moth, and to the house of Judah as rottenness. When Ephraim saw his sickness, and Judah saw his wound, then went

Ephraim to the Assyrian, and sent to King Jareb: yet could he not heal you, nor cure you of your wound. For I will be unto Ephraim as a lion, and as a young lion to the house of Judah: I, even I, will tear and go away; I will take away, and none shall rescue him. I will go and return to my place, till they acknowledge their offence, and seek my face: in their affliction they will seek me early.   —Hosea 4:1–9, 17–19; 5.

"LET US RETURN TO THE LORD AND HE SHALL BE TO US AS THE MORNING": THE PEOPLE MAKE A WEAK ATTEMPT TO REPENT

"Come, and let us return unto the LORD: for he hath torn, and he will heal us; he hath smitten, and he will bind us up. After two days will he revive us: in the third day he will raise us up, and we shall live in his sight. Then shall we know, if we follow on to know the LORD: his going forth is prepared as the morning; and he shall come unto us as the rain, as the latter and former rain unto the earth."

THE REPENTANCE OF THE PEOPLE IS TOO SHALLOW: THEY THINK TOO LIGHTLY OF THEIR SINS

O Ephraim, what shall I do unto thee? O Judah, what shall I do unto thee? For your goodness is as a morning cloud, and as the early dew it goeth away. Therefore have I hewed them by the prophets; I have slain them by the words of my mouth: and thy judgments are as the light that goeth forth. For I desired mercy, and not sacrifice; and the knowledge of God more than burnt offerings. But they like men have transgressed the covenant: there have they dealt treacherously against me. Gilead is a city of them that work iniquity, and is polluted with blood. And as

WOMAN GRINDING GRAIN
Photograph by
Professor E. J. Goodspeed
This woman is grinding grain in the stone mill to make bread.

troops of robbers wait for a man, so the company of priests murder in the way by consent: for they commit lewdness. I have seen an horrible thing in the house of Israel: there is the whoredom of Ephraim, Israel is defiled. Also, O Judah, he hath set an harvest for thee, when I returned the captivity of my people. —Hosea 6.

THE LORD WOULD HEAL BUT THEIR SINS ARE
ONLY THE MORE DISCOVERED

When I would have healed Israel, then the iniquity of Ephraim was discovered, and the wickedness of Samaria: for they commit falsehood; and the thief cometh in, and the troop of robbers spoileth without. And they consider not in their hearts that I remember all their wickedness: now their own doings have beset them about; they are before my face. They make the king glad with their wickedness, and the princes with their lies. They are all adulterers, as an oven heated by the baker, who ceaseth from raising after he hath kneaded the dough, until it be leavened. In the day of our king the princes have made him sick with bottles of wine; he stretched out his hand with scorners. For they have made ready their heart like an oven, whiles they lie in wait: their baker sleepeth all the night; in the morning it burneth as a flaming fire. They are all hot as an oven, and have devoured their judges; all their kings are fallen: there is none among them that calleth unto me.

GOING TO THE BAKER'S

Photograph by
Professor Lewis Bayles Paton

This woman with the attractive little girl is on her way with her big bowl of dough to have it baked at the public baker's. In the eastern cities those who engage in various trades lived on the same street. This woman is going to Bakers' Street with her bread.

"Then Zedekiah, the king, commanded that they should commit Jeremiah into the court of the prison, and that they should give him daily a piece of bread out of the bakers' street, until all the bread in the city was spent. Thus Jeremiah remained in the court of the prison."—*Jeremiah 37:21.*

"Ephraim is a cake (of bread) not turned." —*Hosea 7:8.*

EPHRAIM IS A CAKE NOT TURNED: A SILLY DOVE WITHOUT HEART

Ephraim, he hath mixed himself among the people; Ephraim is a cake not turned. Strangers have devoured his strength, and he knoweth it not: yea, gray hairs are here and there upon him, yet he knoweth not. And the pride of Israel testifieth to his face: and they do not return to the LORD their God, nor seek him for all this. Ephraim also is like a silly dove without heart: they call to Egypt, they go to Assyria. When they shall go, I will spread my net upon them; I will bring them down as the fowls of the heaven; I will chastise them, as their congregation hath heard. Woe unto them! for they have fled from me: destruction unto them! because they have transgressed against me: though I have redeemed them, yet they have spoken lies against me. And they have not cried unto me with their heart, when they howled upon their beds: they assemble themselves for corn and wine, and they rebel against me. Though I have bound and strengthened their arms, yet do they imagine mischief against me. They return, but not to the most High: they are like a deceitful bow: their princes shall fall by the sword for the rage of their tongue: this shall be their derision in the land of Egypt. —Hosea 7.

A People in Decay

Set the trumpet to thy mouth. He shall come as an eagle against the house of the LORD, because they have transgressed my covenant, and trespassed against my law. Israel shall cry unto me, "My God, we know thee." Israel hath cast off the thing that is good: the enemy shall pursue him. They have set up kings, but not by me: they have made princes, and I knew it not: of their silver and their gold have they made them idols, that they may be cut off. Thy calf, O Samaria, hath cast thee off; mine anger is kindled against them: how long will it be ere they attain to innocency? For from Israel was it also: the workman made it; therefore it is not God: but the calf of Samaria shall be broken in pieces. For they have sown the wind, and they shall reap the whirlwind: it hath no stalk: the bud shall yield no meal: if so be it yield, the strangers shall swallow it up.   Israel is swallowed up: now shall they be among the Gentiles as a vessel wherein is no pleasure.   For they are gone up to Assyria, a wild ass alone by himself: Ephraim hath hired lovers.   Yea, though they have hired among the nations, now will I gather them, and they shall sorrow a little for the burden of the king of princes.   Because Ephraim hath made many altars to sin, altars shall be unto him to sin. I have written to him the great things of my law, but they were counted as a strange thing.   They sacrifice flesh for the sacrifices of mine offerings, and eat it; but the LORD accepteth them not, now will he remember their iniquity, and visit their sins: they shall return to Egypt.   For Israel hath forgotten his Maker, and buildeth temples; and Judah hath multiplied fenced cities: but I will send a fire upon his cities, and it shall devour the palaces thereof.   —Hosea 8.

THE FEASTS SHALL BRING NO LONGER JOY

Rejoice not, O Israel, for joy, as other people: for thou hast gone a whoring from thy God, thou hast loved a reward upon every corn-floor.   The floor and the wine-press shall not feed them, and the new wine shall fail in her.   They shall not dwell in the LORD's land; but Ephraim shall return to Egypt, and they shall eat unclean things in Assyria.   They shall not offer wine offerings to the LORD, neither shall they be pleasing unto him: their sacrifices shall be unto them as the bread of mourners; all that eat thereof shall be polluted: for their bread for their soul shall not come into the house of the LORD.   What will ye do in the solemn day, and in the day of the feast of the LORD?   For, lo, they are gone because of destruction: Egypt shall gather them up, Memphis shall bury them: the pleasant places for their silver, nettles shall possess them: thorns shall be in their tabernacles. The days of visitation are come, the days of recompence are come; Israel shall know it: the prophet is a fool, the spiritual man is mad, for the multitude of thine iniquity, and the great hatred. The watchman of Ephraim was with my God: but the prophet is a snare of a fowler in all his ways, and hatred in the house of his God. They have deeply corrupted themselves, as in the days of Gibeah: therefore he will remember their iniquity, he will visit their sins.

SOCIAL CORRUPTION AND ITS CONSEQUENCES

I found Israel like grapes in the wilderness; I saw your fathers as the first-ripe in the fig-tree at her first time: but they went to Baal-peor, and separated themselves unto that shame; and their abominations were according as they loved. As for Ephraim, their glory shall fly away like a bird, from the birth, and from the womb, and from the conception. Though they bring up their children, yet will I bereave them, that there shall not be a man left: yea, woe also to them when I depart from them! Ephraim, as I saw Tyrus, is planted in a pleasant place: but Ephraim shall bring forth his children to the murderer. Give them, O LORD: what wilt thou give? Give them a mis-carrying womb and dry breasts. All their wickedness is in Gilgal: for there I hated them: for the wickedness of their doings I will drive them out of mine house, I will love them no more: all their princes are revolters. Ephraim is smitten, their root is dried up, they shall bear no fruit: yea, though they bring forth, yet will I slay even the beloved fruit of their womb. My God will cast them away, because they did not hearken unto him: and they shall be wanderers among the nations.

"ISRAEL IS AN EMPTY VINE": HER IDOLS AND KINGS
ARE USELESS

Israel is an empty vine, he bringeth forth fruit unto himself: according to the multitude of his fruit he hath increased the altars; according to the goodness of his land they have made goodly images. Their heart is divided; now shall they be found faulty: he shall break down their altars, he shall spoil their images. For now they shall say, "We have no king, because we feared not the LORD; what then should a king do to us?" They have spoken words, swearing falsely in making a covenant: thus judgment springeth up as hemlock in the furrows of the field. The inhabitants of Samaria shall fear because of the calves of Beth-aven: for the people thereof shall mourn over it, and the priests thereof that rejoiced on it, for the glory thereof, because it is departed from it. It shall be also carried unto Assyria for a present to King Jareb: Ephraim shall receive shame, and Israel shall be ashamed of his own counsel. As for Samaria, her king is cut off as the foam upon the water. The high places also of Aven, the sin of Israel, shall be destroyed: the thorn and the thistle shall come up on their altars; and they shall say to the mountains, "Cover us"; and to the hills, "Fall on us." O Israel, thou hast sinned from the days of Gibeah: there they stood: the battle in Gibeah against the children of iniquity did not overtake them. It is in my desire that I should chastise them; and the people shall be gathered against them, when they shall bind themselves in their two furrows. And Ephraim is as an heifer that is taught, and loveth to tread out the corn; but I passed over upon her fair neck: I will make Ephraim to ride; Judah shall plow, and Jacob shall break his clods. Sow to yourselves in righteousness, reap in mercy; break up your fallow ground: for it is time to seek the LORD, till he come and rain righteousness upon you. Ye have plowed wickedness; ye have reaped iniquity; ye have eaten the fruit of lies: because thou didst trust in thy way, in the multitude of thy mighty men. Therefore shall a tumult arise among thy people, and all thy fortresses shall be spoiled, as Shalman spoiled Beth-arbel in the day of battle: the mother was dashed in pieces upon her children. So shall Beth-el do unto you because of your great wickedness: in a morning shall the king of Israel utterly be cut off. —Hosea 9; 10.

A RIFT IN THE CLOUDS OF SIN: "WHEN ISRAEL WAS A CHILD I LOVED HIM," AND GOD'S LOVE CAN NOT LET ISRAEL GO. HOSEA'S CLEAR VISION

"When Israel was a child, then I loved him, and called my son out of Egypt. As they called them, so they went from them: they sacrificed unto Baalim, and burned incense to graven images. I taught Ephraim also to go, taking them by their arms; but they knew not that I healed them. I drew them with cords of a man, with bands of love: and I was to them as they that take off the yoke on their jaws, and I laid meat unto them. He shall not return into the land of Egypt, but the Assyrian shall be his king, because they refused to return. And the sword shall abide on his cities, and shall consume his branches, and devour them, because of their own counsels. And my people are bent to backsliding from me: though they called them to the most High, none at all would exalt him. How shall I give thee up, Ephraim? How shall I deliver thee, Israel? How shall I make thee as Admah? How shall I set thee as Zeboim? Mine heart is turned within me, my repentings are kindled together. I will not execute the fierceness of mine anger, I will not return to destroy Ephraim: for I am God, and not man; the Holy One in the midst of thee: and I will not enter into the city. They shall walk after the LORD: he shall roar like a lion: when he shall roar, then the children shall tremble from the west. They shall tremble as a bird out of Egypt, and as a dove out of the land of Assyria: and I will place them in their houses," saith the LORD. "Ephraim compasseth me about with lies, and the house of Israel with deceit: but Judah yet ruleth with God, and is faithful with the saints."

— Hosea 11.

THE VISION FADES—ISRAEL LIKENED TO JACOB

Ephraim feedeth on wind, and followeth after the east wind: he daily increaseth lies and desolation; and they do make a covenant with the Assyrians, and oil is carried into Egypt. The LORD hath also a controversy with Judah, and will punish Jacob according to his ways; according to his doings will he recompense him. He took his brother by the heel in the womb, and by his strength he had power with God: yea, he had power over the angel, and prevailed: he wept, and made supplication unto him: he found him in Beth-el, and there he spake with us; even the LORD God of hosts; the LORD is his memorial. Therefore turn thou to thy God: keep mercy and judgment, and wait on thy God continually. He is a merchant, the balances of deceit are in his hand: he loveth to oppress. And Ephraim said, "Yet I am become rich, I have found me out substance: in all my labours they shall find none iniquity in me that were sin." And I that am the LORD thy God from the land of Egypt will yet make thee to dwell in tabernacles, as in the days of the solemn feast. I have also spoken by the prophets, and I have multiplied

visions, and used similitudes, by the ministry of the
prophets. Is there iniquity in Gilead? Surely they are
vanity: they sacrifice bullocks in Gilgal; yea, their
altars are as heaps in the furrows of the fields. And
Jacob fled into the country of Syria, and Israel served
for a wife, and for a wife he kept sheep. And by a
prophet the LORD brought Israel out of Egypt, and by
a prophet was he preserved. Ephraim provoked him
to anger most bitterly: therefore shall he leave his
blood upon him, and his reproach shall his LORD return
unto him.   — Hosea 12.

THE PROPHET'S LAST LAMENT FOR EPHRAIM'S FALL

THE NATION IS FINALLY DOOMED

When Ephraim spake trembling, he exalted himself
in Israel; but when he offended in Baal, he died. And
now they sin more and more, and have made them
molten images of their silver, and idols according to
their own understanding, all of it the work of the crafts-
men: they say of them, "Let the men that sacrifice
kiss the calves." Therefore they shall be as the morning cloud, and as the early dew that passeth away, as
the chaff that is driven with the whirlwind out of the
floor, and as the smoke out of the chimney. Yet I
am the LORD thy God from the land of Egypt, and
thou shalt know no god but me: for there is no saviour
beside me.

I did know thee in the wilderness, in the land of
great drought. According to their pasture, so were
they filled; they were filled, and their heart was exalted;
therefore have they forgotten me. Therefore I will be
unto them as a lion: as a leopard by the way will I
observe them: I will meet them as a bear that is bereaved of her whelps, and will rend the caul of their

heart, and there will I devour them like a lion: the wild beast shall tear them. O Israel, thou hast destroyed thyself; but in me is thine help. I will be thy king: where is any other that may save thee in all thy cities? and thy judges of whom thou saidst, "Give me a king and princes?" I gave thee a king in mine anger, and took him away in my wrath. The iniquity of Ephraim is bound up; his sin is hid. The sorrows of a

THE BEAUTIFUL HILL COUNTRY OF LEBANON

Photograph by
Professor Lewis Bayles Paton

As the supports of a great oak run up above the ground so the gradual hills of Galilee rise up from Esdraelon and Jordan upon that tremendous northern mountain range.

"I will be as the dew unto Israel:
He shall grow as the lily,
And cast forth his roots as Lebanon.
His branches shall spread,
And his beauty shall be as the olive-tree,
And his smell as Lebanon.
They that dwell under his shadow shall return;
They shall revive as the corn, and grow as the vine:
The scent thereof shall be as the wine of Lebanon."
—*Hosea 14:5–7*.

travailing woman shall come upon him: he is an unwise son; for he should not stay long in the place of the breaking forth of children.

I will ransom them from the power of the grave; I will redeem them from death: O death, I will be thy plagues; O grave, I will be thy destruction: repentance shall be hid from mine eyes. Though he be fruitful among his brethren, an east wind shall come, the wind of the LORD shall come up from the wilderness, and his spring shall become dry, and his fountain shall be dried up: he shall spoil the treasure of all pleasant vessels. Samaria shall become desolate; for she hath rebelled against her God: they shall fall by the sword: their infants shall be dashed in pieces, and their women with child shall be ripped up.   — Hosea 13.

THE GREAT ASSURANCE REPEATED: THE PROPHET STILL HOPES FOR RESTORATION THROUGH REPENTANCE

O Israel, return unto the LORD thy God; for thou hast fallen by thine iniquity. Take with you words, and turn to the LORD: say unto him, "Take away all iniquity, and receive us graciously: so will we render the calves of our lips. Asshur shall not save us; we will not ride upon horses: neither will we say any more to the work of our hands, 'Ye are our gods': for in thee the fatherless findeth mercy."

THE LORD IS MERCIFUL

I will heal their backsliding, I will love them freely: for mine anger is turned away from him. I will be as the dew unto Israel: he shall grow as the lily, and cast forth his roots as Lebanon. His branches shall spread, and his beauty shall be as the olive-tree, and his smell as Lebanon. They that dwell under his shadow shall return;

they shall revive as the corn, and grow as the vine: the scent thereof shall be as the wine of Lebanon. Ephraim shall say, "What have I to do any more with idols?" I have heard him, and observed him: I am like a green fir-tree. From me is thy fruit found. Who is wise, and he shall understand these things; prudent, and he shall know them? For the ways of the LORD are right, and the just shall walk in them: but the transgressors shall fall therein. —Hosea 14.

VIEW OF SAMARIA WITH RUINS OF THE WALL
AND CITY IN FOREGROUND
Photograph by Professor George R. Berry

"Samaria shall become desolate for she hath rebelled against her God"—
Hosea Chapter 13. See opposite page.

Isaiah, Prophet, Statesman, Poet

I

Isaiah was the greatest figure in the history of the Kingdom of Judah, the greatest prophet, the greatest statesman. He was also a reformer, a poet, an orator, a religious seer. He was not like Amos and Micah, a man of the soil, a shepherd or a farmer. He always lived in the city; he was a friend of kings and of the wealthy class. In that respect, he resembled Washington or Roosevelt rather than Lincoln. He was perhaps even more a statesman than a prophet, a statesman possessing a profound religious conviction, basing statecraft upon faith, upon confidence in the divine guidance rather than upon the wisdom of man.

In order to understand the great political sermons of Isaiah, the world situation must be kept in view. The eastern Mediterranean country was occupied by a number of small states, strong, virile, possessing an intense national spirit, — the Northern and Southern Kingdoms, Syria with its capital at Damascus, the federated Philistine cities, Moab, Edom. Each of these states was antagonistic to the others. The territory of each was always fair prey for conquest. War was as much an occupation as husbandry or commerce. Outside this circle of little states were the great empires, — Egypt on the south, Assyria on the north. Egypt and Assyria were rivals for world dominion; the little states were merely pawns in the great game of war and conquest. They lay in the path of the rival armies. They possessed valuable territory which might be the spoil of war. Individually weak, they were potentially dangerous if they should unite. A well-knit and determined confederacy would seriously menace the supremacy of the great powers. The fatal obstacle to the formation of such a confederacy was the traditional inherited hatred and jealousy of these little peoples. It was hard to make warm friends of people like the Philistines and the Hebrews, who had hated each other and fought each other for centuries. Yet it was always an alluring possibility. The yoke of Assyria was very heavy. The burden of the tribute was hard to bear.

There was always a nationalist party, which favored resistance, the formation of a confederacy, secret pacts with one or the other of the great foes. The people of this party called themselves patriotic, and in a sense they were. The other party, to which the prophets belonged, was the peace party. Their attitude was that resistance was hopeless: it was dangerous to attempt to make leagues and confederacies and secret treaties: bear the yoke patiently for a while; trust in God rather than in alliances with heathen states; develop the state until it should be worthy of independence. Above all, the demand of the prophets was for reform, the purging of the nation of its social evils, its injustice. "This way lies the path of national greatness," they said. One party was the party of political expediency, of freedom gained through diplomacy, alliance with other peoples, not on a basis of righteousness, but of bribery and selfish expediency. This party would absolutely ignore the question of morality. "Morality," they said, "has nothing to do with politics." To this attitude the prophets were passionately opposed. Their message was: "Morality, righteousness, has everything to do not only with politics but with every concern of human life. A nation may be temporarily prosperous and successful, but unless it is righteous, its doom is sealed."

Isaiah, in the course of his long career of forty years, was the leader of the peace party, — not peace at any price, not peace with dishonor, but peace because in that way only could the nation escape slavery and maintain a spiritual independence. His efforts were in the main successful. He kept the nation from entangling alliances; he saved Judah from captivity, and secured a national existence for her which lasted for a hundred years after Northern Israel had paid the price of following the opposite course.

Isaiah was a great religious genius, an evangelical preacher of faith in God, in the coming of the Messiah, of "God the infinitely near," as well as "God the infinitely high," exalted in righteousness, inaccessible in holiness.

> "Seek ye the Lord while he may be found
> Call ye upon him while he is near:
> Let the wicked forsake his way,
> And the unrighteous man his thoughts:
> And let him return unto the Lord,
> And he will have mercy upon him;
> And to our God,
> For he will abundantly pardon." Isa. 55:7

The Prophecy of Isaiah

Part I

The vision of Isaiah, the son of Amoz, which he saw concerning Judah and Jerusalem in the days of Uzziah, Jotham, Ahaz, and Hezekiah, Kings of Judah.

THE CALL OF ISAIAH

IN the year that King Uzziah died, I saw also the LORD sitting upon a throne, high and lifted up, and his train filled the temple. Above it stood the seraphim: each one had six wings; with twain he covered his face, and with twain he covered his feet, and with twain he did fly.

And one cried unto another, and said, "Holy, holy, holy, is the LORD of hosts: the whole earth is full of his glory." And the posts of the door moved at the voice of him that cried, and the house was filled with smoke.

Then said I, "Woe is me! for I am undone; because I am a man of unclean lips, and I dwell in the midst of a people of unclean lips: for mine eyes have seen the King, the LORD of hosts."

Then flew one of the seraphim unto me, having a live coal in his hand, which he had taken with the tongs from off the altar: and he laid it upon my mouth, and said, "Lo, this hath touched thy lips; and thine iniquity is taken away, and thy sin purged."

Also I heard the voice of the LORD, saying, "Whom shall I send, and who will go for us?"

Then said I, "Here am I; send me."

THE PROPHETS
JEREMIAH   JONAH   ISAIAH   HABAKKUK

From the Frieze in the Boston Public Library,
Boston, Massachusetts
By John S. Sargent. From a Copley Print
Copyrighted by Curtis and Cameron, Inc.,
Boston, Massachusetts

THIS great mural painting adorns the
walls of the Public Library at Boston,
Massachusetts. The figures of the "goodly fellowship of the prophets" are painted
with great vigor and spiritual understanding.

And he said, "Go, and tell this people, 'Hear ye indeed, but understand not; and see ye indeed, but perceive not.' Make the heart of this people fat, and make their ears heavy, and shut their eyes; lest they see with their eyes, and hear with their ears, and understand with their heart, and convert, and be healed."

Then said I, "Lord, how long?"

And he answered, "Until the cities be wasted without inhabitant, and the houses without man, and the land be utterly desolate, and the Lord have removed men far away, and there be a great forsaking in the midst of the land. But yet in it shall be a tenth, and it shall return, and shall be eaten: as a teil-tree, and as an oak, whose substance is in them, when they cast their leaves: so the holy seed shall be the substance thereof."

— Isaiah 6.

A Sermon Which Gives Isaiah's Great Message

Hear, O heavens, and give ear, O earth: for the Lord hath spoken:

"I have nourished and brought up children, and they have rebelled against me. The ox knoweth his owner, and the ass his master's crib: but Israel doth not know, my people doth not consider."

Ah, sinful nation! a people laden with iniquity, a seed of evildoers, children that are corrupters: they have forsaken the Lord, they have provoked the Holy One of Israel unto anger, they are gone away backward.

Why should ye be stricken any more? Ye will revolt more and more: the whole head is sick, and the whole heart faint. From the sole of the foot even unto the head there is no soundness in it; but wounds, and bruises, and putrifying sores: they have not been closed, neither bound up, neither mollified with ointment. Your country is desolate, your cities are burned with fire: your land, strangers devour it in your presence, and it is desolate, as overthrown by strangers. And the daughter of Zion is left as a cottage in a vineyard, as a lodge in a garden of cucumbers, as a besieged city. Except the LORD of hosts had left unto us a very small remnant, we should have been as Sodom, and we should have been like unto Gomorrah.

Hear the word of the LORD, ye rulers of Sodom; give ear unto the law of our God, ye people of Gomorrah.

"To what purpose is the multitude of your sacrifices unto me?" saith the LORD: "I am full of the burnt offerings of rams, and the fat of fed beasts; and I delight not in the blood of bullocks, or of lambs, or of he goats. When ye come to appear before me, who hath required this at your hand, to tread my courts? Bring no more vain oblations; incense is an abomination unto me; the new moons and Sabbaths, the calling of assemblies, I cannot away with; it is iniquity, even the solemn meeting. Your new moons and your appointed feasts my soul hateth: they are a trouble unto me; I am weary to bear them. And when ye spread forth your hands, I will hide mine eyes from you: yea, when ye make many prayers, I will not hear: your hands are full of blood.

"Wash you, make you clean; put away the evil of your doings from before mine eyes; cease to do evil; learn to do well; seek judgment, relieve the oppressed, judge the fatherless, plead for the widow.

"Come now, and let us reason together," saith the LORD: "though your sins be as scarlet, they shall be as white as snow; though they be red like crimson, they

shall be as wool. If ye be willing and obedient, ye shall
eat the good of the land: but if ye refuse and rebel, ye
shall be devoured with the sword": for the mouth of the
LORD hath spoken it.   —Isaiah 1:1-20.

A PICTURE OF AN EVIL CITY

How is the faithful city become an harlot! it was
full of judgment; righteousness lodged in it; but now
murderers. Thy silver is become dross, thy wine mixed
with water: thy princes are rebellious, and companions
of thieves: every one loveth gifts, and followeth after
rewards: they judge not the fatherless, neither doth
the cause of the widow come unto them.

Therefore saith the Lord, the LORD of hosts, the
mighty One of Israel, "Ah, I will ease me of mine
adversaries, and avenge me of mine enemies: and I
will turn my hand upon thee, and purely purge away
thy dross, and take away all thy tin: and I will restore
thy judges as at the first, and thy counsellors as at the
beginning: afterward thou shalt be called, 'The city
of righteousness, the faithful city.' Zion shall be redeemed with judgment, and her converts with righteousness.

"And the destruction of the transgressors and of the
sinners shall be together, and they that forsake the
LORD shall be consumed. For they shall be ashamed
of the oaks which ye have desired, and ye shall be confounded for the gardens that ye have chosen. For ye
shall be as an oak whose leaf fadeth, and as a garden
that hath no water. And the strong shall be as tow,
and the maker of it as a spark, and they shall both burn
together, and none shall quench them."   —Isaiah 1:21-31.

The word that Isaiah, the son of Amoz saw concerning Judah and Jerusalem.

The Three Jerusalems

And it shall come to pass in the last days, that the mountain of the LORD's house shall be established in the top of the mountains, and shall be exalted above the hills; and all nations shall flow unto it.

THE IDEAL JERUSALEM

And many people shall go and say, "Come ye, and let us go up to the mountain of the LORD, to the house of the God of Jacob; and he will teach us of his ways, and we will walk in his paths: for out of Zion shall go forth the law, and the word of the LORD from Jerusalem."

And he shall judge among the nations, and shall rebuke many people: and they shall beat their swords into plowshares, and their spears into pruninghooks: nation shall not lift up sword against nation, neither shall they learn war any more. O house of Jacob, come ye, and let us walk in the light of the LORD.

THE ACTUAL JERUSALEM

Therefore thou hast forsaken thy people, the house of Jacob, because they be replenished from the east, and are soothsayers like the Philistines, and they please themselves in the children of strangers. Their land also is full of silver and gold, neither is there any end of their treasures; their land is also full of horses, neither is there any end of their chariots: their land also is full of idols; they worship the work of their own hands, that which their own fingers have made: and the mean man boweth down, and the great man humbleth himself: therefore forgive them not.

Enter into the rock, and hide thee in the dust, for fear of the LORD, and for the glory of his majesty. The lofty looks of man shall be humbled, and the haughtiness of men shall be bowed down, and the LORD alone shall be exalted in that day. For the day of the LORD of hosts shall be upon every one that is proud and lofty, and upon every one that is lifted up; and he shall be brought low: and upon all the cedars of Lebanon, that are high and lifted up, and upon all the oaks of Bashan, and upon all the high mountains, and upon all the hills that are lifted up, and upon every high tower, and upon every fenced wall, and upon all the ships of Tarshish, and upon all pleasant pictures. And the loftiness of man shall be bowed down, and the haughtiness of men shall be made low: and the LORD alone shall be exalted in that day. And the idols he shall utterly abolish. And they shall go into the holes of the rocks, and into the caves of the earth, for fear of the LORD, and for the glory of his majesty, when he ariseth to shake terribly the earth. In that day a man shall cast his idols of silver, and his idols of gold, which they made each one for himself to worship, to the moles and to the bats; to go into the clefts of the rocks, and into the tops of the ragged rocks, for fear of the LORD, and for the glory of his majesty, when he ariseth to shake terribly the earth. Cease ye from man, whose breath is in his nostrils: for wherein is he to be accounted of?

DISASTER IS SURE TO COME UPON JERUSALEM
FOR HER SINS

For, behold, the LORD, the LORD of hosts, doth take away from Jerusalem and from Judah the stay and the staff, the whole stay of bread, and the whole stay of water, the mighty man, and the man of war, the judge, and the prophet, and the prudent, and the ancient, the captain of fifty, and the honourable man, and the counsellor, and the cunning artificer, and the eloquent orator. And I will give children to be their princes, and babes shall rule over them. And the people shall be oppressed, every one by another, and every one by his neighbour: the child shall behave himself proudly against the ancient, and the base against the honourable; when a man shall take hold of his brother of the house of his father, saying, "Thou hast clothing, be thou our ruler, and let this ruin be under thy hand."

In that day shall he swear, saying, "I will not be an healer; for in my house is neither bread nor clothing: make me not a ruler of the people."

JERUSALEM IS RUINED.

For Jerusalem is ruined, and Judah is fallen: because their tongue and their doings are against the LORD to provoke the eyes of his glory.

The show of their countenance doth witness against them; and they declare their sin as Sodom, they hide it not. Woe unto their soul! For they have rewarded evil unto themselves. Say ye to the righteous, that it shall be well with him: for they shall eat the fruit of their doings. Woe unto the wicked! It shall be ill with him: for the reward of his hands shall be given him.

As for my people, children are their oppressors, and women rule over them. O my people, they which lead thee cause thee to err, and destroy the way of thy paths. The LORD standeth up to plead, and standeth to judge the people. The LORD will enter into judgment with the ancients of his people, and the princes thereof: for ye have eaten up the vineyard; the spoil of the poor is in your houses.

"What mean ye that ye beat my people to pieces, and grind the faces of the poor?" saith the Lord GOD of hosts.

PUNISHMENT OF THE DAUGHTERS OF ZION

Moreover the LORD saith, "Because the daughters of Zion are haughty, and walk with stretched forth necks and wanton eyes, walking and mincing as they go, and making a tinkling with their feet: therefore the LORD will smite with a scab the crown of the head of the daughters of Zion."

In that day the LORD will take away the bravery of their tinkling ornaments about their feet, and their cauls, and their round tires like the moon, the chains, and the bracelets, and the mufflers, the bonnets, and the ornaments of the legs, and the headbands, and the tablets, and the earrings, the rings, and nose jewels, the changeable suits of apparel, and the mantles, and the wimples, and the crisping pins, the glasses, and the fine linen, and the hoods, and the veils. And it shall come to pass, that instead of sweet smell there shall be stink; and instead of a girdle a rent; and instead of well set hair baldness; and instead of a stomacher a girding of sackcloth; and burning instead of beauty. Thy men shall fall by the sword, and thy mighty in the war. And her gates shall lament and mourn; and she being desolate shall sit upon the ground.

And in that day seven women shall take hold of one man, saying, "We will eat our own bread, and wear our own apparel: only let us be called by thy name, to take away our reproach."

THE PURIFIED JERUSALEM

In that day shall the branch of the LORD be beautiful and glorious, and the fruit of the earth shall be excellent and comely for them that are escaped of Israel. And it shall come to pass, that he that is left in Zion, and he that remaineth in Jerusalem, shall be called holy, even every one that is written among the living in Jerusalem: when the LORD shall have washed away the filth of the daughters of Zion, and shall have purged the blood of Jerusalem from the midst thereof by the spirit of judgment, and by the spirit of burning. And the LORD will create upon every dwelling place of Mount Zion, and upon her assemblies, a cloud and smoke by day, and the shining of a flaming fire by night: for upon all the glory shall be a defence. And there shall be a tabernacle for a shadow in the daytime from the heat, and for a place of refuge, and for a covert from storm and from rain. — Isaiah 2; 3; 4.

A SONG OF THE VINEYARD

Now I will sing to my wellbeloved a song of my beloved touching his vineyard.

My wellbeloved hath a vineyard in a very fruitful hill:
And he fenced it, and gathered out the stones thereof,
And planted it with the choicest vine,
And built a tower in the midst of it,
And also made a wine-press therein:
And he looked that it should bring forth grapes.
And it brought forth wild grapes.

And now, O inhabitants of Jerusalem, and men of Judah, judge, I pray you, betwixt me and my vineyard. What could have been done more to my vineyard, that I have not done in it? Wherefore, when I looked that it should bring forth grapes, brought it forth wild grapes? And now go to; I will tell you what I will do to my vineyard: I will take away the hedge thereof, and it shall be eaten up; and break down the wall thereof, and it shall be trodden down: and I will lay it waste: it shall not be

Isaiah—Detail of Sistine Chapel Ceiling

By Michelangelo Buonarroti (1475-1564)
In the Sistine Chapel of the Vatican, Rome
Photograph by Anderson, Rome

IN this artistic conception of the prophet Isaiah we see a young man depicted in that moment of spiritual life which is inspiration itself. After reading the life and work of Isaiah, do you find that Michelangelo's conception is as true as it is beautiful? Compare this with the modern representation by John Singer Sargent on page 56.

This magnificent figure of the prophet Isaiah is just one in a vast scheme of fresco paintings covering the ceiling of the Sistine Chapel. The great Michelangelo was commissioned to carry out this tremendous task by Pope Julius II. The artist worked at it four years single-handed and is said to have come out of it temporarily crippled and with eyes distorted from the constant strain of looking upward. This vast work, transcendent in artistic beauty and intellectual conception, remains a marvel which can hardly be matched anywhere.

The Sistine Chapel is a long, narrow building lighted by high, round-arched windows. The ceiling is long and curved, and its painted surface is estimated to be 10,000 square feet. Michelangelo divided this huge expanse of ceiling into nine rectangular spaces in which he represented the most important events recorded in Genesis. These spaces are supported and connected by figures of athletes and by a painted architectural framework. A little lower in the curve of the ceiling, enthroned impressively in this painted architecture, are twelve great seated figures of prophets and sibyls of which this picture is one.

You will find other illustrations from the Sistine Chapel on pages 308, 358, 402 and 422.

ESAIAS

pruned, nor digged; but there shall come up briers and thorns: I will also command the clouds that they rain no rain upon it. For the vineyard of the LORD of hosts is the house of Israel, and the men of Judah his pleasant plant: and he looked for judgment, but behold oppression; for righteousness, but behold a cry.

Woe unto them that join house to house, that lay field to field, till there be no place, that they may be placed alone in the midst of the earth! In mine ears said the LORD of hosts, "Of a truth many houses shall be desolate, even great and fair, without inhabitant. Yea, ten acres of vineyard shall yield one bath, and the seed of an homer shall yield an ephah."

Woe unto them that rise up early in the morning, that they may follow strong drink; that continue until night, till wine inflame them! And the harp, and the viol, the tabret, and pipe, and wine, are in their feasts: but they regard not the work of the LORD, neither consider the operation of his hands.

Therefore my people are gone into captivity, because they have no knowledge: and their honourable men are famished, and their multitude dried up with thirst. Therefore hell hath enlarged herself, and opened her mouth without measure: and their glory, and their multitude, and their pomp, and he that rejoiceth, shall descend into it. And the mean man shall be brought down, and the mighty man shall be humbled, and the eyes of the lofty shall be humbled: but the LORD of hosts shall be exalted in judgment, and God that is holy shall be sanctified in righteousness. Then shall the lambs feed after their manner, and the waste places of the fat ones shall strangers eat.

Woe unto them that draw iniquity with cords of vanity, and sin as it were with a cart rope: that say,

"Let him make speed, and hasten his work, that we may see it: and let the counsel of the Holy One of Israel draw nigh and come, that we may know it!"

Woe unto them that call evil good, and good evil; that put darkness for light, and light for darkness; that put bitter for sweet, and sweet for bitter!

Woe unto them that are wise in their own eyes, and prudent in their own sight!

Woe unto them that are mighty to drink wine, and men of strength to mingle strong drink: which justify the wicked for reward, and take away the righteousness of the righteous from him! Therefore as the fire devoureth the stubble, and the flame consumeth the chaff, so their root shall be as rottenness, and their blossom shall go up as dust: because they have cast away the law of the LORD of hosts, and despised the word of the Holy One of Israel. Therefore is the anger of the LORD kindled against his people, and he hath stretched forth his hand against them, and hath smitten them: and the hills did tremble, and their carcasses were torn in the midst of the streets. For all this his anger is not turned away, but his hand is stretched out still.

And he will lift up an ensign to the nations from far, and will hiss unto them from the end of the earth: and, behold, they shall come with speed swiftly: none shall be weary nor stumble among them; none shall slumber nor sleep; neither shall the girdle of their loins be loosed, nor the latchet of their shoes be broken: whose arrows are sharp, and all their bows bent, their horses' hoofs shall be counted like flint, and their wheels like a whirlwind: their roaring shall be like a lion, they shall roar like young lions: yea, they shall roar, and lay hold of the prey, and shall carry it away safe, and none shall deliver it. And in that day they shall roar against them like the roaring of the sea: and if one look unto the land, behold darkness and sorrow, and the light is darkened in the heavens thereof.

— Isaiah 5.

THE PLOT AGAINST JUDAH. HOW ISAIAH TRIED TO KEEP UP THE COURAGE OF A FRIGHTENED KING AND PEOPLE

In the days of Isaiah the Mediterranean countries were all paying tribute to Assyria. During the reign of Ahaz, Syria and Northern Israel formed a plot to win their freedom and tried to force Judah to enter it. If Judah refused, they threatened to invade the land and seat a new king on the throne, the son of Tabeal. Ahaz was terrified, and the people with him. He dared not enter the conspiracy for fear of Assyria's vengeance, and if he stayed out, he feared the invasion of Syria. Isaiah met him as he went to look after the water supply of Jerusalem in case of a siege, and tried to instill some confidence into the panic-stricken king. He urged him to trust Jehovah, and offered him a sign of Jehovah's power. The king refused, for he had already sent messengers to ask aid of Assyria. The prophet knew this, and ended with a threat that Assyria would bring disaster.

And it came to pass in the days of Ahaz, the son of Jotham, the son of Uzziah, King of Judah, that Rezin, the king of Syria, and Pekah, the son of Remaliah, King of Israel, went up toward Jerusalem to war against it, but could not prevail against it.

And it was told the house of David, saying, "Syria is confederate with Ephraim." And his heart was moved, and the heart of his people, as the trees of the wood are moved with the wind.

Then said the LORD unto Isaiah, "Go forth now to meet Ahaz, thou, and Shear-jashub, thy son, at the end of the conduit of the upper pool in the highway of the fuller's field; and say unto him, 'Take heed, and be quiet; fear not, neither be fainthearted for the two tails of these smoking firebrands, for the fierce anger of Rezin with Syria, and of the son of Remaliah.

HOUSETOPS OF JERUSALEM
Photograph by W. A. Pottenger expressly for The Book of Life
The ancient city with its towers and flat-topped houses must have looked not unlike the modern city shown in the picture.

Because Syria, Ephraim, and the son of Remaliah, have taken evil counsel against thee, saying, "Let us go up against Judah, and vex it, and let us make a breach therein for us, and set a king in the midst of it, even the son of Tabeal": thus saith the Lord God: 'It shall not stand, neither shall it come to pass. For the head of Syria is Damascus, and the head of Damascus is Rezin. And the head of Ephraim is Samaria, and the head of Samaria is Remaliah's son. If ye will not believe, surely ye shall not be established.'"

Moreover the Lord spake again unto Ahaz, saying, "Ask thee a sign of the Lord thy God; ask it either in the depth, or in the height above."

But Ahaz said, "I will not ask, neither will I tempt the Lord."

And he said, "Hear ye now, O house of David: Is it a small thing for you to weary men, but will ye

weary my God also? Therefore the LORD himself
shall give you a sign; behold, a virgin shall conceive,
and bear a son, and shall call his name Immanuel.
Butter and honey shall he eat, that he may know to
refuse the evil, and choose the good. For before the
child shall know to refuse the evil, and choose the good,
the land that thou abhorrest shall be forsaken of both
her kings. The LORD shall bring upon thee, and upon
thy people, and upon thy father's house, days that
have not come, from the day that Ephraim departed
from Judah; even the king of Assyria.

"And it shall come to pass in that day, that the LORD
shall hiss for the fly that is in the uttermost part of
the rivers of Egypt, and for the bee that is in the land
of Assyria. And they shall come, and shall rest all of
them in the desolate valleys, and in the holes of the
rocks, and upon all thorns, and upon all bushes. In
the same day shall the LORD shave with a razor that is
hired, namely, by them beyond the river, by the king
of Assyria, the head, and the hair of the feet: and it
shall also consume the beard. And it shall come to
pass in that day, that a man shall nourish a young cow,
and two sheep; and it shall come to pass, for the abundance of milk that they shall give he shall eat butter:
for butter and honey shall every one eat that is left
in the land. And it shall come to pass in that day,
that every place shall be, where there were a thousand
vines at a thousand silverlings, it shall even be for
briers and thorns. With arrows and with bows shall
men come thither; because all the land shall become
briers and thorns. And on all hills that shall be digged
with the mattock, there shall not come thither the fear
of briers and thorns: but it shall be for the sending
forth of oxen, and for the treading of lesser cattle."

Moreover the LORD said unto me, "Take thee a great roll, and write in it with a man's pen concerning Maher-shalal-hash-baz," (swift spoil, speedy prey).

And I took unto me faithful witnesses to record, Uriah, the priest, and Zechariah, the son of Jeberechiah. And I went unto the prophetess; and she conceived, and bare a son.

Then said the LORD to me, "Call his name Maher-shalal-hash-baz. For before the child shall have knowledge to cry, 'My father,' and 'my mother,' the riches of Damascus and the spoil of Samaria shall be taken away before the king of Assyria."

The LORD spake also unto me again, saying: "Forasmuch as this people refuseth the waters of Shiloah that go softly, and rejoice in Rezin and Remaliah's son; now therefore, behold, the LORD bringeth up upon them the waters of the river, strong and many, even the king of Assyria, and all his glory: and he shall come up over all his channels, and go over all his banks: and he shall pass through Judah; he shall overflow and go over, he shall reach even to the neck and the stretching out of his wings shall fill the breadth of thy land, O Immanuel."

Associate yourselves, O ye people, and ye shall be broken in pieces; and give ear, all ye of far countries: gird yourselves, and ye shall be broken in pieces; gird yourselves, and ye shall be broken in pieces. Take counsel together, and it shall come to naught; speak the word, and it shall not stand: for God is with us.

For the LORD spake thus to me with a strong hand, and instructed me that I should not walk in the way of this people, saying, "Say ye not, 'A confederacy,' to all them to whom this people shall say, 'A confederacy'; neither fear ye their fear, nor be afraid. Sanctify the LORD of hosts himself; and let him be your fear, and let him be your dread. And he shall be for a sanctuary; but for a stone of stumbling and for a rock of offence to both the houses of Israel, for a gin and for a snare to the inhabitants of Jerusalem. And many among them shall stumble, and fall, and be broken, and be snared, and be taken. "Bind up the testimony, seal the law among my disciples."

And I will wait upon the LORD, that hideth his face from the house of Jacob, and I will look for him. Behold, I and the children whom the LORD hath given me are for signs and for wonders in Israel from the LORD of hosts, which dwelleth in Mount Zion.

And when they shall say unto you, "Seek unto them that have familiar spirits, and unto wizards that peep, and that mutter: should not a people seek unto their God? for the living to the dead?" To the law and to the testimony! If they speak not according to this word, it is because there is no light in them. And they shall pass through it, hardly bestead and hungry: and it shall come to pass, that when they shall be hungry, they shall fret themselves, and curse their king and their God, and look upward. And they shall look unto the earth; and behold trouble and darkness, dimness of anguish; and they shall be driven to darkness.

Nevertheless the dimness shall not be such as was in her vexation, when at the first he lightly afflicted the land of Zebulun and the land of Naphtali, and afterward did more grievously afflict her by the way of the sea, beyond Jordan, in Galilee of the nations. The people that walked in darkness have seen a great light: they that dwell in the land of the shadow of death, upon them hath the light shined.

—Isaiah 7; 8; 9: 1, 2.

The Hope of a Great King

Thou hast multiplied the nation, and not increased the joy: they joy before thee according to the joy in harvest, and as men rejoice when they divide the spoil. For thou hast broken the yoke of his burden, and the staff of his shoulder, the rod of his oppressor, as in the day of Midian. For every battle of the warrior is with confused noise, and garments rolled in blood; but this shall be with burning and fuel of fire.

For unto us a child is born, unto us a son is given: and the government shall be upon his shoulder: and his name shall be called Wonderful, Counsellor, The mighty God, The everlasting Father, The Prince of Peace. Of the increase of his government and peace there shall be no end, upon the throne of David, and upon his kingdom, to order it, and to establish it with judgment and with justice from henceforth even forever. The zeal of the LORD of hosts will perform this.

— Isaiah 9:3–7.

Punishments Past and Future

The LORD sent a word into Jacob, and it hath lighted upon Israel. And all the people shall know, even Ephraim and the inhabitant of Samaria, that say in the pride and stoutness of heart, "The bricks are fallen down, but we will build with hewn stones: the sycamores are cut down, but we will change them into cedars." Therefore the LORD shall set up the adversaries of Rezin against him, and join his enemies together; the Syrians before, and the Philistines behind; and they shall devour Israel with open mouth. For all this his anger is not turned away, but his hand is stretched out still.

For the people turneth not unto him that smiteth them, neither do they seek the LORD of hosts. Therefore the LORD will cut off from Israel head and tail, branch and rush, in one day. The ancient and honourable, he is the head; and the prophet that teacheth lies, he is the tail. For the leaders of this people cause them to err; and they that are led of them are destroyed. Therefore the LORD shall have no joy in their young men, neither shall have mercy on their fatherless and widows: for every one is an hypocrite and an evildoer, and every mouth speaketh folly. For all this his anger is not turned away, but his hand is stretched out still.

For wickedness burneth as the fire: it shall devour the briers and thorns, and shall kindle in the thickets of the forest, and they shall mount up like the lifting up of smoke. Through the wrath of the LORD of hosts is the land darkened, and the people shall be as the fuel of the fire: no man shall spare his brother. And he shall snatch on the right hand, and be hungry; and he shall eat on the left hand, and they shall not be satisfied: they shall eat every man the flesh of his own arm: Manasseh, Ephraim; and Ephraim, Manasseh: and they together shall be against Judah. For all this his anger is not turned away, but his hand is stretched out still.

Woe unto them that decree unrighteous decrees, and that write grievousness which they have prescribed; to turn aside the needy from judgment, and to take away the right from the poor of my people, that widows may be their prey, and that they may rob the fatherless! And what will ye do in the day of visitation, and in the desolation which shall come from far? To whom will ye flee for help? And where will ye leave your glory? Without me they shall bow down under the prisoners, and they shall fall under the slain. For all this his anger is not turned away, but his hand is stretched out still. — Isaiah 9:8-10:4.

Though Boastful Assyria Must Punish Israel, Eventually She Must Fall

O Assyrian, the rod of mine anger, and the staff in their hand is mine indignation. I will send him against an hypocritical nation, and against the people of my wrath will I give him a charge, to take the spoil, and to take the prey, and to tread them down like the mire of the streets. Howbeit he meaneth not so, neither doth his heart think so; but it is in his heart to destroy and cut off nations not a few. For he saith, "Are not my princes altogether kings? Is not Calno as Carchemish? Is not Hamath as Arpad? Is not Samaria as Damascus? As my hand hath found the kingdoms of the idols, and whose graven images did excel them of Jerusalem and of Samaria; shall I not, as I have done unto Samaria and her idols, so do to Jerusalem and her idols?"

Wherefore it shall come to pass, that when the LORD hath performed his whole work upon Mount Zion and on Jerusalem, I will punish the fruit of the stout heart of the king of Assyria, and the glory of his high looks. For he saith, "By the strength of my hand I have done it, and by my wisdom; for I am prudent: and I have removed the bounds of the people, and have robbed their treasures, and I have put down the inhabitants like a valiant man: and my hand hath found as a nest the riches of the people: and as one gathereth eggs that are left, have I gathered all the earth; and there was none that moved the wing, or opened the mouth, or peeped."

Shall the ax boast itself against him that heweth therewith? Or shall the saw magnify itself against him that shaketh it? As if the rod should shake itself against them that lift it up, or as if the staff should lift up itself, as if it were no wood. Therefore shall the LORD, the LORD of hosts, send among his fat ones leanness; and under his glory he shall kindle a burning like the burning of a fire. And the light of Israel shall be for a fire, and his Holy One for a flame: and it shall burn and devour his thorns and his briers in one day; and shall consume the glory of his forest, and of his fruitful field, both soul and body: and they shall be as when a standardbearer fainteth. And the rest of the trees of his forest shall be few, that a child may write them.

And it shall come to pass in that day, that the remnant of Israel, and such as are escaped of the house of Jacob, shall no more again stay upon him that smote them; but shall stay upon the LORD, the Holy One of Israel, in truth. The remnant shall return, even the remnant of Jacob, unto the mighty God. For though thy people Israel be as the sand of the sea, yet a remnant of them shall return: the consumption decreed shall overflow with righteousness. For the Lord GOD of hosts shall make a consumption, even determined, in the midst of all the land.

Therefore thus saith the Lord GOD of hosts, "O my people that dwellest in Zion, be not afraid of the Assyrian: he shall smite thee with a rod, and shall lift up his staff against thee, after the manner of Egypt. For yet a very little while, and the indignation shall cease, and mine anger in their destruction. And the LORD of hosts shall stir up a scourge for him according to the slaughter of Midian at the rock of Oreb: and as his rod was upon the sea, so shall he lift it up after the manner of Egypt. And it shall come to pass in that day, that his burden shall be taken away from off thy shoulder, and his yoke from off thy neck, and the yoke shall be destroyed because of the anointing."

He is come to Aiath, he is passed to Migron; at Michmash he hath laid up his carriages: they are gone over the passage: they have taken up their lodging at Geba; Ramah is afraid; Gibeah of Saul is fled. Lift up thy voice, O daughter of Gallim: cause it to be heard unto Laish, O poor Anathoth! Madmenah is removed; the inhabitants of Gebim gather themselves to flee. As yet shall he remain at Nob that day: he shall shake his hand against the mount of the daughter of Zion, the hill of Jerusalem.

Behold, the Lord, the Lord of hosts, shall lop the bough with terror: and the high ones of stature shall be hewn down, and the haughty shall be humbled. And he shall cut down the thickets of the forest with iron, and Lebanon shall fall by a mighty one.

—Isaiah 10:5–34.

PROPHECIES OF PEACE

And there shall come forth a rod out of the stem of Jesse, and a Branch shall grow out of his roots: and the spirit of the Lord shall rest upon him, the spirit of wisdom and understanding, the spirit of counsel and might, the spirit of knowledge and of the fear of the Lord; and shall make him of quick understanding in the fear of the Lord: and he shall not judge after the sight of his eyes, neither reprove after the hearing of his ears: but with righteousness shall he judge the poor, and reprove with equity for the meek of the earth: and he shall smite the earth with the rod of his mouth, and with the breath of his lips shall he slay the wicked. And righteousness shall be the girdle of his loins, and faithfulness the girdle of his reins. The wolf also shall dwell with the lamb, and the leopard shall lie down with the kid; and the calf and the young lion and the fatling together; and a little child shall lead them.

And the cow and the bear shall feed; their young ones shall lie down together: and the lion shall eat straw like the ox. And the sucking child shall play on the hole of the asp, and the weaned child shall put his hand on the cockatrice' den. They shall not hurt nor destroy in all my holy mountain: for the earth shall be full of the knowledge of the LORD, as the waters cover the sea.

And in that day there shall be a root of Jesse, which shall stand for an ensign of the people; to it shall the Gentiles seek: and his rest shall be glorious.

And it shall come to pass in that day, that the LORD shall set his hand again the second time to recover the remnant of his people, which shall be left, from Assyria, and from Egypt, and from Pathros, and from Cush, and from Elam, and from Shinar, and from Hamath, and from the islands of the sea. And he shall set up an ensign for the nations, and shall assemble the outcasts of Israel, and gather together the dispersed of Judah from the four corners of the earth. The envy also of Ephraim shall depart, and the adversaries of Judah shall be cut off: Ephraim shall not envy Judah, and Judah shall not vex Ephraim; but they shall fly upon the shoulders of the Philistines toward the west; they shall spoil them of the east together: they shall lay their hand upon Edom and Moab; and the children of Ammon shall obey them. And the LORD shall utterly destroy the tongue of the Egyptian Sea; and with his mighty wind shall he shake his hand over the river, and shall smite it in the seven streams, and make men go over dryshod, and there shall be an highway for the remnant of his people, which shall be left, from Assyria; like as it was to Israel in the day that he came up out of the land of Egypt.

And in that day thou shalt say:

"O LORD, I will praise thee:
Though thou wast angry with me,
Thine anger is turned away, and thou com-
fortedst me.
Behold, God is my salvation;
I will trust, and not be afraid:
For the LORD JEHOVAH is my strength and
my song;
He also is become my salvation.
Therefore with joy shall ye draw water
Out of the wells of salvation."

And in that day shall ye say,

"Praise the LORD, call upon his name,
Declare his doings among the people,
Make mention that his name is exalted.
Sing unto the LORD; for he hath done excellent
things:
This is known in all the earth.
Cry out and shout, thou inhabitant of Zion:
For great is the Holy One of Israel in the midst
of thee." —Isaiah 11; 12.

A GREAT SERMON OF WARNING: BABYLON SHALL FALL

Lift ye up a banner upon the high mountain, exalt
the voice unto them, shake the hand, that they may
go into the gates of the nobles. I have commanded
my sanctified ones, I have also called my mighty ones
for mine anger, even them that rejoice in my highness.
The noise of a multitude in the mountains, like as of
a great people; a tumultuous noise of the kingdoms
of nations gathered together: the LORD of hosts mus-
tereth the host of the battle. They come from a far

country, from the end of heaven, even the LORD, and the weapons of his indignation, to destroy the whole land.

Howl ye; for the day of the LORD is at hand; it shall come as a destruction from the Almighty. Therefore shall all hands be faint, and every man's heart shall melt: and they shall be afraid: pangs and sorrows shall take hold of them; they shall be in pain as a woman that travaileth: they shall be amazed one at another; their faces shall be as flames.

Behold, the day of the LORD cometh, cruel both with wrath and fierce anger, to lay the land desolate: and he shall destroy the sinners thereof out of it; for the stars of heaven and the constellations thereof shall not give their light: the sun shall be darkened in his going forth, and the moon shall not cause her light to shine; and I will punish the world for their evil, and the wicked for their iniquity; and I will cause the arrogancy of the proud to cease, and will lay low the haughtiness of the terrible. I will make a man more precious than fine gold; even a man than the golden wedge of Ophir.

Therefore I will shake the heavens, and the earth shall remove out of her place, in the wrath of the LORD of hosts, and in the day of his fierce anger. And it shall be as the chased roe, and as a sheep that no man taketh up: they shall every man turn to his own people, and flee every one into his own land. Every one that is found shall be thrust through; and every one that is joined unto them shall fall by the sword. Their children also shall be dashed to pieces before their eyes; their houses shall be spoiled, and their wives ravished.

Behold, I will stir up the Medes against them, which shall not regard silver; and as for gold, they shall not delight in it. Their bows also shall dash the young men to pieces; and they shall have no pity on the fruit of the womb; their eye shall not spare children. And Babylon, the glory of kingdoms, the beauty of the Chaldees' excellency, shall be as when God overthrew Sodom and Gomorrah. It shall never be inhabited, neither shall it be dwelt in from generation to generation: neither shall the Arabian pitch tent there; neither shall the shepherds make their fold there; but wild beasts of the desert shall lie there; and their houses shall be full of doleful creatures; and owls shall dwell there, and satyrs shall dance there; and the wild beasts of the islands shall cry in their desolate houses, and dragons in their pleasant palaces: and her time is near to come, and her days shall not be prolonged.

For the LORD will have mercy on Jacob, and will yet choose Israel, and set them in their own land: and the strangers shall be joined with them, and they shall cleave to the house of Jacob. And the people shall take them, and bring them to their place: and the house of Israel shall possess them in the land of the LORD for servants and handmaids: and they shall take them captives, whose captives they were; and they shall rule over their oppressors.

And it shall come to pass in the day that the LORD shall give thee rest from thy sorrow, and from thy fear, and from the hard bondage wherein thou wast made to serve, that thou shalt take up this proverb against the king of Babylon, and say, "How hath the oppressor ceased! the golden city ceased!" The LORD hath broken the staff of the wicked, and the sceptre of the rulers. He who smote the people in wrath with a continual stroke, he that ruled the nations in anger, is persecuted, and none hindereth. The whole earth is at rest, and is quiet: they break forth into singing. Yea,

A CEDAR OF LEBANON

Photograph by
Professor Lewis Bayles Paton

One of the magnificent cedars, the last survivors of the mighty forest, the lumber from which went to build the palaces of Solomon and the ships of his fleet.

"He heweth him down cedars, and taketh the cypress and the oak, which he strengtheneth for himself among the trees of the forest: he planteth an ash, and the rain doth nourish it.

"Then shall it be for a man to burn: for he will take thereof, and warm himself; yea, he kindleth it, and baketh bread; yea, he maketh a god, and worshipeth it; he maketh it a graven image, and falleth down thereto." — *Isaiah 44:14, 15.*

the fir-trees rejoice at thee, and the cedars of Lebanon, saying, "Since thou art laid down, no feller is come up against us."

Hell from beneath is moved for thee to meet thee at thy coming: it stirreth up the dead for thee, even all the chief ones of the earth; it hath raised up from their thrones all the kings of the nations.

All they shall speak and say unto thee, "Art thou also become weak as we? Art thou become like unto us? Thy pomp is brought down to the grave, and the noise of thy viols: the worm is spread under thee, and the worms cover thee."

How art thou fallen from heaven, O Lucifer, son of the morning! How art thou cut down to the ground, which didst weaken the nations! For thou hast said in thine heart, "I will ascend into heaven, I will exalt my throne above the stars of God: I will sit also upon the mount of the congregation, in the sides of the north: I will ascend above the heights of the clouds; I will be like the most High." Yet thou shalt be brought down to hell, to the sides of the pit.

They that see thee shall narrowly look upon thee, and consider thee, saying, "Is this the man that made the earth to tremble, that did shake kingdoms; that made the world as a wilderness, and destroyed the cities thereof; that opened not the house of his prisoners?"

All the kings of the nations, even all of them, lie in glory, every one in his own house. But thou art cast out of thy grave like an abominable branch, and as the raiment of those that are slain, thrust through with a sword, that go down to the stones of the pit; as a carcass trodden under feet. Thou shalt not be joined with them in burial, because thou hast destroyed thy land, and slain thy people: the seed of evildoers shall never be renowned.

Prepare slaughter for his children for the iniquity of their fathers; that they do not rise, nor possess the land, nor fill the face of the world with cities.

"For I will rise up against them," saith the LORD of hosts, "and cut off from Babylon the name, and remnant, and son, and nephew," saith the LORD. "I will also make it a possession for the bittern, and pools of water: and I will sweep it with the besom of destruction," saith the LORD of hosts. —Isaiah 13; 14:1-23.

The Prophet Pronounces Doom Upon Various Nations of the Earth

DOOM OF ASSYRIA

The LORD of hosts hath sworn, saying, "Surely as I have thought, so shall it come to pass; and as I have purposed, so shall it stand: that I will break the Assyrian in my land, and upon my mountains tread him under foot: then shall his yoke depart from off them, and his burden depart from off their shoulders." This is the purpose that is purposed upon the whole earth: and this is the hand that is stretched out upon all the nations. For the LORD of hosts hath purposed, and who shall disannul it? And his hand is stretched out, and who shall turn it back?

In the year that King Ahaz died was this burden.

DOOM OF PALESTINA

Rejoice not thou, whole Palestina, because the rod of him that smote thee is broken: for out of the serpent's root shall come forth a cockatrice, and his fruit shall be a fiery flying serpent. And the firstborn of the poor shall feed, and the needy shall lie down in safety: and I will kill thy root with famine, and he shall slay thy remnant.

Howl, O gate; cry, O city; thou, whole Palestina, art dissolved: for there shall come from the north a smoke, and none shall be alone in his appointed times. What shall one then answer the messengers of the nation? That the LORD hath founded Zion, and the poor of his people shall trust in it.   —Isaiah 14:24–32.

THE BURDEN OF MOAB

Because in the night Ar of Moab is laid waste, and brought to silence; because in the night Kir of Moab is laid waste, and brought to silence; he is gone up to Bajith, and to Dibon, the high places, to weep: Moab shall howl over Nebo, and over Medeba: on all their heads shall be baldness, and every beard cut off. In their streets they shall gird themselves with sackcloth: on the tops of their houses, and in their streets, every one shall howl, weeping abundantly. And Heshbon shall cry, and Elealeh: their voice shall be heard even unto Jahaz: therefore the armed soldiers of Moab shall cry out; his life shall be grievous unto him.

My heart shall cry out for Moab; his fugitives shall flee unto Zoar, an heifer of three years old: for by the mounting up of Luhith with weeping shall they go it up; for in the way of Horonaim they shall raise up a cry of destruction. For the waters of Nimrim shall be desolate: for the hay is withered away, the grass faileth, there is no green thing. Therefore the abundance they have gotten, and that which they have laid up, shall they carry away to the brook of the willows. For the cry is gone round about the borders of Moab; the howling thereof unto Eglaim, and the howling thereof unto Beer-elim; for the waters of Dimon shall be full of blood: for I will bring more upon Dimon, lions upon him that escapeth of Moab, and upon the remnant of the land.

Send ye the lamb to the ruler of the land from Sela to the wilderness, unto the mount of the daughter of Zion. For it shall be, that, as a wandering bird cast out of the nest, so the daughters of Moab shall be at the fords of Arnon. Take counsel, execute judgment; make thy shadow as the night in the midst of the noonday; hide

the outcasts; betray not him that wandereth. Let mine
outcasts dwell with thee, Moab; be thou a covert to them
from the face of the spoiler: for the extortioner is at an
end, the spoiler ceaseth, the oppressors are consumed out
of the land. And in mercy shall the throne be established:
and he shall sit upon it in truth in the tabernacle of
David, judging, and seeking judgment, and hasting
righteousness.

We have heard of the pride of Moab; he is very proud:
even of his haughtiness, and his pride, and his wrath:
but his lies shall not be so. Therefore shall Moab howl
for Moab, every one shall howl: for the foundations of
Kir-hareseth shall ye mourn; surely they are stricken.
For the fields of Heshbon languish, and the vine of Sibmah: the lords of the heathen have broken down the
principal plants thereof, they are come even unto Jazer,
they wandered through the wilderness: her branches are
stretched out, they are gone over the sea.

Therefore I will bewail with the weeping of Jazer the
vine of Sibmah: I will water thee with my tears, O
Heshbon, and Elealeh: for the shouting for thy summer
fruits and for thy harvest is fallen; and gladness is taken
away, and joy out of the plentiful field; and in the vineyards there shall be no singing, neither shall there be
shouting: the treaders shall tread out no wine in their
presses; I have made their vintage shouting to cease.
Wherefore my bowels shall sound like an harp for Moab,
and mine inward parts for Kir-haresh.

And it shall come to pass, when it is seen that Moab
is weary on the high place, that he shall come to his
sanctuary to pray; but he shall not prevail.

This is the word that the LORD hath spoken concerning Moab since that time. But now the LORD hath spoken,
saying, "Within three years, as the years of an hireling,

and the glory of Moab shall be contemned, with all that great multitude; and the remnant shall be very small and feeble."   —Isaiah 15; 16.

THE BURDEN OF DAMASCUS

"Behold, Damascus is taken away from being a city, and it shall be a ruinous heap. The cities of Aroer are forsaken : they shall be for flocks, which shall lie down, and none shall make them afraid. The fortress also shall cease from Ephraim, and the kingdom from Damascus, and the remnant of Syria: they shall be as the glory of the children of Israel," saith the LORD of hosts. And in that day it shall come to pass, that the glory of Jacob shall be made thin, and the fatness of his flesh shall wax lean. And it shall be as when the harvestman gathereth the corn, and reapeth the ears with his arm; and it shall be as he that gathereth ears in the valley of Rephaim.

"Yet gleaning grapes shall be left in it, as the shaking of an olive-tree, two or three berries in the top of the uppermost bough, four or five in the outmost fruitful branches thereof," saith the LORD God of Israel. At that day shall a man look to his Maker, and his eyes shall have respect to the Holy One of Israel, and he shall not look to the altars, the work of his hands, neither shall respect that which his fingers have made, either the groves, or the images. In that day shall his strong cities be as a forsaken bough, and an uppermost branch, which they left because of the children of Israel: and there shall be desolation. Because thou hast forgotten the God of thy salvation, and hast not been mindful of the rock of thy strength, therefore shalt thou plant pleasant plants, and shalt set it with strange slips: in the day shalt thou make thy plant to grow, and in the morning shalt thou make thy seed to flourish: but the harvest shall be a heap in the day of grief and of desperate sorrow.

A SONG OF DOOM

Woe to the multitude of many people,
Which make a noise like the noise of the seas;
And to the rushing of nations,
That make a rushing like the rushing of mighty
waters!
The nations shall rush like the rushing of many
waters:
But God shall rebuke them, and they shall flee far
off,
And shall be chased as the chaff of the mountains
before the wind,
And like a rolling thing before the whirlwind;
And behold at eveningtide trouble;
And before the morning he is not.
This is the portion of them that spoil us,
And the lot of them that rob us.   —Isaiah 17.

THE DOOM OF ETHIOPIA

Woe to the land shadowing with wings, which is beyond the rivers of Ethiopia: that sendeth ambassadors by
the sea, even in vessels of bulrushes upon the waters,
saying, "Go, ye swift messengers, to a nation scattered
and peeled, to a people terrible from their beginning
hitherto; a nation meted out and trodden down, whose
land the rivers have spoiled!"

All ye inhabitants of the world, and dwellers on the
earth, see ye, when he lifteth up an ensign on the mountains; and when he bloweth a trumpet, hear ye. For so
the LORD said unto me, "I will take my rest, and I will
consider in my dwelling place like a clear heat upon
herbs, and like a cloud of dew in the heat of harvest."
For afore the harvest, when the bud is perfect, and the

sour grape is ripening in the flower, he shall both cut off the sprigs with pruning hooks, and take away and cut down the branches. They shall be left together unto the fowls of the mountains, and to the beasts of the earth: and the fowls shall summer upon them, and all the beasts of the earth shall winter upon them.

In that time shall the present be brought unto the LORD of hosts of a people scattered and peeled, and from a people terrible from their beginning hitherto; a nation meted out and trodden under foot, whose land the rivers have spoiled, to the place of the name of the LORD of hosts, the Mount Zion. —Isaiah 18.

THE BURDEN OF EGYPT

Behold, the LORD rideth upon a swift cloud, and shall come into Egypt: and the idols of Egypt shall be moved at his presence, and the heart of Egypt shall melt in the midst of it. "And I will set the Egyptians against the Egyptians: and they shall fight every one against his brother, and every one against his neighbour; city against

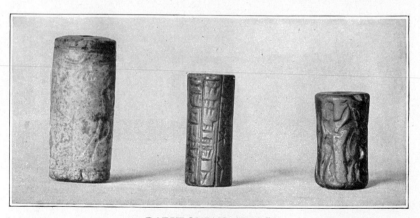

BABYLONIAN SEALS

By courtesy of the Metropolitan Museum of Art
These seals of baked clay were used perhaps for public documents.

city, and kingdom against kingdom. And the spirit of
Egypt shall fail in the midst thereof; and I will destroy
the counsel thereof: and they shall seek to the idols, and
to the charmers, and to them that have familiar spirits,
and to the wizards. And the Egyptians will I give over
into the hand of a cruel lord; and a fierce king shall rule
over them," saith the Lord, the LORD of hosts.

And the waters shall fail from the sea, and the river
shall be wasted and dried up; and they shall turn the
rivers far away; and the brooks of defence shall be
emptied and dried up: the reeds and flags shall wither;
the paper reeds by the brooks, by the mouth of the brooks,
and everything sown by the brooks, shall wither, be
driven away, and be no more. The fishers also shall
mourn, and all they that cast angle into the brooks shall
lament, and they that spread nets upon the waters shall
languish; moreover they that work in fine flax, and they
that weave networks, shall be confounded; and they
shall be broken in the purposes thereof, all that make
sluices and ponds for fish.

Surely the princes of Zoan are fools, the counsel of
the wise counsellors of Pharaoh is become brutish: how
say ye unto Pharaoh, "I am the son of the wise, the son
of ancient kings?" Where are they? Where are thy wise
men? And let them tell thee now, and let them know
what the LORD of hosts hath purposed upon Egypt.

The princes of Zoan are become fools, the princes of
Noph are deceived; they have also seduced Egypt, even
they that are the stay of the tribes thereof. The LORD
hath mingled a perverse spirit in the midst thereof: and
they have caused Egypt to err in every work thereof, as
a drunken man staggereth in his vomit; neither shall
there be any work for Egypt, which the head or tail,
branch or rush, may do.

In that day shall Egypt be like unto women: and it shall be afraid and fear because of the shaking of the hand of the LORD of hosts, which he shaketh over it. And the land of Judah shall be a terror unto Egypt, every one that maketh mention thereof shall be afraid in himself, because of the counsel of the LORD of hosts, which he hath determined against it.

In that day shall five cities in the land of Egypt speak the language of Canaan, and swear to the LORD of hosts; one shall be called, The City of Destruction.

AN ALTAR OF THE LORD IN EGYPT

In that day shall there be an altar to the LORD in the midst of the land of Egypt, and a pillar at the border thereof to the LORD; and it shall be for a sign and for a witness unto the LORD of hosts in the land of Egypt: for they shall cry unto the LORD because of the oppressors, and he shall send them a saviour, and a great one, and he shall deliver them. And the LORD shall be known to Egypt, and the Egyptians shall know the LORD in that day, and shall do sacrifice and oblation; yea, they shall vow a vow unto the LORD, and perform it. And the LORD shall smite Egypt: he shall smite and heal it: and they shall return even to the LORD, and he shall be intreated of them, and shall heal them.

In that day shall there be a highway out of Egypt to Assyria, and the Assyrian shall come into Egypt, and the Egyptian into Assyria, and the Egyptians shall serve with the Assyrians.

In that day shall Israel be the third with Egypt and with Assyria, even a blessing in the midst of the land: whom the LORD of hosts shall bless, saying, "Blessed be Egypt, my people, and Assyria, the work of my hands, and Israel, mine inheritance." —Isaiah 19.

An Acted Sermon on the Occasion of the Fall of Ashdod

Ten years after the fall of Samaria the Mediterranean states once more attempted to plot for freedom from Assyria. This time the Philistine city of Ashdod was the center of the conspiracy. Egypt promised help, and the plotters tried to bring in Judah. Isaiah tried to show the hopelessness of the scheme.

In the year that Tartan came unto Ashdod, when Sargon, the king of Assyria, sent him, and fought against Ashdod, and took it; at the same time spake the LORD by Isaiah, the son of Amoz, saying, "Go and loose the sackcloth from off thy loins, and put off thy shoe from thy foot." And he did so, walking naked and barefoot.

And the LORD said, "Like as my servant Isaiah hath walked naked and barefoot three years for a sign and wonder upon Egypt and upon Ethiopia; so shall the king of Assyria lead away the Egyptians prisoners, and the Ethiopians captives, young and old, naked and barefoot, even with their buttocks uncovered, to the shame of Egypt. And they shall be afraid and ashamed of Ethiopia, their expectation, and of Egypt, their glory. And the inhabitant of this isle shall say in that day, 'Behold, such is our expectation, whither we flee for help to be delivered from the king of Assyria: and how shall we escape?'"

— Isaiah 20.

Further Dooms Pronounced

THE BURDEN OF THE DESERT OF THE SEA

As whirlwinds in the south pass through; so it cometh from the desert, from a terrible land. A grievous vision is declared unto me; the treacherous dealer dealeth treacherously, and the spoiler spoileth. Go up, O Elam: besiege, O Media; all the sighing thereof, have I made to cease. Therefore are my loins filled with pain: pangs have taken hold upon me, as the pangs of a woman that travaileth: I was bowed down at the hearing of it; I was dismayed at the seeing of it. My heart panted, fearfulness affrighted me: the night of my pleasure hath he turned into fear unto me.

Prepare the table, watch in the watchtower, eat, drink: arise, ye princes, and anoint the shield. For thus hath the LORD said unto me, "Go, set a watchman, let him declare what he seeth." And he saw a chariot with a couple of horsemen, a chariot of asses, and a chariot of camels; and he hearkened diligently with much heed: and he cried "A lion: My lord, I stand continually upon the watchtower in the daytime, and I am set in my ward whole nights: and, behold, here cometh a chariot of men, with a couple of horsemen."

And he answered and said, "Babylon is fallen, is fallen; and all the graven images of her gods he hath broken unto the ground."

O my threshing, and the corn of my floor: that which I have heard of the LORD of hosts, the God of Israel, have I declared unto you.

THE BURDEN OF DUMAH

He calleth to me out of Seir, "Watchman, what of the night? Watchman, what of the night?"

The watchman said, "The morning cometh, and also the night: if ye will enquire, enquire ye: return, come."

THE BURDEN UPON ARABIA

In the forest in Arabia shall ye lodge, O ye traveling companies of Dedanim. The inhabitants of the land of Tema brought water to him that was thirsty, they prevented with their bread him that fled. For they fled from the swords, from the drawn sword, and from the bent bow, and from the grievousness of war. For thus hath the LORD said unto me, "Within a year, according to the years of an hireling, and all the glory of Kedar shall fail: and the residue of the number of archers, the mighty men of the children of Kedar, shall be diminished: for the LORD God of Israel hath spoken it." —Isaiah 21.

THE BURDEN OF THE VALLEY OF VISION

What aileth thee now, that thou art wholly gone up to the housetops? Thou that art full of stirs, a tumultuous city, a joyous city: thy slain men are not slain with the sword, nor dead in battle. All thy rulers are fled together, they are bound by the archers: all that are found in thee are bound together, which have fled from far. Therefore said I, "Look away from me; I will weep bitterly, labour not to comfort me, because of the spoiling of the daughter of my people.

"For it is a day of trouble, and of treading down, and of perplexity by the Lord GOD of hosts in the valley of vision, breaking down the walls, and of crying to the mountains. And Elam bare the quiver with chariots of men and horsemen, and Kir uncovered the shield. And it shall come to pass, that thy choicest valleys shall be full of chariots, and the horsemen shall set themselves in array at the gate."

And he discovered the covering of Judah, and thou didst look in that day to the armour of the house of the forest. Ye have seen also the breaches of the city of David, that they are many: and ye gathered together the waters of the lower pool; and ye have numbered the houses of Jerusalem, and the houses have ye broken down to fortify the wall. Ye made also a ditch between the two walls for the water of the old pool: but ye have not looked unto the maker thereof, neither had respect unto him that fashioned it long ago.

And in that day did the Lord GOD of hosts call to weeping, and to mourning, and to baldness, and to girding with sackcloth: and behold joy and gladness, slaying oxen, and killing sheep, eating flesh, and drinking wine: "Let us eat and drink; for to-morrow we shall die." And it was revealed in mine ears by the LORD of hosts, "Surely this iniquity shall not be purged from you till ye die," saith the Lord GOD of hosts.

SHEBNA AND ELIAKIM

Thus saith the Lord GOD of hosts, "Go, get thee unto this treasurer, even unto Shebna, which is over the house, and say, 'What hast thou here? And whom hast thou here, that thou hast hewed thee out a sepulcher here, as he that heweth him out a sepulcher on high, and that graveth an habitation for himself in a rock? Behold, the LORD will carry thee away with a mighty captivity, and will surely cover thee. He will surely violently turn and toss thee like a ball into a large country: there shalt thou die, and there the chariots of thy glory shall be the shame of thy lord's house; and I will drive thee from thy station, and from thy state shall he pull thee down. And it shall come to pass in that day, that I will call my servant Eliakim, the son of Hilkiah: and I will clothe him with thy robe, and strengthen him with thy girdle, and I will commit thy government into his hand: and he shall be a father to the inhabitants of Jerusalem, and to the house of Judah. And the key of the house of David will I lay upon his shoulder; so he shall open, and none shall shut; and he shall shut, and none shall open; and I will fasten him as a nail in a sure place; and he shall be for a glorious throne to his father's house. And they shall hang upon him all the glory of his father's house, the offspring and the issue, all vessels of small quantity, from the vessels of cups, even to all the vessels of flagons. In that day, saith the LORD of hosts, shall the nail that is fastened in the sure place be removed, and be cut down, and fall; and the burden that was upon it shall be cut off: for the LORD hath spoken it.'"

—Isaiah 22.

THE BURDEN OF TYRE

Howl, ye ships of Tarshish, for it is laid waste, so that there is no house, no entering in: from the land of Chittim it is revealed to them. Be still, ye inhabitants of the isle; thou whom the merchants of Zidon, that pass over the sea, have replenished. And by great waters the seed of Sihor, the harvest of the river, is her revenue; and she is a mart of nations. Be thou ashamed, O Zidon: for the sea hath spoken, even the strength of the sea, saying, "I travail not, nor bring forth children, neither do I nourish up young men, nor bring up virgins." As at the report concerning Egypt, so shall they be sorely pained at the report of Tyre.

Pass ye over to Tarshish; howl, ye inhabitants of the isle. Is this your joyous city, whose antiquity is of ancient days? Her own feet shall carry her afar off to sojourn.

Who hath taken this counsel against Tyre, the crowning city, whose merchants are princes, whose traffickers are the honourable of the earth? The LORD of hosts hath purposed it, to stain the pride of all glory, and to bring into contempt all the honourable of the earth. Pass through thy land as a river, O daughter of Tarshish: there is no more strength. He stretched out his hand over the sea, he shook the kingdoms: the LORD hath given a commandment against the merchant city, to destroy the strongholds thereof. And he said, "Thou shalt no more rejoice." O thou oppressed virgin, daughter of Zidon: arise, pass over to Chittim; there also shalt thou have no rest.

Behold the land of the Chaldeans; this people was not, till the Assyrian founded it for them that dwell in the wilderness: they set up the towers thereof, they raised up the palaces thereof; and he brought it to ruin.

Howl, ye ships of Tarshish: for your strength is laid waste.

And it shall come to pass in that day, that Tyre shall be forgotten seventy years, according to the days of one king: after the end of seventy years shall Tyre sing as an harlot. Take an harp, go about the city, thou harlot that hast been forgotten; make sweet melody, sing many songs, that thou mayest be remembered.

And it shall come to pass after the end of seventy years, that the LORD will visit Tyre, and she shall turn to her hire, and shall commit fornication with all the kingdoms of the world upon the face of the earth. And her merchandise and her hire shall be holiness to the LORD: it shall not be treasured nor laid up; for her merchandise shall be for them that dwell before the LORD, to eat sufficiently, and for durable clothing. —Isaiah 23.

PRESENT DESTRUCTION AND FINAL HOPE

This group of prophecies, very unlike anything else in Isaiah, is sometimes supposed to come from a much later time. Its outlook is over the whole earth, but the writer comes back from the consideration of a shattered world to a confident hope in the God of Israel. It has a lesson of trust in the overruling power of God which is of great value to our own age.

Behold, the LORD maketh the earth empty, and maketh it waste, and turneth it upside down, and scattereth abroad the inhabitants thereof. And it shall be, as with the people, so with the priest; as with the servant, so with his master; as with the maid, so with her mistress; as with the buyer, so with the seller; as with the lender, so with the borrower; as with the taker of usury, so with the giver of usury to him. The land shall be utterly emptied, and utterly spoiled: for the LORD hath spoken this word. The earth mourneth and fadeth away, the world languisheth and fadeth away, the haughty people of the earth do languish. The earth also is defiled under the inhabitants thereof; because they have transgressed the laws, changed the ordinance, broken the everlasting covenant; therefore hath the curse devoured the earth, and they that dwell therein are desolate: therefore the inhabitants of the earth are burned, and few men left. The new wine mourneth, the vine languisheth, all the merryhearted do sigh; the mirth of tabrets ceaseth, the noise of them that rejoice endeth, the joy of the harp ceaseth; they shall not drink wine with a song; strong drink shall be bitter to them that drink it. The city of confusion is broken down: every house is shut up, that no man may come in. There is a crying for wine in the streets; all joy is darkened, the mirth of the land is gone. In the city is left desolation, and the gate is smitten with destruction.

When thus it shall be in the midst of the land among the people, there shall be as the shaking of an olive-tree, and as the gleaning grapes when the vintage is done. They shall lift up their voice, they shall sing for the majesty of the LORD, they shall cry aloud from the sea: "Wherefore glorify ye the LORD in the fires, even the name of the LORD God of Israel in the isles of the sea."

From the uttermost part of the earth have we heard songs, even glory to the righteous. But I said, "My leanness, my leanness! woe unto me! the treacherous dealers have dealt treacherously; yea, the treacherous dealers have dealt very treacherously."

Fear, and the pit, and the snare, are upon thee, O inhabitant of the earth. And it shall come to pass, that he who fleeth from the noise of the fear shall fall into the pit; and he that cometh up out of the midst of the pit shall be taken in the snare: for the windows from on high are open, and the foundations of the earth do shake. The earth is utterly broken down, the earth is clean dissolved, the earth is moved exceedingly. The earth shall reel to and fro like a drunkard, and shall be removed like a cottage; and the transgression thereof shall be heavy upon it; and it shall fall, and not rise again.

And it shall come to pass in that day, that the LORD shall punish the host of the high ones that are on high, and the kings of the earth upon the earth. And they shall be gathered together, as prisoners are gathered in the pit, and shall be shut up in the prison, and after many days shall they be visited. Then the moon shall be confounded, and the sun ashamed, when the LORD of hosts shall reign in Mount Zion, and in Jerusalem, and before his ancients gloriously.

O LORD, thou art my God; I will exalt thee, I will praise thy name; for thou hast done wonderful things; thy counsels of old are faithfulness and truth. For thou hast made of a city an heap; of a defenced city a ruin: a palace of strangers to be no city; it shall never be built; therefore shall the strong people glorify thee, the city of the terrible nations shall fear thee. For thou hast been a strength to the poor, a strength to the needy in his distress, a refuge from the storm, a shadow from the heat, when the blast of the terrible ones is as a storm against the wall. Thou shalt bring down the noise of strangers, as the heat in a dry place; even the heat with the shadow of a cloud: the branch of the terrible ones shall be brought low.

And in this mountain shall the LORD of hosts make unto all people a feast of fat things, a feast of wines on the lees, of fat things full of marrow, of wines on the lees well refined. And he will destroy in this mountain the face of the covering cast over all people, and the veil that is spread over all nations. He will swallow up death in victory; and the Lord GOD will wipe away tears from off all faces; and the rebuke of his people shall he take away from off all the earth: for the LORD hath spoken it.

And it shall be said in that day: "Lo, this is our God; we have waited for him, and he will save us: this is the LORD; we have waited for him, we will be glad and rejoice in his salvation." For in this mountain shall the hand of the LORD rest, and Moab shall be trodden down under him, even as straw is trodden down for the dunghill. And he shall spread forth his hands in the midst of them, as he that swimmeth spreadeth forth his hands to swim: and he shall bring down their pride together with the spoils of their hands; and the fortress of the high fort of thy walls shall he bring down, lay low, and bring to the ground, even to the dust. — Isaiah 24; 25.

A SONG IN THE LAND OF JUDAH

In that day shall this song be sung in the land of Judah:
> We have a strong city;
> Salvation will God appoint for walls and bulwarks.
> Open ye the gates,
> That the righteous nation which keepeth the truth
> may enter in.

Thou wilt keep him in perfect peace,
Whose mind is stayed on thee: because he trusteth
in thee.
Trust ye in the LORD for ever:
For in the LORD JEHOVAH is everlasting strength:
For he bringeth down them that dwell on high;
The lofty city, he layeth it low;
He layeth it low, even to the ground;
He bringeth it even to the dust.
The foot shall tread it down,
Even the feet of the poor,
And the steps of the needy.
The way of the just is uprightness:
Thou, most upright, dost weigh the path of the just.
Yea, in the way of thy judgments, O LORD,
Have we waited for thee;
The desire of our soul is to thy name,
And to the remembrance of thee.
With my soul have I desired thee in the night;
Yea, with my spirit within me will I seek thee early:
For when thy judgments are in the earth,
The inhabitants of the world will learn righteousness.
Let favour be shewed to the wicked,
Yet will he not learn righteousness:
In the land of uprightness will he deal unjustly,
And will not behold the majesty of the LORD.
LORD, when thy hand is lifted up, they will not see:
But they shall see, and be ashamed for their envy at
the people;
Yea, the fire of thine enemies shall devour them.
LORD, thou wilt ordain peace for us:
For thou also hast wrought all our works in us.
O LORD our God, other lords beside thee have had
dominion over us:

But by thee only will we make mention of thy name.
They are dead, they shall not live,
They are deceased, they shall not rise:
Therefore hast thou visited and destroyed them,
And made all their memory to perish.
Thou hast increased the nation, O LORD,
Thou hast increased the nation:
Thou art glorified:
Thou hadst removed it far unto all the ends of the
    earth.
LORD, in trouble have they visited thee,
They poured out a prayer when thy chastening was
    upon them.
Like as a woman with child,
That draweth near the time of her delivery,
Is in pain, and crieth out in her pangs;
So have we been in thy sight, O LORD.
We have been with child, we have been in pain,
We have as it were brought forth wind;
We have not wrought any deliverance in the earth;
Neither have the inhabitants of the world fallen.
Thy dead men shall live, together with my dead
    body shall they arise.
Awake and sing, ye that dwell in dust:
For thy dew is as the dew of herbs,
And the earth shall cast out the dead.
Come, my people, enter thou into thy chambers,
And shut thy doors about thee:
Hide thyself as it were for a little moment,
Until the indignation be overpast.
For, behold, the LORD cometh out of his place
To punish the inhabitants of the earth for their
    iniquity:
The earth also shall disclose her blood,

And shall no more cover her slain.

In that day the LORD with his sore and great and
strong sword

Shall punish leviathan, the piercing serpent,

Even leviathan, that crooked serpent;

And he shall slay the dragon that is in the sea.

In that day sing ye unto her: A vineyard of red wine.

I the LORD do keep it;

I will water it every moment:

Lest any hurt it, I will keep it night and day.

Fury is not in me:

Who would set the briers and thorns against me in
battle?

I would go through them, I would burn them together.

Or let him take hold of my strength,

That he may make peace with me;

And he shall make peace with me.

He shall cause them that come of Jacob to take root:

Israel shall blossom and bud, and fill the face of the
world with fruit.

Hath he smitten him, as he smote those that smote
him?

Or is he slain according to the slaughter of them that
are slain by him?

In measure, when it shooteth forth, thou wilt debate
with it:

He stayeth his rough wind in the day of the east wind.

By this therefore shall the iniquity of Jacob be
purged;

And this is all the fruit to take away his sin;

When he maketh all the stones of the altar as chalk-
stones that are beaten in sunder,

The groves and images shall not stand up.

Yet the defenced city shall be desolate,
And the habitation forsaken, and left like a wilder-
ness:
There shall the calf feed, and there shall he lie down,
And consume the branches thereof.
When the boughs thereof are withered they shall be
broken off:
The women come, and set them on fire:
For it is a people of no understanding:
Therefore he that made them will not have mercy on
them,
And he that formed them will shew them no favour.
And it shall come to pass in that day,
That the LORD shall beat off from the channel of the
river unto the stream of Egypt,
And ye shall be gathered one by one, O ye children
of Israel.
And it shall come to pass in that day,
That the great trumpet shall be blown,
And they shall come which were ready to perish in
the land of Assyria,
And the outcasts in the land of Egypt,
And shall worship the LORD in the holy mount at
Jerusalem. — Isaiah 26; 27.

A SERMON AT THE TIME OF THE FALL OF THE NORTHERN KINGDOM

Ten years after the plot of Northern Israel and Syria against
Assyria, another plot arose. Again the Assyrian armies came to
Israel, and this time destroyed Samaria and put an end to the
Northern Kingdom. The course of events was watched closely
from Judah. Isaiah took occasion to warn his people by the events
at Samaria. "You see the disaster there," he said. "You also
have sinned, and stand in danger of the same disaster here." This
precedes the acted sermon given on page 93.

Woe to the crown of pride, to the drunkards of
Ephraim, whose glorious beauty is a fading flower, which
are on the head of the fat valleys of them that are overcome with wine! Behold, the LORD hath a mighty and
strong one, which as a tempest of hail and a destroying
storm, as a flood of mighty waters overflowing, shall cast
down to the earth with the hand. The crown of pride,
the drunkards of Ephraim, shall be trodden under feet:
and the glorious beauty, which is on the head of the fat
valley, shall be a fading flower, and as the hasty fruit before the summer; which when he that looketh upon it
seeth, while it is yet in his hand he eateth it up.

In that day shall the LORD of hosts be for a crown of
glory, and for a diadem of beauty, unto the residue of his
people, and for a spirit of judgment to him that sitteth
in judgment, and for strength to them that turn the
battle to the gate.

But they also have erred through wine, and through
strong drink are out of the way; the priest and the
prophet have erred through strong drink, they are swallowed up of wine, they are out of the way through strong
drink; they err in vision, they stumble in judgment. For
all tables are full of vomit and filthiness, so that there is
no place clean.

Whom shall he teach knowledge and whom shall he
make to understand doctrine? Them that are weaned
from the milk, and drawn from the breasts. For precept
must be upon precept, precept upon precept; line upon
line, line upon line; here a little, and there a little; for
with stammering lips and another tongue will he speak
to this people. To whom he said, "This is the rest wherewith ye may cause the weary to rest; and this is the
refreshing": yet they would not hear. But the word
of the LORD was unto them precept upon precept,

precept upon precept; line upon line, line upon line; here a little, and there a little; that they might go, and fall backward, and be broken, and snared, and taken. Wherefore hear the word of the LORD, ye scornful men, that rule this people which is in Jerusalem.

A COVENANT WITH DEATH

Because ye have said,

"We have made a covenant with death, and with hell are we at agreement; when the overflowing scourge shall pass through, it shall not come unto us: for we have made lies our refuge, and under falsehood have we hid ourselves: therefore thus saith the Lord GOD, 'Behold, I lay in Zion for a foundation a stone, a tried stone, a precious corner stone, a sure foundation: he that believeth shall not make haste. Judgment also will I lay to the line, and righteousness to the plummet: and the hail shall sweep away the refuge of lies, and the waters shall overflow the hiding place.'"

And your covenant with death shall be disannulled, and your agreement with hell shall not stand; when the overflowing scourge shall pass through, then ye shall be trodden down by it. From the time that it goeth forth it shall take you: for morning by morning shall it pass over, by day and by night: and it shall be a vexation only to understand the report. For the bed is shorter than that a man can stretch himself on it: and the covering narrower than that he can wrap himself in it. For the LORD shall rise up as in Mount Perazim, he shall be wroth as in the valley of Gibeon, that he may do his work, his strange work; and bring to pass his act, his strange act. Now therefore be ye not mockers, lest your bands be made strong: for I have heard from the Lord GOD of hosts a consumption, even determined upon the whole earth.

Give ye ear, and hear my voice; hearken, and hear my speech. Doth the plowman plow all day to sow? Doth he open and break the clods of his ground? When he hath made plain the face thereof, doth he not cast abroad the fitches, and scatter the cummin, and cast in the principal wheat and the appointed barley and the rye in their place? For his God doth instruct him to discretion, and doth teach him. For the fitches are not threshed with a threshing instrument, neither is a cart wheel turned about upon the cummin; but the fitches are beaten out with a staff, and the cummin with a rod. Bread corn is bruised; because he will not ever be threshing it, nor break it with the wheel of his cart, nor bruise it with his horsemen. This also cometh forth from the Lord of hosts, which is wonderful in counsel, and excellent in working. — Isaiah 28.

Sermons at the Time of Sennacherib's Great Invasion

Isaiah's Warning not to Revolt: "Woe to Ariel, the City of David"

About ten years after the revolt in which Ashdod was the leader, still another plot against Assyria was formed. This time Judah was deeply implicated. King Hezekiah became a leader in the plot, in spite of the strong opposition of Isaiah. The plan was to combine the armies of Tyre, Sidon, certain of the Philistine cities, and Judah, and so be able to meet the Assyrian forces. Egypt, as usual, promised help, and, as usual, failed to give it. What had happened before happened now. The Assyrian army moved upon the west and attacked the separate states before they could combine. They invaded Judah, captured many cities, and at last invested Jerusalem. In its extremity the city became panic-stricken, and Isaiah had to urge them not to surrender. The history of these events is given in Volume 3. See page 93.

From this time of stress we have two series of sermons by Isaiah. The first was given before the invasion, when Isaiah is trying to show the people their helplessness before Assyria, and the uselessness of relying on Egypt, upon whose promises for help he pours contempt. The Hebrews are already sending their treasures to "a people that cannot profit," but it will be of no avail. The second series of sermons was spoken when the Assyrians were already in Palestine, and there was danger that the Hebrews would surrender Jerusalem in their panic. He tries to put some courage into the poor, panic-stricken people. He urges that God is yet stronger than Assyria, and will "break the Assyrian on these mountains." These fragments of sermons are the most vigorous and fiery that we have from Isaiah. We can feel in them the throbbing pulse of the terrific crisis in which they were spoken.

Woe to Ariel, to Ariel, the city where David dwelt! Add ye year to year; let them kill sacrifices. Yet I will distress Ariel, and there shall be heaviness and sorrow: and it shall be unto me as Ariel. And I will camp against thee round about, and will lay siege against thee with a mount, and I will raise forts against thee. And thou shalt be brought down, and shalt speak out of the ground, and thy speech shall be low out of the dust, and thy voice shall be, as of one that hath a familiar spirit, out of the ground, and thy speech shall whisper out of the dust. Moreover the multitude of thy strangers shall be like small dust, and the multitude of the terrible ones shall be as chaff that passeth away: yea, it shall be at an instant suddenly. Thou shalt be visited of the LORD of hosts with thunder, and with earthquake, and great noise, with storm and tempest, and the flame of devouring fire.

And the multitude of all the nations that fight against Ariel, even all that fight against her and her munition, and that distress her, shall be as a dream of a night vision. It shall even be as when an hungry man dreameth, and, behold, he eateth; but he awaketh, and his soul is empty: or as when a thirsty man dreameth, and, behold, he drinketh; but he awaketh, and, behold, he is faint, and his soul hath appetite: so shall the multitude of all the nations be, that fight against Mount Zion.

Stay yourselves, and wonder; cry ye out, and cry: they are drunken, but not with wine; they stagger, but not with strong drink. For the LORD hath poured out upon you the spirit of deep sleep, and hath closed your eyes: the prophets and your rulers, the seers hath he covered. And the vision of all is become unto you as the words of a book that is sealed, which men deliver to one that is learned, saying, "Read this, I pray thee": and he saith, "I cannot; for it is sealed": and the book is delivered to him that is not learned, saying, "Read this, I pray thee": and he saith, "I am not learned."

Wherefore the LORD said, "Forasmuch as this people draw near me with their mouth, and with their lips do honour me, but have removed their heart far from me, and their fear toward me is taught by the precept of men: therefore, behold, I will proceed to do a marvellous work among this people, even a marvellous work and a wonder: for the wisdom of their wise men shall perish, and the understanding of their prudent men shall be hid."

Woe unto them that seek deep to hide their counsel from the LORD, and their works are in the dark, and they say, "Who seeth us? And who knoweth us?" Surely your turning of things upside down shall be esteemed as the potter's clay: for shall the work say of him that made it, "He made me not"? or shall the thing framed say of him that framed it, "He had no understanding"?

Is it not yet a very little while, and Lebanon shall be turned into a fruitful field, and the fruitful field shall be esteemed as a forest? And in that day shall the deaf hear the words of the book, and the eyes of the blind shall see out of obscurity, and out of darkness. The meek also shall increase their joy in the LORD, and the poor among men shall rejoice in the Holy One of Israel. For the terrible one is brought to naught, and the scorner is consumed, and all that watch for iniquity are cut off: that make a man an offender for a word, and lay a snare for him that reproveth in the gate, and turn aside the just for a thing of naught. Therefore thus saith the LORD, who redeemed Abraham, concerning the house of Jacob, "Jacob shall not now be ashamed, neither shall his face now wax pale. But when he seeth his children, the work of mine hands, in the midst of him, they shall sanctify my name, and sanctify the Holy One of Jacob, and shall fear the God of Israel. They also that erred in spirit shall come to understanding, and they that murmured shall learn doctrine."   — Isaiah 29.

THE HELP OF EGYPT WILL BE IN VAIN: "WOE TO THE REBELLIOUS PEOPLE"

THE HEBREWS HAVE SENT TO BUY HELP FROM EGYPT

"Woe to the rebellious children," saith the LORD, "that take counsel, but not of me; and that cover with a covering, but not of my spirit, that they may add sin to sin: that walk to go down into Egypt, and have not asked at my mouth; to strengthen themselves in the strength of Pharaoh, and to trust in the shadow of Egypt!"

Therefore shall the strength of Pharaoh be your shame, and the trust in the shadow of Egypt your confusion. For his princes were at Zoan, and his ambassadors came to Hanes. They were all ashamed of a people that could not profit them, nor be an help nor profit, but a shame, and also a reproach.

THE BURDEN OF THE BEASTS OF THE SOUTH

Into the land of trouble and anguish, from whence come the young and old lion, the viper and fiery flying serpent, they will carry their riches upon the shoulders of young asses, and their treasures upon the bunches of camels, to a people that shall not profit them. For the Egyptians shall help in vain, and to no purpose: therefore have I cried concerning this, "Their strength is to sit still."

Now go, write it before them in a table, and note it in a book, that it may be for the time to come forever and ever: that this is a rebellious people, lying children, children that will not hear the law of the LORD: which say to the seers, "See not"; and to the prophets, "Prophesy not unto us right things, speak unto us smooth things, prophesy deceits: get you out of the way, turn aside out of the path, cause the Holy One of Israel to cease from before us."

Wherefore thus saith the Holy One of Israel, "Because ye despise this word, and trust in oppression and perverseness, and stay thereon: therefore this iniquity shall be to you as a breach ready to fall, swelling out in a high wall, whose breaking cometh suddenly at an instant."

And he shall break it as the breaking of the potters' vessel that is broken in pieces; he shall not spare: so that there shall not be found in the bursting of it a sherd to take fire from the hearth, or to take water withal out of the pit.

For thus saith the Lord GOD, the Holy One of Israel: "In returning and rest shall ye be saved; in quietness and in confidence shall be your strength": and ye would not.

But ye said, "No; for we will flee upon horses"; therefore shall ye flee: and, "We will ride upon the swift"; therefore shall they that pursue you be swift. One thousand shall flee at the rebuke of one; at the rebuke of five shall ye flee: till ye be left as a beacon upon the top of a mountain, and as an ensign on an hill.

And therefore will the LORD wait, that he may be gracious unto you, and therefore will he be exalted, that he may have mercy upon you: for the LORD is a God of judgment: blessed are all they that wait for him. For the people shall dwell in Zion at Jerusalem: thou shalt weep no more: he will be very gracious unto thee at the voice of thy cry; when he shall hear it, he will answer thee. And though the LORD give you the bread of adversity, and the water of affliction, yet shall not thy teachers be removed into a corner any more, but thine eyes shall see thy teachers:

ASHUR-NASIR-PAL

Photograph by courtesy of the Metropolitan Museum of Art, New York. Bas-relief in Alabaster from the Royal Palace at Nimrud

This is a fine portrait sculpture of one of the great kings of Assyria. Other pictures of Assyrian sculpture will be found at 3:315. The ornament which the king wears on his wrist looks very much like a modern wrist watch.

and thine ears shall hear a word behind thee, saying, "This is the way, walk ye in it, when ye turn to the right hand, and when ye turn to the left."

Ye shall defile also the covering of thy graven images of silver, and the ornament of thy molten images of gold: thou shalt cast them away as an unclean thing; thou shalt say unto it, "Get thee hence." Then shall he give the rain of thy seed, that thou shalt sow the ground withal; and bread of the increase of the earth, and it shall be fat and plenteous: in that day shall thy cattle feed in large pastures. The oxen likewise and the young asses that ear the ground shall eat clean provender, which hath been winnowed with the shovel and with the fan. And there shall be upon every high mountain, and upon every high hill, rivers and streams of waters in the day of the great slaughter, when the towers fall. Moreover the light of the moon shall be as the light of the sun, and the light of the sun shall be sevenfold, as the light of seven days, in the day that the LORD bindeth up the breach of his people, and healeth the stroke of their wound.

Behold, the name of the LORD cometh from far, burning with his anger, and the burden thereof is heavy: his lips are full of indignation, and his tongue as a devouring fire: and his breath, as an overflowing stream, shall reach to the midst of the neck, to sift the nations with the sieve of vanity: and there shall be a bridle in the jaws of the people, causing them to err. Ye shall have a song, as in the night when a holy solemnity is kept; and gladness of heart, as when one goeth with a pipe to come into the mountain of the LORD, to the mighty One of Israel. And the LORD shall cause his glorious voice to be heard, and shall show the lighting down of his arm, with the indignation of his anger, and with the flame of a devouring fire, with scattering, and tempest, and hailstones. For through the voice of the LORD shall the Assyrian be beaten down, which smote with a rod. And in every place where the grounded staff shall pass, which the LORD shall lay upon him, it shall be with tabrets and harps: and in battles of shaking will he fight with it. For Tophet is ordained of old; yea, for the king it is prepared; he hath made it deep and large: the pile thereof is fire and much wood; the breath of the LORD, like a stream of brimstone, doth kindle it. — Isaiah 30.

WOE TO THEM THAT SEEK HELP FROM EGYPT AGAINST ASSYRIA

Woe to them that go down to Egypt for help; and stay on horses, and trust in chariots, because they are many; and in horsemen, because they are very strong; but they look not unto the Holy One of Israel, neither seek the LORD! Yet he also is wise, and will bring evil, and will not call back his words: but will arise against the house of the evildoers, and against the help of them that work iniquity. Now the Egyptians are men, and not God; and their horses flesh, and not spirit. When the LORD shall stretch out his hand, both he that helpeth shall fall, and he that is holpen shall fall down, and they all shall fail together. For thus hath the LORD spoken unto me, "Like as the lion and the young lion roaring on his prey, when a multitude of shepherds is called forth against him, he will not be afraid of their voice, nor abase himself for the noise of them: so shall the LORD of hosts come down to fight for Mount Zion, and for the hill thereof. As birds flying, so will the LORD of hosts defend Jerusalem; defending also he will deliver it; and passing over he will preserve it.

Turn ye unto him from whom the children of Israel have deeply revolted. For in that day every man shall cast away his idols of silver, and his idols of gold, which your own hands have made unto you for a sin.

"Then shall the Assyrian fall with the sword, not of a mighty man; and the sword, not of a mean man, shall devour him: but he shall flee from the sword, and his young men shall be discomfited. And he shall pass over to his stronghold for fear, and his princes shall be afraid

BABYLONIAN "BOOKS"
By courtesy of the Metropolitan Museum of Art, New York

Whole libraries of these Babylonian records have been recovered. They relate to a variety of subjects, not only records of State, but personal accounts and intimate personal letters.

of the ensign," saith the LORD, whose fire is in Zion, and his furnace in Jerusalem. —Isaiah 31.

THE SHADOW OF A GREAT ROCK IN A WEARY LAND

Behold, a king shall reign in righteousness, and princes shall rule in judgment. And a man shall be as an hiding place from the wind, and a covert from the tempest; as rivers of water in a dry place, as the shadow of a great rock in a weary land. And the eyes of them that see shall not be dim, and the ears of them that hear shall hearken. The heart also of the rash shall understand knowledge, and the tongue of the stammerers shall be ready to speak plainly. The vile person shall be no more called liberal, nor the churl said to be bountiful. For the vile person will speak villany, and his heart will work

Assyrian Forces Capturing a City

By courtesy of the British Museum, London

In this picture, the attack upon the city is still going on, but a breach has been made on the walls and the captives are already being taken out. Three captive women and a child are shown and oxen, spoils of war. The king is drawing his bow. A soldier with a pointed helmet defends him with his shield. One attendant holds a quiver full of arrows; another holds a canopy over the king's head.

iniquity, to practise hypocrisy, and to utter error against the LORD, to make empty the soul of the hungry, and he will cause the drink of the thirsty to fail. The instruments also of the churl are evil: he deviseth wicked devices to destroy the poor with lying words, even when the needy speaketh right. But the liberal deviseth liberal things; and by liberal things shall he stand.

RISE UP, YE WOMEN THAT ARE AT EASE

Rise up, ye women that are at ease; hear my voice, ye careless daughters; give ear unto my speech. Many days and years shall ye be troubled, ye careless women: for the vintage shall fail, the gathering shall not come. Tremble, ye women that are at ease; be troubled, ye careless ones: strip you, and make you bare, and gird sackcloth upon your loins. They shall lament for the teats, for the pleasant fields, for the fruitful vine. Upon the land of my people shall come up thorns and briers; yea, upon all the houses of joy in the joyous city: because the palaces shall be forsaken; the multitude of the city shall be left; the forts and towers shall be for dens forever, a joy of wild asses, a pasture of flocks; until the spirit be poured upon us from on high, and the wilderness be a fruitful field, and the fruitful field be counted for a forest. Then judgment shall dwell in the wilderness, and righteousness remain in the fruitful field. And the work of righteousness shall be peace; and the effect of righteousness quietness and assurance for ever. And my people shall dwell in a peaceable habitation, and in sure dwellings, and in quiet resting places; when it shall hail, coming down on the forest; and the city shall be low in a low place. Blessed are ye that sow beside all waters, that send forth thither the feet of the ox and the ass.

—Isaiah 32.

Jerusalem Shall Be a City of Peace and Quiet

Woe to thee that spoilest, and thou wast not spoiled; and dealest treacherously, and they dealt not treacherously with thee! When thou shalt cease to spoil, thou shalt be spoiled; and when thou shalt make an end to deal treacherously, they shall deal treacherously with thee. O Lord, be gracious unto us; we have waited for thee: be thou their arm every morning, our salvation also in the time of trouble. At the noise of the tumult the people fled; at the lifting up of thyself the nations were scattered. And your spoil shall be gathered like the gathering of the caterpiller: as the running to and fro of locusts shall he run upon them. The Lord is exalted; for he dwelleth on high: he hath filled Zion with judgment and righteousness. And wisdom and knowledge shall be the stability of thy times, and strength of salvation: the fear of the Lord is his treasure. Behold, their valiant ones shall cry without: the ambassadors of peace shall weep bitterly. The highways lie waste, the wayfaring man ceaseth: he hath broken the covenant, he hath despised the cities, he regardeth no man. The earth mourneth and languisheth: Lebanon is ashamed and hewn down: Sharon is like a wilderness; and Bashan and Carmel shake off their fruits.

"Now will I rise," saith the Lord; "now will I be exalted; now will I lift up myself. Ye shall conceive chaff, ye shall bring forth stubble: your breath, as fire, shall devour you. And the people shall be as the burnings of lime: as thorns cut up shall they be burned in the fire. Hear, ye that are far off, what I have done; and, ye that are near, acknowledge my might."

The sinners in Zion are afraid; fearfulness hath surprised the hypocrites. Who among us shall dwell with

The King in the Royal Chariot Passing a Fortress

By courtesy of the British Museum, London

In this picture, the king, followed by his personal attendant, is himself driving the two-horse chariot. He is passing a fortress and people are seen on the walls.

the devouring fire? Who among us shall dwell with everlasting burnings? He that walketh righteously, and
speaketh uprightly; he that despiseth the gain of oppres-
sions, that shaketh his hands from holding of bribes, that
stoppeth his ears from hearing of blood, and shutteth his
eyes from seeing evil; he shall dwell on high: his place of
defence shall be the munitions of rocks: bread shall be
given him; his waters shall be sure. Thine eyes shall see
the king in his beauty: they shall behold the land that is
very far off. Thine heart shall meditate terror. Where is
the scribe? Where is the receiver? Where is he that counted
the towers? Thou shalt not see a fierce people, a people
of a deeper speech than thou canst perceive; of a stammering tongue, that thou canst not understand. Look
upon Zion, the city of our solemnities: thine eyes shall
see Jerusalem, a quiet habitation, a tabernacle that shall
not be taken down; not one of the stakes thereof shall
ever be removed, neither shall any of the cords thereof
be broken. But there the glorious LORD will be unto us
a place of broad rivers and streams; wherein shall go no
galley with oars, neither shall gallant ship pass thereby.
For the LORD is our judge, the LORD is our lawgiver, the
LORD is our king; he will save us. Thy tacklings are
loosed; they could not well strengthen their mast, they
could not spread the sail: then is the prey of a great spoil
divided; the lame take the prey. And the inhabitant shall
not say, "I am sick": the people that dwell therein shall
be forgiven their iniquity.   — Isaiah 33.

DESTRUCTION: THE INDIGNATION OF THE LORD
IS UPON ALL NATIONS

Come near, ye nations, to hear; and hearken, ye
people: let the earth hear, and all that is therein; the
world, and all things that come forth of it. For the

indignation of the LORD is upon all nations, and his fury upon all their armies: he hath utterly destroyed them, he hath delivered them to the slaughter. Their slain also shall be cast out, and their stink shall come up out of their carcasses, and the mountains shall be melted with their blood. And all the host of heaven shall be dissolved, and the heavens shall be rolled together as a scroll: and all their host shall fall down, as the leaf falleth off from the vine, and as a falling fig from the fig-tree. For my sword shall be bathed in heaven: behold, it shall come down upon Idumea, and upon the people of my curse, to judgment. The sword of the LORD is filled with blood, it is made fat with fatness, and with the blood of lambs and goats, with the fat of the kidneys of rams: for the LORD hath a sacrifice in Bozrah, and a great slaughter in the land of Idumea. And the unicorns shall come down with them, and the bullocks with the bulls; and their land shall be soaked with blood, and their dust made fat with fatness. For it is the day of the LORD's vengeance, and the year of recompences for the controversy of Zion. And the streams thereof shall be turned into pitch, and the dust thereof into brimstone, and the land thereof shall become burning pitch. It shall not be quenched night nor day; the smoke thereof shall go up forever; from generation to generation it shall lie waste; none shall pass through it forever and ever.

But the cormorant and the bittern shall possess it; the owl also and the raven shall dwell in it: and he shall stretch out upon it the line of confusion, and the stones of emptiness. They shall call the nobles thereof to the kingdom, but none shall be there, and all her princes shall be nothing. And thorns shall come up in her palaces, nettles and brambles in the fortresses thereof: and it shall be an habitation of dragons, and a court for owls. The

The King Returning from Battle

By courtesy of the Metropolitan Museum
of Art, New York

This picture shows the fittings of the chariot,
the elaborate harness of the royal chariot
and the manner in which the horses' tails
and manes were tied. The figure of a god
is shown very clearly. The circle expresses
eternity; the wings, omnipresence; and the
human figure, wisdom and intelligence.

wild beasts of the desert shall also meet with the wild
beasts of the island, and the satyr shall cry to his fellow;
the screech owl also shall rest there, and find for herself
a place of rest. There shall the great owl make her nest,
and lay, and hatch, and gather under her shadow: there
shall the vultures also be gathered, every one with her
mate.

Seek ye out of the book of the LORD, and read: no
one of these shall fail, none shall want her mate: for my
mouth it hath commanded, and his spirit it hath gathered
them. And he hath cast the lot for them, and his hand
hath divided it unto them by line: they shall possess it
forever, from generation to generation shall they dwell
therein.   — Isaiah 34.

A Sermon of Restoration: the Wilderness and the Solitary Place Shall Rejoice

The wilderness and the solitary place shall be glad
for them; and the desert shall rejoice, and blossom as the
rose. It shall blossom abundantly, and rejoice even with
joy and singing: the glory of Lebanon shall be given
unto it, the excellency of Carmel and Sharon, they shall
see the glory of the LORD, and the excellency of our God.
Strengthen ye the weak hands, and confirm the feeble
knees. Say to them that are of a fearful heart, "Be
strong, fear not: behold, your God will come with vengeance, even God with a recompence; he will come and
save you."

Then the eyes of the blind shall be opened, and the
ears of the deaf shall be unstopped. Then shall the lame
man leap as an hart, and the tongue of the dumb sing:
for in the wilderness shall waters break out, and streams
in the desert. And the parched ground shall become a
pool, and the thirsty land springs of water: in the

habitation of dragons, where each lay, shall be grass with reeds and rushes. And an highway shall be there, and a way, and it shall be called "The way of holiness"; the unclean shall not pass over it; but it shall be for those: the wayfaring men, though fools, shall not err therein. No lion shall be there, nor any ravenous beast shall go up thereon, it shall not be found there; but the redeemed shall walk there: and the ransomed of the LORD shall return, and come to Zion with songs and everlasting joy upon their heads: they shall obtain joy and gladness, and sorrow and sighing shall flee away. — Isaiah 35.

The Prophecy of Isaiah

PART II

With the 39th chapter of Isaiah, the political sermons of the prophet come to a close. The style changes. It was exalted at times; now it becomes sublime. The field of action changes. It is no longer the recital of the struggle of the little nation of Judah for individual freedom; the field is the world.

But God has not deserted his people. There will come a redeemer, a saviour. Such a saviour had been represented in earlier days as a conqueror; now the sublime thought is expressed that he is a suffering saviour, "A man of sorrows and acquainted with grief." This is the supreme height of inspired prophetic thought, the idea of a God who loves the world so much that he can suffer with it and for it, in order to heal it and redeem it. There is still the idea of a redeemed people, but it includes all the peoples of the world who shall come thronging to Zion, voluntarily and gladly.

There are many phrases so happy, so full of beauty, that they have become an inseparable part of the religious thought and speech of the world in all ages: "Comfort ye, comfort ye, my people"; "Ho, everyone that thirsteth, come ye to the waters"; "For as the heavens are higher than the earth, so are my ways higher than your ways and my thoughts than your thoughts"; "For,' he said, "surely they are my people, children that will not lie'; so he was their saviour"; "Arise, shine, for thy light is come and the glory of the Lord is risen upon thee"; and the incomparable 53rd chapter, every word of which is full of the most exalted religious feeling. No one can read it without realizing that it came true in a marvellous way in the experience of him who came to be the Saviour of the world, "to give his life a ransom for many." The whole section forms one of the most splendid pieces of religious literature. These are the mountain summits of thought, of the expression of the spirit in its relation to the divine. We stand upon such summits with awe; and we depart, feeling that we have been with God in the mount of vision.

The differences between the first and the second parts of Isaiah are so great that the question has arisen whether the beautiful poems of the second part are not by later prophets, whose writings were added to those of Isaiah as supplementing his hopes for the nation. The important thing, however, is not the problem of who wrote them, but the rich value they have for religious life.

The Prophecy of Isaiah

"HE SHALL FEED HIS FLOCK LIKE A SHEPHERD"

"COMFORT ye, comfort ye my people," saith
  your God.
  "Speak ye comfortably to Jerusalem,
  And cry unto her,
That her warfare is accomplished,
That her iniquity is pardoned:
For she hath received of the LORD's hand
Double for all her sins."

The voice of him that crieth in the wilderness,
"Prepare ye the way of the LORD,
Make straight in the desert a highway for our God.
Every valley shall be exalted,
And every mountain and hill shall be made low:
And the crooked shall be made straight,
And the rough places plain:
And the glory of the LORD shall be revealed,
And all flesh shall see it together:
For the mouth of the LORD hath spoken it."
The voice said, "Cry."

And he said, "What shall I cry?
All flesh is grass,
And all the goodliness thereof is as the flower of the
field:
The grass withereth,
The flower fadeth:
Because the spirit of the LORD bloweth upon it:
Surely the people is grass.
The grass withereth, the flower fadeth:
But the word of our God shall stand forever."

O Zion, that bringest good tidings,
Get thee up into the high mountain;
O Jerusalem, that bringest good tidings,
Lift up thy voice with strength;
Lift it up, be not afraid;
Say unto the cities of Judah, "Behold your God!"

Behold, the Lord GOD will come with strong hand,
And his arm shall rule for him:
Behold, his reward is with him,
And his work before him.
He shall feed his flock like a shepherd:
He shall gather the lambs with his arm,
And carry them in his bosom,
And shall gently lead those that are with young.

"To Whom Then Will Ye Liken God?"

Who hath measured the waters in the hollow of his
hand,
And meted out heaven with the span,
And comprehended the dust of the earth in a measure,
And weighed the mountains in scales,
And the hills in a balance?

Who hath directed the Spirit of the LORD,
Or being his counsellor hath taught him?
With whom took he counsel,
And who instructed him,
And taught him in the path of judgment,
And taught him knowledge,
And shewed to him the way of understanding?
Behold, the nations are as a drop of a bucket,
And are counted as the small dust of the balance:
Behold, he taketh up the isles as a very little thing.
And Lebanon is not sufficient to burn,
Nor the beasts thereof sufficient for a burnt offering.
All nations before him are as nothing;
And they are counted to him less than nothing, and
    vanity.

To whom then will ye liken God?
Or what likeness will ye compare unto him?
The workman melteth a graven image,
And the goldsmith spreadeth it over with gold,
And casteth silver chains.
He that is so impoverished that he hath no oblation
Chooseth a tree that will not rot;
He seeketh unto him a cunning workman to prepare
    a graven image,
That shall not be moved.
Have ye not known?
Have ye not heard?
Hath it not been told you from the beginning?
Have ye not understood from the foundations of the
    earth?
It is he that sitteth upon the circle of the earth,
And the inhabitants thereof are as grasshoppers;
That stretcheth out the heavens as a curtain,

And spreadeth them out as a tent to dwell in:
That bringeth the princes to nothing;
He maketh the judges of the earth as vanity.
Yea, they shall not be planted;
Yea, they shall not be sown:
Yea, their stock shall not take root in the earth:
And he shall also blow upon them,
And they shall wither,
And the whirlwind shall take them away as stubble.

"To whom then will ye liken me,
Or shall I be equal?" saith the Holy One.
Lift up your eyes on high,
And behold who hath created these things,
That bringeth out their host by number:
He calleth them all by names by the greatness of his
    might,
For that he is strong in power;
Not one faileth.
Why sayest thou, O Jacob, and speakest, O Israel,
"My way is hid from the LORD,
And my judgment is passed over from my God?"

Hast thou not known?
Hast thou not heard,
That the everlasting God, the LORD,
The Creator of the ends of the earth,
Fainteth not, neither is weary?

There is no searching of his understanding.
He giveth power to the faint;
And to them that have no might he increaseth
    strength.
Even the youths shall faint and be weary,

And the young men shall utterly fall:
But they that wait upon the LORD shall renew their
  strength;
They shall mount up with wings as eagles;
They shall run, and not be weary;
And they shall walk, and not faint. — Isaiah 40.

"FEAR NOT, FOR I AM WITH THEE"

THE HELP OF THE LORD IS NEAR

Keep silence before me, O islands; and let the people renew their strength: let them come near; then let them speak: let us come near together to judgment. Who raised up the righteous man from the east, called him to his foot, gave the nations before him, and made him rule over kings? He gave them as the dust to his sword, and as driven stubble to his bow. He pursued them, and passed safely; even by the way that he had not gone with his feet. Who hath wrought and done it, calling the generations from the beginning? I, the LORD, the first, and with the last; I am he. The isles saw it, and feared; the ends of the earth were afraid, drew near, and came. They helped every one his neighbour; and every one said to his brother, "Be of good courage." So the carpenter encouraged the goldsmith, and he that smootheth with the hammer him that smote the anvil, saying, "It is ready for the soldering"; and he fastened it with nails, that it should not be moved. But thou, Israel, art my servant, Jacob whom I have chosen, the seed of Abraham, my friend. Thou whom I have taken from the ends of the earth, and called thee from the chief men thereof, and said unto thee, "Thou art my servant"; I have chosen thee, and not cast thee away.

Fear thou not; for I am with thee:
Be not dismayed; for I am thy God:
I will strengthen thee;
Yea, I will help thee;
Yea, I will uphold thee with the right
    hand of my righteousness.

Behold, all they that were incensed against thee shall
be ashamed and confounded: they shall be as nothing;
and they that strive with thee shall perish. Thou shalt
seek them, and shalt not find them, even them that contended with thee: they that war against thee shall be as
nothing, and as a thing of naught. For I, the LORD thy
God, will hold thy right hand, saying unto thee, "Fear
not; I will help thee."

"Fear not, thou worm Jacob, and ye men of Israel; I
will help thee," saith the LORD, and thy redeemer, the
Holy One of Israel.

Behold, I will make thee a new sharp threshing instrument having teeth: thou shalt thresh the mountains,
and beat them small, and shalt make the hills as chaff.
Thou shalt fan them, and the wind shall carry them
away, and the whirlwind shall scatter them: and thou
shalt rejoice in the LORD, and shalt glory in the Holy
One of Israel. When the poor and needy seek water, and
there is none, and their tongue faileth for thirst, I, the
LORD, will hear them; I, the God of Israel, will not forsake
them. I will open rivers in high places, and fountains in
the midst of the valleys: I will make the wilderness a
pool of water, and the dry land springs of water. I will
plant in the wilderness the cedar, the shittah-tree, and
the myrtle, and the oil-tree; I will set in the desert the
fir-tree, and the pine, and the box-tree together: that
they may see. and know, and consider, and understand

together, that the hand of the Lord hath done this, and the Holy One of Israel hath created it.

"Produce your cause," saith the Lord; "bring forth your strong reasons," saith the King of Jacob. "Let them bring them forth, and shew us what shall happen: let them shew the former things, what they be, that we may consider them, and know the latter end of them; or declare us things for to come. Shew the things that are to come hereafter, that we may know that ye are gods: yea, do good, or do evil, that we may be dismayed, and behold it together. Behold, ye are of nothing, and your work of naught: an abomination is he that chooseth you I have raised up one from the north, and he shall come: from the rising of the sun shall he call upon my name: and he shall come upon princes as upon mortar, and as the potter treadeth clay. Who hath declared from the beginning, that we may know? and beforetime, that we may say, 'He is righteous'? yea, there is none that sheweth, yea, there is none that declareth, yea, there is none that heareth your words.

"The first shall say to Zion, 'Behold, behold them': and I will give to Jerusalem one that bringeth good tidings. For I beheld, and there was no man; even among them, and there was no counsellor, that, when I asked of them, could answer a word. Behold, they are all vanity; their works are nothing: their molten images are wind and confusion."   — Isaiah 41.

"Sing unto the Lord a New Song"

Behold my servant, whom I uphold;
Mine elect, in whom my soul delighteth;
I have put my spirit upon him:
He shall bring forth judgment to the Gentiles.
He shall not cry, nor lift up,

Nor cause his voice to be heard in the street.
A bruised reed shall he not break,
And the smoking flax shall he not quench:
He shall bring forth judgment unto truth.
He shall not fail nor be discouraged,
Till he have set judgment in the earth:
And the isles shall wait for his law.

Thus saith God the LORD,
He that created the heavens, and stretched them out;
He that spread forth the earth, and that which
    cometh out of it;
He that giveth breath unto the people upon it,
And spirit to them that walk therein:
"I the LORD have called thee in righteousness,
And will hold thine hand, and will keep thee,
And give thee for a covenant of the people,
For a light of the Gentiles;
To open the blind eyes,
To bring out the prisoners from the prison,
And them that sit in darkness out of the prison house.
I am the LORD: that is my name:
And my glory will I not give to another,
Neither my praise to graven images."

Behold, the former things are come to pass,
And new things do I declare:
Before they spring forth I tell you of them.

Sing unto the LORD a new song,
And his praise from the end of the earth,
Ye that go down to the sea, and all that is therein;
The isles, and the inhabitants thereof.

Let the wilderness and the cities thereof lift up their
    voice,
The villages that Kedar doth inhabit:
Let the inhabitants of the rock sing,
Let them shout from the top of the mountains.
Let them give glory unto the LORD,
And declare his praise in the islands.
The LORD shall go forth as a mighty man,
He shall stir up jealousy like a man of war:
He shall cry, yea, roar;
He shall prevail against his enemies.

I have long time holden my peace;
I have been still, and refrained myself:
Now will I cry like a travailing woman;
I will destroy and devour at once.
I will make waste mountains and hills,
And dry up all their herbs;
And I will make the rivers islands,
And I will dry up the pools.
And I will bring the blind by a way that they knew
    not;
I will lead them in paths that they have not known:
I will make darkness light before them,
And crooked things straight.
These things will I do unto them,
And not forsake them.

They shall be turned back,
They shall be greatly ashamed,
That trust in graven images,
That say to the molten images, "Ye are our gods."
Hear, ye deaf; and look, ye blind, that ye may see.
Who is blind, but my servant?

Or deaf, as my messenger that I sent?
Who is blind as he that is perfect,
And blind as the LORD's servant?
Seeing many things, thou observest not;
Opening the ears, he heareth not.
The LORD is well pleased for his righteousness' sake;
He will magnify the law,
And make it honourable.
But this is a people robbed and spoiled;
They are all of them snared in holes,
And they are hid in prison houses:
They are for a prey, and none delivereth;
For a spoil, and none saith, "Restore."

Who among you will give ear to this?
Who will hearken and hear for the time to come?
Who gave Jacob for a spoil, and Israel to the robbers?
Did not the LORD, he against whom we have sinned?
For they would not walk in his ways,
Neither were they obedient unto his law.
Therefore he hath poured upon him the fury of his
     anger,
And the strength of battle:
And it hath set him on fire round about,
Yet he knew not;
And it burned him, yet he laid it not to heart.

Isaiah 42.

"I WILL NOT REMEMBER THY SINS"

But now thus saith the LORD that created thee, O
Jacob, and he that formed thee, O Israel, "Fear not: for
I have redeemed thee, I have called thee by thy name;
thou art mine. When thou passest through the waters,
I will be with thee; and through the rivers, they shall
not overflow thee: when thou walkest through the fire,

thou shalt not be burned; neither shall the flame kindle upon thee. For I am the LORD thy God, the Holy One of Israel, thy Saviour: I gave Egypt for thy ransom, Ethiopia and Seba for thee. Since thou wast precious in my sight, thou hast been honourable, and I have loved thee: therefore will I give men for thee, and people for thy life. Fear not: for I am with thee: I will bring thy seed from the east, and gather thee from the west; I will say to the north, 'Give up'; and to the south, 'Keep not back: bring my sons from far, and my daughters from the ends of the earth; even every one that is called by my name: for I have created him for my glory, I have formed him; yea, I have made him.'"

Bring forth the blind people that have eyes, and the deaf that have ears. Let all the nations be gathered together, and let the people be assembled: who among them can declare this, and shew us former things? Let them bring forth their witnesses, that they may be justified: or let them hear, and say, "It is truth."

"Ye are my witnesses," saith the LORD, "and my servant whom I have chosen: that ye may know and believe me, and understand that I am he: before me there was no God formed, neither shall there be after me. I, even I, am the LORD; and beside me there is no saviour. I have declared, and have saved, and I have shewed, when there was no strange god among you: therefore ye are my witnesses," saith the LORD, "that I am God. Yea, before the day was I am he; and there is none that can deliver out of my hand: I will work, and who shall let it?"

Thus saith the LORD, your redeemer, the Holy One of Israel: "For your sake I have sent to Babylon, and have brought down all their nobles, and the Chaldeans, whose cry is in the ships. I am the LORD, your Holy One, the creator of Israel, your King."

THE LORD MAKETH A PATH IN THE SEA

Thus saith the LORD, which maketh a way in the sea, and a path in the mighty waters; which bringeth forth the chariot and horse, the army and the power: "They shall lie down together, they shall not rise: they are extinct, they are quenched as tow.

"Remember ye not the former things, neither consider the things of old. Behold, I will do a new thing; now it shall spring forth; shall ye not know it? I will even make a way in the wilderness, and rivers in the desert. The beast of the field shall honour me, the dragons and the owls: because I give waters in the wilderness, and rivers in the desert, to give drink to my people, my chosen. This people have I formed for myself; they shall shew forth my praise.

"But thou hast not called upon me, O Jacob; but thou hast been weary of me, O Israel. Thou hast not brought me the small cattle of thy burnt offerings; neither has thou honoured me with thy sacrifices. I have not caused thee to serve with an offering, nor wearied thee with incense. Thou hast bought me no sweet cane with money, neither hast thou filled me with the fat of thy sacrifices: but thou hast made me to serve with thy sins, thou hast wearied me with thine iniquities. I, even I, am he that blotteth out thy transgressions for mine own sake, and will not remember thy sins. Put me in remembrance: let us plead together: declare thou, that thou mayest be justified. Thy first father hath sinned, and thy teachers have transgressed against me. Therefore I have profaned the princes of the sanctuary, and have given Jacob to the curse, and Israel to reproaches."

— Isaiah 43.

"Hear, O Jacob, My Servant"

Yet now hear, O Jacob, my servant; and Israel, whom I have chosen: thus saith the LORD that made thee, and formed thee from the womb, which will help thee: "Fear not, O Jacob, my servant; and thou, Jesurun, whom I have chosen. For I will pour water upon him that is thirsty, and floods upon the dry ground: I will pour my spirit upon thy seed, and my blessing upon thine offspring: and they shall spring up as among the grass, as willows by the water courses.

"One shall say, 'I am the LORD's'; and another shall call himself by the name of Jacob; and another shall subscribe with his hand unto the LORD, and surname himself by the name of Israel."

Thus saith the LORD, the King of Israel, and his redeemer, the LORD of hosts: "I am the first, and I am the last; and beside me there is no God. And who, as I, shall call, and shall declare it, and set it in order for me since I appointed the ancient people? And the things that are coming, and shall come, let them shew unto them. Fear ye not, neither be afraid: have not I told thee from that time, and have declared it? Ye are even my witnesses. Is there a God beside me? Yea, there is no God; I know not any.

"They that make a graven image are all of them vanity; and their delectable things shall not profit; and they are their own witnesses; they see not, nor know; that they may be ashamed. Who hath formed a god, or molten a graven image that is profitable for nothing? Behold, all his fellows shall be ashamed: and the workmen, they are of men: let them all be gathered together, let them stand up; yet they shall fear, and they shall be ashamed together. The smith with the tongs both worketh in the coals, and fashioneth it with hammers, and worketh it with the strength of his arms: yea, he is hungry, and his strength faileth: he drinketh no water, and is faint. The carpenter stretcheth out his rule; he marketh it out with a line; he fitteth it with planes, and he marketh it out with the compass, and maketh it after the figure of a man, according to the beauty of a man; that it may remain in the house. He heweth him down cedars, and taketh the cypress and the oak, which he strengtheneth for himself among the trees of the forest: he planteth an ash, and the rain doth nourish it. Then shall it be for a man to burn: for he will take thereof, and warm himself; yea, he kindleth it, and baketh bread; yea, he maketh a god, and worshipeth it; he maketh it a graven image, and falleth down thereto. He burneth part thereof in the fire; with part thereof he eateth flesh; he roasteth roast, and is satisfied: yea, he warmeth himself, and saith, 'Aha, I am warm, I have seen the fire': and the residue thereof he maketh a god, even his graven image: he falleth down unto it, and worshipeth it, and prayeth unto it, and saith, 'Deliver me; for thou art my god.'

"They have not known nor understood: for he hath shut their eyes, that they cannot see; and their hearts, that they cannot understand. And none considereth in his heart, neither is there knowledge nor understanding to say, 'I have burned part of it in the fire; yea, also I have baked bread upon the coals thereof; I have roasted flesh, and eaten it: and shall I make the residue thereof an abomination? Shall I fall down to the stock of a tree?' He feedeth on ashes: a deceived heart hath turned him aside, that he cannot deliver his soul, nor say, 'Is there not a lie in my right hand?'

"Remember these, O Jacob and Israel; for thou art my servant: I have formed thee; thou art my servant: O Israel, thou shalt not be forgotten of me. I have blotted out, as a thick cloud, thy transgressions, and, as a cloud, thy sins: return unto me; for I have redeemed thee."

> Sing, O ye heavens;
> For the LORD hath done it:
> Shout, ye lower parts of the earth:
> Break forth into singing, ye mountains,
> O forest, and every tree therein:
> For the LORD hath redeemed Jacob,
> And glorified himself in Israel.

Thus saith the LORD, thy redeemer, and he that formed thee from the womb, "I am the LORD that maketh all things; that stretcheth forth the heavens alone; that spreadeth abroad the earth by myself; that frustrateth the tokens of the liars, and maketh diviners mad; that turneth wise men backward, and maketh their knowledge foolish; that confirmeth the word of his servant, and performeth the counsel of his messengers; that saith to Jerusalem, 'Thou shalt be inhabited'; and to the cities of Judah, 'Ye shall be built, and I will raise up the decayed places thereof': that saith to the deep, 'Be dry, and I will dry up thy rivers': that saith of Cyrus, 'He is my shepherd, and shall perform all my pleasure': even saying to Jerusalem, 'Thou shalt be built'; and to the temple, 'Thy foundation shall be laid.'" — Isaiah 44.

"I Am the Lord; There Is None Else"

Thus saith the LORD to his anointed, to Cyrus, whose right hand I have holden, to subdue nations before him; and I will loose the loins of kings, to open before him the two leaved gates; and the gates shall not be shut.

> "I will go before thee, and make the crooked places
> straight:

I will break in pieces the gates of brass,
And cut in sunder the bars of iron:
And I will give thee the treasures of darkness,
And hidden riches of secret places,
That thou mayest know that I, the LORD,
Which call thee by thy name, am the God of Israel.
For Jacob, my servant's sake, and Israel, mine elect,
I have even called thee by thy name:
I have surnamed thee,
Though thou hast not known me.

I am the LORD, and there is none else,
There is no God beside me:
I girded thee, though thou hast not known me:
That they may know from the rising of the sun,
And from the west,
That there is none beside me.
I am the LORD, and there is none else.
I form the light, and create darkness·
I make peace, and create evil:
I, the LORD, do all these things.
Drop down, ye heavens, from above,
And let the skies pour down righteousness:
Let the earth open,
And let them bring forth salvation,
And let righteousness spring up together;
I, the LORD, have created it."

Woe unto him that striveth with his Maker!
Let the potsherd strive with the potsherds of the
    earth.
Shall the clay say to him that fashioneth it,
'What makest thou?'
Or thy work, 'He hath no hands'?

Woe unto him that saith unto his father,
'What begettest thou?'
Or to the woman,
'What hast thou brought forth?'

Thus saith the LORD, the Holy One of Israel,
And his Maker, "Ask me of things to come concerning my sons,
And concerning the work of my hands command ye me.
I have made the earth, and created man upon it:
I, even my hands, have stretched out the heavens,
And all their host have I commanded.
I have raised him up in righteousness,
And I will direct all his ways:
He shall build my city, and he shall let go my captives,
Not for price nor reward," saith the LORD of hosts.

Thus saith the LORD, "The labour of Egypt, and merchandise of Ethiopia and of the Sabeans, men of stature, shall come over unto thee, and they shall be thine: they shall come after thee; in chains they shall come over, and they shall fall down unto thee, they shall make supplication unto thee, saying, 'Surely God is in thee; and there is none else, there is no God. Verily thou art a God that hidest thyself, O God of Israel, the Saviour.' They shall be ashamed, and also confounded, all of them: they shall go to confusion together that are makers of idols. But Israel shall be saved in the LORD with an everlasting salvation: ye shall not be ashamed nor confounded, world without end."

For thus saith the LORD that created the heavens, God himself that formed the earth and made it; he hath established it, he created it not in vain, he formed

it to be inhabited: "I am the LORD; and there is none
else. I have not spoken in secret, in a dark place of the
earth: I said not unto the seed of Jacob, 'Seek ye me in
vain.' I, the LORD, speak righteousness, I declare things
that are right.

I AM GOD AND THERE IS NONE ELSE

"Assemble yourselves and come; draw near together,
ye that are escaped of the nations: they have no knowledge that set up the wood of their graven image, and pray
unto a god that cannot save. Tell me, and bring them
near; yea, let them take counsel together: who hath declared this from ancient time? Who hath told it from that
time? Have not I, the LORD? And there is no God else beside me; a just God and a Saviour; there is none beside
me. Look unto me, and be ye saved, all the ends of the
earth: for I am God, and there is none else. I have
sworn by myself, the word is gone out of my mouth in
righteousness, and shall not return, that unto me every
knee shall bow, every tongue shall swear. 'Surely,' shall
one say, 'in the LORD have I righteousness and strength:
even to him shall men come; and all that are incensed
against him shall be ashamed. In the LORD shall all the
seed of Israel be justified, and shall glory.'

"Bel boweth down, Nebo stoopeth, their idols were
upon the beasts, and upon the cattle: your carriages
were heavy loaden; they are a burden to the weary beast.
They stoop, they bow down together; they could not deliver the burden, but themselves are gone into captivity.

"Hearken unto me, O house of Jacob, and all the remnant of the house of Israel, which are borne by me from
the belly, which are carried from the womb: and even to
your old age I am he; and even to hoar hairs will I carry
you: I have made, and I will bear; even I will carry,
and will deliver you.

"To whom will ye liken me, and make me equal, and compare me, that we may be like? They lavish gold out of the bag, and weigh silver in the balance, and hire a goldsmith; and he maketh it a god: they fall down, yea, they worship. They bear him upon the shoulder, they carry him, and set him in his place, and he standeth; from his place shall he not remove: yea, one shall cry unto him, yet can he not answer, nor save him out of his trouble. Remember this, and shew yourselves men: bring it again to mind, O ye transgressors. Remember the former things of old: for I am God, and there is none else; I am God, and there is none like me, declaring the end from the beginning, and from ancient times the things that are not yet done, saying, 'My counsel shall stand, and I will do all my pleasure': calling a ravenous bird from the east, the man that executeth my counsel from a far country: yea, I have spoken it, I will also bring it to pass; I have purposed it, I will also do it.

"Hearken unto me, ye stouthearted, that are far from righteousness: I bring near my righteousness; it shall not be far off, and my salvation shall not tarry: and I will place salvation in Zion for Israel my glory.   —Isaiah 45; 46.

The Fate of Babylon

"Come down, and sit in the dust, O virgin daughter of Babylon, sit on the ground: there is no throne, O daughter of the Chaldeans: for thou shalt no more be called tender and delicate. Take the millstones, and grind meal: uncover thy locks, make bare the leg, uncover the thigh, pass over the rivers. Thy nakedness shall be uncovered, yea, thy shame shall be seen: I will take vengeance, and I will not meet thee as a man. As for our redeemer, the LORD of hosts is his name, the Holy One of Israel. Sit thou silent, and get thee into darkness, O daughter of the

Chaldeans: for thou shalt no more be called, 'The lady of kingdoms.'

"I was wroth with my people, I have polluted mine inheritance, and given them into thine hand: thou didst shew them no mercy; upon the ancient has thou very heavily laid thy yoke. And thou saidst, 'I shall be a lady forever': so that thou didst not lay these things to thy heart, neither didst remember the latter end of it. Therefore hear now this, thou that art given to pleasures, that dwellest carelessly, that sayest in thine heart, 'I am, and none else beside me; I shall not sit as a widow, neither shall I know the loss of children': but these two things shall come to thee in a moment in one day, the loss of children, and widowhood: they shall come upon thee in their perfection for the multitude of thy sorceries, and for the great abundance of thine enchantments.

"For thou hast trusted in thy wickedness: thou hast said, 'None seeth me.' Thy wisdom and thy knowledge, it hath perverted thee; and thou hast said in thine heart, 'I am, and none else beside me.'

"Therefore shall evil come upon thee; thou shalt not know from whence it riseth: and mischief shall fall upon thee; thou shalt not be able to put it off: and desolation shall come upon thee suddenly, which thou shalt not know. Stand now with thine enchantments, and with the multitude of thy sorceries, wherein thou hast laboured from thy youth; if so be thou shalt be able to profit, if so be thou mayest prevail. Thou art wearied in the multitude of thy counsels. Let now the astrologers, the stargazers, the monthly prognosticators, stand up, and save thee from these things that shall come upon thee. Behold, they shall be as stubble; the fire shall burn them; they shall not deliver themselves from the power of the flame: there shall not be a coal to warm at, nor fire to sit before it. Thus shall they be unto thee with whom thou hast laboured, even thy merchants, from thy youth: they shall wander every one to his quarter; none shall save thee.　　　　　　　　　　　　　　　— Isaiah 47.

The Exiles Shall Go Forth with Singing

"Hear ye this, O house of Jacob, which are called by the name of Israel, and are come forth out of the waters of Judah, which swear by the name of the LORD, and make mention of the God of Israel, but not in truth, nor in righteousness. For they call themselves of the holy city, and stay themselves upon the God of Israel, The LORD of hosts is his name. I have declared the former things from the beginning; and they went forth out of my mouth and I shewed them; I did them suddenly, and they came to pass. Because I knew that thou art obstinate, and thy neck is an iron sinew, and thy brow brass; I have even from the beginning declared it to thee; before it came to pass I shewed it thee: lest thou shouldest say, 'Mine idol hath done them, and my graven image, and my molten image, hath commanded them.' Thou hast heard, see all this; and will not ye declare it? I have shewed thee new things from this time, even hidden things, and thou didst not know them. They are created now, and not from the beginning; even before the day when thou heardest them not; lest thou shouldest say, 'Behold, I knew them.' Yea, thou heardest not; yea, thou knewest not; yea, from that time that thine ear was not opened: for I knew that thou wouldest deal very treacherously, and wast called a transgressor from the womb.

"For my name's sake will I defer mine anger, and for my praise will I refrain for thee, that I cut thee not off. Behold, I have refined thee, but not with silver; I have chosen thee in the furnace of affliction. For mine own sake, even for mine own sake, will I do it: for how should my name be polluted? And I will not give my glory unto another.

"Hearken unto me, O Jacob and Israel, my called; I am he; I am the first, I also am the last. Mine hand also hath laid the foundation of the earth, and my right hand hath spanned the heavens: when I call unto them, they stand up together. All ye, assemble yourselves, and hear; which among them hath declared these things? The LORD hath loved him: he will do his pleasure on Babylon, and his arm shall be on the Chaldeans. I, even I, have spoken; yea, I have called him: I have brought him, and he shall make his way prosperous.

"Come ye near unto me, hear ye this; I have not spoken in secret from the beginning; from the time that it was, there am I: and now the Lord GOD, and his Spirit, hath sent me. Thus saith the LORD, thy Redeemer, the Holy One of Israel: I am the LORD thy God which teacheth thee to profit, which leadeth thee by the way that thou shouldest go. O that thou hadst hearkened to my commandments! Then had thy peace been as a river, and thy righteousness as the waves of the sea: thy seed also had been as the sand, and the offspring of thy bowels like the gravel thereof; his name should not have been cut off nor destroyed from before me."

Go ye forth of Babylon, flee ye from the Chaldeans, with a voice of singing declare ye, tell this, utter it even to the end of the earth; say ye, "The LORD hath redeemed his servant Jacob. And they thirsted not when he led them through the deserts: he caused the waters to flow out of the rock for them: he clave the rock also, and the waters gushed out."

"There is no peace," saith the LORD, "unto the wicked." — Isaiah 48.

The Future Glory of Israel: The Lord Hath Comforted His People

Listen, O isles, unto me; and hearken, ye people, from far; the LORD hath called me from the womb; from the bowels of my mother hath he made mention of my name. And he hath made my mouth like a sharp sword; in the shadow of his hand hath he hid me, and made me a polished shaft; in his quiver hath he hid me; and said unto me, "Thou art my servant, O Israel, in whom I will be glorified."

Then I said, "I have laboured in vain, I have spent my strength for naught, and in vain: yet surely my judgment is with the LORD, and my work with my God."

"And now," saith the LORD that formed me from the womb to be his servant, to bring Jacob again to him, "though Israel be not gathered, yet shall I be glorious in the eyes of the LORD, and my God shall be my strength."

And he said, "It is a light thing that thou shouldest be my servant to raise up the tribes of Jacob, and to restore the preserved of Israel: I will also give thee for a light to the Gentiles, that thou mayest be my salvation unto the end of the earth."

Thus saith the LORD, the Redeemer of Israel, and his Holy One, to him whom man despiseth, to him whom the nation abhorreth, to a servant of rulers, "Kings shall see and arise, princes also shall worship, because of the LORD that is faithful, and the Holy One of Israel, and he shall choose thee."

Thus saith the LORD, "In an acceptable time have I heard thee, and in a day of salvation have I helped thee: and I will preserve thee, and give thee for a covenant of the people, to establish the earth, to cause to inherit the desolate heritages; that thou mayest say to the prisoners 'Go forth'; to them that are in darkness, 'Shew yourselves.' They shall feed in the ways, and their pastures shall be in all high places. They shall not hunger nor thirst; neither shall the heat nor sun smite them: for he that hath mercy on them shall lead them, even by the springs of water shall he guide them. And I will make all my mountains a way, and my highways shall be exalted. Behold, these shall come from far: and, lo, these from the north and from the west; and these from the land of Sinim."

Sing, O heavens;
And be joyful, O earth;
And break forth into singing, O mountains:
For the LORD hath comforted his people,
And will have mercy upon his afflicted.

But Zion said, "The LORD hath forsaken me, and my Lord hath forgotten me."

"Can a woman forget her sucking child, that she should not have compassion on the son of her womb? Yea, they may forget, yet will I not forget thee. Behold, I have graven thee upon the palms of my hands; thy walls are continually before me. Thy children shall make haste; thy destroyers and they that made thee waste shall go forth of thee.

"Lift up thine eyes round about, and behold: all these gather themselves together, and come to thee. As I live," saith the LORD, "thou shalt surely clothe thee with them all, as with an ornament, and bind them on thee, as a bride doeth. For thy waste and thy desolate places, and the land of thy destruction, shall even now be too narrow by reason of the inhabitants, and they that swallowed thee up shall be far away. The children which thou shalt have, after thou hast lost the other, shall say again

in thine ears, 'The place is too strait for me: give place
to me that I may dwell.' Then shalt thou say in thine
heart, 'Who hath begotten me these, seeing I have lost
my children, and am desolate, a captive, and removing to
and fro? And who hath brought up these? Behold, I was
left alone; these, where had they been?'"

Thus saith the Lord GOD, "Behold, I will lift up mine
hand to the Gentiles, and set up my standard to the
people: and they shall bring thy sons in their arms, and
thy daughters shall be carried upon their shoulders. And
kings shall be thy nursing fathers, and their queens thy
nursing mothers: they shall bow down to thee with their
face toward the earth, and lick up the dust of thy feet;
and thou shalt know that I am the LORD: for they shall
not be ashamed that wait for me."

Shall the prey be taken from the mighty, or the lawful
captive delivered? But thus saith the LORD, "Even the
captives of the mighty shall be taken away, and the prey
of the terrible shall be delivered: for I will contend with
him that contendeth with thee, and I will save thy children. And I will feed them that oppress thee with their
own flesh; and they shall be drunken with their own
blood, as with sweet wine: and all flesh shall know that
I, the LORD, am thy Saviour and thy Redeemer, the
mighty One of Jacob."   — Isaiah 49.

"Trust in the Name of the Lord"

Thus saith the LORD, "Where is the bill of your
mother's divorcement, whom I have put away? Or which
of my creditors is it to whom I have sold you? Behold, for
your iniquities have ye sold yourselves, and for your transgressions is your mother put away. Wherefore, when I
came, was there no man; when I called, was there none
to answer? Is my hand shortened at all, that it cannot

redeem? Or have I no power to deliver? Behold, at my rebuke I dry up the sea, I make the rivers a wilderness: their fish stinketh, because there is no water, and dieth for thirst. I clothe the heavens with blackness, and I make sackcloth their covering."

The Lord GOD hath given me the tongue of the learned, that I should know how to speak a word in season to him that is weary: he wakeneth morning by morning, he wakeneth mine ear to hear as the learned.

The Lord GOD hath opened mine ear, and I was not rebellious, neither turned away back. I gave my back to the smiters, and my cheeks to them that plucked off the hair: I hid not my face from shame and spitting. For the Lord GOD will help me; therefore shall I not be confounded: therefore have I set my face like a flint, and I know that I shall not be ashamed. He is near that justifieth me; who will contend with me? Let us stand together: who is mine adversary? Let him come near to me. Behold, the Lord GOD will help me; who is he that shall condemn me? Lo, they all shall wax old as a garment; the moth shall eat them up. Who is among you that feareth the LORD, that obeyeth the voice of his servant, that walketh in darkness, and hath no light? Let him trust in the name of the LORD, and stay upon his God. Behold, all ye that kindle a fire, that compass yourselves about with sparks: walk in the light of your fire, and in the sparks that ye have kindled. This shall ye have of mine hand; ye shall lie down in sorrow.

— Isaiah 50.

"THE RIGHTEOUSNESS OF THE LORD IS FOREVER"

Hearken to me, ye that follow after righteousness, ye that seek the LORD: look unto the rock whence ye are hewn, and to the hole of the pit whence ye are digged.

Look unto Abraham, your father, and unto Sarah that
bare you: for I called him alone, and blessed him, and
increased him. For the LORD shall comfort Zion: he will
comfort all her waste places; and he will make her wilderness like Eden, and her desert like the garden of the
LORD; joy and gladness shall be found therein, thanksgiving, and the voice of melody.

Hearken unto me, my people; and give ear unto me,
O my nation: for a law shall proceed from me, and I
will make my judgment to rest for a light of the people.
My righteousness is near; my salvation is gone forth,
and mine arms shall judge the people; the isles shall
wait upon me, and on mine arm shall they trust. Lift
up your eyes to the heavens, and look upon the earth
beneath: for the heavens shall vanish away like smoke,
and the earth shall wax old like a garment, and they that
dwell therein shall die in like manner: but my salvation
shall be forever, and my righteousness shall not be
abolished.

Hearken unto me, ye that know righteousness, the
people in whose heart is my law; fear ye not the reproach
of men, neither be ye afraid of their revilings. For the
moth shall eat them up like a garment, and the worm
shall eat them like wool: but my righteousness shall be
forever, and my salvation from generation to generation.

Awake, awake, put on strength, O arm of the LORD;
Awake, as in the ancient days,
In the generations of old.
Art thou not it that hath cut Rahab,
And wounded the dragon?
Art thou not it which hath dried the sea,
The waters of the great deep;
That hath made the depths of the sea

A way for the ransomed to pass over?
Therefore the redeemed of the LORD shall return,
And come with singing unto Zion;
And everlasting joy shall be upon their head:
They shall obtain gladness and joy;
And sorrow and mourning shall flee away.

I, even I, am he that comforteth you: who art thou,
that thou shouldest be afraid of a man that shall die, and
of the son of man which shall be made as grass; and
forgettest the LORD, thy maker, that hath stretched forth
the heavens, and laid the foundations of the earth; and
hast feared continually every day because of the fury of
the oppressor, as if he were ready to destroy? And where
is the fury of the oppressor? The captive exile hasteneth
that he may be loosed, and that he should not die in the
pit, nor that his bread should fail. But I am the LORD
thy God, that divided the sea, whose waves roared: The
LORD of hosts is his name. And I have put my words in
thy mouth, and I have covered thee in the shadow of
mine hand, that I may plant the heavens, and lay the
foundations of the earth, and say unto Zion, "Thou art
my people."

Awake, awake, stand up, O Jerusalem,
Which hast drunk at the hand of the LORD the cup of
    his fury;
Thou hast drunken the dregs of the cup of trembling,
    and wrung them out.
There is none to guide her
Among all the sons whom she hath brought forth;
Neither is there any that taketh her by the hand
Of all the sons that she hath brought up.
These two things are come unto thee;
Who shall be sorry for thee?

Desolation, and destruction,
And the famine, and the sword:
By whom shall I comfort thee?
Thy sons have fainted,
They lie at the head of all the streets,
As a wild bull in a net:
They are full of the fury of the LORD,
The rebuke of thy God.

Therefore hear now this, thou afflicted, and drunken, but not with wine: thus saith thy Lord, the LORD, and thy God that pleadeth the cause of his people, "Behold, I have taken out of thine hand the cup of trembling, even the dregs of the cup of my fury; thou shalt no more drink it again: but I will put it into the hand of them that afflict thee; which have said to thy soul, 'Bow down, that we may go over': and thou hast laid thy body as the ground, and as the street, to them that went over."

— Isaiah 51.

"AWAKE, AWAKE, O ZION"

Awake, awake; put on thy strength, O Zion;
Put on thy beautiful garments, O Jerusalem, the
　　holy city:
For henceforth there shall no more come into thee
　　the uncircumcised and the unclean.
Shake thyself from the dust:
Arise, and sit down, O Jerusalem:
Loose thyself from the bands of thy neck, O captive
　　daughter of Zion.

For thus saith the LORD, "Ye have sold yourselves for naught; and ye shall be redeemed without money."
For thus saith the Lord GOD, "My people went down aforetime into Egypt to sojourn there; and the Assyrian

oppressed them without cause. Now therefore, what have I here," saith the LORD, "that my people is taken away for naught? They that rule over them make them to howl," saith the LORD; "and my name continually every day is blasphemed. Therefore my people shall know my name: therefore they shall know in that day that I am he that doth speak: behold, it is I."

How beautiful upon the mountains are the feet of him
That bringeth good tidings, that publisheth peace;
That bringeth good tidings of good, that publisheth
    salvation;
That saith unto Zion, "Thy God reigneth!"
Thy watchmen shall lift up the voice;
With the voice together shall they sing:
For they shall see eye to eye,
When the LORD shall bring again Zion.
Break forth into joy, sing together,
Ye waste places of Jerusalem:
For the LORD hath comforted his people,
He hath redeemed Jerusalem
The Lord hath made bare his holy arm
In the eyes of all the nations;
And all the ends of the earth
Shall see the salvation of our God.
Depart ye, depart ye, go ye out from thence,
Touch no unclean thing;
Go ye out of the midst of her;
Be ye clean, that bear the vessels of the LORD.
For ye shall not go out with haste,
Nor go by flight:
For the LORD will go before you;
And the God of Israel will be your rereward.

Behold, my servant shall deal prudently, he shall be exalted and extolled, and be very high. As many were astonied at thee; his visage was so marred more than any man, and his form more than the sons of men: so shall he sprinkle many nations; the kings shall shut their mouths at him: for that which had not been told them shall they see; and that which they had not heard shall they consider.

— Isaiah 52.

"The Man of Sorrows" and His High Reward

Who hath believed our report?
And to whom is the arm of the Lord revealed?
For he shall grow up before him as a tender plant,
And as a root out of a dry ground:
He hath no form nor comeliness; and when we shall
   see him,
There is no beauty that we should desire him.
He is despised and rejected of men;
A man of sorrows, and acquainted with grief:
And we hid as it were our faces from him;
He was despised, and we esteemed him not.
Surely he hath borne our griefs,
And carried our sorrows:
Yet we did esteem him stricken,
Smitten of God, and afflicted.
But he was wounded for our transgressions,
He was bruised for our iniquities:
The chastisement of our peace was upon him;
And with his stripes we are healed.
All we like sheep have gone astray;
We have turned every one to his own way;
And the Lord hath laid on him
The iniquity of us all.
He was oppressed,
And he was afflicted,

Yet he opened not his mouth:
He is brought as a lamb to the slaughter,
And as a sheep before her shearers is dumb,
So he openeth not his mouth.
He was taken from prison and from judgment:
And who shall declare his generation?
For he was cut off out of the land of the living:
For the transgression of my people was he stricken.
And he made his grave with the wicked,
And with the rich in his death;
Because he had done no violence,
Neither was any deceit in his mouth.
Yet it pleased the LORD to bruise him;
He hath put him to grief:
When thou shalt make his soul an offering for sin,
He shall see his seed, he shall prolong his days,
And the pleasure of the LORD shall prosper in his
    hand.
He shall see of the travail of his soul, and shall be
    satisfied:
By his knowledge shall my righteous servant justify
    many;
For he shall bear their iniquities.
Therefore will I divide him a portion with the great,
And he shall divide the spoil with the strong;
Because he hath poured out his soul unto death:
And he was numbered with the transgressors;
And he bare the sin of many,
And made intercession for the transgressors.

— Isaiah 53.

THE EVERLASTING MERCY

"Sing, O barren, thou that didst not bear; break forth
into singing, and cry aloud, thou that didst not travail

with child: for more are the children of the desolate than the children of the married wife," saith the LORD.

"Enlarge the place of thy tent, and let them stretch forth the curtains of thine habitations: spare not, lengthen thy cords, and strengthen thy stakes; for thou shalt break forth on the right hand and on the left; and thy seed shall inherit the Gentiles, and make the desolate cities to be inhabited. Fear not; for thou shalt not be ashamed: neither be thou confounded; for thou shalt not be put to shame: for thou shalt forget the shame of thy youth, and shalt not remember the reproach of thy widowhood any more. For thy Maker is thine husband; the LORD of hosts is his name; and thy Redeemer the Holy One of Israel; the God of the whole earth shall he be called. For the LORD hath called thee as a woman forsaken and grieved in spirit, and a wife of youth, when thou wast refused," saith thy God.

"For a small moment have I forsaken thee; but with great mercies will I gather thee. In a little wrath I hid my face from thee for a moment; but with everlasting kindness will I have mercy on thee," saith the LORD thy Redeemer.

"For this is as the waters of Noah unto me: for as I have sworn that the waters of Noah should no more go over the earth; so have I sworn that I would not be wroth with thee, nor rebuke thee. For the mountains shall depart, and the hills be removed; but my kindness shall not depart from thee, neither shall the covenant of my peace be removed," saith the LORD that hath mercy on thee.

"O thou afflicted, tossed with tempest, and not comforted, behold, I will lay thy stones with fair colours, and lay thy foundations with sapphires. And I will make thy windows of agates, and thy gates of carbuncles, and all thy borders of pleasant stones. And all thy children shall be taught of the LORD; and great shall be the peace of thy children. In righteousness shalt thou be established: thou shalt be far from oppression; for thou shalt not fear: and from terror; for it shall not come near thee. Behold, they shall surely gather together, but not by me: whosoever shall gather together against thee shall fall for thy sake. Behold, I have created the smith that bloweth the coals in the fire, and that bringeth forth an instrument for his work; and I have created the waster to destroy. No weapon that is formed against thee shall prosper; and every tongue that shall rise against thee in judgment thou shalt condemn. This is the heritage of the servants of the LORD, and their righteousness is of me," saith the LORD.

— Isaiah 54.

"HO, EVERY ONE THAT THIRSTETH"

Ho, every one that thirsteth, come ye to the waters,
And he that hath no money;
Come ye, buy, and eat;
Yea, come, buy wine and milk
Without money and without price.
Wherefore do ye spend money for that which is not
  bread?
And your labour for that which satisfieth not?

Hearken diligently unto me,
And eat ye that which is good,
And let your soul delight itself in fatness.
Incline your ear, and come unto me:
Hear, and your soul shall live;
And I will make an everlasting covenant with you,
Even the sure mercies of David.

Behold, I have given him for a witness to the people, a leader and commander to the people. Behold, thou shalt call a nation that thou knowest not, and nations that knew not thee shall run unto thee because of the LORD thy God, and for the Holy One of Israel; for he hath glorified thee.

> Seek ye the LORD while he may be found
> Call ye upon him while he is near:
> Let the wicked forsake his way,
> And the unrighteous man his thoughts:
> And let him return unto the LORD,
> And he will have mercy upon him;
> And to our God,
> For he will abundantly pardon.

"For my thoughts are not your thoughts, neither are your ways my ways," saith the LORD.

"For as the heavens are higher than the earth, so are my ways higher than your ways, and my thoughts than your thoughts. For as the rain cometh down, and the snow from heaven, and returneth not thither, but watereth the earth, and maketh it bring forth and bud, that it may give seed to the sower, and bread to the eater: so shall my word be that goeth forth out of my mouth: it shall not return unto me void, but it shall accomplish that which I please, and it shall prosper in the thing whereto I sent it."

> For ye shall go out with joy,
> And be led forth with peace:
> The mountains and the hills shall break forth before
>   you into singing,
> And all the trees of the field shall clap their hands.

Instead of the thorn shall come up the fir-tree,
And instead of the brier shall come up the myrtle-
tree:
And it shall be to the LORD for a name,
For an everlasting sign that shall not be cut off.

— Isaiah 55

"KEEP YE JUDGMENT, AND DO JUSTICE"

Thus saith the LORD, "Keep ye judgment, and do justice: for my salvation is near to come, and my righteousness to be revealed. Blessed is the man that doeth this, and the son of man that layeth hold on it; that keepeth the Sabbath from polluting it, and keepeth his hand from doing any evil.

"Neither let the son of the stranger, that hath joined himself to the LORD, speak, saying, 'The LORD hath utterly separated me from his people': neither let the eunuch say, 'Behold, I am a dry tree.'

"For thus saith the LORD unto the eunuchs that keep my Sabbaths, and choose the things that please me, and take hold of my covenant; 'Even unto them will I give in mine house and within my walls a place and a name better than of sons and of daughters: I will give them an everlasting name, that shall not be cut off. Also the sons of the stranger, that join themselves to the LORD, to serve him, and to love the name of the LORD, to be his servants, every one that keepeth the Sabbath from polluting it, and taketh hold of my covenant; even them will I bring to my holy mountain, and make them joyful in my house of prayer: their burnt offerings and their sacrifices shall be accepted upon mine altar; for mine house shall be called an house of prayer for all people.'"

The Lord GOD which gathereth the outcasts of Israel saith, "Yet will I gather others to him, beside those that are gathered unto him."

All ye beasts of the field, come to devour, yea, all ye beasts in the forest.

His watchmen are blind: they are all ignorant, they are all dumb dogs, they cannot bark; sleeping, lying down, loving to slumber. Yea, they are greedy dogs which can never have enough, and they are shepherds that cannot understand: they all look to their own way, every one for his gain, from his quarter. "Come ye," say they, "I will fetch wine, and we will fill ourselves with strong drink; and to-morrow shall be as this day, and much more abundant."

— Isaiah 56.

"The Righteous Perisheth"

The righteous perisheth, and no man layeth it to heart: and merciful men are taken away, none considering that the righteous is taken away from the evil to come. He shall enter into peace: they shall rest in their beds, each one walking in his uprightness. But draw near hither, ye sons of the sorceress, the seed of the adulterer and the whore. Against whom do ye sport yourselves? Against whom make ye a wide mouth, and draw out the tongue? Are ye not children of transgression, a seed of falsehood, enflaming yourselves with idols under every green tree, slaying the children in the valleys under the clifts of the rocks? Among the smooth stones of the stream is thy portion; they, they are thy lot: even to them hast thou poured a drink offering, thou hast offered a meat offering. Should I receive comfort in these? Upon a lofty and high mountain hast thou set thy bed: even thither wentest thou up to offer sacrifice. Behind the doors also and the posts hast thou set up thy remembrance: for thou hast discovered thyself to another than me, and art gone up; thou hast enlarged thy bed, and made thee a covenant with them; thou lovedst their bed where thou sawest it. And thou wentest to the king with ointment, and didst increase thy perfumes, and didst send thy messengers far off, and didst debase thyself even unto hell. Thou art wearied in the greatness of thy way; yet saidst thou not, "There is no hope": thou hast found the life of thine hand; therefore thou wast not grieved. And of whom hast thou been afraid or feared, that thou hast lied, and hast not remembered me, nor laid it to thy heart? Have not I held my peace even of old, and thou fearest me not? I will declare thy righteousness, and thy works; for they shall not profit thee.

When thou criest, let thy companies deliver thee; but the wind shall carry them all away; vanity shall take them: but he that putteth his trust in me shall possess the land, and shall inherit my holy mountain; and shall say, "Cast ye up, cast ye up, prepare the way, take up the stumblingblock out of the way of my people."

For thus saith the high and lofty One that inhabiteth eternity, whose name is Holy: "I dwell in the high and holy place, with him also that is of a contrite and humble spirit, to revive the spirit of the humble, and to revive the heart of the contrite ones. For I will not contend forever, neither will I be always wroth: for the spirit should fail before me, and the souls which I have made. For the iniquity of his covetousness was I wroth, and smote him: I hid me, and was wroth, and he went on frowardly in the way of his heart. I have seen his ways, and will heal him: I will lead him also, and restore comforts unto him and to his mourners. I create the fruit of the lips. Peace, peace to him that is far off, and to him that is near," saith the LORD: "and I will heal him. But the wicked are like the troubled sea, when it cannot rest, whose waters cast up mire and dirt. There is no peace," saith my God, "to the wicked." — Isaiah 57.

"Cry Aloud, Spare not"

Cry aloud, spare not, lift up thy voice like a trumpet, and shew my people their transgression, and the house of Jacob their sins. Yet they seek me daily, and delight to know my ways, as a nation that did righteousness, and forsook not the ordinance of their God: they ask of me the ordinances of justice; they take delight in approaching to God.

"Wherefore have we fasted," say they, "and thou seest not? Wherefore have we afflicted our soul, and thou takest no knowledge?" Behold, in the day of your fast ye find pleasure, and exact all your labours. Behold, ye fast for strife and debate, and to smite with the fist of wickedness: ye shall not fast as ye do this day, to make your voice to be heard on high. Is it such a fast that I have chosen, a day for a man to afflict his soul? Is it to bow down his head as a bulrush, and to spread sackcloth and ashes under him? Wilt thou call this a fast, and an acceptable day to the Lord? Is not this the fast that I have chosen: to loose the bands of wickedness, to undo the heavy burdens, and to let the oppressed go free, and that ye break every yoke? Is it not to deal thy bread to the hungry, and that thou bring the poor that are cast out to thy house; When thou seest the naked, that thou cover him; and that thou hide not thyself from thine own flesh?

Then shall thy light break forth as the morning, and thine health shall spring forth speedily: and thy righteousness shall go before thee; the glory of the Lord shall be thy rereward. Then shalt thou call, and the Lord shall answer; thou shalt cry, and he shall say, "Here I am." If thou take away from the midst of thee the yoke, the putting forth of the finger, and speaking vanity; and if thou draw out thy soul to the hungry, and satisfy the afflicted soul; then shall thy light rise in obscurity, and thy darkness be as the noon day: and the LORD shall guide thee continually, and satisfy thy soul in drought, and make fat thy bones: and thou shalt be like a watered garden, and like a spring of water, whose waters fail not. And they that shall be of thee shall build the old waste places: thou shalt raise up the foundations of many generations; and thou shalt be called, "The repairer of the breach, The restorer of paths to dwell in."

If thou turn away thy foot from the Sabbath, from doing thy pleasure on my holy day; and call the Sabbath a delight, the holy of the LORD, honourable; and shalt honour him, not doing thine own ways, nor finding thine own pleasure, nor speaking thine own words: then shalt thou delight thyself in the LORD; and I will cause thee to ride upon the high places of the earth, and feed thee with the heritage of Jacob, thy father: for the mouth of the LORD hath spoken it.   — Isaiah 58.

"THE LORD'S HAND IS NOT SHORTENED"

Behold, the LORD's hand is not shortened, that it cannot save; neither his ear heavy, that it cannot hear: but your iniquities have separated between you and your God, and your sins have hid his face from you, that he will not hear. For your hands are defiled with blood, and your fingers with iniquity; your lips have spoken lies, your tongue hath muttered perverseness. None calleth for justice, nor any pleadeth for truth: they trust in vanity, and speak lies; they conceive mischief, and bring forth iniquity. They hatch cockatrice' eggs, and weave the spider's web: he that eateth of their eggs dieth, and that which is crushed breaketh out into a viper. Their webs shall not become garments, neither shall they cover themselves with their works: their works are works of iniquity, and the act of violence is in their hands. Their feet run to evil, and they make haste to shed innocent blood: their thoughts are thoughts of iniquity; wasting and destruction are in their paths. The way of peace they know not; and there is no judgment in their goings: they have made them crooked paths: whosoever goeth therein shall not know peace.

Therefore is judgment far from us, neither doth justice overtake us: we wait for light, but behold obscurity; for brightness, but we walk in darkness. We grope for the wall like the blind, and we grope as if we had no eyes: we stumble at noon day as in the night; we are in desolate places as dead men. We roar all like bears, and mourn sore like doves: we look for judgment, but there is none; for salvation, but it is far off from us. For our transgressions are multiplied before thee, and our sins testify against us: for our transgressions are with us; and as for our iniquities, we know them; in transgressing and lying against the LORD, and departing away from our God, speaking oppression and revolt, conceiving and uttering from the heart words of falsehood. And judgment is turned away backward, and justice standeth afar off: for truth is fallen in the street, and equity cannot enter. Yea, truth faileth; and he that departeth from evil maketh himself a prey: and the LORD saw it, and it displeased him that there was no judgment.

And he saw that there was no man, and wondered that there was no intercessor: therefore his arm brought salvation unto him; and his righteousness, it sustained him. For he put on righteousness as a breastplate, and an helmet of salvation upon his head; and he put on the garments of vengeance for clothing, and was clad with zeal as a cloke. According to their deeds, accordingly he will repay, fury to his adversaries, recompence to his enemies; to the islands he will repay recompence. So shall they fear the name of the LORD from the west, and his glory from the rising of the sun. When the enemy shall come in like a flood, the Spirit of the LORD shall lift up a standard against him.

"And the Redeemer shall come to Zion, and unto them that turn from transgression in Jacob," saith the LORD. "As for me, this is my covenant with them," saith the LORD: "My spirit that is upon thee, and my words which I have put in thy mouth, shall not depart out of thy mouth, nor out of the mouth of thy seed, nor out of the mouth of thy seed's seed," saith the LORD, "from henceforth and forever." — Isaiah 59.

ARISE, SHINE FOR THY LIGHT IS COME

Arise, shine; for thy light is come,
And the glory of the LORD is risen upon thee.
For, behold, the darkness shall cover the earth,
And gross darkness the people:
But the LORD shall arise upon thee,
And his glory shall be seen upon thee.
And the Gentiles shall come to thy light,
And kings to the brightness of thy rising.
Lift up thine eyes round about, and see:
All they gather themselves together, they come to
    thee:
Thy sons shall come from far,
And thy daughters shall be nursed at thy side.
Then thou shalt see, and flow together,
And thine heart shall fear, and be enlarged;
Because the abundance of the sea shall be converted
    unto thee,
The forces of the Gentiles shall come unto thee.

The multitude of camels shall cover thee,
The dromedaries of Midian and Ephah;
All they from Sheba shall come:
They shall bring gold and incense;
And they shall shew forth the praises of the LORD.
All the flocks of Kedar shall be gathered together
    unto thee,
The rams of Nebaioth shall minister unto thee:
They shall come up with acceptance on mine altar,
And I will glorify the house of my glory.
Who are these that fly as a cloud,
And as the doves to their windows?
Surely the isles shall wait for me,
And the ships of Tarshish first,
To bring thy sons from far,
Their silver and their gold with them,
Unto the name of the LORD thy God,
And to the Holy One of Israel,
Because he hath glorified thee.
And the sons of strangers shall build up thy walls,
And their kings shall minister unto thee:
For in my wrath I smote thee,
But in my favour have I had mercy on thee.
Therefore thy gates shall be open continually;
They shall not be shut day nor night,
That men may bring unto thee the forces of the
    Gentiles,
And that their kings may be brought.
For the nation and kingdom that will not serve thee
    shall perish;
Yea, those nations shall be utterly wasted.
The glory of Lebanon shall come unto thee,
The fir-tree, the pine-tree, and the box together,
To beautify the place of my sanctuary;

And I will make the place of my feet glorious.
The sons also of them that afflicted thee
Shall come bending unto thee;
And all they that despised thee
Shall bow themselves down at the soles of thy feet;
And they shall call thee, "The city of the LORD,"
"The Zion of the Holy One of Israel."
Whereas thou hast been forsaken and hated,
So that no man went through thee,
I will make thee an eternal excellency,
A joy of many generations.
Thou shalt also suck the milk of the Gentiles,
And shalt suck the breast of kings:
And thou shalt know that I, the LORD, am thy Saviour
And thy Redeemer, the mighty One of Jacob.
For brass I will bring gold,
And for iron I will bring silver,
And for wood brass,
And for stones iron:
I will also make thy officers peace,
And thine exactors righteousness.
Violence shall no more be heard in thy land,
Wasting nor destruction within thy borders;
But thou shalt call thy walls "Salvation," and thy
    gates "Praise."
The sun shall be no more thy light by day;
Neither for brightness shall the moon give light unto
    thee:
But the LORD shall be unto thee an everlasting light,
And thy God thy glory.
Thy sun shall no more go down;
Neither shall thy moon withdraw itself:
For the LORD shall be thine everlasting light,
And the days of thy mourning shall be ended.

Thy people also shall be all righteous:
They shall inherit the land forever,
The branch of my planting,
The work of my hands,
That I may be glorified.
A little one shall become a thousand,
And a small one a strong nation:
I, the LORD, will hasten it in his time. — Isaiah 60.

THE MESSAGE OF THE LORD'S ANOINTED

The Spirit of the Lord GOD is upon me;
Because the LORD hath anointed me to preach good
    tidings unto the meek;
He hath sent me to bind up the brokenhearted,
To proclaim liberty to the captives,
And the opening of the prison to them that are bound;
To proclaim the acceptable year of the LORD,
And the day of vengeance of our God;
To comfort all that mourn;
To appoint unto them that mourn in Zion,
To give unto them beauty for ashes,
The oil of joy for mourning,
The garment of praise for the spirit of heaviness;
That they might be called trees of righteousness,
The planting of the LORD,
That he might be glorified.

And they shall build the old wastes,
They shall raise up the former desolations,
And they shall repair the waste cities,
The desolations of many generations.
And strangers shall stand and feed your flocks,
And the sons of the alien shall be your plowmen and
    your vinedressers.

But ye shall be named the Priests of the Lord:
Men shall call you the "Ministers of our God":
Ye shall eat the riches of the Gentiles,
And in their glory shall ye boast yourselves.

For your shame ye shall have double;
And for confusion they shall rejoice in their portion:
Therefore in their land they shall possess the double:
Everlasting joy shall be unto them.
For I, the Lord, love judgment,
I hate robbery for burnt offering;
And I will direct their work in truth,
And I will make an everlasting covenant with them.
And their seed shall be known among the Gentiles,
And their offspring among the people:
All that see them shall acknowledge them,
That they are the seed which the Lord hath blessed.
I will greatly rejoice in the Lord,
My soul shall be joyful in my God;
For he hath clothed me with the garments of
    salvation,
He hath covered me with the robe of righteousness,
As a bridegroom decketh himself with ornaments,
And as a bride adorneth herself with her jewels.
For as the earth bringeth forth her bud,
And as the garden causeth the things that are sown
    in it to spring forth;
So the Lord God will cause righteousness and praise
    to spring forth before all the nations.
— Isaiah 61.

"Thou Shalt no More Be Called Forsaken"

For Zion's sake will I not hold my peace, and for Jerusalem's sake I will not rest, until the righteousness thereof go forth as brightness, and the salvation thereof as a lamp that burneth. And the Gentiles shall see thy righteousness, and all kings thy glory: and thou shalt be called by a new name, which the mouth of the LORD shall name. Thou shalt also be a crown of glory in the hand of the LORD, and a royal diadem in the hand of thy God. Thou shalt no more be termed "Forsaken"; neither shall thy land any more be termed "Desolate": but thou shalt be called Hephzi-bah, and thy land, Beulah: for the LORD delighteth in thee, and thy land shall be married.

For as a young man marrieth a virgin, so shall thy sons marry thee: and as the bridegroom rejoiceth over the bride, so shall thy God rejoice over thee. I have set watchmen upon thy walls, O Jerusalem, which shall never hold their peace day nor night: ye that make mention of the LORD, keep not silence. And give him no rest, till he establish, and till he make Jerusalem a praise in the earth. The LORD hath sworn by his right hand, and by the arm of his strength, "Surely I will no more give thy corn to be meat for thine enemies; and the sons of the stranger shall not drink thy wine, for the which thou hast laboured: but they that have gathered it shall eat it, and praise the LORD; and they that have brought it together shall drink it in the courts of my holiness."

Go through, go through the gates; prepare ye the way of the people; cast up, cast up the highway; gather out the stones; lift up a standard for the people. Behold, the LORD hath proclaimed unto the end of the world, "Say ye to the daughter of Zion, 'Behold, thy salvation cometh; behold, his reward is with him, and his work before him.'"

And they shall call them, "The holy people, The redeemed of the LORD": and thou shalt be called, "Sought out, A city not forsaken." ~ Isaiah 62.

"Who Is This that Cometh from Edom?"

The Doom of Edom

Who is this that cometh from Edom,
With dyed garments from Bozrah?
This that is glorious in his apparel,
Traveling in the greatness of his strength?
I that speak in righteousness, mighty to save.
Wherefore art thou red in thine apparel,
And thy garments like him that treadeth in the
 winefat?
I have trodden the wine-press alone;
And of the people there was none with me:
For I will tread them in mine anger, and trample them
 in my fury;
And their blood shall be sprinkled upon my garments,
And I will stain all my raiment.
For the day of vengeance is in mine heart,
And the year of my redeemed is come.
And I looked, and there was none to help;
And I wondered that there was none to uphold:
Therefore mine own arm brought salvation unto me;
And my fury, it upheld me.
And I will tread down the people in mine anger,
And make them drunk in my fury,
And I will bring down their strength to the earth.

Thanksgiving for Ancient Days

I will mention the loving kindnesses of the Lord,
And the praises of the Lord,
According to all that the Lord hath bestowed on us,
And the great goodness toward the house of Israel,
Which he hath bestowed on them according to his
 mercies,

And according to the multitude of his lovingkind-
    nesses.
For he said, "Surely they are my people,
Children that will not lie":
So he was their Saviour.
In all their affliction he was afflicted,
And the angel of his presence saved them:
In his love and in his pity he redeemed them;
And he bare them, and carried them all the days of
    old.

But they rebelled, and vexed his holy Spirit:
Therefore he was turned to be their enemy,
And he fought against them.
Then he remembered the days of old,
Moses, and his people, saying,
"Where is he that brought them up out of the sea
    with the shepherd of his flock?
Where is he that put his holy Spirit within him:
That led them by the right hand of Moses with his
    glorious arm,
Dividing the water before them,
To make himself an everlasting name:
That led them through the deep,
As an horse in the wilderness,
That they should not stumble?"
As a beast goeth down into the valley,
The Spirit of the LORD caused him to rest:
So didst thou lead thy people,
To make thyself a glorious name.

"RETURN, FOR THY SERVANTS' SAKE"
Look down from heaven,
And behold from the habitation of thy holiness and
    of thy glory:

Where is thy zeal and thy strength,
The sounding of thy bowels and of thy mercies to-
    ward me?
Are they restrained?

Doubtless thou art our father, though Abraham be
    ignorant of us, and Israel acknowledge us not:
Thou, O LORD, art our father, our redeemer;
Thy name is from everlasting.
O LORD, why hast thou made us to err from thy ways,
And hardened our heart from thy fear?
Return, for thy servants' sake,
The tribes of thine inheritance.

The people of thy holiness have possessed it but a
    little while:
Our adversaries have trodden down thy sanctuary.
We are thine: thou never barest rule over them;
They were not called by thy name.   — Isaiah 63.

"THOU ART OUR FATHER. WE ARE THE CLAY AND THOU THE POTTER"

Oh that thou wouldest rend the heavens, that thou
wouldest come down, that the mountains might flow down
at thy presence, as when the melting fire burneth, the
fire causeth the waters to boil, to make thy name known
to thine adversaries, that the nations may tremble at thy
presence! When thou didst terrible things which we
looked not for, thou camest down, the mountains flowed
down at thy presence. For since the beginning of the
world men have not heard, nor perceived by the ear,
neither hath the eye seen, O God, beside thee, what he
hath prepared for him that waiteth for him. Thou meetest
him that rejoiceth and worketh righteousness, those that

remember thee in thy ways: behold, thou art wroth; for we have sinned: in those is continuance, and we shall be saved. But we are all as an unclean thing, and all our righteousnesses are as filthy rags; and we all do fade as a leaf; and our iniquities, like the wind, have taken us away. And there is none that calleth upon thy name, that stirreth up himself to take hold of thee: for thou hast hid thy face from us, and hast consumed us, because of our iniquities. But now, O Lord, thou art our father; we are the clay, and thou our potter; and we all are the work of thy hand.

Be not wroth very sore, O Lord, neither remember iniquity for ever: behold, see, we beseech thee, we are all thy people. Thy holy cities are a wilderness, Zion is a wilderness, Jerusalem a desolation. Our holy and our beautiful house, where our fathers praised thee, is burned up with fire: and all our pleasant things are laid waste. Wilt thou refrain thyself for these things, O Lord? Wilt thou hold thy peace, and afflict us very sore?

I am sought of them that asked not for me; I am found of them that sought me not: I said, "Behold me, behold me," unto a nation that was not called by my name. I have spread out my hands all the day unto a rebellious people, which walketh in a way that was not good, after their own thoughts; a people that provoketh me to anger continually to my face; that sacrificeth in gardens, and burneth incense upon altars of brick; which remain among the graves, and lodge in the monuments, which eat swine's flesh, and broth of abominable things is in their vessels; which say, "Stand by thyself, come not near to me; for I am holier than thou." These are a smoke in my nose, a fire that burneth all the day.

Behold, it is written before me: "I will not keep silence, but will recompense, even recompense into their bosom, your iniquities, and the iniquities of your fathers together," saith the LORD, "which have burned incense upon the mountains, and blasphemed me upon the hills: therefore will I measure their former work into their bosom."

Thus saith the LORD, "As the new wine is found in the cluster and one saith, 'Destroy it not; for a blessing is in it': so will I do for my servants' sakes, that I may not destroy them all. And I will bring forth a seed out of Jacob, and out of Judah an inheritor of my mountains: and mine elect shall inherit it, and my servants shall dwell there. And Sharon shall be a fold of flocks, and the valley of Achor a place for the herds to lie down in, for my people that have sought me. But ye are they that forsake the LORD, that forget my holy mountain, that prepare a table for that troop, and that furnish the drink offering unto that number. Therefore will I number you to the sword, and ye shall all bow down to the slaughter: because when I called, ye did not answer; when I spake, ye did not hear; but did evil before mine eyes, and did choose that wherein I delighted not."

Therefore thus saith the Lord GOD, "Behold, my servants shall eat, but ye shall be hungry: behold, my servants shall drink, but ye shall be thirsty: behold, my servants shall rejoice, but ye shall be ashamed: behold, my servants shall sing for joy of heart, but ye shall cry for sorrow of heart, and shall howl for vexation of spirit. And ye shall leave your name for a curse unto my chosen: for the Lord GOD shall slay thee, and call his servants by another name: that he who blesseth himself in the earth shall bless himself in the God of truth; and he that sweareth in the earth shall swear by the God of truth; because the former troubles are forgotten, and because they are hid from mine eyes.   — Isaiah 64: 65:1-16.

THE NEW HEAVENS AND THE NEW EARTH

"For, behold, I create new heavens and a new earth: and the former shall not be remembered, nor come into mind. But be ye glad and rejoice forever in that which I create: for, behold, I create Jerusalem a rejoicing, and her people a joy. And I will rejoice in Jerusalem, and joy in my people: and the voice of weeping shall be no more heard in her, nor the voice of crying. There shall be no more thence an infant of days, nor an old man that hath not filled his days: for the child shall die an hundred years old; but the sinner being an hundred years old shall be accursed. And they shall build houses, and inhabit them; and they shall plant vineyards, and eat the fruit of them. They shall not build, and another inhabit; they shall not plant, and another eat: for as the days of a tree are the days of my people, and mine elect shall long enjoy the work of their hands. They shall not labour in vain, nor bring forth for trouble; for they are the seed of the blessed of the LORD, and their offspring with them. And it shall come to pass, that before they call, I will answer; and while they are yet speaking, I will hear. The wolf and the lamb shall feed together, and the lion shall eat straw like the bullock: and dust shall be the serpent's meat. They shall not hurt nor destroy in all my holy mountain," saith the LORD.

Thus saith the LORD, "The heaven is my throne, and the earth is my footstool: where is the house that ye build unto me? And where is the place of my rest? For all those things hath mine hand made, and all those things have been," saith the LORD: "but to this man will I look, even to him that is poor and of a contrite spirit, and trembleth at my word. He that killeth an ox is as if he slew a man; he that sacrificeth a lamb, as if he cut off a dog's neck; he that offereth an oblation, as if he

offered swine's blood; he that burneth incense, as if he
blessed an idol. Yea, they have chosen their own ways,
and their soul delighteth in their abominations. I also
will choose their delusions, and will bring their fears upon
them; because when I called, none did answer; when I
spake, they did not hear: but they did evil before mine
eyes, and chose that in which I delighted not."

Hear the word of the LORD, ye that tremble at his
word: "Your brethren that hated you, that cast you out
for my name's sake, said, 'Let the LORD be glorified': but
he shall appear to your joy, and they shall be ashamed."

A voice of noise from the city, a voice from the temple,
a voice of the LORD that rendereth recompence to his
enemies. Before she travailed, she brought forth; before
her pain came, she was delivered of a man child. Who
hath heard such a thing? Who hath seen such things?
Shall the earth be made to bring forth in one day? Or
shall a nation be born at once? For as soon as Zion travailed, she brought forth her children. "Shall I bring to
the birth, and not cause to bring forth?" saith the LORD:
"Shall I cause to bring forth, and shut the womb?"
saith thy God. Rejoice ye with Jerusalem, and be glad
with her, all ye that love her: rejoice for joy with her, all
ye that mourn for her: that ye may suck, and be satisfied with the breasts of her consolations; that ye may milk
out, and be delighted with the abundance of her glory.

For thus saith the LORD, "Behold, I will extend peace
to her like a river, and the glory of the Gentiles like a
flowing stream: then shall ye suck, ye shall be borne upon
her sides, and be dandled upon her knees. As one whom
his mother comforteth, so will I comfort you; and ye
shall be comforted in Jerusalem. And when ye see this
your heart shall rejoice, and your bones shall flourish like
an herb: and the hand of the LORD shall be known

toward his servants, and his indignation toward his enemies. For, behold, the LORD will come with fire, and with his chariots like a whirlwind, to render his anger with fury, and his rebuke with flames of fire. For by fire and by his sword will the LORD plead with all flesh: and the slain of the LORD shall be many. They that sanctify themselves, and purify themselves in the gardens behind one tree in the midst, eating swine's flesh, and the abomination, and the mouse, shall be consumed together," saith the LORD.

"For I know their works and their thoughts: it shall come, that I will gather all nations and tongues; and they shall come, and see my glory. And I will set a sign among them, and I will send those that escape of them unto the nations, to Tarshish, Pul, and Lud, that draw the bow, to Tubal, and Javan, to the isles afar off, that have not heard my fame, neither have seen my glory; and they shall declare my glory among the Gentiles. And they shall bring all your brethren for an offering unto the LORD out of all nations upon horses, and in chariots, and in litters, and upon mules, and upon swift beasts, to my holy mountain Jerusalem," saith the LORD, "as the children of Israel bring an offering in a clean vessel into the house of the LORD. And I will also take of them for priests and for Levites," saith the LORD.

"For as the new heavens and the new earth, which I will make, shall remain before me," saith the LORD, "so shall your seed and your name remain. And it shall come to pass, that from one new moon to another, and from one Sabbath to another, shall all flesh come to worship before me," saith the LORD.

"And they shall go forth, and look upon the carcasses of the men that have transgressed against me: for their worm shall not die, neither shall their fire be quenched; and they shall be an abhorring unto all flesh."

—Isaiah 65:17-25; 66.

THE PROPHETS

MICAH   HAGGAI   MALACHI   ZECHARIAH

From the Frieze in the Boston Public Library,
Boston, Massachusetts
By John S. Sargent. From a Copley Print
Copyrighted by Curtis and Cameron, Inc.,
Boston, Massachusetts

THIS great mural painting adorns the walls
of the Public Library at Boston, Massachusetts. The figures of the "goodly fellowship of the prophets" are painted with great
vigor and spiritual understanding. For
other portions of this frieze, see pages 30,
56, and 412 of this volume.

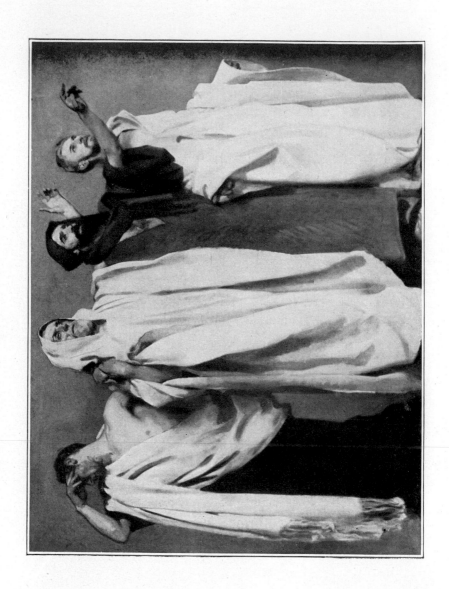

Micah

The Prophet of the Poor

The home of Amos was in the wild and rugged country of eastern Palestine. Across the breadth of the land in the fair and fertile foot-hills which look down upon the Plain of the Philistines and the sea, lived, thirty years later, another prophet of the people, Micah, the farmer.

In Jerusalem, Isaiah, the city statesman-prophet, was thundering against the evils of the day. Here, in the little village of Moresheth, which has long since disappeared, lived, at the outposts of the country, the gateway of Jerusalem, a man who was one of the greatest of the inspired leaders of the people.

The oppression of the poor, the demand for social justice, was his great theme. Like Amos, he speaks of the coming doom of his nation, and like Amos, he bases his prediction of disaster upon the nation itself. The same conditions which prevailed in Samaria were to be found in Jerusalem, and not only in Jerusalem, but in all the country, in his own little town, among the farmers of the fat valleys and the shepherds on the hills. The avarice of the rich reached out and laid its fingers upon every smallest hut. As in the days before the French Revolution, before the Servile Wars of the Roman Empire, the Peasants' Rising in England, the Russian Revolution, injustice and oppression were more keenly felt and more bitterly resented in the country than in the city. In Judah after the prosperous reign of Uzziah, evil conditions had become acute. There were war-profiteers in those days, as in every age. Isaiah had protested, "Woe upon them that join house to house, that lay field to field, till there be no place." He meant that the rich had bought up field after field until there was no room for the common people, the small holders of land; and Micah condemns the same injustice: "They covet fields and seize them and houses and take them away, and they oppress a man and his house, even a man and his heritage. The women of my people they cast out of their pleasant houses: from the young children ye take away my glory forever." The greed of the rich and powerful, the exploitation of women and little children,—these are not the sins of Micah's age alone, but of every age.

There are three great passages in Micah which make his prophecy one of the most notable and distinguished documents in human history. He turns away from the blood and brutality of the wars of his own age and he prophesies in words which have never lost their power to move men. He sees the dawn of universal peace: "And he shall judge among many people, and rebuke strong nations afar off; and they shall beat their swords into plowshares and their spears into pruning-hooks: nation shall not lift up a sword against nation, neither shall they learn war any more. But they shall sit every man under his vine and under his fig-tree; and none shall make them afraid: for the mouth of the Lord of hosts hath spoken it."

He realizes that first the king must come who will lead the people to the happy future: "This man shall be our peace;" and he predicts, in words which have ever since been cherished in the heart of humanity, the very place where the Prince of Peace is to be born: "But thou, Bethlehem Ephratah, though thou be little among the thousands of Judah, yet out of thee shall he come forth unto me that is to be ruler in Israel; whose goings forth have been from of old, from everlasting."

The third passage which rises to the most sublime heights has been called "the greatest saying of the Old Testament": "Wherewith shall I come before the LORD, and bow myself before the high God? Shall I come before him with burnt offerings, with calves of a year old? Will the LORD be pleased with thousands of rams, or with ten thousands of rivers of oil? Shall I give my firstborn for my transgression, the fruit of my body for the sin of my soul? He hath showed thee, O man, what is good: and what doth the LORD require of thee, but to do justly, and to love mercy, and to walk humbly with thy God?"

The Book of Micah was the favorite of Theodore Roosevelt, as it has been and must always be the inspiration of all those who sincerely pity the sufferings of the poor, who look and work for the coming of the day of social justice and righteousness and the salvation of mankind.

The Prophecy of Micah

The word of the Lord that came to Micah, the Morasthite, in the days of Jotham, Ahaz, and Hezekiah, Kings of Judah, which he saw concerning Samaria and Jerusalem.

THE COMING DESTRUCTION OF ISRAEL AND JUDAH

HEAR, all ye people; hearken, O earth, and all that therein is: and let the Lord GOD be witness against you, the LORD from his holy temple. For, behold, the LORD cometh forth out of his place, and will come down, and tread upon the high places of the earth. And the mountains shall be molten under him, and the valleys shall be cleft, as wax before the fire, and as the waters that are poured down a steep place. For the transgression of Jacob is all this, and for the sins of the house of Israel. What is the transgression of Jacob? Is it not Samaria? And what are the high places of Judah? Are they not Jerusalem? Therefore I will make Samaria as an heap of the field, and as plantings of a vineyard: and I will pour down the stones thereof into the valley, and I will discover the foundations thereof. And all the graven images thereof shall be beaten to pieces, and all the hires thereof shall be burned with the fire, and all the idols thereof will I lay desolate: for she gathered it of the hire of an harlot, and they shall return to the hire of an harlot. Therefore I will wail and howl, I will go stripped and naked: I will make a wailing like the dragons, and mourning as the owls. For her wound is incurable; for it is come unto

PLOWING IN PALESTINE
Photograph by
Professor Lewis Bayles Paton

This shows the very primitive plow still in use in Palestine. Micah, the farmer, doubtless much resembled this farmer as he tilled his fields in the foothills of Judea.

Judah; he is come unto the gate of my people, even to Jerusalem.

Declare ye it not at Gath, weep ye not at all: in the house of Aphrah roll thyself in the dust. Pass ye away, thou inhabitant of Saphir, having thy shame naked: the inhabitant of Zaanan came not forth in the mourning of Beth-ezel; he shall receive of you his standing. For the inhabitant of Maroth waited carefully for good: but evil came down from the LORD unto the gate of Jerusalem. O thou inhabitant of Lachish, bind the chariot to the swift beast: she is the beginning of the sin to the daughter of Zion: for the transgressions of Israel were found in thee. Therefore shalt thou give presents to Moresheth-gath: the houses of Achzib shall be a lie to the kings of Israel. Yet will I bring an heir unto thee, O inhabitant of Mareshah: he shall come unto Adullam, the glory of Israel. Make thee bald, and poll thee for thy delicate children; enlarge thy baldness as the eagle; for they are gone into captivity from thee. —Micah 1.

JUDAH AND ISRAEL PURSUE THEIR SELFISH WAYS: "WOE TO THEM THAT COVET FIELDS AND TAKE THEM BY VIOLENCE"

Woe to them that devise iniquity, and work evil upon their beds! When the morning is light, they practise it, because it is in the power of their hand. And they covet fields, and take them by violence; and houses, and take them away: so they oppress a man and his house, even a man and his heritage.

Therefore thus saith the LORD: "Behold, against this family do I devise an evil, from which ye shall not remove your necks; neither shall ye go haughtily: for this time is evil."

In that day shall one take up a parable against you, and lament with a doleful lamentation, and say, "We be utterly spoiled: he hath changed the portion of my people: how hath he removed it from me! Turning away, he hath divided our fields." Therefore thou shalt have none that shall cast a cord by lot in the congregation of the LORD.

"Prophesy ye not," say they to them that prophesy: "they shall not prophesy to them, that they shall not take shame."

O thou that art named the house of Jacob, is the spirit of the LORD straitened? Are these his doings? Do not my words do good to him that walketh uprightly? Even of late my people is risen up as an enemy: ye pull off the robe with the garment from them that pass by securely as men averse from war. The women of my people have ye cast out from their pleasant houses; from their children have ye taken away my glory forever. Arise ye, and depart; for this is not your rest: because it is polluted, it shall destroy you, even with a sore destruction. If a man walking in the spirit and falsehood do lie, saying, "I will prophesy unto thee of wine and of strong drink"; he shall even be the prophet of this people.

I will surely assemble, O Jacob, all of thee; I will surely gather the remnant of Israel; I will put them together as the sheep of Bozrah, as the flock in the midst of their fold: they shall make great noise by reason of the multitude of men. The breaker is come up before them: they have broken up, and have passed through the gate, and are gone out by it: and their king shall pass before them, and the LORD on the head of them. —Micah 2.

"WOE TO THEM WHO EAT THE FLESH OF MY PEOPLE"

And I said, "Hear, I pray you, O heads of Jacob, and ye princes of the house of Israel: Is it not for you to know judgment, who hate the good, and love the evil; who pluck off their skin from off them, and their flesh from off their bones; who also eat the flesh of my people, and flay their skin from off them; and they break their bones, and chop them in pieces, as for the pot, and as flesh within the caldron? Then shall they cry unto the LORD, but he will not hear them: he will even hide his face from them at that time, as they have behaved themselves ill in their doings."

Thus saith the LORD concerning the prophets that make my people err, that bite with their teeth, and cry, "Peace"; and he that putteth not into their mouths, they even prepare war against him: "Therefore night shall be unto you, that ye shall not have a vision; and it shall be dark unto you, that ye shall not divine; and the sun shall go down over the prophets, and the day shall be dark over them. Then shall the seers be ashamed, and the diviners confounded: yea, they shall all cover their lips; for there is no answer of God."

But truly I am full of power by the spirit of the LORD, and of judgment, and of might, to declare unto Jacob his transgression, and to Israel his sin. Hear this, I pray you, ye heads of the house of Jacob, and princes of the house of Israel, that abhor judgment, and pervert all equity. They build up Zion with blood, and Jerusalem with iniquity. The heads thereof judge for reward, and the priests thereof teach for hire, and the prophets thereof divine for money: yet will they lean upon the LORD, and say, "Is not the LORD among us? None evil can come upon us." Therefore shall Zion for your sake be plowed as a field, and Jerusalem shall become heaps, and the mountain of the house as the high places of the forest.

—Micah 3.

"THE MOUNTAIN OF THE LORD'S HOUSE"

But in the last days it shall come to pass, that the mountain of the house of the LORD shall be established in the top of the mountains, and it shall be exalted above the hills; and people shall flow unto it. And many nations shall come, and say, "Come, and let us go up to the mountain of the LORD, and to the house of the God of Jacob; and he will teach us of his ways, and we will walk in his paths: for the law shall go forth of Zion, and the word of the LORD from Jerusalem."

"THEY SHALL BEAT THEIR SWORDS INTO PLOWSHARES AND THEIR SPEARS INTO PRUNINGHOOKS"

And he shall judge among many people, and rebuke strong nations afar off; and they shall beat their swords into plowshares, and their spears into pruninghooks: nation shall not lift up a sword against nation, neither shall they learn war any more. But they shall sit every man under his vine and under his fig-tree; and none shall make them afraid: for the mouth of the LORD of hosts hath spoken it. For all people will walk every one in the name of his god, and we will walk in the name of the LORD our God forever and ever.

"In that day," saith the LORD, "will I assemble her that halteth, and I will gather her that is driven out, and her that I have afflicted; and I will make her that halted a remnant, and her that was cast far off a strong nation: and the LORD shall reign over them in Mount Zion from henceforth, even forever."

THE KINGDOM SHALL COME TO JERUSALEM

And thou, O tower of the flock, the stronghold of the daughter of Zion, unto thee shall it come, even the first dominion; the kingdom shall come to the daughter of Jerusalem. Now why dost thou cry out aloud? Is there no king in thee? Is thy counsellor perished? For pangs have taken thee as a woman in travail. Be in pain, and labour to bring forth, O daughter of Zion, like a woman in travail: for now shalt thou go forth out of the city, and thou shalt dwell in the field, and thou shalt go even to Babylon; there shalt thou be delivered; there the LORD shall redeem thee from the hand of thine enemies.

Now also many nations are gathered against thee, that say, "Let her be defiled, and let our eye look upon Zion." But they know not the thoughts of the LORD, neither understand they his counsel: for he shall gather them as the sheaves into the floor. Arise and thresh, O daughter of Zion: for I will make thine horn iron, and I will make thy hoofs brass: and thou shalt beat in pieces many people: and I will consecrate their gain unto the LORD, and their substance unto the Lord of the whole earth.

—Micah 4.

"Out of Thee, Bethlehem Ephratah, Shall Come Forth a Ruler in Israel"

Now gather thyself in troops, O daughter of troops: he hath laid siege against us: they shall smite the judge of Israel with a rod upon the cheek. But thou, Bethlehem Ephratah, though thou be little among the thousands of Judah, yet out of thee shall he come forth unto me that is to be ruler in Israel; whose goings forth have been from of old, from everlasting. Therefore will he give them up, until the time that she which travaileth hath brought forth: then the remnant of his brethren shall return unto the children of Israel. And he shall stand and feed in the strength of the Lord, in the majesty of the name of the Lord his God; and they shall abide: for now shall he be great unto the ends of the earth. And this man shall be the peace, when the Assyrian shall come into our land: and when he shall tread in our palaces, then shall we raise against him seven shepherds, and eight principal men. And they shall waste the land of Assyria with the sword, and the land of Nimrod in the entrances thereof: thus shall he deliver us from the Assyrian, when he cometh into our land, and when he treadeth within our borders. And the remnant of Jacob shall be in the midst of many people as a dew from the Lord, as the showers upon the grass, that tarrieth not for man, nor waiteth for the sons of men. And the remnant of Jacob shall be among the Gentiles in the midst of many people as a lion among the beasts of the forest, as a young lion among the flocks of sheep: who, if he go through, both treadeth down, and teareth in pieces, and none can deliver. Thine hand shall be lifted up upon thine adversaries, and all thine enemies shall be cut off.

"And it shall come to pass in that day," saith the
LORD, "that I will cut off thy horses out of the midst of
thee, and I will destroy thy chariots: and I will cut off the
cities of thy land, and throw down all thy strongholds:
and I will cut off witchcrafts out of thine hand; and
thou shalt have no more soothsayers: thy graven images
also will I cut off, and thy standing images out of the
midst of thee; and thou shalt no more worship the work
of thine hands. And I will pluck up thy groves out of
the midst of thee: so will I destroy thy cities. And I
will execute vengeance in anger and fury upon the heathen,
such as they have not heard." —Micah 5.

THE WORDS OF JEHOVAH, THE SINFUL PEOPLE, AND THE PROPHET

Hear ye now what the LORD saith: arise, contend thou
before the mountains, and let the hills hear thy voice.
Hear ye, O mountains, the LORD's controversy, and ye
strong foundations of the earth: for the LORD hath a
controversy with his people, and he will plead with
Israel.

"O my people, what have I done unto thee and
wherein have I wearied thee? Testify against me. For I
brought thee up out of the land of Egypt, and redeemed
thee out of the house of servants; and I sent before thee
Moses, Aaron, and Miriam. O my people, remember now
what Balak, King of Moab, consulted, and what Balaam,
the son of Beor, answered him from Shittim unto Gilgal;
that ye may know the righteousness of the LORD."

HOW SHALL WE COME BEFORE THE LORD?

"Wherewith shall I come before the LORD, and bow
myself before the high God? Shall I come before him with
burnt offerings, with calves of a year old? Will the LORD

be pleased with thousands of rams, or with ten thousands of rivers of oil? shall I give my firstborn for my transgression, the fruit of my body for the sin of my soul?"

"THE LORD REQUIRES THEE TO DO JUSTLY AND TO LOVE MERCY AND TO WALK HUMBLY WITH THY GOD"

He hath shewed thee, O man, what is good; and what doth the LORD require of thee, but to do justly, and to love mercy, and to walk humbly with thy God? The LORD's voice crieth unto the city, and the man of wisdom shall see thy name: hear ye the rod, and who hath appointed it. Are there yet the treasures of wickedness in the house of the wicked, and the scant measure that is abominable? Shall I count them pure with the wicked balances, and with the bag of deceitful weights? For the rich men thereof are full of violence, and the inhabitants thereof have spoken lies, and their tongue is deceitful in their mouth. Therefore also will I make thee sick in smiting thee, in making thee desolate because of thy sins. Thou shalt eat, but not be satisfied; and thy casting down shall be in the midst of thee; and thou shalt take hold, but shalt not deliver; and that which thou deliverest will I give up to the sword. Thou shalt sow, but thou shalt not reap; thou shalt tread the olives, but thou shalt not anoint thee with oil; and sweet wine, but shalt not drink wine. For the statutes of Omri are kept, and all the works of the house of Ahab, and ye walk in their counsels; that I should make thee a desolation, and the inhabitants thereof an hissing: therefore ye shall bear the reproach of my people.

"THE GOOD MAN IS PERISHED OUT OF THE EARTH"

Woe is me! for I am as when they have gathered the summer fruits, as the grapegleanings of the vintage:

there is no cluster to eat: my soul desired the first-ripe fruit. The good man is perished out of the earth: and there is none upright among men: they all lie in wait for blood; they hunt every man his brother with a net. That they may do evil with both hands earnestly, the prince asketh, and the judge asketh for a reward; and the great man, he uttereth his mischievous desire: so they wrap it up. The best of them is as a brier: the most upright is sharper than a thorn hedge: the day of thy watchmen and thy visitation cometh; now shall be their perplexity.

Trust ye not in a friend, put ye not confidence in a guide: keep the doors of thy mouth from her that lieth in thy bosom. For the son dishonoureth the father, the daughter riseth up against her mother, the daughter-in-law against her mother-in-law; a man's enemies are the men of his own house.　　　　　Micah 6; 7:1–6.

A Psalm of Hope

Therefore I will look unto the Lord;
I will wait for the God of my salvation: my God
　　will hear me.
Rejoice not against me, O mine enemy:
When I fall, I shall arise;
When I sit in darkness, the Lord shall be a light
　　unto me.
I will bear the indignation of the Lord, because I
　　have sinned against him,
Until he plead my cause, and execute judgment for
　　me:
He will bring me forth to the light,
And I shall behold his righteousness.
Then she that is mine enemy shall see it,
And shame shall cover her which said unto me,

"Where is the LORD thy God?" Mine eyes shall behold her:
Now shall she be trodden down as the mire of the streets.
In the day that thy walls are to be built,
In that day shall the decree be far removed.
In that day also he shall come even to thee from Assyria,
And from the fortified cities, and from the fortress even to the river,
And from sea to sea, and from mountain to mountain.
Notwithstanding the land shall be desolate
Because of them that dwell therein,
For the fruit of their doings.
Feed thy people with thy rod, the flock of thine heritage,
Which dwell solitarily in the wood,
In the midst of Carmel:
Let them feed in Bashan and Gilead, as in the days of old.
According to the days of thy coming out of the land of Egypt
Will I shew unto him marvellous things.
The nations shall see and be confounded at all their might:
They shall lay their hand upon their mouth,
Their ears shall be deaf.
They shall lick the dust like a serpent,
They shall move out of their holes like worms of the earth:
They shall be afraid of the LORD our God,
And shall fear because of thee.
Who is a God like unto thee,

That pardoneth iniquity,
And passeth by the transgression of the remnant
    of his heritage?
He retaineth not his anger forever,
Because he delighteth in mercy:
He will turn again, he will have compassion upon us;
He will subdue our iniquities;
And thou wilt cast all their sins into the depths of
    the sea.
Thou wilt perform the truth to Jacob,
And the mercy to Abraham,
Which thou hast sworn unto our fathers from the
    days of old.   Micah 7:7–20.

Zephaniah

THE WATCHMAN OF JEHOVAH

After the days of Isaiah and Micah, the voice of the prophet was not heard for a period of seventy-five years. The party of re-action, which had bitterly opposed Isaiah, came into power; and their puppet-king, Manasseh, persecuted the followers of Jehovah. Then came Josiah with his reforms. Again the conditions were favorable to prophecy and a group of three: Zephaniah, Nahum, and Ha-bakkuk, made their contribution to prophetic literature.

On the whole, they do not possess the vigor of utterance, the spiritual fervor, the commanding power of the earlier prophets. Zephaniah was a prince of the royal house of Hezekiah. During the days of Josiah, the fear of Assyria had become a memory. But danger always threatened from the north. During the time of Zephaniah, an invasion of the wild Scythian tribes from the north threatened Palestine. Like a flood pouring over a dam, they broke over the northern mountains, down into the Mesopotamian plain and then marched by the old road of invasion toward Egypt. It was a tribal movement, a migration; they came with their wagons and their herds, sweeping on in a resistless tide. They were bought off and turned back by the ruler of Egypt. They did not penetrate to the hills of Judea; but Zephaniah, whose name means, "whom Jehovah protects," took the opportunity to deliver his message of the Day of Judgment and Wrath, not only upon Judah, but upon the world. "I will utterly consume," is his message. A new deluge is about to descend upon the earth.

The language which he uses is direct, sombre, not without power. In times of threatening danger, it has often been recalled. During the Middle Ages, a great hymn, "Dies Irae," was based upon the words of Zephaniah.

The Prophecy of Zephaniah

The word of the Lord which came unto Zephaniah, the son of Cushi, the son of Gedaliah, the son of Amariah, the son of Hizkiah, in the days of Josiah, the son of Amon, King of Judah.

The Doom of Israel

"I WILL utterly consume all things from off the land,' saith the LORD.

"I will consume man and beast; I will consume the fowls of the heaven, and the fishes of the sea, and the stumblingblocks with the wicked; and I will cut off man from off the land," saith the LORD. "I will also stretch out mine hand upon Judah, and upon all the inhabitants of Jerusalem; and I will cut off the remnant of Baal from this place, and the name of the Chemarims with the priests; and them that worship the host of heaven upon the housetops; and them that worship and that swear by the LORD, and that swear by Malcham; and them that are turned back from the LORD; and those that have not sought the LORD, nor enquired for him. Hold thy peace at the presence of the Lord GOD: for the day of the LORD is at hand: for the LORD hath prepared a sacrifice, he hath bid his guests.

"And it shall come to pass in the day of the LORD's sacrifice, that I will punish the princes, and the king's children, and all such as are clothed with strange apparel. In the same day also will I punish all those that leap on the threshold, which fill their masters' houses with violence and deceit. And it shall come to pass in that day,"

saith the LORD, "that there shall be the noise of a cry
from the fish gate, and an howling from the second, and
a great crashing from the hills.

"Howl, ye inhabitants of Maktesh, for all the merchant people are cut down; all they that bear silver are
cut off. And it shall come to pass at that time, that I
will search Jerusalem with candles, and punish the men
that are settled on their lees: that say in their heart,
'The LORD will not do good, neither will he do evil.'
Therefore their goods shall become a booty, and their
houses a desolation: they shall also build houses, but
not inhabit them; and they shall plant vineyards, but
not drink the wine thereof.

"THE DAY OF WRATH: OF CLOUDS AND THICK DARKNESS"

"The great day of the LORD is near, it is near, and
hasteth greatly, even the voice of the day of the LORD:
the mighty man shall cry there bitterly. That day is a day
of wrath, a day of trouble and distress, a day of wasteness
and desolation, a day of darkness and gloominess, a day
of clouds and thick darkness, a day of the trumpet and
alarm against the fenced cities, and against the high
towers. And I will bring distress upon men, that they
shall walk like blind men, because they have sinned against
the LORD: and their blood shall be poured out as dust,
and their flesh as the dung. Neither their silver nor their
gold shall be able to deliver them in the day of the LORD's
wrath; but the whole land shall be devoured by the fire
of his jealousy: for he shall make even a speedy rid-
dance of all them that dwell in the land.   — Zephaniah 1.

THE DOOM OF OTHER NATIONS

"Gather yourselves together, yea, gather together,
O nation not desired; before the decree bring forth,

before the day pass as the chaff, before the fierce anger
of the LORD come upon you, before the day of the LORD's
anger come upon you. Seek ye the LORD, all ye meek
of the earth, which have wrought his judgment; seek
righteousness, seek meekness: it may be ye shall be hid
in the day of the LORD's anger.

"For Gaza shall be forsaken, and Ashkelon a desolation: they shall drive out Ashdod at the noon day, and
Ekron shall be rooted up. Woe unto the inhabitants
of the sea coast, the nation of the Cherethites! The word
of the LORD is against you; O Canaan, the land of the
Philistines, I will even destroy thee, that there shall be
no inhabitant. And the sea coast shall be dwellings and
cottages for shepherds, and folds for flocks. And the
coast shall be for the remnant of the house of Judah;
they shall feed thereupon: in the houses of Ashkelon
shall they lie down in the evening: for the LORD their
God shall visit them, and turn away their captivity.

"I have heard the reproach of Moab, and the revilings
of the children of Ammon, whereby they have reproached
my people, and magnified themselves against their
border. Therefore as I live," saith the Lord of hosts,
the God of Israel, "surely Moab shall be as Sodom, and
the children of Ammon as Gomorrah, even the breeding
of nettles, and saltpits, and a perpetual desolation: the
residue of my people shall spoil them, and the remnant
of my people shall possess them. This shall they have
for their pride, because they have reproached and magnified themselves against the people of the LORD of hosts.
The LORD will be terrible unto them: for he will famish
all the gods of the earth; and men shall worship him,
every one from his place, even all the isles of the heathen.

"Ye Ethiopians also, ye shall be slain by my sword.
And he will stretch out his hand against the north, and

destroy Assyria; and will make Nineveh a desolation, and dry like a wilderness. And flocks shall lie down in the midst of her, all the beasts of the nations: both the cormorant and the bittern shall lodge in the upper lintels of it; their voice shall sing in the windows; desolation shall be in the thresholds: for he shall uncover the cedar work. This is the rejoicing city that dwelt carelessly, that said in her heart, 'I am, and there is none beside me': how is she become a desolation, a place for beasts to lie down in! Every one that passeth by her shall hiss, and wag his hand.

—Zephaniah 2.

HOPE

"THE JUST LORD IS IN THE MIDST OF HER"

"Woe to her that is filthy and polluted, to the oppressing city! She obeyed not the voice; she received not correction; she trusted not in the LORD; she drew not near to her God. Her princes within her are roaring lions; her judges are evening wolves; they gnaw not the bones till the morrow. Her prophets are light and treacherous persons: her priests have polluted the sanctuary, they have done violence to the law. The just LORD is in the midst thereof; he will not do iniquity: every morning doth he bring his judgment to light, he faileth not; but the unjust knoweth no shame. I have cut off the nations: their towers are desolate; I made their streets waste, that none passeth by: their cities are destroyed, so that there is no man, that there is none inhabitant.

"I said, 'Surely thou wilt fear me, thou wilt receive instruction'; so their dwelling should not be cut off, howsoever I punished them: but they rose early, and corrupted all their doings.

"Therefore wait ye upon me," saith the LORD, "until the day that I rise up to the prey: for my determination is to gather the nations, that I may assemble the kingdoms, to pour upon them mine indignation, even all my fierce anger: for all the earth shall be devoured with the fire of my jealousy. For then will I turn to the people a pure language, that they may all call upon the name of the LORD, to serve him with one consent. From beyond the rivers of Ethiopia my suppliants, even the daughter of my dispersed, shall bring mine offering. In that day shalt thou not be ashamed for all thy doings, wherein thou hast transgressed against me: for then I will take away out of the midst of thee them that rejoice in thy pride, and thou shalt no more be haughty because of my holy mountain. I will also leave in the midst of thee an afflicted and poor people, and they shall trust in the name of the LORD. The remnant of Israel shall not do iniquity, nor speak lies; neither shall a deceitful tongue be found in their mouth: for they shall feed and lie down, and none shall make them afraid.

A SONG OF TRUST

"Sing, O daughter of Zion; shout, O Israel;
Be glad and rejoice with all the heart, O daughter of
    Jerusalem.
The LORD hath taken away thy judgments,
He hath cast out thine enemy:
The King of Israel, even the LORD, is in the midst of thee:
Thou shalt not see evil any more.
In that day it shall be said to Jerusalem, 'Fear thou not':
And to Zion, 'Let not thine hands be slack.'
The LORD thy God in the midst of thee is mighty;
He will save, he will rejoice over thee with joy;
He will rest in his love, he will joy over thee with singing.
I will gather them that are sorrowful for the solemn
    assembly,

Who are of thee, to whom the reproach of it was a burden.

Bchold, at that time I will undo all that afflict thee:

And I will save her that halteth, and gather her that was
    driven out;

And I will get them praise and fame in every land where
    they have been put to shame.

At that time will I bring you again, even in the time that
    I gather you:

For I will make you a name and a praise among all people
    of the earth,

When I turn back your captivity before your eyes,"
    saith the LORD.   — Zephaniah 3.

Nahum

The Prophet of the Doom of Assyria

Great Nineveh was about to fall! The capital of that ruthless power which had been for so long the terror of all the smaller states was doomed. Assyria was about to receive the same treatment which she had visited upon others.

The Book of Nahum is a poem in which the speaker exults in the face of the hated nation. "It is one great 'At Last!' The old Lion is at bay. The Besieger of the World is at last besieged; every cruelty he has inflicted upon men is now to be turned upon himself." The book contains wonderful descriptions of the siege of an ancient city.

Assyrian Forces Besieging a City

By courtesy of the British Museum, London

In this vigorous picture, unfortunately somewhat mutilated, the king with his armorbearer is seen on the right. A great military tower with a battering ram is attacking the walls. A catapult is also seen and two men are bringing up stones for ammunition. Two soldiers on the left are undermining a wall. The besieged are vigorously defending the city. Killed and wounded soldiers are falling from the walls.

The Prophecy of Nahum

The burden of Nineveh. The book of the vision of Nahum the Elkoshite.

"THE LORD HATH HIS WAY IN THE WHIRLWIND"

GOD is jealous, and the LORD revengeth; the LORD revengeth, and is furious; the LORD will take vengeance on his adversaries, and he reserveth wrath for his enemies. The LORD is slow to anger, and great in power, and will not at all acquit the wicked: the LORD hath his way in the whirlwind and in the storm, and the clouds are the dust of his feet. He rebuketh the sea, and maketh it dry, and drieth up all the rivers: Bashan languisheth, and Carmel, and the flower of Lebanon languisheth. The mountains quake at him, and the hills melt, and the earth is burned at his presence, yea, the world, and all that dwell therein. Who can stand before his indignation? And who can abide in the fierceness of his anger? His fury is poured out like fire, and the rocks are thrown down by him. The LORD is good, a stronghold in the day of trouble; and he knoweth them that trust in him. But with an overrunning flood he will make an utter end of the place thereof, and darkness shall pursue his enemies. What do ye imagine against the LORD? He will make an utter end: affliction shall not rise up the second time. For while they be folden together as thorns, and while they are drunken as drunkards, they shall be devoured as stubble fully dry. There is one come out of thee, that imagineth evil against the LORD, a wicked counsellor.

LION HUNT BAS-RELIEF FROM THE PALACE OF
ASHURBANIPAL, 686–626 B.C.

*By courtesy of the Metropolitan Museum of Art, New York, and the
British Museum, London*

Notice the splendid action and the fine modeling of the figures of this famous sculpture: the leaping lions, the horses at full speed. Notice how the second figure from the left is giving his horse rein; a spare horse is being held in reserve by a servant. The Sculpture is continued on the next page.

This sculpture is of the epoch of the greatest power of Assyria when Israel had gone into captivity, and even Egypt was under Assyrian rule.

Thus saith the LORD: "Though they be quiet, and likewise many, yet thus shall they be cut down, when he shall pass through. Though I have afflicted thee, I will afflict thee no more. For now will I break his yoke from off thee, and will burst thy bonds in sunder. And the LORD hath given a commandment concerning thee, that no more of thy name be sown: out of the house of thy gods will I cut off the graven image and the molten image: I will make thy grave; for thou art vile. Behold upon the mountains the feet of him that bringeth good tidings, that publisheth peace! O Judah, keep thy solemn feasts, perform thy vows: for the wicked shall no more pass through thee; he is utterly cut off.   —Nahum 1.

THE BESIEGED CITY

"He that dasheth in pieces is come up before thy face: keep the munition, watch the way, make thy loins strong, fortify thy power mightily. For the LORD hath

turned away the excellency of Jacob, as the excellency of Israel: for the emptiers have emptied them out, and marred their vine branches. The shield of his mighty men is made red, the valiant men are in scarlet: the chariots shall be with flaming torches in the day of his preparation, and the fir-trees shall be terribly shaken. The chariots shall rage in the streets, they shall justle one against another in the broad ways: they shall seem like torches, they shall run like the lightnings. He shall recount his worthies; they shall stumble in their walk; they shall make haste to the wall thereof, and the defence shall be prepared. The gates of the rivers shall be opened, and the palace shall be dissolved. And Huzzab shall be led away captive, she shall be brought up, and her maids shall lead her as with the voice of doves, tabering upon their breasts. But Nineveh is of old like a pool of water: yet they shall flee away. Stand, stand, shall they cry; but none shall look back. Take ye the spoil of silver, take the spoil of gold: for there is none end of the store and glory out of all the pleasant furniture. She is empty, and void, and waste: and the heart melteth, and the knees smite together, and much pain is in all loins, and the faces of them all gather blackness. Where is the dwelling of the lions and the feeding place of the young lions, where the lion, even the old lion, walked, and the lion's whelp, and none made them afraid? The lion did tear in pieces enough for his whelps, and strangled for his lionesses, and filled his holes with prey, and his dens with ravin. Behold, I am against thee," saith the LORD of hosts, "and I will burn her chariots in the smoke, and the sword shall devour thy young lions: and I will cut off thy prey from the earth, and the voice of thy messengers shall no more be heard. —Nahum 2.

WOE TO THE BLOODY CITY

"Woe to the bloody city! it is all full of lies and robbery; the prey departeth not; the noise of a whip, and the noise of the rattling of the wheels, and of the pransing horses, and of the jumping chariots. The horseman lifteth up both the bright sword and the glittering spear: and there is a multitude of slain, and a great number of carcasses; and there is none end of their corpses; they stumble upon their corpses: because of the multitude of the whoredoms of the wellfavoured harlot, the mistress of witchcrafts, that selleth nations through her whoredoms, and families through her witchcrafts. Behold, I am against thee," saith the LORD of hosts; "and I will discover thy skirts upon thy face, and I will shew the nations thy nakedness, and the kingdoms thy shame. And I will cast abominable filth upon thee, and make thee vile, and will set thee as a gazingstock. And it shall come to pass, that all they that look upon thee shall flee from thee, and say, 'Nineveh is laid waste: who will bemoan her?' Whence shall I seek comforters for thee? Art thou better than populous No, that was situate among the rivers, that had the waters round about it, whose rampart was the sea, and her wall was from the sea? Ethiopia and Egypt were her strength, and it was infinite; Put and Lubim were thy helpers. Yet was she carried away, she went into captivity: her young children also

Assyrian Lion

In the Louvre, Paris

This magnificent sculptured lion is typical of Assyrian sculpture.

were dashed in pieces at the top of all the streets: and they cast lots for her honourable men, and all her great men were bound in chains. Thou also shalt be drunken: thou shalt be hid, thou also shalt seek strength because of the enemy. All thy strongholds shall be like fig-trees with the first-ripe figs: if they be shaken, they shall even fall into the mouth of the eater. Behold, thy people in the midst of thee are women: the gates of thy land shall be set wide open unto thine enemies: the fire shall devour thy bars. Draw thee waters for the siege, fortify thy strongholds: go into clay, and tread the mortar, make strong the brickkiln. There shall the fire devour thee; the sword shall cut thee off, it shall eat thee up like the cankerworm: make thyself many as the cankerworm, make thyself many as the locusts. Thou hast multiplied thy merchants above the stars of heaven: the cankerworm spoileth, and fleeth away. Thy crowned are as the locusts, and thy captains as the great grasshoppers, which camp in the hedges in the cold day, but when the sun ariseth they flee away, and their place is not known where they are. Thy shepherds slumber, O king of Assyria: thy nobles shall dwell in the dust: thy people is scattered upon the mountains, and no man gathereth them. There is no healing of thy bruise; thy wound is grievous: all that hear the bruit of thee shall clap the hands over thee: for upon whom hath not thy wickedness passed continually?" —Nahum 3.

Habakkuk

The great city of Nineveh fell in the year 606 B.C. The next year, in the battle of Carchemish, the conquering power of Babylon overthrew the forces of the Egyptians. Babylon became the supreme empire of the world. This brought, however, no satisfaction to the little kingdom of Judah. Another cruel dominating power was substituted for Assyria. It mattered not what nation was master of the world. Judah was the corn between the millstones, to be ground exceeding fine.

The prophecy of Habakkuk deals with the problem of the delayed deliverance of God for his people. The older prophets proclaimed the destruction of evil, the triumph of goodness. The promise seemed to fail. "Wait," says Habakkuk; "the dawn of God's triumph may be long delayed, but it will come; the wicked will be punished and righteousness will be rewarded."

The Prophecy of Habakkuk

The burden which Habakkuk, the prophet, did see.

The Eternal Problem of Justice Delayed, of Sin and Evil: "Why?"

O LORD, how long shall I cry, and thou wilt not hear! even cry out unto thee of violence, and thou wilt not save! Why dost thou shew me iniquity, and cause me to behold grievance? For spoiling and violence are before me: and there are that raise up strife and contention. Therefore the law is slacked, and judgment doth never go forth: for the wicked doth compass about the righteous; therefore wrong judgment proceedeth.

"Behold ye among the heathen, and regard, and wonder marvellously: for I will work a work in your days, which ye will not believe, though it be told you. For, lo, I raise up the Chaldeans, that bitter and hasty nation, which shall march through the breadth of the land, to possess the dwellingplaces that are not theirs. They are terrible and dreadful: their judgment and their dignity shall proceed of themselves. Their horses also are swifter than the leopards, and are more fierce than the evening wolves: and their horsemen shall spread themselves, and their horsemen shall come from far; they shall fly as the eagle that hasteth to eat. They shall come all for violence: their faces shall sup up as the east wind, and they shall gather the captivity as the sand. And they shall scoff at the kings, and the princes shall be a scorn unto them: they shall deride every stronghold;

for they shall heap dust, and take it. Then shall his mind change, and he shall pass over, and offend, imputing this his power unto his god."

Art thou not from everlasting, O LORD my God, mine Holy One? We shall not die. O LORD, thou hast ordained them for judgment; and, O mighty God, thou hast established them for correction. Thou art of purer eyes than to behold evil, and canst not look on iniquity: wherefore lookest thou upon them that deal treacherously, and holdest thy tongue when the wicked devoureth the man that is more righteous than he and makest men as the fishes of the sea, as the creeping things, that have no ruler over them? They take up all of them with the angle, they catch them in their net, and gather them in their drag: therefore they rejoice and are glad. Therefore they sacrifice unto their net, and burn incense unto their drag; because by them their portion is fat, and their meat plenteous. Shall they therefore empty their net, and not spare continually to slay the nations?

—Habakkuk 1.

THE ANSWER: "THE JUST SHALL LIVE BY FAITH"

I will stand upon my watch, and set me upon the tower and will watch to see what he will say unto me, and what I shall answer when I am reproved.

"THAT HE MAY RUN THAT READETH IT"

And the LORD answered me, and said, "Write the vision, and make it plain upon tables, that he may run that readeth it. For the vision is yet for an appointed time, but at the end it shall speak, and not lie: though it tarry, wait for it; because it will surely come, it will not tarry. Behold, his soul which is lifted up is not upright in him: but the just shall live by his faith.

"Yea also, because he transgresseth by wine, he is a proud man, neither keepeth at home, who enlargeth his desire as hell, and is as death, and cannot be satisfied, but gathereth unto him all nations, and heapeth unto him all people: shall not all these take up a parable against him, and a taunting proverb against him, and say, 'Woe to him that increaseth that which is not his! How long? and to him that ladeth himself with thick clay!' Shall they not rise up suddenly that shall bite thee, and awake that shall vex thee, and thou shalt be for booties unto them? Because thou hast spoiled many nations, all the remnant of the people shall spoil thee; because of men's blood, and for the violence of the land, of the city, and of all that dwell therein.

"Woe to him that coveteth an evil covetousness to his house, that he may set his nest on high, that he may be delivered from the power of evil! Thou hast consulted shame to thy house by cutting off many people, and hast sinned against thy soul. For the stone shall cry out of the wall, and the beam out of the timber shall answer it.

"WOE TO HIM THAT BUILDETH A TOWN WITH BLOOD"

"Woe to him that buildeth a town with blood, and establisheth a city by iniquity! Behold, is it not of the LORD of hosts that the people shall labour in the very fire, and the people shall weary themselves for very vanity? For the earth shall be filled with the knowledge of the glory of the LORD, as the waters cover the sea.

"WOE TO HIM THAT GIVETH HIS NEIGHBOUR DRINK!"

"Woe unto him that giveth his neighbour drink, that puttest thy bottle to him, and makest him drunken also, that thou mayest look on their nakedness! Thou art filled with shame for glory: drink thou also, and let thy foreskin be uncovered: the cup of the LORD's right hand shall be turned unto thee, and shameful spewing shall be on thy glory. For the violence of Lebanon shall cover thee, and the spoil of beasts, which made them afraid, because of men's blood, and for the violence of the land, of the city, and of all that dwell therein.

"What profiteth the graven image that the maker thereof hath graven it; the molten image, and a teacher of lies, that the maker of his work trusteth therein, to make dumb idols? Woe unto him that saith to the wood, 'Awake'; to the dumb stone, 'Arise, it shall teach'! Behold, it is laid over with gold and silver, and there is no breath at all in the midst of it. But the LORD is in his holy temple: let all the earth keep silence before him."

— Habakkuk 2.

A PRAYER OF HABAKKUK

A prayer of Habakkuk, the prophet, upon Shigionoth.

O LORD, I have heard thy speech, and was afraid:
O LORD, revive thy work in the midst of the years,
In the midst of the years make known;
In wrath remember mercy.
God came from Teman, and the Holy One from Mount
 Paran.
His glory covered the heavens, and the earth was full of
 his praise.
And his brightness was as the light;
He had horns coming out of his hand:
And there was the hiding of his power.
Before him went the pestilence,
And burning coals went forth at his feet.
He stood, and measured the earth:
He beheld and drove asunder the nations;

And the everlasting mountains were scattered, the per-
petual hills did bow:
His ways are everlasting.
I saw the tents of Cushan in affliction:
And the curtains of the land of Midian did tremble.
Was the LORD displeased against the rivers?
Was thine anger against the rivers?
Was thy wrath against the sea,
That thou didst ride upon thine horses and thy chariots
of salvation?
Thy bow was made quite naked, according to the oaths
of the tribes, even thy word.
Thou didst cleave the earth with rivers.
The mountains saw thee, and they trembled:
The overflowing of the water passed by:
The deep uttered his voice, and lifted up his hands on
high.
The sun and moon stood still in their habitation:
At the light of thine arrows they went,
And at the shining of thy glittering spear.
Thou didst march through the land in indignation,
Thou didst thresh the heathen in anger.
Thou wentest forth for the salvation of thy people,
Even for salvation with thine anointed;
Thou woundedst the head out of the house of the
wicked,
By discovering the foundation unto the neck.
Thou didst strike through with his staves the head of his
villages:
They came out as a whirlwind to scatter me:
Their rejoicing was as to devour the poor secretly.
Thou didst walk through the sea with thine horses,
Through the heap of great waters.
When I heard, my belly trembled;

My lips quivered at the voice:
Rottenness entered into my bones, and I trembled in
    myself,
That I might rest in the day of trouble:
When he cometh up unto the people,
He will invade them with his troops.
Although the fig-tree shall not blossom, neither shall
    fruit be in the vines:
The labour of the olive shall fail, and the fields shall yield
    no meat;
The flock shall be cut off from the fold, and there shall
    be no herd in the stalls:
Yet I will rejoice in the LORD,
I will joy in the God of my salvation.

The LORD God is my strength
And he will make my feet like hinds' feet,
And he will make me to walk upon mine high
places.
[To the chief singer on my stringed instruments.]

— Habakkuk 3.

Jeremiah

THE MAN WHO SUFFERED FOR HIS COUNTRY

There are few books in the Bible so little read and understood as Jeremiah; yet there are few so worthy of attention and study. The popular conception of Jeremiah is that of the "weeping prophet," a figure of pessimism and despair. He was nothing of the kind. He was active, brave, hopeful,—a noble and splendid personality. There are those who think that he was no less great than Isaiah. His style is less poetical and exalted than that of Isaiah. It is simple, pleading prose, eloquent with feeling rather than with poetry. The book is a collection of sermons and historical statements which might be called "The Life and Times of Jeremiah."

The work of Jeremiah began in 626 B.C., and ended in exile in Egypt, when Jeremiah was an old man, broken by his labors for his country. Jeremiah was a prophet-statesman like Isaiah, and his message to Judah was the same: the nation must repent and reform, it must avoid entangling alliances with other peoples. In his single-hearted devotion to this cause, Jeremiah suffered imprisonment, the jibes and taunts of his countrymen, exile and death in Egypt. Few characters make so strong an appeal to the sympathy and sense of the heroic as does that of Jeremiah. He deserves to have a high place in the affection of all readers of the Old Testament.

The Prophecy of Jeremiah

The words of Jeremiah, the son of Hilkiah of the priests that were in Anathoth in the land of Benjamin: to whom the word of the Lord came in the days of Josiah, the son of Amon, King of Judah, in the thirteenth year of his reign. It came also in the days of Jehoiakim, the son of Josiah, King of Judah, unto the end of the eleventh year of Zedekiah, the son of Josiah, King of Judah, unto the carrying away of Jerusalem captive in the fifth month.

The Call of Jeremiah

THEN the word of the Lord came unto me, saying, "Before I formed thee in the belly I knew thee; and before thou camest forth out of the womb I sanctified thee, and I ordained thee a prophet unto the nations."

Then said I, "Ah, Lord God! behold, I cannot speak: for I am a child."

But the Lord said unto me, "Say not, 'I am a child': for thou shalt go to all that I shall send thee, and whatsoever I command thee thou shalt speak. Be not afraid of their faces: for I am with thee to deliver thee," saith the Lord. Then the Lord put forth his hand, and touched my mouth. And the Lord said unto me, "Behold, I have put my words in thy mouth. See, I have this day set thee over the nations and over the kingdoms, to root out, and to pull down, and to destroy, and to throw down, to build, and to plant.

THE ALMOND ROD

Moreover the word of the LORD came unto me, saying, "Jeremiah, what seest thou?"

And I said, "I see a rod of an almond-tree."

Then said the LORD unto me, "Thou hast well seen: for I will hasten my word to perform it."

THE BOILING POT

And the word of the LORD came unto me the second time, saying, "What seest thou?"

And I said, "I see a seething pot; and the face thereof is toward the north."

Then the LORD said unto me, "Out of the north an evil shall break forth upon all the inhabitants of the land. For, lo, I will call all the families of the kingdoms of the north," saith the LORD: "and they shall come, and they shall set every one his throne at the entering of the gates of Jerusalem, and against all the walls thereof round about, and against all the cities of Judah. And I will utter my judgments against them touching all their wickedness, who have forsaken me, and have burned incense unto other gods, and worshiped the works of their own hands.

"Thou therefore gird up thy loins, and arise, and speak unto them all that I command thee: be not dismayed at their faces, lest I confound thee before them. For, behold, I have made thee this day a defenced city, and an iron pillar, and brasen walls against the whole land, against the kings of Judah, against the princes thereof, against the priests thereof, and against the people of the land. And they shall fight against thee; but they shall not prevail against thee; for I am with thee," saith the LORD "to deliver thee."   — Jeremiah 1

The Love of the Lord for His City of Jerusalem

Moreover the word of the Lord came to me, saying, "Go and cry in the ears of Jerusalem, saying, 'Thus saith the Lord: "I remember thee, the kindness of thy youth, the love of thine espousals, when thou wentest after me in the wilderness, in a land that was not sown. Israel was holiness unto the Lord, and the firstfruits of his increase: all that devour him shall offend; evil shall come upon them," saith the Lord.'"

Hear ye the word of the Lord, O house of Jacob, and all the families of the house of Israel: thus saith the Lord,

THE SITE OF THE TOWN OF ANATHOTH

Photograph by Professor Lewis Bayles Paton

Jeremiah, the prophet, was brought up in the hill town of Anathoth, a little to the northeast of Jerusalem, across Scopus and over a deep valley. It is the last village eastward before you reach the desert and from it the land falls away in broken barren hills to the north end of the Dead Sea. The vision of that wild desert was burnt into the prophet's mind.

"I beheld, and lo, the fruitful place was a wilderness, and all the cities thereof were broken down at the presence of the Lord, and by his fierce anger."—*Jeremiah 4:26.*

"What iniquity have your fathers found in me, that they are gone far from me, and have walked after vanity, and are become vain? Neither said they, 'Where is the LORD that brought us up out of the land of Egypt, that led us through the wilderness, through a land of deserts and of pits, through a land of drought, and of the shadow of death, through a land that no man passed through, and where no man dwelt?' And I brought you into a plentiful country, to eat the fruit thereof and the goodness thereof; but when ye entered, ye defiled my land, and made mine heritage an abomination.

ROAD ON THE WAY FROM JERUSALEM TO THE NORTH

Photograph by W. A. Pottenger expressly for The Book of Life

This is the country north of Jerusalem with which Jeremiah was familiar in his early days.

"The priests said not, 'Where is the LORD?' and they that handle the law knew me not: the pastors also transgressed against me, and the prophets prophesied by Baal, and walked after things that do not profit.

"Wherefore I will yet plead with you," saith the LORD, "and with your children's children will I plead. For pass over the isles of Chittim, and see; and send unto Kedar, and consider diligently, and see if there be such a thing. Hath a nation changed their gods, which are yet no gods? But my people have changed their glory for that which doth not profit. Be astonished, O ye heavens, at this, and be horribly afraid, be ye very desolate," saith the LORD.

"For my people have committed two evils; they have forsaken me, the fountain of living waters, and hewed them out cisterns, broken cisterns, that can hold no water.

"Is Israel a servant? Is he a homeborn slave? Why is he spoiled? The young lions roared upon him, and yelled, and they made his land waste: his cities are burned without inhabitant. Also the children of Noph and Tahapanes have broken the crown of thy head. Hast thou not procured this unto thyself, in that thou hast forsaken the LORD thy God, when he led thee by the way? And now what hast thou to do in the way of Egypt, to drink the water of Sihor? Or what hast thou to do in the way of Assyria, to drink the waters of the river? Thine own wickedness shall correct thee, and thy backslidings shall reprove thee: know therefore and see that it is an evil thing and bitter, that thou hast forsaken the LORD thy God, and that my fear is not in thee," saith the Lord GOD of hosts.

"For of old time I have broken thy yoke, and burst thy bands; and thou saidst, 'I will not transgress'; when upon every high hill and under every green tree thou wanderest, playing the harlot. Yet I had planted thee a noble vine, wholly a right seed: how then art thou turned into the degenerate plant of a strange vine unto me? For though thou wash thee with nitre, and take thee much soap, yet thine iniquity is marked before me," saith the Lord GOD. "How canst thou say, 'I am not polluted, I have not gone after Baalim?' See thy way in the valley, know what thou hast done: thou art a swift dromedary traversing her ways; a wild ass used to the wilderness, that snuffeth up the wind at her pleasure; in her occasion who can turn her away? All they that seek her will not weary themselves; in her month they shall find her.

"Withhold thy foot from being unshod, and thy throat from thirst: but thou saidst, 'There is no hope: no; for I have loved strangers, and after them will I go.' As the thief is ashamed when he is found, so is the house of Israel ashamed; they, their kings, their princes, and their priests, and their prophets, saying to a stock, 'Thou art my father'; and to a stone, 'Thou hast brought me forth': for they have turned their back unto me, and not their face: but in the time of their trouble they will say, 'Arise, and save us.'

"But where are thy gods that thou hast made thee? Let them arise, if they can save thee in the time of thy trouble: for according to the number of thy cities are thy gods, O Judah. Wherefore will ye plead with me? Ye all have transgressed against me," saith the LORD.

"In vain have I smitten your children; they received no correction: your own sword hath devoured your prophets, like a destroying lion. O generation, see ye the word of the LORD. Have I been a wilderness unto Israel, a land of darkness? Wherefore say my people, 'We are lords; we will come no more unto thee?' Can a maid forget her ornaments, or a bride her attire? Yet my people have forgotten me days without number. Why trimmest thou thy way to seek love? Therefore hast thou also taught the wicked ones thy ways. Also in thy skirts is found the blood of the souls of the poor innocents: I have not found it by secret search, but upon all these. Yet thou sayest, 'Because I am innocent, surely his anger shall turn from me.' Behold, I will plead with thee, because thou sayest, 'I have not sinned.' Why gaddest thou about so much to change thy way? Thou also shalt be ashamed of Egypt, as thou wast ashamed of Assyria. Yea, thou shalt go forth from him, and thine hands upon thine head: for the LORD hath

rejected thy confidences, and thou shalt not prosper in
them."

—Jeremiah 2.

"Fear the Lord Who Hath Placed the Sand as a Perpetual Bound for the Sea"

And it shall come to pass when ye shall say, "Wherefore doeth the Lord our God all these things unto us?"
then shalt thou answer them, "Like as ye have forsaken
me, and served strange gods in your land, so shall ye
serve strangers in a land that is not yours."

Declare this in the house of Jacob, and publish it in
Judah, saying, "Hear now this, O foolish people, and
without understanding; which have eyes, and see not;
which have ears, and hear not: 'Fear ye not me?' saith
the Lord: 'will ye not tremble at my presence, which
have placed the sand for the bound of the sea by a perpetual decree, that it cannot pass it: and though the
waves thereof toss themselves, yet can they not prevail;
though they roar, yet can they not pass over it?'"

But this people hath a revolting and a rebellious heart;
they are revolted and gone. "Neither say they in their
heart, Let us now fear the Lord our God, that giveth
rain, both the former and the latter, in his season: he
reserveth unto us the appointed weeks of the harvest."

Your iniquities have turned away these things, and
your sins have withholden good things from you. For
among my people are found wicked men: they lay wait,
as he that setteth snares; they set a trap, they catch men.
As a cage is full of birds, so are their houses full of deceit:
therefore they are become great, and waxen rich. They
are waxen fat, they shine: yea, they overpass the deeds
of the wicked: they judge not the cause, the cause of the
fatherless, yet they prosper; and the right of the needy
do they not judge.

"Shall I not visit for these things?" saith the LORD: "Shall not my soul be avenged on such a nation as this?"

A wonderful and horrible thing is committed in the land: the prophets prophesy falsely, and the priests bear rule by their means; and my people love to have it so: and what will ye do in the end thereof?   —Jeremiah 5:19–31.

"They Say, 'Peace, Peace,' when There Is no Peace"

O ye children of Benjamin, gather yourselves to flee out of the midst of Jerusalem, and blow the trumpet in Tekoa, and set up a sign of fire in Beth-haccerem: for evil appeareth out of the north, and great destruction. I have likened the daughter of Zion to a comely and delicate woman. The shepherds with their flocks shall come unto her; they shall pitch their tents against her round about; they shall feed every one in his place. Prepare ye war against her; arise, and let us go up at noon. Woe unto us! for the day goeth away, for the shadows of the evening are stretched out. Arise, and let us go by night, and let us destroy her palaces.

For thus hath the LORD of hosts said, "Hew ye down trees, and cast a mount against Jerusalem: this is the city to be visited; she is wholly oppression in the midst of her. As a fountain casteth out her waters, so she casteth out her wickedness: violence and spoil is heard in her; before me continually is grief and wounds. Be thou instructed, O Jerusalem, lest my soul depart from thee; lest I make thee desolate, a land not inhabited."

Thus saith the LORD of hosts, "They shall thoroughly glean the remnant of Israel as a vine: turn back thine hand as a grapegatherer into the baskets."

To whom shall I speak, and give warning, that they may hear? Behold, their ear is uncircumcised, and they cannot hearken: behold, the word of the LORD is unto them a reproach; they have no delight in it. Therefore I am full of the fury of the LORD; I am weary with holding in: I will pour it out upon the children abroad, and upon the assembly of young men together: for even the husband with the wife shall be taken, the aged with him that is full of days. And their houses shall be turned unto others, with their fields, and wives together: "for I will stretch out my hand upon the inhabitants of the land," saith the LORD. For from the least of them even unto the greatest of them every one is given to covetousness; and from the prophet even unto the priest every one dealeth falsely. They have healed also the hurt of the daughter of my people slightly, saying, "Peace, peace"; when there is no peace.

"Were they ashamed when they had committed abomination? Nay, they were not at all ashamed, neither could they blush: therefore they shall fall among them that fall: at the time that I visit them they shall be cast down," saith the LORD.

Thus saith the LORD, "Stand ye in the ways, and see, and ask for the old paths, where is the good way, and walk therein, and ye shall find rest for your souls."

But they said, "We will not walk therein."

"Also I set watchmen over you, saying, 'Hearken to the sound of the trumpet.'"

But they said, "We will not hearken."

"Therefore hear, ye nations, and know, O congregation, what is among them. Hear, O earth: behold, I will bring evil upon this people, even the fruit of their thoughts, because they have not hearkened unto my words, nor to my law, but rejected it. To what purpose cometh there to me incense from Sheba, and the sweet cane from a far country? Your burnt offerings are not acceptable, nor your sacrifices sweet unto me."

Therefore thus saith the LORD, "Behold, I will lay stumbling blocks before this people, and the fathers and the sons together shall fall upon them; the neighbour and his friend shall perish."

Thus saith the LORD, "Behold, a people cometh from the north country, and a great nation shall be raised from the sides of the earth. They shall lay hold on bow and spear; they are cruel, and have no mercy; their voice roareth like the sea; and they ride upon horses, set in array as men for war against thee, O daughter of Zion."

We have heard the fame thereof: our hands wax feeble: anguish hath taken hold of us, and pain, as of a woman in travail. Go not forth into the field, nor walk by the way; for the sword of the enemy and fear is on every side.

O daughter of my people, gird thee with sackcloth, and wallow thyself in ashes: make thee mourning, as for an only son, most bitter lamentation: for the spoiler shall suddenly come upon us. I have set thee for a tower and a fortress among my people, that thou mayest know and try their way. They are all grievous revolters, walking with slanders: they are brass and iron; they are all corrupters. The bellows are burned, the lead is consumed of the fire; the founder melteth in vain: for the wicked are not plucked away. Reprobate silver shall men call them, because the LORD hath rejected them.

—Jeremiah 6.

THE LORD DESIRES REPENTANCE AND JUSTICE

The word that came to Jeremiah from the LORD, saying, "Stand in the gate of the LORD's house, and proclaim there this word, and say, 'Hear the word of the

LORD, all ye of Judah, that enter in at these gates to worship the LORD.'"

Thus saith the LORD of hosts, the God of Israel, "Amend your ways and your doings, and I will cause you to dwell in this place. Trust ye not in lying words, saying, 'The temple of the LORD, The temple of the LORD, The temple of the LORD, are these.' For if ye thoroughly amend your ways and your doings; if ye thoroughly execute judgment between a man and his neighbour; if ye oppress not the stranger, the fatherless, and the widow, and shed not innocent blood in this place, neither walk after other gods to your hurt: then will I cause you to dwell in this place, in the land that I gave to your fathers, forever and ever.

"Behold, ye trust in lying words, that cannot profit. Will ye steal, murder, and commit adultery, and swear falsely, and burn incense unto Baal, and walk after other gods whom ye know not; and come and stand before me in this house, which is called by my name and say, 'We are delivered to do all these abominations?' Is this house, which is called by my name, become a den of robbers in your eyes? Behold, even I have seen it," saith the LORD.

"But go ye now unto my place which was in Shiloh, where I set my name at the first, and see what I did to it for the wickedness of my people Israel. And now, because ye have done all these works," saith the LORD, "and I spake unto you, rising up early and speaking, but ye heard not; and I called you, but ye answered not; therefore will I do unto this house, which is called by my name, wherein ye trust, and unto the place which I gave to you and to your fathers, as I have done to Shiloh. And I will cast you out of my sight, as I have cast out all your brethren, even the whole seed of Ephraim. Therefore pray not thou for this people, neither lift up cry nor prayer for them, neither make intercession to me: for I will not hear thee.

"Seest thou not what they do in the cities of Judah and in the streets of Jerusalem? The children gather wood, and the fathers kindle the fire, and the women knead their dough, to make cakes to the queen of heaven, and to pour out drink offerings unto other gods, that they may provoke me to anger. Do they provoke me to anger?" saith the LORD: "Do they not provoke themselves to the confusion of their own faces?"

Therefore thus saith the Lord GOD: "Behold, mine anger and my fury shall be poured out upon this place, upon man, and upon beast, and upon the trees of the field, and upon the fruit of the ground; and it shall burn, and shall not be quenched."

Thus saith the LORD of hosts, the God of Israel: "Put your burnt offerings unto your sacrifices, and eat flesh. For I spake not unto your fathers, nor commanded them in the day that I brought them out of the land of Egypt, concerning burnt offerings or sacrifices: but this thing commanded I them, saying, 'Obey my voice, and I will be your God, and ye shall be my people: and walk ye in all the ways that I have commanded you, that it may be well unto you.' But they hearkened not, nor inclined their ear, but walked in the counsels and in the imagination of their evil heart, and went backward, and not forward. Since the day that your fathers came forth out of the land of Egypt unto this day I have even sent unto you all my servants the prophets, daily rising up early and sending them: yet they hearkened not unto me, nor inclined their ear, but hardened their neck: they did worse than their fathers. Therefore thou shalt speak all these words unto them; but they will not hearken to thee: thou shalt also call unto them; but they will not answer thee. But thou shalt say unto them, 'This is a nation that obeyeth not the voice of the LORD their God, nor receiveth correction: truth is perished, and is cut off from their mouth.'"

Cut off thine hair, O Jerusalem, and cast it away, and take up a lamentation on high places; for the LORD hath rejected and forsaken the generation of his wrath.

"For the children of Judah have done evil in my sight," saith the LORD: "They have set their abominations in the house which is called by my name, to pollute it. And they have built the high places of Tophet, which is in the valley of the son of Hinnom, to burn their sons and their daughters in the fire; which I commanded them not, neither came it into my heart. Therefore, behold, the days come," saith the LORD, "that it shall no more be called Tophet, nor 'the valley of the son of Hinnom,' but 'the valley of slaughter' for they shall bury in Tophet, till there be no place. And the carcasses of this people shall be meat for the fowls of the heaven, and for the beasts of the earth; and none shall fray them away. Then will I cause to cease from the cities of Judah, and from the streets of Jerusalem, the voice of mirth, and the voice of gladness, the voice of the bridegroom, and the voice of the bride: for the land shall be desolate." —Jeremiah 7.

"Is There no Balm in Gilead?"

"At that time," saith the LORD, "they shall bring out the bones of the kings of Judah, and the bones of his princes, and the bones of the priests, and the bones of the prophets, and the bones of the inhabitants of Jerusalem, out of their graves: and they shall spread them before the sun, and the moon, and all the host of heaven, whom they have loved, and whom they have served, and after whom they have walked, and whom they have sought, and whom they have worshiped: they shall not be gathered, nor be buried; they shall be for dung upon the face of the earth. And death shall be chosen rather than life by all the residue of them that remain of this evil family, which remain in all the places whither I have driven them," saith the LORD of hosts.

"Moreover thou shalt say unto them, 'Thus saith the LORD: "Shall they fall, and not arise? Shall he turn away, and not return? Why then is this people of Jerusalem slidden back by a perpetual backsliding? They hold fast deceit, they refuse to return. I hearkened and heard, but they spake not aright: no man repented him of his wickedness, saying, 'What have I done?' Every one turned to his course, as the horse rusheth into the battle."'"

Yea, the stork in the heaven knoweth her appointed times; and the turtle and the crane and the swallow observe the time of their coming; but my people know not the judgment of the LORD. How do ye say, "We are wise, and the law of the LORD is with us?" Lo, certainly in vain made he it; the pen of the scribes is in vain. The wise men are ashamed, they are dismayed and taken: lo, they have rejected the word of the LORD; and what wisdom is in them? Therefore will I give their wives unto others, and their fields to them that shall inherit them: for every one from the least even unto the greatest is given to covetousness, from the prophet even unto the priest every one dealeth falsely. For they have healed the hurt of the daughter of my people slightly, saying, "Peace, peace"; when there is no peace.

"Were they ashamed when they had committed abomination? Nay, they were not at all ashamed, neither could they blush: therefore shall they fall among them that fall: in the time of their visitation they shall be cast down," saith the LORD.

"I will surely consume them," saith the LORD: "There shall be no grapes on the vine, nor figs on the fig-tree, and the leaf shall fade; and the things that I have given them shall pass away from them." Why do we sit still? Assemble yourselves, and let us enter into the defenced cities, and let us be silent there: for the LORD our God hath put us to silence, and given us water of gall to drink, because we have sinned against the LORD. We looked for peace, but no good came; and for a time of health, and behold trouble! The snorting of his horses was heard from Dan: the whole land trembled at the sound of the neighing of his strong ones; for they are come, and have devoured the land, and all that is in it; the city, and those that dwell therein.

"For, behold, I will send serpents, cockatrices, among you, which will not be charmed, and they shall bite you," saith the LORD.

When I would comfort myself against sorrow, my heart is faint in me. Behold the voice of the cry of the daughter of my people because of them that dwell in a far country: "Is not the LORD in Zion? Is not her king in her?" Why have they provoked me to anger with their graven images, and with strange vanities? The harvest is past, the summer is ended, and we are not saved. For the hurt of the daughter of my people am I hurt; I am black; astonishment hath taken hold on me. Is there no balm in Gilead; is there no physician there? Why then is not the health of the daughter of my people recovered?　—Jeremiah 8.

THE PROPHET MOURNS FOR HIS PEOPLE

Oh that my head were waters, and mine eyes a fountain of tears, that I might weep day and night for the slain of the daughter of my people! Oh that I had in the wilderness a lodging place of wayfaring men; that I might leave my people, and go from them! For they be all adulterers, an assembly of treacherous men. And they bend their tongues like their bow for lies: but they are not valiant for the truth upon the earth: "For they proceed from evil to evil, and they know not me," saith the LORD. Take ye heed every one of his neighbour, and trust ye not in any brother: for every brother will utterly supplant, and every neighbour will walk with slanders. And they will deceive every one his neighbour, and will not speak the truth: they have taught their tongue to speak lies, and weary themselves to commit iniquity. "Thine habitation is in the midst of deceit; through deceit they refuse to know me," saith the LORD.

Therefore thus saith the LORD of hosts, "Behold, I will melt them, and try them; for how shall I do for the daughter of my people? Their tongue is as an arrow shot out; it speaketh deceit: one speaketh peaceably to his neighbour with his mouth, but in heart he layeth his wait. Shall I not visit them for these things?" saith the LORD: "Shall not my soul be avenged on such a nation as this? For the mountains will I take up a weeping and wailing, and for the habitations of the wilderness a lamentation, because they are burned up, so that none can pass through them; neither can men hear the voice of the cattle; both the fowl of the heavens and the beast are fled; they are gone. And I will make Jerusalem heaps, and a den of dragons; and I will make the cities of Judah desolate, without an inhabitant."

Who is the wise man, that may understand this? And who is he to whom the mouth of the LORD hath spoken, that he may declare it, for what the land perisheth and is burned up like a wilderness, that none passeth through? And the LORD saith, "Because they have forsaken my law which I set before them, and have not obeyed my voice, neither walked therein; but have walked after the imagination of their own heart, and after Baalim, which their fathers taught them: therefore thus saith the LORD of hosts, the God of Israel: 'Behold, I will feed them, even this people, with wormwood, and give them water of gall to drink. I will scatter them also among the heathen, whom neither they nor their fathers have known: and I will send a sword after them, till I have consumed them.'"

Thus saith the LORD of hosts, "Consider ye, and call for the mourning women, that they may come; and send for cunning women, that they may come: and let them make haste, and take up a wailing for us, that our eyes may run down with tears, and our eyelids gush out with waters. For a voice of wailing is heard out of Zion: 'How are we spoiled! we are greatly confounded, because we have forsaken the land, because our dwellings have cast us out.'"

Yet hear the word of the LORD, O ye women, and let your ear receive the word of his mouth, and teach your daughters wailing, and every one her neighbour lamentation. For death is come up into our windows, and is entered into our palaces, to cut off the children from without, and the young men from the streets. Speak, "Thus saith the LORD, 'Even the carcasses of men shall fall as dung upon the open field, and as the handful after the harvestman, and none shall gather them.'"

Thus saith the LORD, "Let not the wise man glory in his wisdom, neither let the mighty man glory in his might, let not the rich man glory in his riches: but let him that glorieth glory in this, that he understandeth and knoweth me, that I am the LORD which exercise lovingkindness, judgment, and righteousness, in the earth: for in these things I delight," saith the LORD.

"Behold, the days come," saith the LORD, "that I will punish all them which are circumcised with the uncircumcised: Egypt, and Judah, and Edom, and the children of Ammon, and Moab, and all that are in the utmost corners, that dwell in the wilderness: for all these nations are uncircumcised, and all the house of Israel are uncircumcised in the heart."

—Jeremiah 9.

THE IDOL MAKERS

Hear ye the word which the LORD speaketh unto you, O house of Israel: Thus saith the LORD, "Learn not the way of the heathen, and be not dismayed at the signs of heaven; for the heathen are dismayed at them. For the customs of the people are vain: for one cutteth a tree out of the forest, the work of the hands of the workman, with the ax. They deck it with silver and with gold; they fasten it with nails and with hammers, that it move not. They are upright as the palm-tree, but speak not: they must needs be borne, because they cannot go. Be not afraid of them; for they cannot do evil, neither also is it in them to do good."

Forasmuch as there is none like unto thee, O LORD; thou art great, and thy name is great in might. Who would not fear thee, O King of nations? For to thee doth it appertain: forasmuch as among all the wise men of the nations, and in all their kingdoms, there is none like unto thee. But they are altogether brutish and foolish: the stock is a doctrine of vanities. Silver spread into plates is brought from Tarshish, and gold from Uphaz, the work of the workman, and of the hands of the founder: blue and purple is their clothing: they are all the work of cunning men. But the LORD is the true God, he is the living God, and an everlasting king: at his wrath the earth shall tremble, and the nations shall not be able to abide his indignation.

Thus shall ye say unto them, "The gods that have not made the heavens and the earth, even they shall perish from the earth, and from under these heavens. He hath made the earth by his power, he hath established the world by his wisdom, and hath stretched out the heavens by his discretion. When he uttereth his voice, there is a multitude of waters in the heavens, and he causeth the vapours to ascend from the ends of the earth; he maketh lightnings with rain, and bringeth forth the wind out of his treasures. Every man is brutish in his knowledge: every founder is confounded by the graven image: for his molten image is falsehood, and there is no breath in them. They are vanity, and the work of errors: in the time of their visitation they shall perish. The portion of Jacob is not like them: for he is the former of all things; and Israel is the rod of his inheritance: The LORD of hosts is his name."

Gather up thy wares out of the land, O inhabitant of the fortress. For thus saith the LORD, "Behold, I will sling out the inhabitants of the land at this once, and will distress them that they may find it so."

Woe is me for my hurt! my wound is grievous: but I said, "Truly this is a grief, and I must bear it. My tabernacle is spoiled, and all my cords are broken: my children are gone forth of me, and they are not: there is none to stretch forth my tent any more, and to set up my curtains. For the pastors are become brutish, and have not sought the LORD: therefore they shall not prosper, and all their flocks shall be scattered. Behold, the noise of the bruit is come, and a great commotion out of the north country, to make the cities of Judah desolate, and a den of dragons."

O LORD, I know that the way of man is not in himself: it is not in man that walketh to direct his steps. O LORD, correct me, but with judgment; not in thine anger, lest thou bring me to nothing. Pour out thy fury upon the heathen that know thee not, and upon the families that call not on thy name: for they have eaten up Jacob, and devoured him, and consumed him, and have made his habitation desolate. —Jeremiah 10.

JUDAH HAS DISOBEYED THE COVENANT

The word that came to Jeremiah from the LORD, saying, "Hear ye the words of this covenant, and speak unto the men of Judah, and to the inhabitants of Jerusalem; and say thou unto them, 'Thus saith the LORD God of Israel: "Cursed be the man that obeyeth not the words of this covenant, which I commanded your fathers in the day that I brought them forth out of the land of Egypt, from the iron furnace, saying, 'Obey my voice, and do them, according to all which I command you: so shall ye be my people, and I will be your God: that I may perform the oath which I have sworn unto your fathers, to give them a land flowing with milk and honey, as it is this day.'"'"

Then answered I, and said, "So be it, O LORD."

Then the LORD said unto me, "Proclaim all these words in the cities of Judah, and in the streets of Jerusalem, saying, 'Hear ye the words of this covenant, and do them. For I earnestly protested unto your fathers in the day that I brought them up out of the land of Egypt, even unto this day, rising early and protesting, saying, "Obey my voice." Yet they obeyed not, nor inclined their ear, but walked every one in the imagination of their evil heart: therefore I will bring upon them all the words of this covenant, which I commanded them to do; but they did them not.'"

And the LORD said unto me, "A conspiracy is found among the men of Judah, and among the inhabitants of Jerusalem. They are turned back to the iniquities of their forefathers, which refused to hear my words; and they went after other gods to serve them: the house of Israel and the house of Judah have broken my covenant which I made with their fathers."

Therefore thus saith the LORD, "Behold, I will bring evil upon them, which they shall not be able to escape; and though they shall cry unto me, I will not hearken unto them.

"Then shall the cities of Judah and inhabitants of Jerusalem go, and cry unto the gods unto whom they offer incense: but they shall not save them at all in the time of their trouble. For according to the number of thy cities were thy gods, O Judah; and according to the number of the streets of Jerusalem have ye set up altars to that shameful thing, even altars to burn incense unto Baal. Therefore pray not thou for this people, neither lift up a cry or prayer for them: for I will not hear them in the time that they cry unto me for their trouble. What hath my beloved to do in mine house, seeing she hath wrought lewdness with many, and the holy flesh is passed from thee? When thou doest evil, then thou rejoicest. The LORD called thy name, 'A green olive-tree, fair, and of goodly fruit:' with the noise of a great tumult he hath kindled fire upon it, and the branches of it are broken. For the LORD of hosts, that planted thee, hath pronounced evil against thee, for the evil of the house of Israel and of the house of Judah, which they have done against themselves to provoke me to anger in offering incense unto Baal."

And the LORD hath given me knowledge of it, and I know it: then thou shewedst me their doings. But I was like a lamb or an ox that is brought to the slaughter; and I knew not that they had devised devices against me, saying, "Let us destroy the tree with the fruit thereof, and let us cut him off from the land of the living, that his name may be no more remembered." But, O LORD of hosts, that judgest righteously, that triest the reins and the heart, let me see thy vengeance on them: for unto thee have I revealed my cause.

Therefore thus saith the LORD of the men of Anathoth, that seek thy life, saying, "Prophesy not in the name of the LORD, that thou die not by our hand": therefore thus saith the LORD of hosts, "Behold, I will punish them: the young men shall die by the sword; their sons and their daughters shall die by famine: and there shall be no remnant of them: for I will bring evil upon the men of Anathoth, even the year of their visitation."

—Jeremiah 11.

They Have Sown Wheat but Reap Thorns

Righteous art thou, O LORD, when I plead with thee: yet let me talk with thee of thy judgments: wherefore doth the way of the wicked prosper? Wherefore are all they happy that deal very treacherously? Thou hast planted them, yea, they have taken root: they grow, yea, they bring forth fruit: thou art near in their mouth, and far from their reins. But thou, O LORD, knowest me: thou hast seen me, and tried mine heart toward thee: pull them out like sheep for the slaughter, and prepare them for the day of slaughter. How long shall the land mourn, and the herbs of every field wither, for the wickedness of them that dwell therein? The beasts are consumed, and the birds; because they said, "He shall not see our last end."

If thou hast run with the footmen, and they have wearied thee, then how canst thou contend with horses? And if in the land of peace, wherein thou trustedst, they wearied thee, then how wilt thou do in the swelling of Jordan? For even thy brethren, and the house of thy father, even they have dealt treacherously with thee; yea, they have called a multitude after thee: believe them not, though they speak fair words unto thee.

I have forsaken mine house, I have left mine heritage; I have given the dearly beloved of my soul into the hand of her enemies. Mine heritage is unto me as a lion in the forest; it crieth out against me: therefore have I hated it. Mine heritage is unto me as a speckled bird, the birds round about are against her; come ye, assemble all the beasts of the field, come to devour. Many pastors have destroyed my vineyard, they have trodden my portion under foot, they have made my pleasant portion a desolate wilderness. They have made it desolate, and being desolate it mourneth unto me; the whole land is made desolate, because no man layeth it to heart. The spoilers are come upon all high places through the wilderness: for the sword of the LORD shall devour from the one end of the land even to the other end of the land: no flesh shall have peace. They have sown wheat, but shall reap thorns: they have put themselves to pain, but shall not profit: and they shall be ashamed of your revenues because of the fierce anger of the LORD.

Thus saith the LORD against all mine evil neighbours, that touch the inheritance which I have caused my people Israel to inherit: "Behold, I will pluck them out of their land, and pluck out the house of Judah from among them. And it shall come to pass, after that I have plucked them out I will return, and have compassion on them, and will bring them again, every man to his

heritage, and every man to his land. And it shall come
to pass, if they will diligently learn the ways of my people,
to swear by my name, 'The LORD liveth': as they taught
my people to swear by Baal; then shall they be built in
the midst of my people. But if they will not obey, I
will utterly pluck up and destroy that nation," saith the
LORD.   — Jeremiah 12.

THE LESSON OF THE LINEN GIRDLE

Jeremiah used symbolism and acted prophecies more frequently
than any previous prophet. Notice how abundant such symbolism
is from this point on. Always striking, often spectacular, it made
his message more vivid to the people than anything else could have
done.

Thus saith the LORD unto me, "Go and get thee a
linen girdle, and put it upon thy loins, and put it not in
water."

So I got a girdle according to the word of the LORD,
and put it on my loins. And the word of the LORD came
unto me the second time, saying, "Take the girdle that
thou hast got, which is upon thy loins, and arise, go to
Euphrates, and hide it there in a hole of the rock."

So I went, and hid it by Euphrates, as the LORD
commanded me. And it came to pass after many days,
that the LORD said unto me, "Arise, go to Euphrates,
and take the girdle from thence, which I commanded thee
to hide there."

Then I went to Euphrates, and digged, and took the
girdle from the place where I had hid it: and, behold,
the girdle was marred, it was profitable for nothing.

Then the word of the LORD came unto me, saying,
"Thus saith the LORD, 'After this manner will I mar the
pride of Judah, and the great pride of Jerusalem. This
evil people, which refuse to hear my words, which walk

in the imagination of their heart, and walk after other gods, to serve them, and to worship them, shall even be as this girdle, which is good for nothing. For as the girdle cleaveth to the loins of a man, so have I caused to cleave unto me the whole house of Israel and the whole house of Judah,' saith the LORD; 'that they might be unto me for a people, and for a name, and for a praise, and for a glory: but they would not hear.'"

— Jeremiah 13:1–11.

"The Sin of Judah Is Written with a Pen of Iron"

The sin of Judah is written with a pen of iron, and with the point of a diamond: it is graven upon the table of their heart, and upon the horns of your altars; whilst their children remember their altars and their groves by the green trees upon the high hills. O my mountain in the field, I will give thy substance and all thy treasures to the spoil, and thy high places for sin, throughout all thy borders. And thou, even thyself, shalt discontinue from thine heritage that I gave thee; and I will cause thee to serve thine enemies in the land which thou knowest not: for ye have kindled a fire in mine anger, which shall burn forever.

Thus saith the LORD: "Cursed be the man that trusteth in man, and maketh flesh his arm, and whose heart departeth from the LORD. For he shall be like the heath in the desert, and shall not see when good cometh; but shall inhabit the parched places in the wilderness, in a salt land and not inhabited. Blessed is the man that trusteth in the LORD, and whose hope the LORD is. For he shall be as a tree planted by the waters, and that spreadeth out her roots by the river, and shall not see when heat cometh, but her leaf shall be green; and shall not be careful in the year of drought, neither shall cease from yielding fruit.

"The heart is deceitful above all things, and desperately wicked: who can know it? I, the LORD, search the heart, I try the reins, even to give every man according to his ways, and according to the fruit of his doings. As the partridge sitteth on eggs, and hatcheth them not; so he that getteth riches, and not by right, shall leave them in the midst of his days, and at his end shall be a fool."

A glorious high throne from the beginning is the place of our sanctuary. O LORD, the hope of Israel, all that forsake thee shall be ashamed, and they that depart from me shall be written in the earth, because they have forsaken the LORD, the fountain of living waters. Heal me, O LORD, and I shall be healed; save me, and I shall be saved: for thou art my praise.

Behold, they say unto me, "Where is the word of the LORD? Let it come now." As for me, I have not hastened from being a pastor to follow thee: neither have I desired the woeful day; thou knowest; that which came out of my lips was right before thee. Be not a terror unto me: thou art my hope in the day of evil. Let them be confounded that persecute me, but let not me be confounded: let them be dismayed, but let not me be dismayed: bring upon them the day of evil, and destroy them with double destruction.

Thus said the LORD unto me: "Go and stand in the gate of the children of the people, whereby the kings of Judah come in, and by the which they go out, and in all the gates of Jerusalem; and say unto them, 'Hear ye the word of the LORD, ye kings of Judah, and all Judah, and all the inhabitants of Jerusalem, that enter in by these gates.

" 'Thus saith the LORD: "Take heed to yourselves, and bear no burden on the Sabbath Day, nor bring it in by the gates of Jerusalem; neither carry forth a burden out of your houses on the Sabbath Day, neither do ye any work, but hallow ye the Sabbath Day, as I commanded your fathers." But they obeyed not, neither inclined their ear, but made their neck stiff, that they might not hear, nor receive instruction.'"

"And it shall come to pass, if ye diligently hearken unto me," saith the LORD, "to bring in no burden through the gates of this city on the Sabbath Day, but hallow the Sabbath Day, to do no work therein; then shall there enter into the gates of this city kings and princes sitting upon the throne of David, riding in chariots and on horses, they, and their princes, the men of Judah, and the inhabitants of Jerusalem: and this city shall remain forever. And they shall come from the cities of Judah, and from the places about Jerusalem, and from the land of Benjamin, and from the plain, and from the mountains, and from the south, bringing burnt offerings, and sacrifices, and meat offerings, and incense, and bringing sacrifices of praise, unto the house of the LORD. But if ye will not hearken unto me to hallow the Sabbath Day, and not to bear a burden, even entering in at the gates of Jerusalem on the Sabbath Day; then will I kindle a fire in the gates thereof, and it shall devour the palaces of Jerusalem, and it shall not be quenched."

—Jeremiah 17.

THE POTTER'S WHEEL

The word which came to Jeremiah from the LORD, saying, "Arise, and go down to the potter's house, and there I will cause thee to hear my words."

Then I went down to the potter's house, and, behold, he wrought a work on the wheels. And the vessel that he made of clay was marred in the hand of the potter: so he made it again another vessel, as seemed good to the potter to make it.

BOYS WITH WATER BOTTLES
Photograph by Professor Lewis Bayles Paton
These three boys have loaded the little donkey with water jars to sell in the town. One of them is taking a drink for himself. These jars are made of the pottery so often spoken of by the prophets.
"Go and get a potter's earthen bottle."   —Jeremiah 19:1.

Then the word of the LORD came to me, saying, "O house of Israel, cannot I do with you as this potter?" saith the LORD. "Behold, as the clay is in the potter's hand, so are ye in mine hand, O house of Israel. At what instant I shall speak concerning a nation, and concerning a kingdom, to pluck up, and to pull down, and to destroy it; if that nation, against whom I have pronounced, turn from their evil, I will repent of the evil that I thought to do unto them. And at what instant I shall speak concerning a nation, and concerning a kingdom, to build and to plant it; if it do evil in my sight, that it obey not my voice, then I will repent of the good, wherewith I said I would benefit them.

"Now therefore go to, speak to the men of Judah, and to the inhabitants of Jerusalem, saying, 'Thus saith the LORD: "Behold, I frame evil against you, and devise a device against you: return ye now every one from his evil way, and make your ways and your doings good."'"

And they said, "There is no hope: but we will walk after our own devices, and we will every one do the imagination of his evil heart."

Therefore thus saith the LORD: "Ask ye now among the heathen, who hath heard such things: the virgin of Israel hath done a very horrible thing. Will a man leave the snow of Lebanon which cometh from the rock of the field? Or shall the cold flowing waters that come from another place be forsaken? Because my people hath forgotten me, they have burned incense to vanity, and they have caused them to stumble in their ways from the ancient paths, to walk in paths, in a way not cast up; to make their land desolate, and a perpetual hissing; every one that passeth thereby shall be astonished, and wag his head. I will scatter them as with an east wind before the enemy; I will shew them the back, and not the face, in the day of their calamity."

Then said they, "Come, and let us devise devices against Jeremiah; for the law shall not perish from the priest, nor counsel from the wise, nor the word from the prophet. Come, and let us smite him with the tongue, and let us not give heed to any of his words."

Give heed to me, O LORD, and hearken to the voice of them that contend with me. Shall evil be recompensed for good? For they have digged a pit for my soul. Remember that I stood before thee to speak good for them, and to turn away thy wrath from them. Therefore deliver up their children to the famine, and pour out their blood by the force of the sword; and let their wives be

bereaved of their children, and be widows; and let their
men be put to death; let their young men be slain by the
sword in battle. Let a cry be heard from their houses,
when thou shalt bring a troop suddenly upon them:
for they have digged a pit to take me, and hid snares
for my feet. Yet, LORD, thou knowest all their counsel
against me to slay me: forgive not their iniquity, neither
blot out their sin from thy sight, but let them be overthrown before thee; deal thus with them in the time of
thine anger.   —Jeremiah 18.

THE BROKEN EARTHEN VESSEL

Thus saith the LORD, "Go and get a potter's earthen
bottle, and take of the ancients of the people, and of the
ancients of the priests; and go forth unto the valley of
the son of Hinnom, which is by the entry of the east gate,
and proclaim there the words that I shall tell thee, and
say, 'Hear ye the word of the LORD, O kings of Judah,
and inhabitants of Jerusalem: Thus saith the LORD of
hosts, the God of Israel; "Behold, I will bring evil upon this
place, the which whosoever heareth, his ears shall tingle.
Because they have forsaken me, and have estranged
this place, and have burned incense in it unto other
gods, whom neither they nor their fathers have known,
nor the kings of Judah, and have filled this place with the
blood of innocents; they have built also the high places
of Baal, to burn their sons with fire for burnt offerings
unto Baal, which I commanded not, nor spake it, neither
came it into my mind: therefore, behold, the days
come," saith the LORD, "that this place shall no more be
called Tophet, nor 'The valley of the son of Hinnom,'
but 'The valley of slaughter.'
"'"And I will make void the counsel of Judah and
Jerusalem in this place; and I will cause them to fall by

the sword before their enemies, and by the hands of them that seek their lives: and their carcasses will I give to be meat for the fowls of the heaven, and for the beasts of the earth. And I will make this city desolate, and an hissing; every one that passeth thereby shall be astonished and hiss because of all the plagues thereof. And I will cause them to eat the flesh of their sons and the flesh of their daughters, and they shall eat every one the flesh of his friend in the siege and straitness, wherewith their enemies, and they that seek their lives, shall straiten them.'''

"Then shalt thou break the bottle in the sight of the men that go with thee, and shalt say unto them, 'Thus saith the LORD of hosts: "Even so will I break this people and this city, as one breaketh a potter's vessel, that cannot be made whole again: and they shall bury them in Tophet, till there be no place to bury. Thus will I do unto this place," saith the LORD, "and to the inhabitants thereof, and even make this city as Tophet: and the houses of Jerusalem, and the houses of the kings of Judah, shall be defiled as the place of Tophet, because of all the houses upon whose roofs they have burned incense unto all the host of heaven, and have poured out drink offerings unto other gods."'"

Then came Jeremiah from Tophet, whither the LORD had sent him to prophesy; and he stood in the court of the LORD's house; and said to all the people, "Thus saith the LORD of hosts, the God of Israel: 'Behold, I will bring upon this city and upon all her towns all the evil that I have pronounced against it, because they have hardened their necks, that they might not hear my words.'"

—Jeremiah 19.

THE CHIEF GOVERNOR PUTS JEREMIAH IN THE STOCKS

Now Pashur, the son of Immer, the priest who was also chief governor in the house of the LORD, heard that

Jeremiah prophesied these things. Then Pashur smote Jeremiah, the prophet, and put him in the stocks that were in the high gate of Benjamin, which was by the house of the LORD. And it came to pass on the morrow, that Pashur brought forth Jeremiah out of the stocks. Then said Jeremiah unto him, "The LORD hath not called thy name Pashur, but Magor-missabib. For thus saith the LORD, 'Behold, I will make thee a terror to thyself, and to all thy friends: and they shall fall by the sword of their enemies, and thine eyes shall behold it: and I will give all Judah into the hand of the king of Babylon, and he shall carry them captive into Babylon, and shall slay them with the sword. Moreover I will deliver all the strength of this city, and all the labours thereof, and all the precious things thereof, and all the treasures of the kings of Judah will I give into the hand of their enemies, which shall spoil them, and take them, and carry them to Babylon. And thou, Pashur, and all that dwell in thine house shall go into captivity: and thou shalt come to Babylon, and there thou shalt die, and shalt be buried there, thou, and all thy friends, to whom thou hast prophesied lies.'"

O LORD, thou hast deceived me, and I was deceived: thou art stronger than I, and hast prevailed: I am in derision daily, every one mocketh me. For since I spake, I cried out, I cried violence and spoil; because the word of the LORD was made a reproach unto me, and a derision, daily. Then I said, "I will not make mention of him, nor speak any more in his name." But his word was in mine heart as a burning fire shut up in my bones, and I was weary with forbearing, and I could not stay.

For I heard the defaming of many, fear on every side. "Report," say they, "and we will report it." All my families watched for my halting, saying, "Peradventure he will be enticed, and we shall prevail against him, and we shall take our revenge on him." But the LORD is with me as a mighty terrible one: therefore my persecutors shall stumble, and they shall not prevail: they shall be greatly ashamed; for they shall not prosper: their everlasting confusion shall never be forgotten.

—Jeremiah 20:1–11.

WOE TO THE UNFAITHFUL SHEPHERDS

"Woe be unto the pastors that destroy and scatter the sheep of my pasture!" saith the LORD. Therefore thus saith the LORD God of Israel against the pastors that feed my people: "Ye have scattered my flock, and driven them away, and have not visited them: behold, I will visit upon you the evil of your doings," saith the LORD. "And I will gather the remnant of my flock out of all countries whither I have driven them, and will bring them again to their folds; and they shall be fruitful and increase. And I will set up shepherds over them which shall feed them: and they shall fear no more, nor be dismayed, neither shall they be lacking," saith the LORD.

"Behold, the days come," saith the LORD, "that I will raise unto David a righteous Branch, and a King shall reign and prosper, and shall execute judgment and justice in the earth. In his days Judah shall be saved, and Israel shall dwell safely: and this is his name whereby he shall be called, THE LORD OUR RIGHTEOUSNESS. Therefore, behold, the days come," saith the LORD, "that they shall no more say, 'The LORD liveth, which brought up the children of Israel out of the land of Egypt'; but, 'The LORD liveth, which brought up and which led the seed of the house of Israel out of the north country, and from all countries whither I had driven them; and they shall dwell in their own land.'"

Mine heart within me is broken because of the prophets; all my bones shake; I am like a drunken man, and like a man whom wine hath overcome, because of the LORD, and because of the words of his holiness. For the land is full of adulterers; for because of swearing the land mourneth; the pleasant places of the wilderness are dried up, and their course is evil, and their force is not right.

"For both prophet and priest are profane; yea, in my house have I found their wickedness," saith the LORD.

"Wherefore their way shall be unto them as slippery ways in the darkness: they shall be driven on and fall therein: for I will bring evil upon them, even the year of their visitation," saith the LORD.

"And I have seen folly in the prophets of Samaria; they prophesied in Baal, and caused my people Israel to err. I have seen also in the prophets of Jerusalem an horrible thing: they commit adultery, and walk in lies: they strengthen also the hands of evildoers, that none doth return from his wickedness: they are all of them unto me as Sodom, and the inhabitants thereof as Gomorrah."

Therefore thus saith the LORD of hosts concerning the prophets: "Behold, I will feed them with wormwood, and make them drink the water of gall: for from the prophets of Jerusalem is profaneness gone forth into all the land."

Thus saith the LORD of hosts, "Hearken not unto the words of the prophets that prophesy unto you: they make you vain: they speak a vision of their own heart, and not out of the mouth of the LORD. They say still unto them that despise me, 'The LORD hath said, "Ye shall have peace"'; and they say unto every one that walketh after the imagination of his own heart, 'No evil shall come upon you.'

"For who hath stood in the counsel of the LORD, and hath perceived and heard his word? Who hath marked his word, and heard it? Behold, a whirlwind of the LORD is gone forth in fury, even a grievous whirlwind: it shall fall grievously upon the head of the wicked. The anger of the LORD shall not return, until he have executed, and till he have performed the thoughts of his heart: in the latter days ye shall consider it perfectly. I have not sent these prophets, yet they ran: I have not spoken to them, yet they prophesied. But if they had stood in my counsel, and had caused my people to hear my words, then they should have turned them from their evil way, and from the evil of their doings.

"Am I a God at hand," saith the LORD, "and not a God afar off? Can any hide himself in secret places that I shall not see him?" saith the LORD. "Do not I fill heaven and earth?" saith the LORD.

"I have heard what the prophets said, that prophesy lies in my name, saying, 'I have dreamed, I have dreamed.' How long shall this be in the heart of the prophets that prophesy lies? Yea, they are prophets of the deceit of their own heart; which think to use my people to forget my name by their dreams which they tell every man to his neighbour, as their fathers have forgotten my name for Baal. The prophet that hath a dream, let him tell a dream; and he that hath my word, let him speak my word faithfully. What is the chaff to the wheat?" saith the LORD.

"Is not my word like as a fire?" saith the LORD; "and like a hammer that breaketh the rock in pieces? Therefore, behold, I am against the prophets," saith the LORD, "that steal my words every one from his neighbour. Behold, I am against the prophets," saith the LORD. "that use their tongues, and say, 'He saith.' Be-

hold, I am against them that prophesy false dreams,"
saith the LORD, "and do tell them, and cause my people
to err by their lies, and by their lightness; yet I sent them
not, nor commanded them: therefore they shall not profit
this people at all," saith the LORD.

"And when this people, or the prophet, or a priest,
shall ask thee, saying, 'What is the burden of the LORD?'
thou shalt then say unto them, 'What burden?' 'I will
even forsake you,'" saith the LORD.

"And as for the prophet, and the priest, and the people,
that shall say, 'The burden of the LORD,' I will even
punish that man and his house.

"Thus shall ye say every one to his neighbour, and
every one to his brother, 'What hath the LORD answered?' and, 'What hath the LORD spoken?' And the
burden of the LORD shall ye mention no more: for every
man's word shall be his burden; for ye have perverted
the words of the living God, of the LORD of hosts our God.

"Thus shalt thou say to the prophet, 'What hath the
LORD answered thee?' and, 'What hath the LORD
spoken?' But since ye say, 'The burden of the LORD'";
therefore thus saith the LORD: "Because ye say this word,
'The burden of the LORD,' and I have sent unto you,
saying, 'Ye shall not say, "The burden of the LORD"';
therefore, behold, I, even I, will utterly forget you, and
I will forsake you, and the city that I gave you and your
fathers, and cast you out of my presence: and I will
bring an everlasting reproach upon you, and a perpetual
shame, which shall not be forgotten." —Jeremiah 23.

THE LESSON OF THE TWO BASKETS OF FIGS

In 597 B.C. Nebuchadnezzar captured Judah, deported the king
and all the leaders of the people, and set a new king, Zedekiah, on
the throne. The former king had lost his throne through revolts

against Babylon; it might be supposed that the new king would have learned a lesson. But before long, plots to revolt began to stir the people. The indignation of Jeremiah was roused. "You fools!" he said. "When all the leaders of the nation were here revolt failed. Now with them gone, what do you hope to accomplish? You are only rotten figs compared with them." But even this blunt and uncomplimentary warning did not keep the foolish people from revolting, as later chapters in Jeremiah show.

The LORD shewed me, and, behold, two baskets of figs were set before the temple of the LORD, after that Nebuchadnezzar, King of Babylon, had carried away captive Jeconiah, the son of Jehoiakim, King of Judah, and the princes of Judah, with the carpenters and smiths, from Jerusalem, and had brought them to Babylon. One basket had very good figs, even like the figs that are first ripe: and the other basket had very naughty figs, which could not be eaten, they were so bad. Then said the LORD unto me, "What seest thou, Jeremiah?"

And I said, "Figs; the good figs, very good; and the evil, very evil, that cannot be eaten, they are so evil."

Again the word of the LORD came unto me, saying, "Thus saith the LORD, the God of Israel: 'Like these good figs, so will I acknowledge them that are carried away captive of Judah, whom I have sent out of this place, into the land of the Chaldeans for their good. For I will set mine eyes upon them for good, and I will bring them again to this land: and I will build them, and not pull them down; and I will plant them, and not pluck them up. And I will give them an heart to know me, that I am the LORD: and they shall be my people, and I will be their God: for they shall return unto me with their whole heart.

"'And as the evil figs, which cannot be eaten, they are so evil'; surely thus saith the LORD, 'so will I give Zedekiah, the king of Judah, and his princes, and the residue of Jerusalem, that remain in this land, and them that dwell in the land of Egypt: and I will deliver them to be removed into all the kingdoms of the earth for their hurt, to be a reproach and a proverb, a taunt and a curse, in all places whither I shall drive them. And I will send the sword, the famine, and the pestilence, among them, till they be consumed from off the land that I gave unto them and to their fathers.'"

—Jeremiah 24.

"This Man Is Not Worthy to Die"

This section seems to follow Chapter 7, p. 235, and to show what was the outcome of that sermon, the most bitter and vigorous in its denunciation of any we have from the long career of Jeremiah.

Then spake Jeremiah unto all the princes and to all the people saying, "The Lord sent me to prophesy against this house and against this city all the words that ye have heard. Therefore now amend your ways and your doings, and obey the voice of the Lord your God; and the Lord will repent him of the evil that he hath pronounced against you. As for me, behold, I am in your hand: do with me as seemeth good and meet unto you. But know ye for certain, that if ye put me to death, ye shall surely bring innocent blood upon yourselves, and upon this city, and upon the inhabitants thereof: for of a truth the Lord hath sent me unto you to speak all these words in your ears."

Then said the princes and all the people unto the priests and to the prophets: "This man is not worthy to die: for he hath spoken to us in the name of the Lord our God."

Then rose up certain of the elders of the land, and spake to all the assembly of the people, saying, "Micah, the Morasthite, prophesied in the days of Hezekiah, King of Judah, and spake to all the people of Judah, saying, 'Thus saith the LORD of hosts: "Zion shall be plowed like a field, and Jerusalem shall become heaps, and the mountain of the house as the high places of a forest."' Did Hezekiah, King of Judah, and all Judah put him at all to death? Did he not fear the LORD, and besought the LORD, and the LORD repented him of the evil which he had pronounced against them? Thus might we procure great evil against our souls.

"And there was also a man that prophesied in the name of the LORD, Urijah, the son of Shemaiah of Kirjath-jearim, who prophesied against this city and against this land according to all the words of Jeremiah: and when Jehoiakim, the king, with all his mighty men, and all the princes, heard his words, the king sought to put him to death: but when Urijah heard it, he was afraid, and fled, and went into Egypt; and Jehoiakim, the king, sent men into Egypt, namely, Elnathan, the son of Achbor, and certain men with him into Egypt. And they fetched forth Urijah out of Egypt, and brought him unto Jehoiakim, the king; who slew him with the sword, and cast his dead body into the graves of the common people."

Nevertheless the hand of Ahikam, the son of Shaphan, was with Jeremiah, that they should not give him into the hand of the people to put him to death.

— Jeremiah 26·12–24.

THE LESSON OF THE YOKES

This is another prophecy showing that revolt against Babylon was planned from the beginning of the reign of Zedekiah.

In the beginning of the reign of Zedekiah, the son of Josiah, King of Judah, came this word unto Jeremiah from the LORD, saying, "Thus saith the LORD to me: 'Make thee bonds and yokes, and put them upon thy neck, and send them to the king of Edom, and to the king of Moab, and to the king of the Ammonites, and to the king of Tyrus, and to the king of Zidon, by the hand of the messengers which come to Jerusalem unto Zedekiah, King of Judah; and command them to say unto their masters, "Thus saith the LORD of hosts, the God of Israel: thus shall ye say unto your masters: 'I have made the earth, the man and the beast that are upon the ground, by my great power and by my outstretched arm, and have given it unto whom it seemed meet unto me. And now have I given all these lands into the hand of Nebuchadnezzar, the king of Babylon, my servant; and the beasts of the field have I given him also to serve him. And all nations shall serve him, and his son, and his son's son, until the very time of his land come: and then many nations and great kings shall serve themselves of him. And it shall come to pass, that the nation and kingdom which will not serve the same Nebuchadnezzar, the king of Babylon, and that will not put their neck under the yoke of the king of Babylon, that nation will I punish,' saith the LORD, 'with the sword, and with the famine, and with the pestilence, until I have consumed them by his hand. Therefore hearken not ye to your prophets, nor to your diviners, nor to your dreamers, nor to your enchanters, nor to your sorcerers, which speak unto you, saying, "Ye shall not serve the king of Babylon": for they prophesy a lie unto you, to remove you far from your land; and that I should drive you out, and ye should perish. But the nations that bring their neck under the yoke of the king of Babylon, and serve him, those will I let remain still in their own land,' saith the LORD; 'and they shall till it, and dwell therein.'""

I spake also to Zedekiah, King of Judah, according to all these words, saying, "Bring your necks under the yoke of the king of Babylon, and serve him and his people, and live. Why will ye die, thou and thy people, by the sword, by the famine, and by the pestilence, as the LORD hath spoken against the nation that will not serve the king of Babylon? Therefore hearken not unto the words of the prophets that speak unto you, saying, 'Ye shall not serve the king of Babylon': for they prophesy a lie unto you.

"'For I have not sent them,' saith the LORD, 'yet they prophesy a lie in my name; that I might drive you out, and that ye might perish, ye, and the prophets that prophesy unto you.'"

Also I spake to the priests and to all this people, saying, "Thus saith the LORD: 'Hearken not to the words of your prophets that prophesy unto you, saying, "Behold, the vessels of the LORD's house shall now shortly be brought again from Babylon": for they prophesy a lie unto you. Hearken not unto them; serve the king of Babylon, and live: wherefore should this city be laid waste? But if they be prophets, and if the word of the LORD be with them, let them now make intercession to the LORD of hosts, that the vessels which are left in the house of the LORD, and in the house of the king of Judah, and at Jerusalem, go not to Babylon.'

"For thus saith the LORD of hosts concerning the pillars, and concerning the sea, and concerning the bases, and concerning the residue of the vessels that remain in this city, which Nebuchadnezzar, King of Babylon, took not, when he carried away captive Jeconiah, the son of Jehoiakim, King of Judah, from Jerusalem to Babylon, and all the nobles of Judah and Jerusalem; yea, thus saith the LORD of hosts, the God of Israel, concerning the vessels that remain in the house of the LORD, and in the house of the king of Judah and of Jerusalem: 'They shall be carried to Babylon, and there shall they be until the day that I visit them,' saith the LORD; 'then will I bring them up, and restore them to this place.'"

And it came to pass the same year, in the beginning of the reign of Zedekiah, King of Judah, in the fourth year, and in the fifth month, that Hananiah, the son of Azur, the prophet, which was of Gibeon, spake unto me in the house of the LORD, in the presence of the priests and of all the people, saying, "Thus speaketh the LORD of hosts, the God of Israel, saying, 'I have broken the yoke of the king of Babylon. Within two full years will I bring again into this place all the vessels of

A TERRACED FIELD IN PALESTINE

Photograph by W. A. Pottenger expressly for The Book of Life

These terraced fields are near the well En Rogel.

"Buy me my field that is in Anathoth, for the right of redemption is thine to buy it." —Jeremiah 32:7.

the LORD's house, that Nebuchadnezzar, King of Babylon, took away from this place, and carried them to Babylon: and I will bring again to this place Jeconiah, the son of Jehoiakim, King of Judah, with all the captives of Judah, that went into Babylon,' saith the LORD: 'for I will break the yoke of the king of Babylon.'"

Then the prophet Jeremiah said unto the prophet Hananiah in the presence of the priests, and in the presence of all the people that stood in the house of the LORD, even the prophet Jeremiah said, "Amen: the LORD do so: the LORD perform thy words which thou hast prophesied, to bring again the vessels of the LORD's house, and all that is carried away captive, from Babylon into this place. Nevertheless hear thou now this word that I speak in thine ears, and in the ears of all the people; the prophets that have been before me and before thee of old prophesied both against many countries, and against great kingdoms, of war, and of evil, and of pestilence. The prophet which prophesieth of peace, when the word of the prophet shall come to pass, then shall the prophet be known, that the LORD hath truly sent him."

Then Hananiah, the prophet, took the yoke from off the prophet Jeremiah's neck, and brake it. And Hananiah spake in the presence of all the people, saying, "Thus saith the LORD: 'Even so will I break the yoke of Nebuchadnezzar, King of Babylon, from the neck of all nations within the space of two full years.'" And the prophet Jeremiah went his way.

Then the word of the LORD came unto Jeremiah, the prophet, after that Hananiah, the prophet, had broken the yoke from off the neck of the prophet Jeremiah, saying, "Go and tell Hananiah, saying, 'Thus saith the LORD: "Thou hast broken the yokes of wood; but thou shalt make for them yokes of iron."'"

"For thus saith the LORD of hosts, the God of Israel: 'I have put a yoke of iron upon the neck of all these nations, that they may serve Nebuchadnezzar, King of Babylon; and they shall serve him: and I have given him the beasts of the field also.'"

Then said the prophet Jeremiah unto Hananiah, the prophet, "Hear now, Hananiah: The LORD hath not sent thee; but thou makest this people to trust in a lie. Therefore thus saith the LORD: "Behold, I will cast thee from off the face of the earth: this year thou shalt die,

because thou hast taught rebellion against the LORD.'"
So Hananiah, the prophet, died the same year in the
seventh month. Jeremiah 27:28.

THE LESSON OF THE FIELD WHICH JEREMIAH BOUGHT

PEACE WILL YET COME TO JUDAH

Jeremiah was not able to stop the revolt of Judah from Babylon; but soon after the rebellion developed the army of Babylon
appeared in Judah and Jerusalem was besieged. Meantime Jeremiah had been imprisoned as a traitor, because of his opposition
to this hopeless war for independence. But even so he does not
despair of the final freedom of Judah, and is willing to redeem the
family property against the far-off day of peace.

And Jeremiah said, "The word of the LORD came
unto me, saying, 'Behold, Hanameel, the son of Shallum,
thine uncle, shall come unto thee, saying, "Buy thee my
field that is in Anathoth: for the right of redemption is
thine to buy it."'"

"So Hanameel, mine uncle's son, came to me in the
court of the prison according to the word of the LORD,
and said unto me, 'Buy my field, I pray thee, that is in
Anathoth, which is in the country of Benjamin: for the
right of inheritance is thine, and the redemption is thine;
buy it for thyself.' Then I knew that this was the word
of the LORD.

"And I bought the field of Hanameel, my uncle's
son, that was in Anathoth, and weighed him the money,
even seventeen shekels of silver. And I subscribed the
evidence, and sealed it, and took witnesses, and weighed
him the money in the balances. So I took the evidence
of the purchase, both that which was sealed according to
the law and custom, and that which was open: and I
gave the evidence of the purchase unto Baruch, the son
of Neriah, the son of Maaseiah, in the sight of Hanameel,

mine uncle's son, and in the presence of the witnesses that subscribed the book of the purchase, before all the Jews that sat in the court of the prison.

"And I charged Baruch before them, saying, 'Thus saith the LORD of hosts, the God of Israel: "Take these evidences, this evidence of the purchase, both which is sealed, and this evidence which is open; and put them in an earthen vessel, that they may continue many days."

"'For thus saith the LORD of hosts, the God of Israel: "Houses and fields and vineyards shall be possessed again in this land."'"

Now when I had delivered the evidence of the purchase unto Baruch, the son of Neriah, I prayed unto the LORD, saying, "Ah, Lord GOD! behold, thou hast made the heaven and the earth by thy great power and stretched out arm, and there is nothing too hard for thee: thou shewest lovingkindness unto thousands, and recompensest the iniquity of the fathers into the bosom of their children after them: the Great, the Mighty God, the LORD of hosts, is his name, great in counsel, and mighty in work: for thine eyes are open upon all the ways of the sons of men: to give every one according to his ways, and according to the fruit of his doings: which hast set signs and wonders in the land of Egypt, even unto this day, and in Israel, and among other men; and hast made thee a name, as at this day; and hast brought forth thy people Israel out of the land of Egypt with signs, and with wonders, and with a strong hand, and with a stretched out arm, and with great terror; and hast given them this land, which thou didst swear to their fathers to give them, a land flowing with milk and honey; and they came in, and possessed it; but they obeyed not thy voice, neither walked in thy law; they have done nothing of all that thou commandedst them to do: therefore thou hast caused all this evil to come upon them.

"Behold the mounts, they are come unto the city to take it; and the city is given into the hand of the Chaldeans, that fight against it, because of the sword, and of the famine, and of the pestilence: and what thou hast spoken is come to pass; and, behold, thou seest it. And thou hast said unto me, O Lord God, 'Buy thee the field for money, and take witnesses; for the city is given into the hand of the Chaldeans.'"

Then came the word of the Lord unto Jeremiah, saying, "Behold, I am the Lord, the God of all flesh: is there anything too hard for me?" Therefore thus saith the Lord: "Behold, I will give this city into the hand of the Chaldeans, and into the hand of Nebuchadnezzar, King of Babylon, and he shall take it: and the Chaldeans, that fight against this city, shall come and set fire on this city, and burn it with the houses, upon whose roofs they have offered incense unto Baal, and poured out drink offerings unto other gods, to provoke me to anger. For the children of Israel and the children of Judah have only done evil before me from their youth: for the children of Israel have only provoked me to anger with the work of their hands," saith the Lord.

"For this city hath been to me as a provocation of mine anger and of my fury from the day that they built it even unto this day; that I should remove it from before my face, because of all the evil of the children of Israel and of the children of Judah, which they have done to provoke me to anger, they, their kings, their princes, their priests, and their prophets, and the men of Judah, and the inhabitants of Jerusalem. And they have turned unto me the back, and not the face: though I taught them, rising up early and teaching them, yet they have not hearkened to receive instruction. But they set their abominations in the house, which is called by my name, to defile it. And they built the high places of Baal, which are in the valley of the son of Hinnom, to cause their sons and their daughters to pass through the fire unto Molech; which I commanded them not, neither came it into my mind, that they should do this abomination, to cause Judah to sin."

And now therefore thus saith the Lord, the God of Israel, concerning this city, whereof ye say, "It shall be delivered into the hand of the king of Babylon by the sword, and by the famine, and by the pestilence": "Behold, I will gather them out of all countries, whither I have driven them in mine anger, and in my fury, and in great wrath; and I will bring them again unto this place, and I will cause them to dwell safely: and they shall be my people, and I will be their God: and I will give them one heart, and one way, that they may fear me forever, for the good of them, and of their children after them: and I will make an everlasting covenant with them, that I will not turn away from them, to do them good; but I will put my fear in their hearts, that they shall not depart from me. Yea, I will rejoice over them to do them good, and I will plant them in this land assuredly with my whole heart and with my whole soul."

For thus saith the Lord: "Like as I have brought all this great evil upon this people, so will I bring upon them all the good that I have promised them. And fields shall be bought in this land, whereof ye say, 'It is desolate without man or beast; it is given into the hand of the Chaldeans.' Men shall buy fields for money, and subscribe evidences, and seal them, and take witnesses in the land of Benjamin, and in the places about Jerusalem, and in the cities of Judah, and in the cities of the mountains, and in the cities of the valley, and in the cities of the south: for I will cause their captivity to return," saith the LORD.   —Jeremiah 32:6–44.

JERUSALEM SHALL BE SAVED

Moreover the word of the LORD came unto Jeremiah the second time, while he was yet shut up in the court of the prison, saying, "Thus saith the LORD, the maker thereof, the LORD that formed it, to establish it: the LORD is his name: 'Call unto me, and I will answer thee, and shew thee great and mighty things, which thou knowest not.'

"For thus saith the LORD, the God of Israel, concerning the houses of this city, and concerning the houses of the kings of Judah, which are thrown down by the mounts, and by the sword: 'They come to fight with the Chaldeans, but it is to fill them with the dead bodies of men, whom I have slain in mine anger and in my fury, and for all whose wickedness I have hid my face from this city. Behold, I will bring it health and cure, and I will cure them, and will reveal unto them the abundance of peace and truth. And I will cause the captivity of Judah and the captivity of Israel to return, and will build them, as at the first. And I will cleanse them from all their iniquity, whereby they have sinned against me; and I will pardon all their iniquities, whereby they have sinned, and whereby they have transgressed against me.

"'And it shall be to me a name of joy, a praise and an honour before all the nations of the earth, which shall hear all the good that I do unto them: and they shall fear and tremble for all the goodness and for all the prosperity that I procure unto it.'

"Thus saith the LORD: 'Again there shall be heard in this place, which ye say shall be desolate without man and without beast, even in the cities of Judah, and in the streets of Jerusalem, that are desolate, without man, and without inhabitant, and without beast, the voice of joy, and the voice of gladness, the voice of the bridegroom, and the voice of the bride, the voice of them that shall say,

> "Praise the LORD of hosts:
> For the LORD is good;
> For his mercy endureth forever":

and of them that shall bring the sacrifice of praise into the house of the LORD. For I will cause to return the captivity of the land, as at the first,' saith the LORD.

"Thus saith the LORD of hosts: 'Again in this place, which is desolate without man and without beast, and in all the cities thereof, shall be an habitation of shepherds causing their flocks to lie down. In the cities of the mountains, in the cities of the vale, and in the cities of the south, and in the land of Benjamin, and in the places about Jerusalem, and in the cities of Judah, shall the flocks pass again under the hands of him that telleth them,' saith the LORD. 'Behold, the days come,' saith the LORD, 'that I will perform that good thing which I have promised unto the house of Israel and to the house of Judah. In those days, and at that time, will I cause the Branch of righteousness to grow up unto David; and he shall execute judgment and righteousness in the land. In those days shall Judah be saved, and Jerusalem shall dwell safely: and this is the name wherewith she shall be called, "The LORD our righteousness."'

"For thus saith the LORD: 'David shall never want a man to sit upon the throne of the house of Israel; neither shall the priests, the Levites, want a man before me to offer burnt offerings, and to kindle meat offerings, and to do sacrifice continually.'"   — Jeremiah 33:1–18.

The Story of Jeremiah's Bravery in the Face of the King and Princes

JEREMIAH WRITES HIS PROPHECIES IN A BOOK

And it came to pass in the fourth year of Jehoiakim, the son of Josiah, King of Judah, that this word came unto Jeremiah from the LORD, saying, "Take thee a roll of a book, and write therein all the words that I have spoken unto thee against Israel, and against Judah, and against all the nations, from the day I spake unto thee, from the days of Josiah, even unto this day. It may be that the house of Judah will hear all the evil which I purpose to do unto them; that they may return every man from his evil way; that I may forgive their iniquity and their sin."

Then Jeremiah called Baruch, the son of Neriah: and Baruch wrote from the mouth of Jeremiah all the words of the LORD, which he had spoken unto him, upon a roll of a book. And Jeremiah commanded Baruch, saying, "I am shut up; I cannot go into the house of the LORD: therefore go thou, and read in the roll, which thou has written from my mouth, the words of the LORD in the ears of the people in the LORD's house upon the fasting day: and also thou shalt read them in the ears of all Judah that come out of their cities. It may be they will present their supplication before the LORD, and will return every one from his evil way: for great is the anger and the fury that the LORD hath pronounced against this people."

And Baruch, the son of Neriah, did according to all that Jeremiah, the prophet, commanded him, reading in the book the words of the LORD in the LORD's house. And it came to pass in the fifth year of Jehoiakim, the son of Josiah, King of Judah, in the ninth month, that they proclaimed a fast before the LORD to all the people in

Jerusalem, and to all the people that came from the cities of Judah unto Jerusalem. Then read Baruch in the book the words of Jeremiah in the house of the LORD, in the chamber of Gemariah, the son of Shaphan, the scribe, in the higher court, at the entry of the new gate of the LORD's house, in the ears of all the people.

When Michaiah, the son of Gemariah, the son of Shaphan, had heard out of the book all the words of the LORD, then he went down into the king's house, into the scribe's chamber: and, lo, all the princes sat there, even Elishama, the scribe, and Delaiah, the son of Shemaiah, and Elnathan, the son of Achbor, and Gemariah, the son of Shaphan, and Zedekiah, the son of Hananiah, and all the princes. Then Michaiah declared unto them all the words that he had heard, when Baruch read the book in the ears of the people.

THE PRINCES FEAR BECAUSE OF THE PROPHET'S WORDS

Therefore all the princes sent Jehudi, the son of Nethaniah, the son of Shelemiah, the son of Cushi, unto Baruch, saying, "Take in thine hand the roll wherein thou hast read in the ears of the people, and come." So Baruch, the son of Neriah, took the roll in his hand, and came unto them.

And they said unto him, "Sit down now, and read it in our ears." So Baruch read it in their ears.

Now it came to pass, when they had heard all the words, they were afraid both one and other, and said unto Baruch, "We will surely tell the king of all these words." And they asked Baruch, saying, "Tell us now, how didst thou write all these words at his mouth?"

Then Baruch answered them, "He pronounced all these words unto me with his mouth, and I wrote them with ink in the book."

Then said the princes unto Baruch, "Go, hide thee, thou and Jeremiah; and let no man know where ye be."

THE KING CUTS JEREMIAH'S BOOK WITH HIS PENKNIFE AND BURNS IT TO ASHES

And they went in to the king into the court, but they laid up the roll in the chamber of Elishama, the scribe, and told all the words in the ears of the king. So the king sent Jehudi to fetch the roll: and he took it out of Elishama, the scribe's, chamber. And Jehudi read it in the ears of the king, and in the ears of all the princes which stood beside the king. Now the king sat in the winter-house in the ninth month: and there was a fire on the hearth burning before him. And it came to pass, that when Jehudi had read three or four leaves, he cut it with the penknife, and cast it into the fire that was on the hearth, until all the roll was consumed in the fire that was on the hearth. Yet they were not afraid, nor rent their garments, neither the king, nor any of his servants that heard all these words. Nevertheless Elnathan and Delaiah and Gemariah had made intercession to the king that he would not burn the roll: but he would not hear them. But the king commanded Jerahmeel, the son of Hammelech, and Seraiah, the son of Azriel, and Shelemiah, the son of Abdeel, to take Baruch, the scribe, and Jeremiah, the prophet: but the LORD hid them.

JEREMIAH WRITES THE BOOK AGAIN

Then the word of the LORD came to Jeremiah, after that the king had burned the roll, and the words which Baruch wrote at the mouth of Jeremiah, saying, "Take thee again another roll, and write in it all the former words that were in the first roll, which Jehoiakim, the king of Judah, hath burned. And thou shalt say to Jehoiakim, King of Judah, 'Thus saith the LORD: "Thou hast burned this roll, saying, 'Why hast thou written therein, saying, "The king of Babylon shall certainly come and destroy this land, and shall cause to cease from thence man and beast?"' "

"'Therefore thus saith the LORD of Jehoiakim, King of Judah: "He shall have none to sit upon the throne of David: and his dead body shall be cast out in the day to the heat, and in the night to the frost. And I will punish him and his seed and his servants for their iniquity; and I will bring upon them, and upon the inhabitants of Jerusalem, and upon the men of Judah, all the evil that I have pronounced against them; but they hearkened not."'"

Then took Jeremiah another roll, and gave it to Baruch, the scribe, the son of Neriah; who wrote therein from the mouth of Jeremiah all the words of the book which Jehoiakim, King of Judah, had burned in the fire: and there were added besides unto them many like words.

—Jeremiah 36.

PHARAOH'S ARMY RAISES THE SIEGE OF JERUSALEM

And King Zedekiah, the son of Josiah, reigned instead of Coniah, the son of Jehoiakim, whom Nebuchadnezzar, King of Babylon, made king in the land of Judah. But neither he, nor his servants, nor the people of the land, did hearken unto the words of the LORD, which he spake by the prophet Jeremiah. And Zedekiah, the king, sent Jehucal, the son of Shelemiah, and Zephaniah, the son of Maaseiah, the priest, to the prophet Jeremiah, saying, "Pray now unto the LORD our God for us."

Now Jeremiah came in and went out among the people: for they had not put him into prison. Then Pharaoh's army was come forth out of Egypt: and when the Chaldeans that besieged Jerusalem heard tidings of them, they departed from Jerusalem.

Then came the word of the LORD unto the prophet Jeremiah, saying, "'Thus saith the LORD, the God of Israel: 'Thus shall ye say to the king of Judah, that sent you unto me to enquire of me: "Behold, Pharaoh's army, which is come forth to help you, shall return to Egypt into their own land. And the Chaldeans shall come again, and fight against this city, and take it, and burn it with fire."'

"Thus saith the LORD: 'Deceive not yourselves, saying, "The Chaldeans shall surely depart from us": for they shall not depart. For though ye had smitten the whole army of the Chaldeans that fight against you, and there remained but wounded men among them, yet should they rise up every man in his tent, and burn this city with fire.'"

JEREMIAH IS ACCUSED OF DESERTING TO THE CHALDEANS

And it came to pass, that when the army of the Chaldeans was broken up from Jerusalem for fear of Pharaoh's army, then Jeremiah went forth out of Jerusalem to go into the land of Benjamin, to separate himself thence in the midst of the people. And when he was in the gate of Benjamin, a captain of the ward was there, whose name was Irijah, the son of Shelemiah, the son of Hananiah; and he took Jeremiah, the prophet, saying, "Thou fallest away to the Chaldeans." Then said Jeremiah, "It is false; I fall not away to the Chaldeans." But he hearkened not to him: so Irijah took Jeremiah, and brought him to the princes. Wherefore the princes were wroth with Jeremiah, and smote him, and put him in prison in the house of Jonathan, the scribe: for they had made that the prison.

JEREMIAH IS PUT INTO THE DUNGEON

When Jeremiah was entered into the dungeon, and into the cabins, and Jeremiah had remained there many days; then Zedekiah, the king, sent, and took him out: and the king asked him secretly in his house, and said, "Is there any word from the LORD?"

And Jeremiah said, "There is: for," said he, "thou shalt be delivered into the hand of the king of Babylon." Moreover Jeremiah said unto King Zedekiah, "What have I offended against thee, or against thy servants, or against this people, that ye have put me in prison? Where are now your prophets which prophesied unto you, saying, 'The king of Babylon shall not come against you, nor against this land?' Therefore hear now, I pray thee, O my lord the king: let my supplication, I pray thee, be accepted before thee; that thou cause me not to return to the house of Jonathan, the scribe, lest I die there."

JEREMIAH IS CONFINED IN THE PRISON COURT

Then Zedekiah, the king, commanded that they should commit Jeremiah into the court of the prison, and that they should give him daily a piece of bread out of the bakers' street, until all the bread in the city were spent. Thus Jeremiah remained in the court of the prison.

Then Shephatiah, the son of Mattan, and Gedaliah, the son of Pashur, and Jucal, the son of Shelemiah, and Pashur, the son of Malchiah, heard the words that Jeremiah had spoken unto all the people, saying, "Thus saith the LORD, 'He that remaineth in this city shall die by the sword, by the famine, and by the pestilence: but he that goeth forth to the Chaldeans shall live; for he shall have his life for a prey, and shall live.'

"Thus saith the LORD, 'This city shall surely be given into the hand of the king of Babylon's army, which shall take it.'"

Therefore the princes said unto the king, "We beseech thee, let this man be put to death: for thus he weakeneth the hands of the men of war that remain in this city, and the hands of all the people, in speaking such words unto them: for this man seeketh not the welfare of this people, but the hurt."

Then Zedekiah, the king, said, "Behold, he is in your hand: for the king is not he that can do anything against you."   —Jeremiah 37; 38:1-5.

JEREMIAH IS CAST INTO THE DUNGEON AND SINKS IN THE MIRE

Then took they Jeremiah, and cast him into the dungeon of Malchiah, the son of Hammelech, that was in the court of the prison: and they let down Jeremiah with cords. And in the dungeon there was no water, but mire: so Jeremiah sunk in the mire.

Now when Ebed-melech, the Ethiopian, one of the eunuchs which was in the king's house, heard that they had put Jeremiah in the dungeon, the king then sitting in the gate of Benjamin, Ebed-melech went forth out of the king's house, and spake to the king, saying, "My lord the king, these men have done evil in all that they have done to Jeremiah, the prophet, whom they have cast into the dungeon; and he is like to die for hunger in the place where he is: for there is no more bread in the city."

Then the king commanded Ebed-melech, the Ethiopian, saying, "Take from hence thirty men with thee, and take up Jeremiah, the prophet, out of the dungeon, before he die."

JEREMIAH IS DRAWN OUT OF THE DUNGEON

So Ebed-melech took the men with him, and went into the house of the king under the treasury, and took thence old cast clouts and old rotten rags, and let them down by cords into the dungeon to Jeremiah. And

Ebed-melech, the Ethiopian, said unto Jeremiah, "Put now these old cast clouts and rotten rags under thine armholes under the cords." And Jeremiah did so. So they drew up Jeremiah with cords, and took him up out of the dungeon: and Jeremiah remained in the court of the prison.

ZEDEKIAH PROMISES TO SAVE THE LIFE OF JEREMIAH

Then Zedekiah, the king, sent, and took Jeremiah, the prophet, unto him into the third entry that is in the house of the LORD: and the king said unto Jeremiah, "I will ask thee a thing; hide nothing from me."

Then Jeremiah said unto Zedekiah, "If I declare it unto thee, wilt thou not surely put me to death? And if I give thee counsel, wilt thou not hearken unto me?"

So Zedekiah, the king, sware secretly unto Jeremiah, saying, "As the LORD liveth, that made us this soul, I will not put thee to death, neither will I give thee into the hand of these men that seek thy life."

Then said Jeremiah unto Zedekiah, "Thus saith the LORD, the God of hosts, the God of Israel: 'If thou wilt assuredly go forth unto the king of Babylon's princes, then thy soul shall live, and this city shall not be burned with fire; and thou shalt live, and thine house: but if thou wilt not go forth to the king of Babylon's princes, then shall this city be given into the hand of the Chaldeans, and they shall burn it with fire, and thou shalt not escape out of their hand.'"

And Zedekiah, the king, said unto Jeremiah, "I am afraid of the Jews that are fallen to the Chaldeans, lest they deliver me into their hand, and they mock me."

But Jeremiah said, "They shall not deliver thee Obey, I beseech thee, the voice of the LORD, which I speak unto thee: so it shall be well unto thee, and thy soul shall live. But if thou refuse to go forth, this is the word that the LORD hath shewed me: and, behold, all the women that are left in the king of Judah's house shall be brought forth to the king of Babylon's princes, and those women shall say, 'Thy friends have set thee on, and have prevailed against thee: thy feet are sunk in the mire, and they are turned away back.' So they shall bring out all thy wives and thy children to the Chaldeans: and thou shalt not escape out of their hand, but shalt be taken by the hand of the king of Babylon: and thou shalt cause this city to be burned with fire."

Then said Zedekiah unto Jeremiah, "Let no man know of these words, and thou shalt not die. But if the princes hear that I have talked with thee, and they come unto thee, and say unto thee, 'Declare unto us now what thou hast said unto the king, hide it not from us, and we will not put thee to death; also what the king said unto thee': then thou shalt say unto them, 'I presented my supplication before the king, that he would not cause me to return to Jonathan's house, to die there.'"

Then came all the princes unto Jeremiah, and asked him: and he told them according to all these words that the king had commanded. So they left off speaking with him; for the matter was not perceived. So Jeremiah abode in the court of the prison until the day that Jerusalem was taken: and he was there when Jerusalem was taken.   —Jeremiah 38:6–28.

THE CAPTURE OF THE CITY BY THE KING OF BABYLON

HOW JEREMIAH WAS SAVED

In the ninth year of Zedekiah, King of Judah, in the tenth month, came Nebuchadnezzar, King of Babylon, and all his army against Jerusalem, and they besieged it.

And in the eleventh year of Zedekiah, in the fourth month, the ninth day of the month, the city was broken up. And all the princes of the king of Babylon came in, and sat in the middle gate, even Nergal-sharezer, Samgar-nebo, Sarsechim, Rab-saris, Rab-mag, with all the residue of the princes of the king of Babylon.

And it came to pass, that when Zedekiah, the king of Judah, saw them, and all the men of war, then they fled, and went forth out of the city by night, by the way of the king's garden, by the gate betwixt the two walls: and he went out the way of the plain. But the Chaldeans' army pursued after them, and overtook Zedekiah in the plains of Jericho: and when they had taken him, they brought him up to Nebuchadnezzar, King of Babylon, to Riblah in the land of Hamath, where he gave judgment upon him. Then the king of Babylon slew the sons of Zedekiah in Riblah before his eyes: also the king of Babylon slew all the nobles of Judah. Moreover he put out Zedekiah's eyes, and bound him with chains, to carry him to Babylon. And the Chaldeans burned the king's house, and the houses of the people, with fire, and brake down the walls of Jerusalem. Then Nebuzar-adan, the captain of the guard, carried away captive into Babylon the remnant of the people that remained in the city, and those that fell away, that fell to him, with the rest of the people that remained. But Nebuzar-adan, the captain of the guard, left the poor of the people, which had nothing, in the land of Judah, and gave them vineyards and fields at the same time.

THE KING OF BABYLON PROTECTS JEREMIAH

Now Nebuchadnezzar, King of Babylon, gave charge concerning Jeremiah to Nebuzar-adan, the captain of the guard, saying, "Take him, and look well to him, and do him no harm; but do unto him even as he shall say unto thee."

So Nebuzar-adan, the captain of the guard, sent, and Nebushasban, Rab-saris, and Nergal-sharezer, Rab-mag, and all the king of Babylon's princes; even they sent, and took Jeremiah out of the court of the prison, and committed him unto Gedaliah, the son of Ahikam, the son of Shaphan, that he should carry him home: so he dwelt among the people.

Now the word of the LORD came unto Jeremiah, while he was shut up in the court of the prison, saying, "Go and speak to Ebed-melech, the Ethiopian, saying, 'Thus saith the LORD of hosts, the God of Israel: "Behold, I will bring my words upon this city for evil, and not for good; and they shall be accomplished in that day before thee. But I will deliver thee in that day," saith the LORD: "and thou shalt not be given into the hand of the men of whom thou art afraid. For I will surely deliver thee, and thou shalt not fall by the sword, but thy life shall be for a prey unto thee: because thou hast put thy trust in me," saith the LORD.'"   Jeremiah 39.

JUDAH A VASSAL-STATE

THE CAPTAIN OF THE GUARD RELEASES JEREMIAH

And the captain of the guard took Jeremiah, and said unto him, "The LORD thy God hath pronounced this evil upon this place. Now the LORD hath brought it, and done according as he hath said: because ye have sinned against the LORD, and have not obeyed his voice, therefore this thing is come upon you. And now, behold, I loose thee this day from the chains which were upon thine hand. If it seem good unto thee to come with me into Babylon, come; and I will look well unto thee: but if it seem ill unto thee to come with me into Babylon, forbear: behold, all the land is before thee: whither it seemeth good and convenient for thee to go, thither go."

Now while he was not yet gone back, he said, "Go back also to Gedaliah, the son of Ahikam, the son of

GROTTO OF JEREMIAH

Photograph by W. A. Pottenger expressly for The Book of Life

This is probably an old quarry. Since the Fifteenth Century there has been a tradition that this is the tomb of Jeremiah.

Shaphan, whom the king of Babylon hath made governor over the cities of Judah, and dwell with him among the people: or go wheresoever it seemeth convenient unto thee to go." So the captain of the guard gave him victuals and a reward, and let him go.

JEREMIAH GOES TO MIZPAH

Then went Jeremiah unto Gedaliah, the son of Ahikam, to Mizpah; and dwelt with him among the people that were left in the land. Now when all the captains of the forces which were in the fields, even they and their men, heard that the king of Babylon had made Gedaliah, the son of Ahikam, governor in the land, and had committed unto him men, and women, and children, and of the poor of the land, of them that were not carried away captive to Babylon; then they came to Gedaliah to Mizpah, even Ishmael, the son of Nethaniah, and Johanan and Jonathan, the sons of Kareah, and Seraiah, the son of Tanhumeth, and the sons of Ephai, the Netophathite, and Jezaniah, the son of a Maachathite, they and their men. And Gedaliah, the son of Ahikam, the son of Shaphan, sware unto them and to their men, saying, "Fear not to serve the Chaldeans: dwell in the land, and serve the king of Babylon, and it shall be well with you. As for me, behold, I will dwell at Mizpah, to serve the Chaldeans, which will come unto us: but ye, gather ye wine, and summer fruits, and oil, and put them in your vessels, and dwell in your cities that ye have taken."

Likewise when all the Jews that were in Moab, and among the Ammonites, and in Edom, and that were in all the countries, heard that the king of Babylon had left a remnant of Judah, and that he had set over them Gedaliah, the son of Ahikam, the son of Shaphan; even all the Jews returned out of all places whither they were driven, and came to the land of Judah, to Gedaliah, unto Mizpah, and gathered wine and summer fruits very much.

Moreover Johanan, the son of Kareah, and all the captains of the forces that were in the fields, came to Gedaliah to Mizpah, and said unto him, "Dost thou certainly know that Baalis, the king of the Ammonites, hath sent Ishmael, the son of Nethaniah, to slay thee?"

But Gedaliah, the son of Ahikam, believed them not.

Then Johanan, the son of Kareah, spake to Gedaliah in Mizpah secretly, saying, "Let me go, I pray thee, and I will slay Ishmael, the son of Nethaniah, and no man shall know it: wherefore should he slay thee, that all the Jews which are gathered unto thee should be scattered, and the remnant in Judah perish?"

But Gedaliah, the son of Ahikam, said unto Johanan, the son of Kareah, "Thou shalt not do this thing: for thou speakest falsely of Ishmael." —Jeremiah 40.

ISHMAEL AND TEN MEN SLAY GEDALIAH, THE GOVERNOR

Now it came to pass in the seventh month, that Ishmael, the son of Nethaniah, the son of Elishama, of the seed royal, and the princes of the king, even ten men with him, came unto Gedaliah, the son of Ahikam, to Mizpah; and there they did eat bread together in Mizpah. Then arose Ishmael, the son of Nethaniah, and the ten men that were with him, and smote Gedaliah, the son of Ahikam, the son of Shaphan, with the sword, and slew him, whom the king of Babylon had made governor over the land. Ishmael also slew all the Jews that were with him, even with Gedaliah, at Mizpah, and the Chaldeans that were found there, and the men of war. And it came to pass the second day after he had slain Gedaliah, and no man knew it, that there came certain from Shechem, from Shiloh, and from Samaria, even fourscore men, having their beards shaven, and their clothes rent, and having cut themselves, with offerings and incense in their hand, to bring them to the house of the LORD. And Ishmael, the son of Nethaniah, went forth from Mizpah to meet them, weeping all along as he went: and it came to pass, as he met them, he said unto them, "Come to Gedaliah, the son of Ahikam."

And it was so, when they came into the midst of the city, that Ishmael, the son of Nethaniah, slew them, and cast them into the midst of the pit, he, and the men that were with him. But ten men were found among them that said unto Ishmael, "Slay us not: for we have treasures in the field, of wheat, and of barley, and of oil, and of honey." So he forbare, and slew them not among their brethren.

Now the pit wherein Ishmael had cast all the dead bodies of the men, whom he had slain because of Gedaliah, was it which Asa, the king, had made for fear of Baasha, King of Israel: and Ishmael, the son of Nethaniah, filled it with them that were slain.

ISHMAEL TAKES THE PEOPLE IN MIZPAH CAPTIVE

Then Ishmael carried away captive all the residue of the people that were in Mizpah, even the king's daughters, and all the people that remained in Mizpah, whom Nebuzar-adan, the captain of the guard, had committed to Gedaliah, the son of Ahikam: and Ishmael, the son of Nethaniah, carried them away captive, and departed to go over to the Ammonites.

But when Johanan, the son of Kareah, and all the captains of the forces that were with him, heard of all the evil that Ishmael, the son of Nethaniah, had done, then they took all the men, and went to fight with Ishmael, the son of Nethaniah, and found him by the great waters that are in Gibeon. Now it came to pass, that when all the people which were with Ishmael saw Johanan, the son of Kareah, and all the captains of the forces that were with him, then they were glad. So all the people that Ishmael had carried away captive from Mizpah cast about and returned, and went unto Johanan, the son of Kareah.

ISHMAEL IS DEFEATED AND ESCAPES WITH EIGHT MEN

But Ishmael, the son of Nethaniah, escaped from Johanan with eight men, and went to the Ammonites.

Then took Johanan, the son of Kareah, and all the captains of the forces that were with him, all the remnant of the people whom he had recovered from Ishmael, the son of Nethaniah, from Mizpah, after that he had slain Gedaliah, the son of Ahikam, even mighty men of war, and the women, and the children, and the eunuchs, whom he had brought again from Gibeon: and they departed, and dwelt in the habitation of Chimham, which is by Beth-lehem, to go to enter into Egypt, because of the Chaldeans: for they were afraid of them, because Ishmael, the son of Nethaniah, had slain Gedaliah, the son of Ahikam, whom the king of Babylon made governor in the land.   —Jeremiah 41.

THE PEOPLE PLAN TO GO TO EGYPT; THEY ASK JEREMIAH'S ADVICE

Then all the captains of the forces, and Johanan, the son of Kareah, and Jezaniah, the son of Hoshaiah, and all the people from the least even unto the greatest, came near, and said unto Jeremiah, the prophet, "Let, we beseech thee, our supplication be accepted before thee, and pray for us unto the LORD thy God, even for all this remnant; for we are left but a few of many, as thine eyes do behold us: that the LORD thy God may shew us the way wherein we may walk, and the thing that we may do."

Then Jeremiah, the prophet, said unto them, "I have heard you; behold, I will pray unto the LORD your God according to your words and it shall come to pass, that whatsoever thing the LORD shall answer you, I will declare it unto you; I will keep nothing back from you."

Then they said to Jeremiah, "The LORD be a true and faithful witness between us, if we do not even according to all things for the which the LORD thy God shall send thee to us. Whether it be good, or whether it be evil,

PYRAMIDS AND SPHINX

THE exile of Jeremiah in the land of the old oppression, while his people were in captivity in Babylon, is one of the interesting and pathetic incidents of Hebrew history.

we will obey the voice of the LORD our God, to whom we send thee; that it may be well with us, when we obey the voice of the LORD our God."

And it came to pass after ten days, that the word of the LORD came unto Jeremiah. Then called he Johanan, the son of Kareah, and all the captains of the forces which were with him, and all the people from the least even to the greatest, and said unto them, "Thus saith the LORD, the God of Israel, unto whom ye sent me to present your supplication before him: 'If ye will still abide in this land, then will I build you, and not pull you down, and I will plant you, and not pluck you up: for I repent me of the evil that I have done unto you. Be not afraid of the king of Babylon, of whom ye are afraid; be not afraid of him,' saith the LORD: 'for I am with you to save you, and to deliver you from his hand. And I will shew mercies unto you, that he may have mercy upon you, and cause you to return to your own land.'

JEREMIAH WARNS THE PEOPLE NOT TO GO INTO EGYPT

"But if ye say, 'We will not dwell in this land, neither obey the voice of the LORD your God,' saying, 'No; but we will go into the land of Egypt, where we shall see no war, nor hear the sound of the trumpet, nor have hunger of bread; and there will we dwell:" now therefore hear the word of the LORD, ye remnant of Judah: thus saith the LORD of hosts, the God of Israel: 'If ye wholly set your faces to enter into Egypt, and go to sojourn there; then it shall come to pass, that the sword, which ye feared, shall overtake you there in the land of Egypt, and the famine, whereof ye were afraid, shall follow close after you there in Egypt; and there ye shall die. So shall it be with all the men that set their faces to go into Egypt to sojourn there; they shall die by the sword, by the famine, and by the pestilence: and none of them shall remain or escape from the evil that I will bring upon them.'

"For thus saith the LORD of hosts, the God of Israel: 'As mine anger and my fury hath been poured forth upon the inhabitants of Jerusalem; so shall my fury be poured forth upon you, when ye shall enter into Egypt: and ye shall be an execration, and an astonishment, and a curse, and a reproach; and ye shall see this place no more.'

"The LORD hath said concerning you, 'O ye remnant of Judah; go ye not into Egypt: know certainly that I have admonished you this day.' For ye dissembled in your hearts, when ye sent me unto the LORD your God, saying, 'Pray for us unto the LORD our God; and according unto all that the LORD our God shall say, so declare unto us, and we will do it.' And now I have this day declared it to you; but ye have not obeyed the voice of the LORD your God, nor any thing for the which he hath sent me unto you. Now therefore know certainly that ye shall die by the sword, by the famine, and by the pestilence, in the place whither ye desire to go and to sojourn."

—Jeremiah 42.

The People Go Down to Egypt in Spite of the Warning of Jeremiah and He Goes With Them

And it came to pass, that when Jeremiah had made an end of speaking unto all the people all the words of the LORD their God, for which the LORD their God had sent him to them, even all these words, then spake Azariah, the son of Hoshaiah, and Johanan, the son of Kareah, and all the proud men, saying unto Jeremiah, "Thou speakest falsely: the LORD our God hath not sent thee to say, 'Go not into Egypt to sojourn there': but Baruch, the son of Neriah, setteth thee on against us, **for**

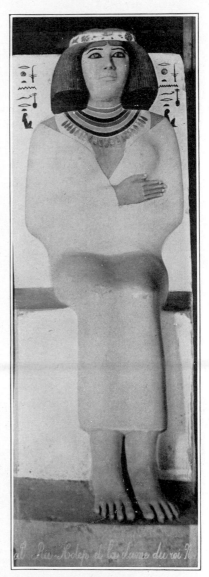

A PRINCE AND PRINCESS OF OLD EGYPT

By courtesy of the British Museum, London

The princess in the arrangement of her hair and her dress has a distinctly
modern look!

to deliver us into the hand of the Chaldeans, that they might put us to death, and carry us away captives into Babylon."

So Johanan, the son of Kareah, and all the captains of the forces, and all the people, obeyed not the voice of the LORD, to dwell in the land of Judah. But Johanan, the son of Kareah, and all the captains of the forces, took all the remnant of Judah, that were returned from all nations, whither they had been driven, to dwell in the land of Judah; even men, and women, and children, and the king's daughters, and every person that Nebuzaradan, the captain of the guard, had left with Gedaliah, the son of Ahikam, the son of Shaphan, and Jeremiah, the prophet, and Baruch, the son of Neriah. So they came into the land of Egypt: for they obeyed not the voice of the LORD: thus came they even to Tahpanhes.

—Jeremiah 43:1-7.

PROPHECIES FROM EGYPT

THE LESSONS OF THE STONES IN THE CLAY OF THE BRICK KILN

Then came the word of the LORD unto Jeremiah in Tahpanhes, saying, "Take great stones in thine hand, and hide them in the clay in the brickkiln, which is at the entry of Pharaoh's house in Tahpanhes, in the sight of the men of Judah; and say unto them, 'Thus saith the LORD of hosts, the God of Israel: "Behold, I will send and take Nebuchadnezzar, the king of Babylon, my servant, and will set his throne upon these stones that I have hid; and he shall spread his royal pavilion over them. And when he cometh, he shall smite the land of Egypt, and deliver such as are for death to death; and such as are for captivity to captivity; and such as are for the sword to the sword. And I will kindle a fire in the houses of the

Queen Teta-Khart

By courtesy of the British Museum, London

THIS queen of ancient Egypt reigned a thousand years before Jeremiah, a dauntless old man, went down to the land of the Nile to spend his last days in exile. At the time of Jeremiah, Egypt had been defeated by Babylon at Carchemish, and the rule of the native princes was drawing to a close.

"He shall smite the land of Egypt and deliver such as are for death to death, and such as are for captivity to captivity, and such as are for the sword to the sword." — *Jeremiah 43:11.*

gods of Egypt; and he shall burn them, and carry them away captives: and he shall array himself with the land of Egypt, as a shepherd putteth on his garment; and he shall go forth from thence in peace. He shall break also the images of Beth-shemesh, that is in the land of Egypt; and the houses of the gods of the Egyptians shall he burn with fire.""" —Jeremiah 43:8-13.

THE PROPHECY AGAINST EGYPT

The word of the LORD which came to Jeremiah, the prophet, against the Gentiles; against Egypt, against the army of Pharaoh-necho, King of Egypt, which was by the river Euphrates in Carchemish, which Nebuchadnezzar, King of Babylon, smote in the fourth year of Jehoiakim, the son of Josiah, King of Judah.

"Order ye the buckler and shield, and draw near to battle. Harness the horses; and get up, ye horsemen

HEAD OF THOTHMES III
(1501–1447 B.C.)

By courtesy of the British Museum, London

This king was one of the most powerful of the Pharaohs. He conquered Syria by repeated raids and brought many Canaanites captive to Egypt before the days of Joseph and Moses, and yet his glory passed. "Pharaoh is but a noise, he hath passed the time appointed."

and stand forth with your helmets; furbish the spears, and put on the brigandines. Wherefore have I seen them dismayed and turned away back? And their mighty ones are beaten down, and are fled apace, and look not back: for fear was round about," saith the LORD.

"Let not the swift flee away, nor the mighty man escape; they shall stumble, and fall toward the north by the river Euphrates. Who is this that cometh up as a flood, whose waters are moved as the rivers? Egypt riseth up like a flood, and his waters are moved like the rivers; and he saith, 'I will go up, and will cover the earth; and I will destroy the city and the inhabitants thereof.' Come up, ye horses; and rage, ye chariots; and let the mighty men come forth; the Ethiopians and the Libyans, that handle the shield; and the Lydians, that handle and bend the bow. For this is the day of the Lord GOD of hosts, a day of vengeance, that he may avenge him of his adversaries: and the sword shall devour, and it shall be satiate and made drunk with their blood: for the Lord GOD of hosts hath a sacrifice in the north country by the river Euphrates. Go up into Gilead, and take balm, O virgin, the daughter of Egypt: in vain shalt thou use many medicines; for thou shalt not be cured. The nations have heard of thy shame, and thy cry hath filled the land: for the mighty man hath stumbled against the mighty, and they are fallen both together.

THE WORD THAT THE LORD SPAKE TO JEREMIAH, THE
PROPHET, HOW NEBUCHADNEZZAR, KING OF BABYLON,
SHOULD COME AND SMITE THE LAND OF EGYPT

"Declare ye in Egypt, and publish in Migdol, and publish in Noph and in Tahpanhes: say ye, 'Stand fast, and prepare thee; for the sword shall devour round about thee.' Why are thy valiant men swept away?

They stood not, because the LORD did drive them. He made many to fall, yea, one fell upon another: and they said, 'Arise, and let us go again to our own people, and to the land of our nativity, from the oppressing sword.' They did cry there, 'Pharaoh, King of Egypt, is but a noise; he hath passed the time appointed.'

"As I live," saith the king, whose name is the LORD of hosts, "surely as Tabor is among the mountains, and as Carmel by the sea, so shall he come. O thou daughter dwelling in Egypt, furnish thyself to go into captivity: for Noph shall be waste and desolate without an inhabitant. Egypt is like a very fair heifer, but destruction cometh; it cometh out of the north. Also her hired men are in the midst of her like fatted bullocks; for they also are turned back, and are fled away together: they did not stand, because the day of their calamity was come upon them, and the time of their visitation. The voice thereof shall go like a serpent; for they shall march with an army, and come against her with axes, as hewers of wood. They shall cut down her forest," saith the LORD, "though it cannot be searched; because they are more than the grasshoppers, and are innumerable. The daughter of Egypt shall be confounded; she shall be delivered into the hand of the people of the north."

The LORD of hosts, the God of Israel, saith: "Behold, I will punish the multitude of No, and Pharaoh, and Egypt, with their gods, and their kings; even Pharaoh, and all them that trust in him: and I will deliver them into the hand of those that seek their lives, and into the hand of Nebuchadnezzar, King of Babylon, and into the hand of his servants: and afterward it shall be inhabited, as in the days of old," saith the LORD.

"But fear not thou, O my servant Jacob, and be not dismayed, O Israel: for, behold, I will save thee from afar off, and thy seed from the land of their captivity; and Jacob shall return, and be in rest and at ease, and none shall make him afraid. Fear thou not, O Jacob, my servant," saith the LORD: "for I am with thee; for I will make a full end of all the nations whither I have driven thee: but I will not make a full end of thee, but correct thee in measure; yet will I not leave thee wholly unpunished."

—Jeremiah 46.

THE PROPHECY AGAINST BABYLON

Thus saith the LORD: "Behold, I will raise up against Babylon, and against them that dwell in the midst of them that rise up against me, a destroying wind; and will send unto Babylon fanners, that shall fan her, and shall empty her land: for in the day of trouble they shall be against her round about. Against him that bendeth let the archer bend his bow, and against him that lifteth himself up in his brigandine: and spare ye not her young men; destroy ye utterly all her host. Thus the slain shall fall in the land of the Chaldeans, and they that are thrust through in her streets. For Israel hath not been forsaken, nor Judah of his God, of the LORD of hosts; though their land was filled with sin against the Holy One of Israel. Flee out of the midst of Babylon, and deliver every man his soul: be not cut off in her iniquity; for this is the time of the LORD's vengeance; he will render unto her a recompence. Babylon hath been a golden cup in the LORD's hand, that made all the earth drunken: the nations have drunken of her wine; therefore the nations are mad. Babylon is suddenly fallen and destroyed: howl for her; take balm for her pain, if so be she may be healed. We would have healed Babylon, but she is not healed: forsake her, and let us go every one into his own country: for her judgment reacheth unto heaven, and is lifted up even to the skies. The LORD hath brought forth our righteousness: come, and let us declare in Zion the word of the LORD our God. Make bright the arrows; gather the shields: the LORD hath raised up the spirit of the kings of the Medes: for his device is against Babylon, to destroy it; because it is the vengeance of the LORD, the vengeance of his temple.

"Set up the standard upon the walls of Babylon, make the watch strong, set up the watchmen, prepare the ambushes: for the LORD hath both devised and done that which he spake against the inhabitants of Babylon. O thou that dwellest upon many waters, abundant in treasures, thine end is come, and the measure of thy covetousness. The LORD of hosts hath sworn by himself, saying, 'Surely I will fill thee with men, as with caterpillers; and they shall lift up a shout against thee.' He hath made the earth by his power, he hath established the world by his wisdom, and hath stretched out the heaven by his understanding. When he uttereth his voice, there is a multitude of waters in the heavens; and he causeth the vapours to ascend from the ends of the earth: he maketh lightnings with rain, and bringeth forth the wind out of his treasures. Every man is brutish by his knowledge; every founder is confounded by the graven image: for his molten image is falsehood, and there is no breath in them. They are vanity, the work of errors: in the time of their visitation they shall perish. The portion of Jacob is not like them; for he is the former of all things: and Israel is the rod of his inheritance: the LORD of hosts is his name. Thou art my battle-ax and weapons of war: for with thee will I break in pieces the nations, and with thee will I destroy kingdoms; and with thee will I break in pieces the horse and his rider; and with thee will I break in pieces the chariot and his rider; with thee also will I break in pieces man and woman; and with thee will

I break in pieces old and young; and with thee will I break in pieces the young man and the maid; I will also break in pieces with thee the shepherd and his flock; and with thee will I break in pieces the husbandman and his yoke of oxen; and with thee will I break in pieces captains and rulers. And I will render unto Babylon and to all the inhabitants of Chaldea all their evil that they have done in Zion in your sight," saith the Lord.

"Behold, I am against thee, O destroying mountain," saith the Lord, which destroyest all the earth: "and I will stretch out mine hand upon thee, and roll thee down from the rocks, and will make thee a burnt mountain. And they shall not take of thee a stone for a corner, nor a stone for foundations; but thou shalt be desolate forever," saith the Lord.

"Set ye up a standard in the land, blow the trumpet among the nations, prepare the nations against her, call together against her the kingdoms of Ararat, Minni, and Ashchenaz; appoint a captain against her; cause the horses to come up as the rough caterpillers. Prepare against her the nations with the kings of the Medes, the captains thereof, and all the rulers thereof, and all the land of his dominion. And the land shall tremble and sorrow: for every purpose of the Lord shall be performed against Babylon, to make the land of Babylon a desolation without an inhabitant. The mighty men of Babylon have foreborn to fight, they have remained in their holds: their might hath failed; they became as women: they have burned her dwellingplaces; her bars are broken. One post shall run to meet another, and one messenger to meet another, to shew the king of Babylon that his city is taken at one end; and that the passages are stopped, and the reeds they have burned with fire, and the men of war are affrighted."

For thus saith the LORD of hosts, the God of Israel: "The daughter of Babylon is like a threshing-floor, it is time to thresh her: yet a little while, and the time of her harvest shall come. Nebuchadnezzar, the king of Babylon, hath devoured me, he hath crushed me, he hath made me an empty vessel, he hath swallowed me up like a dragon, he hath filled his belly with my delicates, he hath cast me out. The violence done to me and to my flesh be upon Babylon, shall the inhabitant of Zion say; and my blood upon the inhabitants of Chaldea, shall Jerusalem say."

Therefore thus saith the LORD: "Behold, I will plead thy cause, and take vengeance for thee; and I will dry up her sea, and make her springs dry. And Babylon shall become heaps, a dwellingplace for dragons, an astonishment, and an hissing, without an inhabitant. They shall roar together like lions: they shall yell as lions' whelps. In their heat I will make their feasts, and I will make them drunken, that they may rejoice, and sleep a perpetual sleep, and not wake," saith the LORD. "I will bring them down like lambs to the slaughter, like rams with he goats. How is Sheshach taken! And how is the praise of the whole earth surprised! How is Babylon become an astonishment among the nations! The sea is come up upon Babylon: she is covered with the multitude of the waves thereof. Her cities are a desolation, a dry land, and a wilderness, a land wherein no man dwelleth, neither doth any son of man pass thereby. And I will punish Bel in Babylon, and I will bring forth out of his mouth that which he hath swallowed up: and the nations shall not flow together any more unto him: yea, the wall of Babylon shall fall. My people, go ye out of the midst of her, and deliver ye every man his soul from the fierce anger of the LORD. And lest your heart faint, and ye fear for the rumour that shall be heard in the land; a rumour shall both come one year, and after that in another year shall come a rumour, and violence in the land, ruler against ruler. Therefore, behold, the days come, that I will do judgment upon the graven images of Babylon: and her whole land shall be confounded, and all her slain shall fall in the midst of her. Then the heaven and the earth, and all that is therein, shall sing for Babylon: for the spoilers shall come unto her from the north," saith the LORD.

"As Babylon hath caused the slain of Israel to fall, so at Babylon shall fall the slain of all the earth. Ye that have escaped the sword, go away, stand not still: remember the LORD afar off, and let Jerusalem come into your mind. We are confounded, because we have heard reproach: shame hath covered our faces: for strangers are come into the sanctuaries of the LORD's house. Wherefore, behold, the days come," saith the LORD, "that I will do judgment upon her graven images: and through all her land the wounded shall groan. Though Babylon should mount up to heaven, and though she should fortify the height of her strength, yet from me shall spoilers come unto her," saith the LORD. "A sound of a cry cometh from Babylon, and great destruction from the land of the Chaldeans: because the LORD hath spoiled Babylon, and destroyed out of her the great voice; when her waves do roar like great waters, a noise of their voice is uttered: because the spoiler is come upon her, even upon Babylon, and her mighty men are taken, every one of their bows is broken: for the Lord GOD of recompences shall surely requite. And I will make drunk her princes, and her wise men, her captains, and her rulers, and her mighty men: and they shall sleep a perpetual sleep, and not wake," saith the King, whose name is the LORD of hosts.

—Jeremiah 51:1–57.

Ezekiel—Detail of Sistine Chapel Ceiling

By Michelangelo Buonarroti (1475-1564)
In the Sistine Chapel of the Vatican, Rome
Photograph by Anderson, Rome

THIS grandly tempestuous figure of the prophet Ezekiel is another of the magnificent characterizations painted by Michelangelo in the Sistine Chapel at Rome. This is just one of hundreds of beings taking part in that marvelous representation of the Christian drama of redemption. Spread on the vast expanse of ceiling is the whole story of the Creation, the Fall, the promised Salvation, and man's continued frailty. The drama closes with Michelangelo's LAST JUDGMENT on the adjoining altar wall. There Christ separates eternally the saved from the damned, echoing the definitive gesture with which God separates light from darkness in the Creation scene overhead.

The fiery Ezekiel is one of an impressive chorus of twelve colossal figures representing prophets and sibyls. They are all conceived as great presences who have seen into divine mysteries. Their size, as Hawthorne has well said, is "necessarily so gigantic because the weight of thought within them is so massive." The very vehemence of Ezekiel's gesture proclaims the power and energy that characterized his spiritual life and his writings. We know that this was a man who had something to say in life, and who said it with all the fervor of an inspired mind.

The stories of the prophets are among the most dramatic in the great gallery of Biblical personalities. Michelangelo's portrayals as well as John Singer Sargent's (see page 412 for his Ezekiel) help us to visualize the living, human persons. Others of Michelangelo's paintings are shown on pages 66, 358, 402 and 422.

EZECHIEL

Ezekiel

When, in 597 B.C., large portions of the upper classes of Judah were deported to Babylon, they entered upon an entirely new life. Economically and socially they fared much better than ordinary captives of oriental wars. They were not sold in the slave markets and scattered, but were treated as enforced colonists, given villages on the fertile Babylonian plain, and allowed to develop their own social and economic life as best they could. Doubtless the new conditions brought certain hardships, and the longing for friends and for the sight of the hills about Jerusalem finds occasional pathetic expression in their literature. But deeper than this homesickness, known to all emigrants the world over, and far more dangerous to the national existence, was the religious peril. How could the Hebrews individually and as a nation keep their faith in Jehovah under these difficult conditions?

There was a young priest among the exiles, Ezekiel, a disciple of Jeremiah, who pondered these problems during five years, and then in 592 B.C., began to give the solution as he said God had given it to him. At intervals for twenty-two years, till 570 B.C., he came forward with messages for the people. These messages all concerned the problem of how to hold faith in God amid the new conditions. He was, like Jeremiah, a patriot, but he could not hope to influence events in Jerusalem. His work lay with the exile community in Babylon; but he did not regard that work as unimportant. Like Jeremiah, he recognized that the exiles were the flower of the nation, and he believed that the hope of the future lay with them.

The style is mostly prosaic, sometimes in the more emotional parts rising into poetry. It is homely, plain, and full of words. One characteristic is the abundant use of vivid parables, allegories, and enacted prophecy. Vision plays a large part, often evidently as a literary device. Babylonian winged images appear in the visions, and the Babylonian influence is also seen in the careful scheme of dating by year and month, so different from the earlier prophetic books.

The Prophecy of Ezekiel

THE CALL OF EZEKIEL: THE VISION OF THE FOUR LIV-
ING CREATURES WHICH EZEKIEL, THE CAPTIVE SAW

NOW it came to pass in the thirtieth year, in the
fourth month, in the fifth day of the month,
as I was among the captives by the river of
Chebar, that the heavens were opened, and I
saw visions of God. In the fifth day of the month,
which was the fifth year of King Jehoiachin's captivity,
the word of the LORD came expressly unto Ezekiel,
the priest, the son of Buzi, in the land of the Chaldeans
by the river Chebar; and the hand of the LORD was there
upon him.

And I looked, and, behold, a whirlwind came out of
the north, a great cloud, and a fire unfolding itself, and a
brightness was about it, and out of the midst thereof as
the colour of amber, out of the midst of the fire. Also
out of the midst thereof came the likeness of four living
creatures. And this was their appearance; they had the
likeness of a man. And every one had four faces, and
every one had four wings. And their feet were straight
feet; and the sole of their feet was like the sole of a calf's
foot: and they sparkled like the colour of burnished brass.
And they had the hands of a man under their wings on
their four sides; and they four had their faces and their
wings. Their wings were joined one to another; they
turned not when they went; they went every one straight
forward. As for the likeness of their faces, they four
had the face of a man, and the face of a lion, on the right
side: and they four had the face of an ox on the left side;

they four also had the face of an eagle. Thus were their
faces: and their wings were stretched upward; two
wings of every one were joined one to another, and two
covered their bodies. And they went every one straight
forward: whither the spirit was to go, thcy wcnt, and
they turned not when they went. As for the likeness
of the living creatures, their appearance was like burning
coals of fire, and like the appearance of lamps: it went
up and down among the living creatures; and the fire
was bright, and out of the fire went forth lightning.
And the living creatures ran and returned as the appearance of a flash of lightning.

Now as I beheld the living creatures, behold one wheel
upon the earth by the living creatures, with his four
faces. The appearance of the wheels and their work was
like unto the colour of a beryl: and they four had one
likeness: and their appearance and their work was as it
were a wheel in the middle of a wheel. When they went,
they went upon their four sides: and they turned not
when they went. As for their rings, they were so high
that they were dreadful; and their rings were full of
eyes round about them four. And when the living creatures went, the wheels went by them: and when the living
creatures were lifted up from the earth, the wheels were
lifted up. Whithersoever the spirit was to go, they went,
thither was their spirit to go; and the wheels were lifted
up over against them: for the spirit of the living creature
was in the wheels. When those went, these went; and
when those stood, these stood; and when those were
lifted up from the earth, the wheels were lifted up over
against them: for the spirit of the living creature was in
the wheels. And the likeness of the firmament upon the
heads of the living creature was as the colour of the terrible crystal, stretched forth over their heads above. And

under the firmament were their wings straight, the one
toward the other: every one had two, which covered
on this side, and every one had two, which covered on
that side, their bodies. And when they went, I heard
the noise of their wings, like the noise of great waters,
as the voice of the Almighty, the voice of speech, as the
noise of an host: when they stood, they let down their
wings. And there was a voice from the firmament that
was over their heads, when they stood, and had let down
their wings.

And above the firmament that was over their heads
was the likeness of a throne, as the appearance of a
sapphire stone: and upon the likeness of the throne was
the likeness as the appearance of a man above upon it.
And I saw as the colour of amber, as the appearance of
fire round about within it, from the appearance of his
loins even upward, and from the appearance of his
loins even downward, I saw as it were the appearance of
fire, and it had brightness round about. As the appearance of the bow that is in the cloud in the day of rain,
so was the appearance of the brightness round about.
This was the appearance of the likeness of the glory of the
LORD. And when I saw it, I fell upon my face, and I
heard a voice of one that spake.   —Ezekiel 1.

EZEKIEL'S COMMISSION

And he said unto me, "Son of man, stand upon thy
feet, and I will speak unto thee." And the spirit entered
into me when he spake unto me, and set me upon my
feet, that I heard him that spake unto me. And he said
unto me, "Son of man, I send thee to the children of
Israel, to a rebellious nation that hath rebelled against
me: they and their fathers have transgressed against me,
even unto this very day. For they are impudent children

and stiffhearted. I do send thee unto them; and thou shalt say unto them, 'Thus saith the Lord God.' And they, whether they will hear, or whether they will forbear, for they are a rebellious house, yet shall know that there hath been a prophet among them. And thou, son of man, be not afraid of them, neither be afraid of their words, though briers and thorns be with thee, and thou dost dwell among scorpions: be not afraid of their words, nor be dismayed at their looks, though they be a rebellious house. And thou shalt speak my words unto them, whether they will hear, or whether they will forbear: for they are most rebellious. But thou, son of man, hear what I say unto thee: be not thou rebellious like that rebellious house: open thy mouth, and eat that I give thee."

THE VISION OF THE BOOK WHICH THE PROPHET ATE AND IT WAS AS SWEET AS HONEY

And when I looked, behold, an hand was sent unto me; and, lo, a roll of a book was therein; and he spread it before me; and it was written within and without: and there was written therein lamentations, and mourning, and woe.

Moreover he said unto me, "Son of man, eat that thou findest; eat this roll, and go speak unto the house of Israel." So I opened my mouth, and he caused me to eat that roll. And he said unto me, "Son of man, cause thy belly to eat, and fill thy bowels with this roll that I give thee." Then did I eat it; and it was in my mouth as honey for sweetness. —Ezekiel 2; 3:1–3.

EZEKIEL'S COMMISSION IS REPEATED

And he said unto me, "Son of man, Go, get thee unto the house of Israel, and speak with my words unto

them. For thou art not sent to a people of a strange
speech and of an hard language, but to the house of
Israel; not to many people of a strange speech and of
an hard language, whose words thou canst not understand. Surely, had I sent thee to them, they would have
hearkened unto thee. But the house of Israel will not
hearken unto thee; for they will not hearken unto me:
for all the house of Israel are impudent and hard-hearted.
Behold, I have made thy face strong against their faces,
and thy forehead strong against their foreheads. As an
adamant harder than flint have I made thy forehead.
Fear them not, neither be dismayed at their looks, though
they be a rebellious house."

Moreover he said unto me, "Son of man, all my words
that I shall speak unto thee receive in thine heart, and
hear with thine ears. And go, get thee to them of the
captivity, unto the children of thy people, and speak
unto them, and tell them, 'Thus saith the Lord GoD';
whether they will hear, or whether they will forbear."

Then the spirit took me up, and I heard behind me
a voice of a great rushing, saying, "Blessed be the glory
of the LORD from his place." I heard also the noise of
the wings of the living creatures that touched one another,
and the noise of the wheels over against them, and a noise
of a great rushing. So the spirit lifted me up, and took
me away, and I went in bitterness, in the heat of my
spirit; but the hand of the LORD was strong upon me.

EZEKIEL RECEIVES A FURTHER COMMAND TO WARN
THE WICKED

Then I came to them of the captivity at Tel-abib, that
dwelt by the river of Chebar, and I sat where they sat,
and remained there astonished among them seven days.
And it came to pass at the end of seven days, that the

word of the LORD came unto me, saying, "Son of man,
I have made thee a watchman unto the house of Israel:
therefore hear the word at my mouth, and give them
warning from me. When I say unto the wicked, 'Thou
shalt surely die'; and thou givest him not warning, nor
speakest to warn the wicked from his wicked way, to save
his life; the same wicked man shall die in his iniquity;
but his blood will I require at thine hand. Yet if thou
warn the wicked, and he turn not from his wickedness,
nor from his wicked way, he shall die in his iniquity;
but thou hast delivered thy soul. Again, when a righteous
man doth turn from his righteousness, and commit
iniquity, and I lay a stumblingblock before him, he shall
die: because thou hast not given him warning, he shall
die in his sin, and his righteousness which he hath done
shall not be remembered; but his blood will I require at
thine hand. Nevertheless if thou warn the righteous
man, that the righteous sin not, and he doth not sin, he
shall surely live, because he is warned; also thou hast
delivered thy soul."

And the hand of the LORD was there upon me; and
he said unto me, "Arise, go forth into the plain, and I
will there talk with thee." Then I arose, and went forth
into the plain: and, behold, the glory of the LORD stood
there, as the glory which I saw by the river of Chebar:
and I fell on my face. Then the spirit entered into me,
and set me upon my feet, and spake with me, and said
unto me, "Go, shut thyself within thine house. But
thou, O son of man, behold, they shall put bands upon
thee, and shall bind thee with them, and thou shalt not
go out among them: and I will make thy tongue cleave
to the roof of thy mouth, that thou shalt be dumb, and
shalt not be to them a reprover: for they are a rebellious
house. But when I speak with thee, I will open thy

mouth, and thou shalt say unto them, 'Thus saith the Lord God.' He that heareth, let him hear; and he that forbeareth, let him forbear: for they are a rebellious house.
—Ezekiel 3:4–27.

Symbols of the Fall of Jerusalem

How Ezekiel is Told to Make with a Tile and Clay and an Iron Pan a Model Plan of a City Besieged with Engines of War

"Thou also, son of man, take thee a tile, and lay it before thee, and portray upon it the city, even Jerusalem: and lay siege against it, and build a fort against it, and cast a mount against it; set the camp also against it, and set battering rams against it round about. Moreover take thou unto thee an iron pan, and set it for a wall of iron between thee and the city: and set thy face against it, and it shall be besieged, and thou shalt lay siege against it. This shall be a sign to the house of Israel. Lie thou also upon thy left side, and lay the iniquity of the house of Israel upon it: according to the number of the days that thou shalt lie upon it thou shalt bear their iniquity. For I have laid upon thee the years of their iniquity, according to the number of the days, three hundred and ninety days: so shalt thou bear the iniquity of the house of Israel. And when thou hast accomplished them, lie again on thy right side, and thou shalt bear the iniquity of the house of Judah forty days: I have appointed thee each day for a year. Therefore thou shalt set thy face toward the siege of Jerusalem, and thine arm shall be uncovered, and thou shalt prophesy against it. And, behold, I will lay bands upon thee, and thou shalt not turn thee from one side to another, till thou hast ended the days of thy siege.
—Ezekiel 4:1–8.

THE SIGN OF THE DIVIDED HAIR

"And thou, son of man, take thee a sharp knife, take thee a barber's razor, and cause it to pass upon thine head and upon thy beard: then take thee balances to weigh, and divide the hair. Thou shalt burn with fire a third part in the midst of the city, when the days of the siege are fulfilled: and thou shalt take a third part, and smite about it with a knife: and a third part thou shalt scatter in the wind; and I will draw out a sword after them. Thou shalt also take thereof a few in number, and bind them in thy skirts. Then take of them again, and cast them into the midst of the fire, and burn them in the fire; for thereof shall a fire come forth into all the house of Israel."

Thus saith the Lord GOD: "This is Jerusalem: I have set it in the midst of the nations and countries that are round about her. And she hath changed my judgments into wickedness more than the nations, and my statutes more than the countries that are round about her: for they have refused my judgments and my statutes, they have not walked in them.

Therefore thus saith the Lord GOD: "Because ye multiplied more than the nations that are round about you, and have not walked in my statutes, neither have kept my judgments, neither have done according to the judgments of the nations that are round about you"; therefore thus saith the Lord GOD: "Behold, I, even I, am against thee, and will execute judgments in the midst of thee in the sight of the nations. And I will do in thee that which I have not done, and whereunto I will not do any more the like, because of all thine abominations. Therefore the fathers shall eat the sons in the midst of thee, and the sons shall eat their fathers; and I will execute judgments in thee, and the whole remnant of thee will I scatter into all the winds. Wherefore, as I live," saith the Lord God: "surely, because thou hast defiled my sanctuary with all thy detestable things, and with all thine abominations, therefore will I also diminish thee; neither shall mine eye spare, neither will I have any pity.

"A third part of thee shall die with the pestilence, and with famine shall they be consumed in the midst of thee: and a third part shall fall by the sword round about thee; and I will scatter a third part into all the winds, and I will draw out a sword after them. Thus shall mine anger be accomplished, and I will cause my fury to rest upon them, and I will be comforted: and they shall know that I, the Lord, have spoken it in my zeal, when I have accomplished my fury in them. Moreover I will make thee waste, and a reproach among the nations that are round about thee, in the sight of all that pass by. So it shall be a reproach and a taunt, an instruction and an astonishment unto the nations that are round about thee, when I shall execute judgments in thee in anger and in fury and in furious rebukes. I, the Lord, have spoken it. When I shall send upon them the evil arrows of famine, which shall be for their destruction, and which I will send to destroy you: and I will increase the famine upon you, and will break your staff of bread: so will I send upon you famine and evil beasts, and they shall bereave thee; and pestilence and blood shall pass through thee; and I will bring the sword upon thee. I, the Lord, have spoken it." —Ezekiel 5.

A PROPHECY OF DESTRUCTION

And the word of the Lord came unto me, saying, "Son of man, set thy face toward the mountains of Israel, and prophesy against them, and say, 'Ye mountains of Israel, hear the word of the Lord GOD: Thus saith the Lord GOD to the mountains, and to the hills, to the rivers, and to the valleys: "Behold, I, even I, will bring a sword upon you, and I will destroy your high places. And your altars shall be desolate, and your images shall be broken: and I will cast down your slain men before your idols. And I will lay the dead carcasses of the children of Israel before their idols.; and I will scatter your bones round about your altars. In all your dwellingplaces the cities shall be laid waste, and the high places shall be desolate; that your altars may be laid waste and made desolate, and your idols may be broken and cease, and your images may be cut down, and your works may be abolished. And the slain shall fall in the midst of you, and ye shall know that I am the LORD.

""""Yet will I leave a remnant, that ye may have some that shall escape the sword among the nations, when ye shall be scattered through the countries. And they that escape of you shall remember me among the nations whither they shall be carried captives, because I am broken with their whorish heart, which hath departed from me, and with their eyes, which go a whoring after their idols: and they shall loathe themselves for the evils which they have committed in all their abominations. And they shall know that I am the LORD, and that I have not said in vain that I would do this evil unto them.""""

Thus saith the Lord GOD: "Smite with thine hand, and stamp with thy foot, and say, 'Alas for all the evil abominations of the house of Israel!' for they shall fall by the sword, by the famine, and by the pestilence. He that is far off shall die of the pestilence; and he that is near shall fall by the sword; and he that remaineth and is besieged shall die by the famine: thus will I accomplish

my fury upon them. Then shall ye know that I am the
LORD, when their slain men shall be among their idols
round about their altars, upon every high hill, in all the
tops of the mountains, and under every green tree, and
under every thick oak, the place where they did offer
sweet savour to all their idols. So will I stretch out my
hand upon them, and make the land desolate, yea, more
desolate than the wilderness toward Diblath, in all their
habitations: and they shall know that I am the LORD."

—Ezekiel 6.

"THE END IS COME"

Moreover the word of the LORD came unto me, saying,
"Also, thou son of man, thus saith the Lord GOD unto
the land of Israel: 'An end, the end is come upon the
four corners of the land. Now is the end come upon thee,
and I will send mine anger upon thee, and will judge thee
according to thy ways, and will recompense upon thee all
thine abominations. And mine eye shall not spare thee,
neither will I have pity: but I will recompense thy ways
upon thee, and thine abominations shall be in the midst
of thee: and ye shall know that I am the LORD.'

"Thus saith the Lord GOD: 'An evil, an only evil,
behold, is come. An end is come, the end is come: it
watcheth for thee; behold, it is come. The morning is
come unto thee, O thou that dwellest in the land: the
time is come, the day of trouble is near, and not the
sounding again of the mountains. Now will I shortly
pour out my fury upon thee, and accomplish mine anger
upon thee: and I will judge thee according to thy ways,
and will recompense thee for all thine abominations.
And mine eye shall not spare, neither will I have pity:
I will recompense thee according to thy ways and thine
abominations that are in the midst of thee; and ye shall
know that I am the LORD that smiteth. Behold the

day, behold, it is come: the morning is gone forth; the rod hath blossomed, pride hath budded. Violence is risen up into a rod of wickedness: none of them shall remain, nor of their multitude, nor of any of theirs: neither shall there be wailing for them. The time is come, the day draweth near: let not the buyer rejoice nor the seller mourn: for wrath is upon all the multitude thereof. For the seller shall not return to that which is sold, although they were yet alive: for the vision is touching the whole multitude thereof, which shall not return; neither shall any strengthen himself in the iniquity of his life. They have blown the trumpet, even to make all ready; but none goeth to the battle: for my wrath is upon all the multitude thereof. The sword is without and the pestilence and the famine within: he that is in the field shall die with the sword; and he that is in the city, famine and pestilence shall devour him.

"'But they that escape of them shall escape, and shall be on the mountains like doves of the valleys, all of them mourning, every one for his iniquity. All hands shall be feeble, and all knees shall be weak as water. They shall also gird themselves with sackcloth, and horror shall cover them; and shame shall be upon all faces, and baldness upon all their heads. They shall cast their silver in the streets, and their gold shall be removed: their silver and their gold shall not be able to deliver them in the day of the wrath of the LORD: they shall not satisfy their souls, neither fill their bowels: because it is the stumblingblock of their iniquity.

"'As for the beauty of his ornament, he set it in majesty: but they made the images of their abominations and of their detestable things therein: therefore have I set it far from them. And I will give it into the hands of the strangers for a prey, and to the wicked of the earth for a spoil; and they shall pollute it. My face will I turn also from them, and they shall pollute my secret place: for the robbers shall enter into it, and defile it.

"'Make a chain: for the land is full of bloody crimes, and the city is full of violence. Wherefore I will bring the worst of the heathen, and they shall possess their houses: I will also make the pomp of the strong to cease; and their holy places shall be defiled. Destruction cometh; and they shall seek peace, and there shall be none. Mischief shall come upon mischief, and rumour shall be upon rumour; then shall they seek a vision of the prophet; but the law shall perish from the priest, and counsel from the ancients. The king shall mourn, and the prince shall be clothed with desolation, and the hands of the people of the land shall be troubled: I will do unto them after their way, and according to their deserts will I judge them; and they shall know that I am the LORD.'"

—Ezekiel 7.

THE FALL OF JERUSALEM IS A PUNISHMENT

THE VISION OF THE VISIT TO JERUSALEM

And it came to pass in the sixth year, in the sixth month, in the fifth day of the month, as I sat in mine house, and the elders of Judah sat before me, that the hand of the Lord GOD fell there upon me. Then I beheld, and lo a likeness as the appearance of fire: from the appearance of his loins even downward, fire; and from his loins even upward, as the appearance of brightness, as the colour of amber. And he put forth the form of an hand, and took me by a lock of mine head; and the spirit lifted me up between the earth and the heaven, and brought me in the visions of God to Jerusalem, to the door of the inner gate that looketh toward the north; where was the seat of the image of jealousy, which provoketh to jealousy. And, behold, the glory of the God of Israel was there, according to the vision that I saw in the plain.

Then said he unto me, "Son of man, lift up thine eyes now the way toward the north." So I lifted up mine eyes the way toward the north, and behold northward at the gate of the altar this image of jealousy in the entry. He said furthermore unto me, "Son of man, seest thou what they do? Even the great abominations that the house of Israel committeth here, that I should go far off from my sanctuary? But turn thee yet again, and thou shalt see greater abominations."

THE DOOR WHICH WAS WITHIN THE WALL

And he brought me to the door of the court; and when I looked, behold a hole in the wall. Then said he unto me, "Son of man, dig now in the wall"; and when I had digged in the wall, behold a door. And he said unto me, "Go in, and behold the wicked abominations that they do here." So I went in and saw; and behold every form of creeping things, and abominable beasts, and all the idols of the house of Israel, portrayed upon the wall round about. And there stood before them seventy men of the ancients of the house of Israel, and in the midst of then stood Jaazaniah, the son of Shaphan, with every man his censer in his hand; and a thick cloud of incense went up. Then said he unto me, "Son of man, hast thou seen what the ancients of the house of Israel do in the dark, every man in the chambers of his imagery? For they say, 'The LORD seeth us not; the LORD hath forsaken the earth.'"

He said also unto me, "Turn thee yet again, and thou shalt see greater abominations that they do." Then he brought me to the door of the gate of the LORD's house which was toward the north; and, behold, there sat women weeping for Tammuz.

Then said he unto me, "Hast thou seen this. O son of man? Turn thee yet again, and thou shalt see greater abominations than these." And he brought me into the inner court of the LORD's house, and, behold, at the door of the temple of the LORD, between the porch and the altar, were about five and twenty men, with their backs toward the temple of the LORD, and their faces toward the east; and they worshiped the sun toward the east.

Then he said unto me, "Hast thou seen this, O son of man? Is it a light thing to the house of Judah that they commit the abominations which they commit here? for they have filled the land with violence, and have returned to provoke me to anger: and, lo, they put the branch to their nose. Therefore will I also deal in fury: mine eyes shall not spare, neither will I have pity: and though they cry in mine ears with a loud voice, yet will I not hear them." —Ezekiel 8.

THE MAN WITH THE WRITER'S INKHORN

He cried also in mine ears with a loud voice, saying, "Cause them that have charge over the city to draw near, even every man with his destroying weapon in his hand."

And, behold, six men came from the way of the higher gate, which lieth toward the north, and every man a slaughter weapon in his hand; and one man among them was clothed with linen, with a writer's inkhorn by his side: and they went in, and stood beside the brasen altar. And the glory of the God of Israel was gone up from the cherub, whereupon he was, to the threshold of the house. And he called to the man clothed with linen, which had the writer's inkhorn by his side; and the LORD said unto him, "Go through the midst of the city, through the midst of Jerusalem, and set a mark upon the foreheads of the men that sigh and that cry for all the abominations that be done in the midst thereof."

And to the others he said in mine hearing, "Go ye after him through the city, and smite: let not your eye spare, neither have ye pity: slay utterly old and young, both maids, and little children, and women: but come not near any man upon whom is the mark; and begin at my sanctuary." Then they began at the ancient men which were before the house.

And he said unto them, "Defile the house, and fill the courts with the slain: go ye forth." And they went forth, and slew in the city.

And it came to pass, while they were slaying them, and I was left, that I fell upon my face, and cried, and said, "Ah, Lord God! wilt thou destroy all the residue of Israel in thy pouring out of thy fury upon Jerusalem?"

Then said he unto me, "The iniquity of the house of Israel and Judah is exceeding great, and the land is full of blood, and the city full of perverseness: for they say, 'The LORD hath forsaken the earth, and the LORD seeth not.' And as for me also, mine eye shall not spare, neither will I have pity, but I will recompense their way upon their head."

And, behold, the man clothed with linen, which had the inkhorn by his side, reported the matter, saying, "I have done as thou hast commanded me."   —Ezekiel 9.

THE VISION OF THE CHERUBIM

Then I looked, and, behold, in the firmament that was above the head of the cherubim there appeared over them as it were a sapphire stone, as the appearance of the likeness of a throne. And he spake unto the man clothed with linen, and said, "Go in between the wheels, even under the cherub, and fill thine hand with coals of fire from between the cherubim, and scatter them over the city." And he went in in my sight. Now the cherubim stood on the right side of the house, when the man went in; and the cloud filled the inner court. Then the glory of the LORD went up from the cherub, and stood over the threshold of the house; and the house was filled with the cloud, and the court was full of the brightness of the LORD's glory. And the sound of the cherubim's wings was heard even to the outer court, as the voice of the Almighty God when he speaketh.

And it came to pass, that when he had commanded the man clothed with linen, saying, "Take fire from between the wheels, from between the cherubim"; then he went in, and stood beside the wheels. And one cherub stretched forth his hand from between the cherubim unto the fire that was between the cherubim, and took thereof, and put it into the hands of him that was clothed with linen: who took it, and went out.

And there appeared in the cherubim the form of a man's hand under their wings. And when I looked, behold the four wheels by the cherubim, one wheel by one cherub, and another wheel by another cherub: and the appearance of the wheels was as the colour of a beryl stone. And as for their appearances, they four had one likeness, as if a wheel had been in the midst of a wheel. When they went, they went upon their four sides; they turned not as they went, but to the place whither the head looked they followed it; they turned not as they went. And their whole body, and their backs, and their hands, and their wings, and the wheels, were full of eyes round about, even the wheels that they four had. As for the wheels, it was cried unto them in my hearing, "O wheel." And every one had four faces: the first face

was the face of a cherub, and the second face was the face
of a man, and the third the face of a lion, and the fourth
the face of an eagle. And the cherubim were lifted up.
This is the living creature that I saw by the river of
Chebar.

And when the cherubim went, the wheels went by
them: and when the cherubim lifted up their wings to
mount up from the earth, the same wheels also turned
not from beside them. When they stood, these stood;
and when they were lifted up, these lifted up themselves
also: for the spirit of the living creature was in them.
Then the glory of the LORD departed from off the threshold of the house, and stood over the cherubim. And the
cherubim lifted up their wings, and mounted up from the
earth in my sight: when they went out, the wheels also
were beside them, and every one stood at the door of the
east gate of the LORD'S house; and the glory of the God
of Israel was over them above. This is the living creature
that I saw under the God of Israel by the river of Chebar;
and I knew that they were the cherubim. Every one had
four faces apiece, and every one four wings; and the
likeness of the hands of a man was under their wings.
And the likeness of their faces was the same faces which
I saw by the river of Chebar, their appearances and themselves: they went every one straight forward.

Moreover the spirit lifted me up, and brought me
unto the east gate of the LORD'S house, which looketh eastward: and behold at the door of the gate five and twenty
men; among whom I saw Jaazaniah, the son of Azur,
and Pelatiah, the son of Benaiah, princes of the people.
Then said he unto me, "Son of man, these are the men
that devise mischief, and give wicked counsel in this city,
which say, 'It is not near; let us build houses: this city
is the caldron, and we be the flesh.'

"Therefore prophesy against them, prophesy, O son of man."

And the Spirit of the LORD fell upon me, and said unto me, "Speak: Thus saith the LORD: 'Thus have ye said, O house of Israel: for I know the things that come into your mind, every one of them. Ye have multiplied your slain in this city, and ye have filled the streets thereof with the slain.',

"Therefore thus saith the Lord GOD: 'Your slain whom ye have laid in the midst of it, they are the flesh, and this city is the caldron: but I will bring you forth out of the midst of it. Ye have feared the sword; and I will bring a sword upon you,' saith the LORD God. 'And I will bring you out of the midst thereof, and deliver you into the hands of strangers, and will execute judgments among you. Ye shall fall by the sword; I will judge you in the border of Israel; and ye shall know that I am the LORD. This city shall not be your caldron, neither shall ye be the flesh in the midst thereof; but I will judge you in the border of Israel: and ye shall know that I am the LORD: for ye have not walked in my statutes, neither executed my judgments, but have done after the manners of the heathen that are round about you.'"

And it came to pass, when I prophesied, that Pelatiah, the son of Benaiah, died. Then fell I down upon my face, and cried with a loud voice, and said, "Ah, Lord GOD! wilt thou make a full end of the remnant of Israel?"

Again the word of the LORD came unto me saying, "Son of man, thy brethren, even thy brethren, the men of thy kindred, and all the house of Israel wholly, are they unto whom the inhabitants of Jerusalem have said, 'Get you far from the LORD: unto us is this land given in possession.'

"Therefore say, 'Thus saith the Lord God: "Although I have cast them far off among the heathen, and although I have scattered them among the countries, yet will I be to them as a little sanctuary in the countries where they shall come."'

"Therefore say, 'Thus saith the Lord God: "I will even gather you from the people, and assemble you out of the countries where ye have been scattered, and I will give you the land of Israel. And they shall come thither, and they shall take away all the detestable things thereof and all the abominations thereof from thence. And I will give them one heart, and I will put a new spirit within you; and I will take the stony heart out of their flesh, and will give them an heart of flesh: that they may walk in my statutes, and keep mine ordinances, and do them: and they shall be my people, and I will be their God. But as for them whose heart walketh after the heart of their detestable things and their abominations, I will recompense their way upon their own heads,'" saith the Lord God."

Then did the cherubim lift up their wings, and the wheels beside them; and the glory of the God of Israel was over them above. And the glory of the LORD went up from the midst of the city, and stood upon the mountain which is on the east side of the city.

Afterwards the spirit took me up, and brought me in a vision by the Spirit of God into Chaldea, to them of the captivity. So the vision that I had seen went up from me. Then I spake unto them of the captivity all the things that the LORD had shewed me.　　—Ezekiel 10; 11.

THE MESSAGE TO THE CAPTIVES

The word of the LORD also came unto me, saying, "Son of man, thou dwellest in the midst of a rebellious house, which have eyes to see, and see not; they have ears to hear, and hear not: for they are a rebellious house. Therefore, thou son of man, prepare thee stuff for removing, and remove by day in their sight; and thou shalt remove from thy place to another place in their sight: it may be they will consider, though they be a rebellious house. Then shalt thou bring forth thy stuff by day in their sight, as stuff for removing: and thou shalt go forth at even in their sight, as they that go forth into captivity. Dig thou through the wall in their sight, and carry out thereby. In their sight shalt thou bear it upon thy shoulders, and carry it forth in the twilight: thou shalt cover thy face, that thou see not the ground: for I have set thee for a sign unto the house of Israel."

And I did so as I was commanded: I brought forth my stuff by day, as stuff for captivity, and in the even I digged through the wall with mine hand; I brought it forth in the twilight, and I bare it upon my shoulder in their sight.

And in the morning came the word of the LORD unto me, saying, "Son of man, hath not the house of Israel, the rebellious house, said unto thee, 'What doest thou?'

"Say thou unto them, 'Thus saith the Lord GOD: "This burden concerneth the prince in Jerusalem, and all the house of Israel that are among them.'''

"Say, 'I am your sign: like as I have done, so shall it be done unto them: they shall remove and go into captivity.' And the prince that is among them shall bear upon his shoulder in the twilight, and shall go forth: they shall dig through the wall to carry out thereby: he shall cover his face, that he see not the ground with his eyes. My net also will I spread upon him, and he shall be taken in my snare: and I will bring him to Babylon to the land of the Chaldeans; yet shall he not see it, though he shall die there. And I will scatter toward every wind all that are about him to help him, and all his bands; and I will draw out the sword after them. And they shall know that I am the LORD, when I shall scatter them among the nations, and disperse them in the countries. But I will leave a few men of them from the sword, from the famine, and from the pestilence; that they may declare all their abominations among the heathen whither they come; and they shall know that I am the LORD."

Moreover the word of the LORD came to me, saying, "Son of man, eat thy bread with quaking, and drink thy water with trembling and with carefulness; and say unto the people of the land, 'Thus saith the Lord GOD of the inhabitants of Jerusalem, and of the land of Israel: "They shall eat their bread with carefulness, and drink their water with astonishment, that her land may be desolate from all that is therein, because of the violence of all them that dwell therein. And the cities that are inhabited shall be laid waste, and the land shall be desolate; and ye shall know that I am the LORD.""'"

And the word of the LORD came unto me, saying, "Son of man, what is that proverb that ye have in the land of Israel, saying, 'The days are prolonged, and every vision faileth'? Tell them therefore, 'Thus saith the Lord GOD: "I will make this proverb to cease, and they shall no more use it as a proverb in Israel; but say unto them, 'The days are at hand, and the effect of every vision.' For there shall be no more any vain vision nor flattering divination within the house of Israel. For I am the LORD: I will speak, and the word that I shall speak shall come to pass; it shall be no more prolonged: for in your days, O rebellious house, will I say the word, and will perform it,"'" saith the Lord GOD.

Again the word of the LORD came to me, saying,

"Son of man, behold, they of the house of Israel say, 'The vision that he seeth is for many days to come, and he prophesieth of the times that are far off.' Therefore say unto them, 'Thus saith the Lord GOD: "There shall none of my words be prolonged any more, but the word which I have spoken shall be done,"'" saith the Lord GOD.

— Ezekiel 12.

SPEAK AGAINST THE PROPHETS

And the word of the LORD came unto me, saying, "Son of man, prophesy against the prophets of Israel that prophesy, and say thou unto them that prophesy out of their own hearts, 'Hear ye the word of the LORD: Thus saith the Lord GOD: "Woe unto the foolish prophets, that follow their own spirit, and have seen nothing! O Israel, thy prophets are like the foxes in the deserts. Ye have not gone up into the gaps, neither made up the hedge for the house of Israel to stand in the battle in the day of the LORD. They have seen vanity and lying divination, saying, 'The LORD saith': and the LORD hath not sent them: and they have made others to hope that they would confirm the word. Have ye not seen a vain vision, and have ye not spoken a lying divination, whereas ye say, 'The LORD saith it'; albeit I have not spoken?"

"'Therefore thus saith the Lord GOD: "Because ye have spoken vanity, and seen lies, therefore, behold, I am against you," saith the Lord GOD. "And mine hand shall be upon the prophets that see vanity, and that divine lies: they shall not be in the assembly of my people, neither shall they be written in the writing of the house of Israel, neither shall they enter into the land of Israel; and ye shall know that I am the Lord GOD. Because, even because they have seduced my people, saying, 'Peace'; and there was no peace; and one built up a wall, and, lo, others daubed it with untempered mortar: say unto them which daub it with untempered mortar, that it shall fall: there shall be an overflowing shower; and ye, O great hailstones, shall fall; and a stormy wind shall rend it. Lo, when the wall is fallen, shall it not be said unto you, "Where is the daubing wherewith ye have daubed it?"

"'Therefore thus saith the Lord GOD: "I will even rend it with a stormy wind in my fury; and there shall be an overflowing shower in mine anger, and great hailstones in my fury to consume it. So will I break down the wall that ye have daubed with untempered mortar, and bring it down to the ground, so that the foundation thereof shall be discovered, and it shall fall, and ye shall be consumed in the midst thereof: and ye shall know that I am the LORD. Thus will I accomplish my wrath upon the wall, and upon them that have daubed it with untempered mortar, and will say unto you, 'The wall is no more, neither they that daubed it'; to wit, the prophets of Israel which prophesy concerning Jerusalem, and which see visions of peace for her, and there is no peace," saith the Lord GOD.'

"Likewise, thou son of man, set thy face against the daughters of thy people, which prophesy out of their own heart; and prophesy thou against them, and say, 'Thus saith the Lord GOD: "Woe to the women that sew pillows to all armholes, and make kerchiefs upon the head of every stature to hunt souls! Will ye hunt the souls of my people, and will ye save the souls alive that come unto you? And will ye pollute me among my people for handfuls of barley and for pieces of bread, to slay the souls that should not die, and to save the souls alive that should not live, by your lying to my people that hear your lies?"'"

"Wherefore thus saith the Lord GOD: 'Behold, I am
against your pillows, wherewith ye there hunt the souls
to make them fly, and I will tear them from your arms,
and will let the souls go, even the souls that ye hunt to
make them fly. Your kerchiefs also will I tear, and
deliver my people out of your hand, and they shall be no
more in your hand to be hunted; and ye shall know that
I am the LORD. Because with lies ye have made the
heart of the righteous sad, whom I have not made sad;
and strengthened the hands of the wicked, that he should
not return from his wicked way, by promising him life:
therefore ye shall see no more vanity, nor divine divi-
nations: for I will deliver my people out of your hand:
and ye shall know that I am the LORD.'" — Ezekiel 13.

A GREAT MESSAGE OF EZEKIEL

"BEHOLD, ALL SOULS ARE MINE"

The word of the LORD came unto me again, saying,
"What mean ye, that ye use this proverb concerning
the land of Israel, saying, 'The fathers have eaten sour
grapes, and the children's teeth are set on edge?' As
I live," saith the Lord GOD, "ye shall not have occasion
any more to use this proverb in Israel. Behold, all souls
are mine; as the soul of the father, so also the soul of the
son is mine: the soul that sinneth, it shall die.

EZEKIEL'S STATEMENT OF PERSONAL RELIGION

"But if a man be just, and do that which is lawful
and right, and hath not eaten upon the mountains,
neither hath lifted up his eyes to the idols of the house
of Israel, neither hath defiled his neighbour's wife, and
hath not oppressed any, but hath restored to the debtor
his pledge, hath spoiled none by violence, hath given

his bread to the hungry, and hath covered the naked with a garment; he that hath not given forth upon usury, neither hath taken any increase, that hath withdrawn his hand from iniquity, hath executed true judgment between man and man, hath walked in my statutes, and hath kept my judgments, to deal truly; he is just, he shall surely live," saith the Lord GOD.

"If he beget a son that is a robber, a shedder of blood, and that doeth the like to any one of these things, and that doeth not any of those duties, but even hath eaten upon the mountains, and defiled his neighbour's wife, hath oppressed the poor and needy, hath spoiled by violence, hath not restored the pledge, and hath lifted up his eyes to the idols, hath committed abomination, hath given forth upon usury, and hath taken increase: shall he then live? He shall not live: he hath done all these abominations; he shall surely die; his blood shall be upon him.

"Now, lo, if he beget a son, that seeth all his father's sins which he hath done, and considereth, and doeth not such like, that hath not eaten upon the mountains, neither hath lifted up his eyes to the idols of the house of Israel, hath not defiled his neighbour's wife, neither hath oppressed any, hath not withholden the pledge, neither hath spoiled by violence, but hath given his bread to the hungry, and hath covered the naked with a garment, that hath taken off his hand from the poor, that hath not received usury nor increase, hath executed my judgments, hath walked in my statutes; he shall not die for the iniquity of his father, he shall surely live.

"As for his father, because he cruelly oppressed, spoiled his brother by violence, and did that which is not good among his people, lo, even he shall die in his iniquity.

SHALL THE SINS OF THE FATHERS BE VISITED UPON THE SONS?
EZEKIEL'S ANSWER

"Yet say ye, 'Why? Doth not the son bear the iniquity of the father?' When the son hath done that which is lawful and right, and hath kept all my statutes, and hath done them, he shall surely live. The soul that sinneth, it shall die. The son shall not bear the iniquity of the father, neither shall the father bear the iniquity of the son: the righteousness of the righteous shall be upon him, and the wickedness of the wicked shall be upon him. But if the wicked will turn from all his sins that he hath committed, and keep all my statutes, and do that which is lawful and right, he shall surely live, he shall not die. All his transgressions that he hath committed, they shall not be mentioned unto him: in his righteousness that he hath done he shall live.

"HAVE I ANY PLEASURE AT ALL THAT THE WICKED SHOULD DIE?"

"Have I any pleasure at all that the wicked should die?" saith the Lord GOD: "and not that he should return from his ways, and live? But when the righteous turneth away from his righteousness, and committeth iniquity, and doeth according to all the abominations that the wicked man doeth, shall he live? All his righteousness that he hath done shall not be mentioned: in his trespass that he hath trespassed, and in his sin that he hath sinned, in them shall he die.

"Yet ye say, 'The way of the LORD is not equal.' Hear now, O house of Israel: Is not my way equal? Are not your ways unequal? When a righteous man turneth away from his righteousness, and committeth iniquity, and dieth in them; for his iniquity that he hath done shall he die. Again, when the wicked man turneth away from his wickedness that he hath committed, and doeth that which is lawful and right, he shall save his soul alive. Because he considereth, and turneth away from all his transgressions that he hath committed, he shall surely live, he shall not die.

"Yet saith the house of Israel, 'The way of the LORD is not equal.' O house of Israel, are not my ways equal? Are not your ways unequal? Therefore I will judge you, O house of Israel, every one according to his ways," saith the Lord GOD. "Repent, and turn yourselves from all your transgressions; so iniquity shall not be your ruin. Cast away from you all your transgressions, whereby ye have transgressed; and make you a new heart and a new spirit: for why will ye die, O house of Israel? For I have no pleasure in the death of him that dieth," saith the Lord GOD: "wherefore turn yourselves, and live ye."

— Ezekiel 18.

THE PROPHECY AGAINST TYRE

And it came to pass in the eleventh year, in the first day of the month, that the word of the LORD came unto me, saying, "Son of man, because that Tyrus hath said against Jerusalem, 'Aha, she is broken that was the gates of the people: she is turned unto me: I shall be replenished, now she is laid waste': therefore thus saith the Lord GOD: 'Behold, I am against thee, O Tyrus, and will cause many nations to come up against thee, as the sea causeth his waves to come up. And they shall destroy the walls of Tyrus, and break down her towers: I will also scrape her dust from her, and make her like the top of a rock. It shall be a place for the spreading of nets in the midst of the sea: for I have spoken it,' saith the Lord GOD: 'and it shall become a spoil to the nations.

ANCIENT CITY OF TYRE

Photograph by Professor Lewis Bayles Paton

Tyre was one of the strongest and wealthiest cities of the eastern world. Hiram, King of Tyre, was the friend of Solomon, but in later years a bitter enmity existed between the Hebrews and the people of Tyre.

The city sustained many sieges, one for thirteen years by Nebuchadnezzar; and a famous resistance was made to Alexander who finally captured the island city by building a gigantic mole from the mainland to its walls. Now it is small and poor but very interesting because of its great history. The Hebrew prophecies are full of warnings to the proud city of Tyre.

And her daughters which are in the field shall be slain by the sword; and they shall know that I am the LORD.'

"For thus saith the Lord GOD: 'Behold, I will bring upon Tyrus Nebuchadnezzar, King of Babylon, a king of kings, from the north, with horses, and with chariots, and with horsemen, and companies, and much people. He shall slay with the sword thy daughters in the field: and he shall make a fort against thee, and cast a mount against thee, and lift up the buckler against thee. And he shall set engines of war against thy walls, and with his axes he shall break down thy towers. By reason of the abundance of his horses their dust shall cover thee: thy walls shall shake at the noise of the horsemen, and of the wheels, and of the chariots, when he shall enter into thy gates, as men enter into a city wherein is made a breach. With the hoofs of his horses shall he tread down all thy streets: he shall slay thy people by the sword, and thy strong garrisons shall go down to the ground. And they shall make a spoil of thy riches, and make a prey of thy merchandise: and they shall break down thy walls, and destroy thy pleasant houses: and they shall lay thy stones and thy timber and thy dust in the midst of the water. And I will cause the noise of thy songs to cease; and the sound of thy harps shall be no more heard. And I will make thee like the top of a rock: thou shalt be a place to spread nets upon; thou shalt be built no more: for I, the Lord, have spoken it,' saith the Lord God.

"Thus saith the Lord God to Tyrus: 'Shall not the isles shake at the sound of thy fall, when the wounded

MODERN SHIP BUILDING ON THE NILE
Photograph by W. A. Pottenger expressly for The Book of Life

These modern Nile boats are probably not unlike the galleys of Tyre in size and general build.

cry, when the slaughter is made in the midst of thee? Then all the princes of the sea shall come down from their thrones, and lay away their robes, and put off their broidered garments: they shall clothe themselves with trembling; they shall sit upon the ground, and shall tremble at every moment, and be astonished at thee. And they shall take up a lamentation for thee, and say to thee, "How art thou destroyed, that wast inhabited of seafaring men, the renowned city, which was strong in the sea, she and her inhabitants, which cause their terror to be on all that haunt it!" Now shall the isles tremble in the day of thy fall; yea, the isles that are in the sea shall be troubled at thy departure.'

"For thus saith the Lord God: 'When I shall make thee a desolate city, like the cities that are not inhabited; when I shall bring up the deep upon thee, and great waters shall cover thee; when I shall bring thee down with them that descend into the pit, with the people of old time, and shall set thee in the low parts of the earth, in places desolate of old, with them that go down to the pit, that thou be not inhabited; and I shall set glory in the land of the living; I will make thee a terror, and thou shalt be no more: though thou be sought for, yet shalt thou never be found again,' saith the Lord God."

—Ezekiel 26.

THE SHIP OF TYRE

The 27th chapter of Ezekiel is a fine description of a great sailing galley. The list of the places from which the materials for the building of the ship came and her lading show Ezekiel's wide knowledge and incidentally it is a little lesson in ancient geography. The planks for the ship came from Senir in the Lebanon country; the masts were tall cedars of Lebanon. The stout oars were made of the oaks of Bashan, the country north and east of the Jordan. The ivory for the rower's benches came from Chittim (Cyprus). The sails were of fine embroidered linen from Egypt. The garments of

the rowers were of purple Tyrian dye from Elishah, perhaps southern
Italy. The seamen were from Sidon and from Arvad, an island city
off the coast of Syria. The pilots were of the city of Tyre itself. The
vessel was calked by men from the ancient seaport of Gebad on the
coast of northern Syria. The armed marines were from Persia, Lud
(perhaps Lydia), and Phut, probably Africa. The ship traded with
Tarshish for silver, iron, tin, and lead; with Javan, Tubal and
Meshech (the location of these places is doubtful, perhaps they were
in the highland regions of Asia Minor) for brass and slaves. From
Dedan, Arabia, and the isles came horns of ivory and ebony. Syria
brought to the great fairs of Tyre emeralds, purple, embroidered
work, fine linen, coral, and agate. Judah brought wheat and honey,
oil and balm. Damascus contributed white wool and wine. Dan
and Javan (location unknown) brought cassia, calamus, and bright
iron. Dedan, perhaps Rhodes, sold precious cloths for chariots.
Arabia and Kedar furnished goats, rams, and lambs. Sheba, in
Arabia, and Raamah, a city of Arabia, brought spices, gold, and precious stones, while Haran, Abraham's old city, Sheba, Canneh, Asshur,
and Chilmod (the latter unidentified) sold "all sorts of things," blue
cloths and embroidered work in cedar chests, richly ornamented.

   The word of the LORD came again unto me, saying,
"Now, thou son of man, take up a lamentation for Tyrus;
         and say unto Tyrus,
'O thou that art situate at the entry of the sea,
  Which art a merchant of the people for many isles,
  Thus saith the Lord God:
"O Tyrus, thou hast said, 'I am of perfect beauty.'
Thy borders are in the midst of the seas,
Thy builders have perfected thy beauty.
They have made all thy ship-boards of fir-trees of Senir:
They have taken cedars from Lebanon to make masts
         for thee.
Of the oaks of Bashan have they made thine oars;
The company of the Ashurites have made thy benches
         of ivory,
Brought out of the isles of Chittim.

Fine linen with broidered work from Egypt was that
    which thou spreadest forth to be thy sail;
Blue and purple from the isles of Elishah was that
    which covered thee.
The inhabitants of Zidon and Arvad were thy mariners:
Thy wise men, O Tyrus, that were in thee, were thy
    pilots.
The ancients of Gebal and the wise men thereof were
    in thee thy calkers:
All the ships of the sea with their mariners were in
    thee to occupy thy merchandise.
They of Persia and of Lud and of Phut were in thine
    army, thy men of war:
They hanged the shield and helmet in thee; they set
    forth thy comeliness.
The men of Arvad with thine army were upon thy
    walls round about,
And the Gammadims were in thy towers:
They hanged their shields upon thy walls round about;
They have made thy beauty perfect.
Tarshish was thy merchant by reason of the multitude
    of all kind of riches;
With silver, iron, tin, and lead, they traded in thy fairs.
Javan, Tubal, and Meshech, they were thy merchants:
They traded the persons of men and vessels of brass
    in thy market.
They of the house of Togarmah traded in thy fairs
    with horses and horsemen and mules.
The men of Dedan were thy merchants:
Many isles were the merchandise of thine hand:
They brought thee for a present horns of ivory and
    ebony.
Syria was thy merchant by reason of the multitude
    of the wares of thy making:

They occupied in thy fairs with emeralds, purple, and broidered work, and fine linen, and coral, and agate.

Judah, and the land of Israel, they were thy merchants:

They traded in thy market wheat of Minnith, and Pannag, and honey, and oil, and balm.

Damascus was thy merchant in the multitude of the wares of thy making, for the multitude of all riches;

In the wine of Helbon, and white wool.

Dan also and Javan going to and fro occupied in thy fairs:

Bright iron, cassia, and calamus, were in thy market.

Dedan was thy merchant in precious clothes for chariots.

Arabia, and all the princes of Kedar, they occupied with thee in lambs, and rams, and goats:

In these were they thy merchants.

The merchants of Sheba and Raamah, they were thy merchants:

They occupied in thy fairs with chief of all spices,

And with all precious stones, and gold.

Haran, and Canneh, and Eden, the merchants of Sheba, Asshur, and Chilmad, were thy merchants.

These were thy merchants in all sorts of things,

In blue clothes, and broidered work, and in chests of rich apparel,

Bound with cords, and made of cedar, among thy merchandise.

The ships of Tarshish did sing of thee in thy market:

And thou wast replenished, and made very glorious in the midst of the seas.

Thy rowers have brought thee into great waters:

The east wind hath broken thee in the midst of the
seas.
Thy riches, and thy fairs, thy merchandise, thy mar-
iners,
And thy pilots, thy calkers, and the occupiers of thy
merchandise,
And all thy men of war, that are in thee,
And in all thy company which is in the midst of thee,
Shall fall into the midst of the seas in the day of thy
ruin.
The suburbs shall shake at the sound of the cry of thy
pilots.
And all that handle the oar, the mariners, and all the
pilots of the sea,
Shall come down from their ships, they shall stand
upon the land;
And shall cause their voice to be heard against thee,
And shall cry bitterly, and shall cast up dust upon
their heads,
They shall wallow themselves in the ashes:
And they shall make themselves utterly bald for thee,
And gird them with sackcloth, and they shall weep for
thee with bitterness of heart and bitter wailing.
And in their wailing they shall take up a lamentation
for thee,
And lament over thee, saying,
'What city is like Tyrus, like the destroyed in the midst
of the sea?
When thy wares went forth out of the seas, thou filledst
many people;
Thou didst enrich the kings of the earth with the mul-
titude of thy riches and of thy merchandise.
In the time when thou shalt be broken by the seas in
the depths of the waters

Thy merchandise and all thy company in the midst
of thee shall fall.
All the inhabitants of the isles shall be astonished at
thee,
And their kings shall be sore afraid,
They shall be troubled in their countenance.
The merchants among the people shall hiss at thee;
Thou shalt be a terror, and never shalt be any
more.'''''   —Ezekiel 27.

"PRIDE GOETH BEFORE A FALL"

The word of the LORD came again unto me, saying,

"Son of man, say unto the prince of Tyrus,
'Thus saith the Lord GOD:
"Because thine heart is lifted up, and thou hast said,
'I am a God, I sit in the seat of God, in the midst of the
seas';
Yet thou art a man, and not God,
Though thou set thine heart as the heart of God:
Behold, thou art wiser than Daniel;
There is no secret that they can hide from thee:
With thy wisdom and with thine understanding thou
hast gotten thee riches,
And hast gotten gold and silver into thy treasures:
By thy great wisdom and by thy traffic hast thou
increased thy riches,
And thine heart is lifted up because of thy riches:"
'Therefore thus saith the Lord GOD:
"Because thou hast set thine heart as the heart of God;
Behold, therefore I will bring strangers upon thee, the
terrible of the nations:
And they shall draw their swords against the beauty
of thy wisdom,
And they shall defile thy brightness.

They shall bring thee down to the pit,
And thou shalt die the deaths of them that are slain in
the midst of the seas.
Wilt thou yet say before him that slayeth thee, 'I am
God'?
But thou shalt be a man, and no God,
In the hand of him that slayeth thee.
Thou shalt die the deaths of the uncircumcised by the
hand of strangers:
For I have spoken it,'" saith the Lord God."

WORDS OF DOOM TO THE KING OF TYRE

Moreover the word of the Lord came unto me, saying,

"Son of man, take up a lamentation upon the king of
Tyrus.
And say unto him, 'Thus saith the Lord God:
"Thou sealest up the sum, full of wisdom, and perfect in
beauty.
Thou hast been in Eden, the garden of God;
Every precious stone was thy covering, the sardius,
topaz, and the diamond,
The beryl, the onyx, and the jasper, the sapphire, the
emerald, and the carbuncle, and gold:
The workmanship of thy tabrets and of thy pipes
Was prepared in thee in the day that thou wast created.
Thou art the anointed cherub that covereth;
And I have set thee so:
Thou wast upon the holy mountain of God;
Thou hast walked up and down in the midst of the
stones of fire.
Thou wast perfect in thy ways from the day that thou
wast created,
Till iniquity was found in thee.

By the multitude of thy merchandise
They have filled the midst of thee with violence, and
    thou hast sinned:
Therefore I will cast thee as profane out of the moun-
    tain of God:
And I will destroy thee, O covering cherub, from the
    midst of the stones of fire.
Thine heart was lifted up because of thy beauty,
Thou hast corrupted thy wisdom by reason of thy
    brightness:
I will cast thee to the ground,
I will lay thee before kings, that they may behold thee.
Thou hast defiled thy sanctuaries by the multitude of
    thine iniquities, by the iniquity of thy traffic;
Therefore will I bring forth a fire from the midst of
    thee,
It shall devour thee, and I will bring thee to ashes upon
    the earth
In the sight of all them that behold thee.
All they that know thee among the people shall be
    astonished at thee:
Thou shalt be a terror, and never shalt thou be any
    more."'"
                                —Ezekiel 28:1–19.

Prophecy Against Zidon

Again the word of the LORD came unto me, saying,
"Son of man, set thy face against Zidon, and prophesy
against it, and say, 'Thus saith the Lord GOD: "Behold,
I am against thee, O Zidon; and I will be glorified in the
midst of thee: and they shall know that I am the LORD,
when I shall have executed judgments in her, and shall be
sanctified in her. For I will send into her pestilence, and
blood into her streets; and the wounded shall be judged

in the midst of her by the sword upon her on every side; and they shall know that I am the LORD.

""'And there shall be no more a pricking brier unto the house of Israel, nor any grieving thorn of all that are round about them, that despised them; and they shall know that I am the Lord GOD."'

"Thus saith the Lord GOD: "When I shall have gathered the house of Israel from the people among whom they are scattered, and shall be sanctified in them in the sight of the heathen; then shall they dwell in their land that I have given to my servant Jacob. And they shall dwell safely therein, and shall build houses, and plant vineyards; yea, they shall dwell with confidence, when I have executed judgments upon all those that despise them round about them; and they shall know that I am the LORD their God."'" — Ezekiel 28:20–26.

A MESSAGE OF PERSONAL RESPONSIBILITY

Again the word of the LORD came unto me, saying, "Son of man, speak to the children of thy people, and say unto them, 'When I bring the sword upon a land, if the people of the land take a man of their coasts, and set him for their watchman: if when he seeth the sword come upon the land, he blow the trumpet, and warn the people; then whosoever heareth the sound of the trumpet, and taketh not warning; if the sword come, and take him away, his blood shall be upon his own head. He heard the sound of the trumpet, and took not warning; his blood shall be upon him. But he that taketh warning shall deliver his soul. But if the watchman see the sword come, and blow not the trumpet, and the people be not warned; if the sword come, and take any person from among them, he is taken away in his iniquity; but his blood will I require at the watchman's hand.'

"I HAVE SET THEE A WATCHMAN UNTO THE HOUSE OF ISRAEL"

"So thou, O son of man, I have set thee a watchman unto the house of Israel; therefore thou shalt hear the word at my mouth, and warn them from me. When I say unto the wicked, 'O wicked man, thou shalt surely die,' if thou dost not speak to warn the wicked from his way, that wicked man shall die in his iniquity; but his blood will I require at thine hand. Nevertheless, if thou warn the wicked of his way to turn from it; if he do not turn from his way, he shall die in his iniquity; but thou hast delivered thy soul.

LET THE WICKED TURN FROM HIS WAY AND LIVE

"Therefore, O thou son of man, speak unto the house of Israel; thus ye speak, saying, 'If our transgressions and our sins be upon us, and we pine away in them, how should we then live?' Say unto them, 'As I live,' saith the Lord GOD, 'I have no pleasure in the death of the wicked; but that the wicked turn from his way and live: turn ye, turn ye from your evil ways; for why will ye die, O house of Israel?'

"Therefore, thou son of man, say unto the children of thy people, 'The righteousness of the righteous shall not deliver him in the day of his transgression': as for the wickedness of the wicked, he shall not fall thereby in the day that he turneth from his wickedness; neither shall the righteous be able to live for his righteousness in the day that he sinneth. When I shall say to the righteous, that he shall surely live; if he trust to his own righteousness, and commit iniquity, all his righteousnesses shall not be remembered; but for his iniquity that he hath committed, he shall die for it. Again, when I say unto the wicked, 'Thou shalt surely die'; if he turn from his sin, and do that which is lawful and right; if the wicked restore the pledge, give again that he had robbed, walk in the statutes of life, without committing iniquity; he shall surely live, he shall not die. None of his sins that he hath committed shall be mentioned unto him: he hath done that which is lawful and right; he shall surely live.'

"Yet the children of thy people say, 'The way of the LORD is not equal': but as for them, their way is not equal. When the righteous turneth from his righteousness, and committeth iniquity, he shall even die thereby. But if the wicked turn from his wickedness, and do that which is lawful and right, he shall live thereby.

"Yet ye say, 'The way of the LORD is not equal.' O ye house of Israel, I will judge you every one after his ways." — Ezekiel 33:1–20.

THE WORD OF THE LORD TO THE SHEPHERDS OF ISRAEL

And the word of the LORD came unto me, saying, "Son of man, prophesy against the shepherds of Israel, prophesy, and say unto them, 'Thus saith the Lord GOD unto the shepherds; "Woe be to the shepherds of Israel that do feed themselves! Should not the shepherds feed the flocks? Ye eat the fat, and ye clothe you with the wool, ye kill them that are fed: but ye feed not the flock. The diseased have ye not strengthened, neither have ye healed that which was sick, neither have ye bound up that which was broken, neither have ye brought again that which was driven away, neither have ye sought that which was lost; but with force and with cruelty have ye ruled them. And they were scattered, because there is no shepherd: and they became meat to all the beasts of the field, when they were scattered.

"MY SHEEP WANDERED AND NONE DID SEEK AFTER THEM"

"'"My sheep wandered through all the mountains, and upon every high hill: yea, my flock was scattered upon all the face of the earth, and none did search or seek after them. Therefore, ye shepherds, hear the word of the LORD: 'As I live,' saith the Lord GOD, 'surely because my flock became a prey, and my flock became meat to every beast of the field, because there was no shepherd, neither did my shepherds search for my flock, but the shepherds fed themselves, and fed not my flock'; therefore, O ye shepherds, hear the word of the LORD; thus saith the Lord GOD: 'Behold, I am against the shepherds; and I will require my flock at their hand, and cause them to cease from feeding the flock; neither shall the shepherds feed themselves any more; for I will deliver my flock from their mouth, that they may not be meat for them.'"

"I, EVEN I, WILL BOTH SEARCH MY SHEEP, AND SEEK THEM OUT"

"'For thus saith the Lord GOD: "Behold, I, even I, will both search my sheep, and seek them out. As a shepherd seeketh out his flock in the day that he is among his sheep that are scattered; so will I seek out my sheep, and will deliver them out of all places where they have been scattered in the cloudy and dark day. And I will bring them out from the people, and gather them from the countries, and will bring them to their own land, and feed them upon the mountains of Israel by the rivers, and in all the inhabited places of the country. I will feed them in a good pasture, and upon the high mountains of Israel shall their fold be: there shall they lie in a good fold, and in a fat pasture shall they feed upon the mountains of Israel. I will feed my flock, and I will cause them to lie down," saith the Lord God.

"I WILL BIND UP THAT WHICH WAS BROKEN"

"'I will seek that which was lost, and bring again that which was driven away, and will bind up that which was broken, and will strengthen that which was sick: but I will destroy the fat and the strong; I will feed them with judgment. And as for you, O my flock,' thus saith the Lord God: 'Behold, I judge between cattle and cattle, between the rams and the he goats. Seemeth it a small thing unto you to have eaten up the good pasture, but ye must tread down with your feet the residue of your pastures and to have drunk of the deep waters, but ye must foul the residue with your feet? And as for my flock, they eat that which ye have trodden with your feet; and they drink that which ye have fouled with your feet.'

"Therefore thus saith the Lord God unto them: 'Behold, I, even I, will judge between the fat cattle and between the lean cattle. Because ye have thrust with side and with shoulder, and pushed all the diseased with your horns, till ye have scattered them abroad; therefore will I save my flock, and they shall no more be a prey; and I will judge between cattle and cattle.

"AND YE MY FLOCK ARE MEN, AND I AM YOUR GOD"

"'And I will set up one shepherd over them, and he shall feed them, even my servant David; he shall feed them, and he shall be their shepherd. And I, the Lord, will be their God, and my servant David a prince among them; I, the Lord, have spoken it. And I will make with them a covenant of peace, and will cause the evil beasts to cease out of the land: and they shall dwell safely in the wilderness, and sleep in the woods. And I will make them and the places round about my hill a blessing; and I will cause the shower to come down in his season; there shall be showers of blessing. And the tree of the field shall yield her fruit, and the earth shall yield her increase, and they shall be safe in their land, and shall know that I am the LORD, when I have broken the bands of their yoke, and delivered them out of the hand of those that served themselves of them. And they shall no more be a prey to the heathen, neither shall the beast of the land devour them; but they shall dwell safely, and none shall make them afraid. And I will raise up for them a plant of renown, and they shall be no more consumed with hunger in the land, neither bear the shame of the heathen any more. Thus shall they know that I, the LORD their God, am with them, and that they, even the house of Israel, are my people,' saith the Lord GOD.

"'And ye my flock, the flock of my pasture, are men and I am your God,' saith the Lord GOD."　　— Ezekiel 34.

THE VISION OF THE VALLEY OF DRY BONES

The hand of the LORD was upon me, and carried me out in the spirit of the LORD, and set me down in the midst of the valley which was full of bones, and caused me to pass by them round about: and, behold, there were very many in the open valley; and, lo, they were very dry.

And he said unto me, "Son of man, can these bones live?"

And I answered, "O Lord GOD, thou knowest."

Again he said unto me, "Prophesy upon these bones, and say unto them, 'O ye dry bones, hear the word of the LORD. Thus saith the Lord GOD unto these bones:

"Behold, I will cause breath to enter into you, and ye shall live: and I will lay sinews upon you, and will bring up flesh upon you, and cover you with skin, and put breath in you, and ye shall live; and ye shall know that I am the LORD.'''

So I prophesied as I was commanded: and as I prophesied, there was a noise, and behold a shaking, and the bones came together, bone to his bone. And when I beheld, lo, the sinews and the flesh came up upon them, and the skin covered them above: but there was no breath in them.

Then said he unto me, "Prophesy unto the wind, prophesy, son of man, and say to the wind, 'Thus saith the Lord GOD: "Come from the four winds, O breath, and breathe upon these slain, that they may live."'"

So I prophesied as he commanded me, and the breath came into them, and they lived, and stood up upon their feet, an exceeding great army.

Then he said unto me, "Son of man, these bones are the whole house of Israel: behold, they say, 'Our bones are dried, and our hope is lost: we are cut off for our parts.' Therefore prophesy and say unto them, 'Thus saith the Lord GOD: "Behold, O my people, I will open your graves, and cause you to come up out of your graves, and bring you into the land of Israel. And ye shall know that I am the LORD, when I have opened your graves, O my people, and brought you up out of your graves, and shall put my spirit in you, and ye shall live, and I shall place you in your own land: then shall ye know that I the LORD have spoken it, and performed it," saith the LORD.'"   Ezekiel 37:1-14.

Haggai and Zechariah

In 538 B.C. Cyrus, the great king of the Medes and Persians, took Babylon, and the Hebrew captives came under his enlightened and comparatively lenient authority. He allowed many of the captive people to return to their own homes, and a company of Hebrews, estimated by Ezra at 42,000, went back to Jerusalem. The returned exiles at once began to rebuild the temple. The Samaritans asked to aid, but were refused, the result of that historic enmity which, beginning in the division between the northern and southern kingdoms, persisted through to the time of Jesus,—"The Jews have no dealings with the Samaritans." Angered by this refusal, the Samaritans secured an order from the government forbidding the building of the temple. The people were deeply discouraged. Life from the physical standpoint in this new colony must have been much harder than it was in Babylon. It is more difficult to build on the ruins of an old life than to be a pioneer in new fields. Meanwhile Darius had conducted a successful revolt in Babylon. He was too busy to concern himself with these Jewish colonists in Palestine.

Under the leadership of two prophets, Haggai and Zechariah, work on the temple was resumed. Haggai's appeal is plain and practical: "Build the Temple"; "Do the task at hand." He emphasizes the responsibility of the people rather than the opposition of the Samaritans and the government. Luxury is beginning to appear. The House of God lies waste. The people are living in ceiled houses. They have forgotten that the Lord is the giver. "The silver is mine, the gold also is mine, saith the Lord of Hosts." It is all plain and direct, straightforward, and sincere: "Go up into the hills and get wood and build." There could hardly be advice more simple and practical. It is the appeal for the House of God which has been made in every generation and needs to be made now in almost every community. It makes this one of the most startlingly modern books in the Bible.

Zechariah was a younger man, a grandson perhaps of one of the returning exiles. His message is the same and yet strikingly different. It is filled with poetic imagery, memories of the glory of great Babylon,

Zechariah—Detail of Sistine Chapel Ceiling

By Michelangelo Buonarroti (1475-1564)
In the Sistine Chapel of the Vatican, Rome
Photograph by Anderson, Rome

HERE we see the prophet Zechariah, aged and venerable, eagerly searching through the pages of a book. He is still after a long life engaged in deep study.

This is but one of the impressive figures with which Michelangelo decorated the Sistine Chapel. The entire ceiling is covered with painted subjects from Christian history and theology. The center portion is divided into nine scenes representing the most important events recorded in Genesis. This great drama of redemption, including the Creation, the Fall, the Flood and the promised Salvation, is witnessed by twelve gigantic figures of prophets and sibyls. The sibyls represent the great priestesses of the pagan world who were believed to see into divine mysteries. The prophets represent the great men of the Hebrew world who had the certain vision of a coming Redeemer. They are among the most wonderful creations in modern art.

On first thought it seems strange to find references to the pagan world in a work portraying Christian faith and beliefs. However, we must remember that Michelangelo was here setting forth the Renaissance understanding of the philosophy of the ancient world. In the eyes of the Italian scholars, the poets and philosophers of Greece and the Fathers and Doctors of the Christian Church alike bore witness to the same Father of all. This dream of unity with the past was cherished by the finest intellects of the Renaissance. It was the common inheritance of Roman and Florentine scholars. Thus Michelangelo was but voicing the highest philosophical aspirations of his age when he placed the sibyls next to the prophets in the Sistine Chapel.

It is interesting to compare Michelangelo's Zechariah with the characterization by the American artist, John Singer Sargent, on page 186. Other paintings by Michelangelo are on pages 66, 308, 402 and 422.

—the seven lamps, the celestial messengers on red and dappled horses, the chariots with horses of various colors, the flying roll, the strange figure of the woman in the barrel. Then there is at the close the fine vision of the glory of the restored Jerusalem, a city which has no walls because the power of God is like a flame which protects it, a city in which little children shall play safely and happily in the streets, where there shall be upon the bells of the horses, "Holiness unto the Lord"; and "the pots in the Lord's house shall be like the bowls before the altar."

We know the very day on which these prophecies were spoken. The years are in the reign of Darius:

	Year	Month	Day
Haggai 1:1–11	2	6	1
Haggai 1:12–15	2	6	24
Haggai 2:1–9	2	7	21
Zechariah 1:1–6	2	8	..
Haggai 2:10–23	2	9	24
Zechariah 1:7 to 6:15	2	11	24
Zechariah 7:1–8:23	4	9	4

It brings these two prophets, the one old, the other filled with the imaginative enthusiasm of youth, much nearer, to be able to think of them as appearing amid the ruins of Jerusalem, on the exact day, walking through those streets where new houses were going up, like the streets of the devastated areas of France, going to the public squares and delivering their appeals to the people to build the House of God first, to subordinate everything to that great work. Their appeals were successful. The people, roused by their entreaties, began to build, and finished the Temple, difficult as the task must have been, in four years.

The Prophecy of Haggai

IN the second year of Darius, the king, in the sixth month, in the first day of the month, came the word of the LORD by Haggai, the prophet, unto Zerubbabel, the son of Shealtiel, governor of Judah, and to Joshua, the son of Josedech, the high priest, saying, "Thus speaketh the LORD of hosts, saying, 'This people say, "The time is not come, the time that the LORD's house should be built."'"

Then came the word of the LORD by Haggai, the prophet, saying, "Is it time for you, O ye, to dwell in your ceiled houses, and this house lie waste?"

Now therefore thus saith the LORD of hosts: "Consider your ways. Ye have sown much, and bring in little; ye eat, but ye have not enough; ye drink, but ye are not filled with drink; ye clothe you, but there is none warm; and he that earneth wages earneth wages to put it into a bag with holes."

Thus saith the LORD of hosts: "Consider your ways. Go up to the mountain, and bring wood, and build the house; and I will take pleasure in it, and I will be glorified," saith the LORD. "Ye looked for much, and lo, it came to little; and when ye brought it home, I did blow upon it. Why?" saith the LORD of hosts. "Because of mine house that is waste, and ye run every man unto his own house. Therefore the heaven over you is stayed from dew, and the earth is stayed from her fruit. And I called for a drought upon the land, and upon the mountains, and upon the corn, and upon the new wine, and upon the oil, and upon that which the ground bringeth forth, and upon men, and upon cattle, and upon all the labour of the hands."

Then Zerubbabel, the son of Shealtiel, and Joshua, the son of Josedech, the high priest, with all the remnant of the people, obeyed the voice of the LORD their God, and the words of Haggai, the prophet, as the LORD their God had sent him, and the people did fear before the LORD. Then spake Haggai, the LORD's messenger, in the LORD's message unto the people, saying, "'I am with you,' saith the LORD."

And the LORD stirred up the spirit of Zerubbabel, the son of Shealtiel, governor of Judah, and the spirit of Joshua, the son of Josedech, the high priest, and the spirit of all the remnant of the people; and they came and did work in the house of the LORD of hosts, their God, in the four and twentieth day of the sixth month, in the second year of Darius, the king.

In the seventh month, in the one and twentieth day of the month, came the word of the LORD by the prophet Haggai, saying, "Speak now to Zerubbabel, the son of Shealtiel, governor of Judah, and to Joshua, the son of Josedech, the high priest, and to the residue of the people, saying, 'Who is left among you that saw this house in her first glory and how do ye see it now? Is it not in your eyes in comparison of it as nothing? Yet now be strong, O Zerubbabel,' saith the LORD; 'and be strong, O Joshua, son of Josedech, the high priest; and be strong, all ye people of the land,' saith the LORD, 'and work: for I am with you,' saith the LORD of hosts: 'According to the word that I covenanted with you when ye came out of Egypt, so my spirit remaineth among you: fear ye not.' For thus saith the LORD of hosts: 'Yet once, it is a little while, and I will shake the heavens, and the earth, and the sea, and the dry land; and I will shake all nations, and the desire of all nations shall come: and I will fill this house with glory,' saith the LORD of hosts. 'The silver is mine, and the gold is mine,' saith the LORD of hosts. 'The glory of this latter house shall be greater than of the former,' saith the LORD of hosts: 'and in this place will I give peace,' saith the LORD of hosts."

In the four and twentieth day of the ninth month, in the second year of Darius, came the word of the LORD by Haggai, the prophet, saying, "Thus saith the LORD of hosts: 'Ask now the priests concerning the law, saying, "If one bear holy flesh in the skirt of his garment, and with his skirt do touch bread, or pottage, or wine, or oil, or any meat, shall it be holy?"'"

And the priests answered and said, "No."

Then said Haggai, "If one that is unclean by a dead body touch any of these, shall it be unclean?"

And the priests answered and said, "It shall be unclean."

Then answered Haggai, and said, "'So is this people, and so is this nation before me,' saith the LORD; 'and so is every work of their hands; and that which they offer there is unclean. And now, I pray you, consider from this day and upward, from before a stone was laid upon a stone in the temple of the LORD: since those days were, when one came to an heap of twenty measures, there were but ten: when one came to the pressfat for to draw out fifty vessels out of the press, there were but twenty.

"'I smote you with blasting and with mildew and with hail in all the labours of your hands; yet ye turned not to me,' saith the LORD. 'Consider now from this day and upward, from the four and twentieth day of the ninth month, even from the day that the foundation of the LORD's temple was laid, consider it. Is the seed yet in the barn? Yea, as yet the vine, and the fig-tree, and the pomegranate, and the olive-tree, hath not brought forth: from this day will I bless you.'"

And again the word of the LORD came unto Haggai in the four and twentieth day of the month, saying, "Speak to Zerubbabel, governor of Judah, saying, 'I will shake the heavens and the earth; and I will overthrow the throne of kingdoms, and I will destroy the strength of the kingdoms of the heathen; and I will overthrow the chariots, and those that ride in them; and the horses and their riders shall come down, every one by the sword of his brother. In that day,' saith the LORD of hosts, 'will I take thee, O Zerubbabel, my servant, the son of Shealtiel,' saith the LORD, 'and will make thee as a signet: for I have chosen thee,' saith the LORD of hosts."

— Haggai 1; 2.

The Prophecy of Zechariah

In the eighth month, in the second year of Darius, came the word of the LORD unto Zechariah, the son of Berechiah, the son of Iddo, the prophet, saying, "The LORD hath been sore displeased with your fathers. Therefore say thou unto them, 'Thus saith the LORD of hosts: "Turn ye unto me," saith the LORD of hosts, "and I will turn unto you," saith the LORD of hosts. "Be ye not as your fathers, unto whom the former prophets have cried, saying, 'Thus saith the LORD of hosts: "Turn ye now from your evil ways, and from your evil doings: but they did not hear, nor hearken unto me,"'" saith the LORD.

"'Your fathers, where are they, and the prophets, do they live forever? But my words and my statutes, which I commanded my servants, the prophets, did they not take hold of your fathers? And they returned and said, "Like as the LORD of hosts thought to do unto us, according to our ways, and according to our doings, so hath he dealt with us."'"

— Zechariah 1:1–6.

THE MEN WHO RODE AT NIGHT UPON RED HORSES, SPECKLED AND WHITE

Upon the four and twentieth day of the eleventh month, which is the month Sebat, in the second year of Darius, came the word of the LORD unto Zechariah, the son of Berechiah, the son of Iddo, the prophet, saying, "I saw by night, and behold a man riding upon a red horse, and he stood among the myrtle-trees that were in the bottom; and behind him were there red horses, speckled, and white."

WINGED BULL

In the Louvre, Paris

THIS sculpture is of the age of Darius, the Persian.

Zechariah very probably took his symbols of winged creatures from the sculptures which he saw in the days of the captivity.

Then said I, "O my lord, what are these?"

And the angel that talked with me said unto me, "I will shew thee what these be."

And the man that stood among the myrtle-trees answered and said, "These are they whom the LORD hath sent to walk to and fro through the earth."

And they answered the angel of the LORD that stood among the myrtle-trees, and said, "We have walked to and fro through the earth, and, behold, all the earth sitteth still, and is at rest."

Then the angel of the LORD answered and said, "O LORD of hosts, how long wilt thou not have mercy on Jerusalem and on the cities of Judah, against which thou hast had indignation these threescore and ten years?"

And the LORD answered the angel that talked with me with good words and comfortable words.

So the angel that communed with me said unto me, "Cry thou, saying, 'Thus saith the LORD of hosts: "I am jealous for Jerusalem and for Zion with a great jealousy. And I am very sore displeased with the heathen that are at ease: for I was but a little displeased, and they helped forward the affliction." '

"Therefore thus saith the LORD: 'I am returned to Jerusalem with mercies: my house shall be built in it,' saith the LORD of hosts, 'and a line shall be stretched forth upon Jerusalem.'

"Cry yet, saying, 'Thus saith the LORD of hosts: "My cities through prosperity shall yet be spread abroad; and the LORD shall yet comfort Zion, and shall yet choose Jerusalem." ' "

Then lifted I up mine eyes, and saw, and behold four horns. And I said unto the angel that talked with me, "What be these?"

And he answered me, "These are the horns which have scattered Judah, Israel, and Jerusalem." And the LORD shewed me four carpenters.

Then said I, "What come these to do?"

And he spake, saying, "These are the horns which have scattered Judah, so that no man did lift up his head: but these are come to fray them, to cast out the horns of the Gentiles, which lifted up their horn over the land of Judah to scatter it." — Zechariah 1:7–21.

THE MAN WITH A MEASURING LINE

I lifted up mine eyes again, and looked, and behold a man with a measuring line in his hand.

Then said I, "Whither goest thou?"

And he said unto me, "To measure Jerusalem, to see what is the breadth thereof, and what is the length thereof."

And, behold, the angel that talked with me went forth, and another angel went out to meet him, and said unto him, "Run, speak to this young man, saying, 'Jerusalem shall be inhabited as towns without walls for the multitude of men and cattle therein: for I,' saith the LORD, 'will be unto her a wall of fire round about, and will be the glory in the midst of her.

"'Ho, ho, come forth, and flee from the land of the north,' saith the LORD: 'for I have spread you abroad as the four winds of the heaven,' saith the LORD. 'Deliver thyself, O Zion, that dwellest with the daughter of Babylon.' For thus saith the LORD of hosts: 'After the glory hath he sent me unto the nations which spoiled you: for he that toucheth you toucheth the apple of his eye. For, behold, I will shake mine hand upon them, and they shall be a spoil to their servants: and ye shall know that the LORD of hosts hath sent me.

KING IN COMBAT WITH A LION

From the Palace of Darius, 521 B.C.
By courtesy of the Metropolitan Museum of
Art, New York

THIS Persian bas-relief of a man in kingly
dress, fighting with a lion, seems more
crude and stiff in execution than the earlier
sculptures from the palace of Ashur-nasi-pal
in Volume 2 and 3.

" 'Sing and rejoice, O daughter of Zion: for, lo, I come, and I will dwell in the midst of thee,' saith the LORD.

" 'And many nations shall be joined to the LORD in that day, and shall be my people: and I will dwell in the midst of thee, and thou shalt know that the LORD of hosts hath sent me unto thee. And the LORD shall inherit Judah his portion in the holy land, and shall choose Jerusalem again. Be silent, O all flesh, before the LORD: for he is raised up out of his holy habitation.' " — Zechariah 2.

The Filthy Garments of the High Priest Changed to Clean

And he shewed me Joshua, the high priest, standing before the angel of the LORD, and Satan standing at his right hand to resist him. And the LORD said unto Satan, "The LORD rebuke thee, O Satan; even the LORD that hath chosen Jerusalem rebuke thee: is not this a brand plucked out of the fire?" Now Joshua was clothed with filthy garments, and stood before the angel. And he answered and spake unto those that stood before him, saying, "Take away the filthy garments from him."

And unto him he said, "Behold, I have caused thine iniquity to pass from thee, and I will clothe thee with change of raiment."

And I said, "Let them set a fair mitre upon his head." So they set a fair mitre upon his head, and clothed him with garments. And the angel of the LORD stood by.

And the angel of the LORD protested unto Joshua, saying, "Thus saith the LORD of hosts: 'If thou wilt walk in my ways, and if thou wilt keep my charge, then thou shalt also judge my house, and shalt also keep my courts, and I will give thee places to walk among these that stand by. Hear now, O Joshua, the high priest, thou, and thy fellows that sit before thee: for they are men wondered at: for, behold, I will bring forth my servant, The BRANCH. For behold the stone that I have laid before Joshua; upon one stone shall be seven eyes: behold, I will engrave the graving thereof,' saith the LORD of hosts, 'and I will remove the iniquity of that land in one day. In that day,' saith the LORD of hosts, 'shall ye call every man his neighbor under the vine and under the fig-tree.'" — Zechariah 3.

THE GOLDEN CANDLESTICK AND THE OLIVE-TREES

And the angel that talked with me came again, and waked me, as a man that is wakened out of his sleep, and said unto me, "What seest thou?"

And I said, "I have looked, and behold a candlestick all of gold, with a bowl upon the top of it, and his seven lamps thereon, and seven pipes to the seven lamps, which are upon the top thereof: and two olive-trees by it, one upon the right side of the bowl, and the other upon the left side thereof."

So I answered and spake to the angel that talked with me, saying, "What are these, my lord?"

Then the angel that talked with me answered and said unto me, "Knowest thou not what these be?"

And I said, "No, my lord."

Then he answered and spake unto me, saying, "This is the word of the LORD unto Zerubbabel, saying, 'Not by might, not by power, but by my spirit,' saith the LORD of hosts. 'Who art thou, O great mountain? Before Zerubbabel thou shalt become a plain: and he shall bring forth the headstone thereof with shoutings, crying, "Grace, grace unto it."'"

Moreover the word of the LORD came unto me, saying, "The hands of Zerubbabel have laid the foundation of this house; his hands shall also finish it; and thou shalt know that the LORD of hosts hath sent me unto you. For who hath despised the day of small things? For they shall rejoice, and shall see the plummet in the hand of Zerubbabel with those seven; they are the eyes of the LORD, which run to and fro through the whole earth."

Then answered I, and said unto him, "What are these two olive-trees upon the right side of the candlestick and upon the left side thereof?" And I answered again, and said unto him, "What be these two olive branches which through the two golden pipes empty the golden oil out of themselves?" And he answered me and said, "Knowest thou not what these be?"

And I said, "No, my lord."

Then said he, "These are the two anointed ones, that stand by the LORD of the whole earth."

— Zechariah 4.

THE FLYING ROLL

Then I turned, and lifted up mine eyes, and looked, and behold a flying roll. And he said unto me, "What seest thou?"

And I answered, "I see a flying roll; the length thereof is twenty cubits, and the breadth thereof ten cubits."

Then said he unto me, "This is the curse that goeth forth over the face of the whole earth: for every one that stealeth shall be cut off as on this side according to it; and every one that sweareth shall be cut off as on that side according to it. 'I will bring it forth,' saith the LORD of hosts, 'and it shall enter into the house of the thief, and into the house of him that sweareth falsely by my name: and it shall remain in the midst of his house, and shall consume it with the timber thereof and the stones thereof.'"

— Zechariah 5:1-4.

The Woman in the Measure

Then the angel that talked with me went forth, and said unto me, "Lift up now thine eyes, and see what is this that goeth forth."

And I said, "What is it?"

And he said, "This is an ephah that goeth forth." He said moreover, "This is their resemblance through all the earth."

And, behold, there was lifted up a talent of lead: and this is a woman that sitteth in the midst of the ephah. And he said, "This is wickedness." And he cast it into the midst of the ephah; and he cast the weight of lead upon the mouth thereof. Then lifted I up mine eyes, and looked, and, behold, there came out two women, and the wind was in their wings; for they had wings like the wings of a stork: and they lifted up the ephah between the earth and the heaven. Then said I to the angel that talked with me, "Whither do these bear the ephah?"

And he said unto me, "To build it an house in the land of Shinar: and it shall be established, and set there upon her own base." — Zechariah 5:5-11.

The Chariots with the Red, Black, Gray, and White Horses

And I turned, and lifted up mine eyes, and looked, and, behold, there came four chariots out from between two mountains; and the mountains were mountains of brass. In the first chariot were red horses; and in the second chariot black horses; and in the third chariot white horses; and in the fourth chariot grisled and bay horses. Then I answered and said unto the angel that talked with me, "What are these, my lord?"

And the angel answered and said unto me, "These are the four spirits of the heavens, which go forth from standing before the LORD of all the earth. The black horses which are therein go forth into the north country; and the white go forth after them; and the grisled go forth toward the south country."

And the bay went forth, and sought to go that they might walk to and fro through the earth: and he said, "Get you hence, walk to and fro through the earth." So they walked to and fro through the earth.

Then cried he upon me, and spake unto me, saying, "Behold, these that go toward the north country have quieted my spirit in the north country." — Zechariah 6:1–8.

THE MAN WHOSE NAME IS "THE BRANCH"

And the word of the LORD came unto me, saying, "Take of them of the captivity, even of Heldai, of Tobijah, and of Jedaiah, which are come from Babylon, and come thou the same day, and go into the house of Josiah, the son of Zephaniah; then take silver and gold, and make crowns, and set them upon the head of Joshua, the son of Josedech, the high priest; and speak unto him, saying, "Thus speaketh the LORD of hosts, saying, "Behold the man whose name is The BRANCH; and he shall grow up out of his place, and he shall build the temple of the LORD: even he shall build the temple of the LORD; and he shall bear the glory, and shall sit and rule upon his throne; and he shall be a priest upon his throne: and the counsel of peace shall be between them both. And the crowns shall be to Helem, and to Tobijah, and to Jedaiah, and to Hen, the son of Zephaniah, for a memorial in the temple of the LORD. And they that are far off shall come and build in the temple of the LORD, and ye shall know that the LORD of hosts hath sent me unto you. And this shall come to pass, if ye will diligently obey the voice of the LORD your God."" — Zechariah 6:9–15.

THE PUNISHMENT OF ISRAEL BECAUSE THE PEOPLE MADE THEIR HEARTS AS ADAMANT

And it came to pass in the fourth year of King Darius, that the word of the LORD came unto Zechariah in the fourth day of the ninth month, even in Chisleu; when they had sent unto the house of God Sherezer and Regemmelech, and their men, to pray before the LORD, and to speak unto the priests which were in the house of the LORD of hosts, and to the prophets, saying, "Should I weep in the fifth month, separating myself, as I have done these so many years?"

Then came the word of the LORD of hosts unto me, saying, "Speak unto all the people of the land, and to the priests, saying, 'When ye fasted and mourned in the fifth and seventh month, even those seventy years, did ye at all fast unto me, even to me? And when ye did eat, and when ye did drink, did not ye eat for yourselves, and drink for yourselves? Should ye not hear the words which the LORD hath cried by the former prophets, when Jerusalem was inhabited and in prosperity, and the cities thereof round about her, when men inhabited the south and the plain?'"

And the word of the LORD came unto Zechariah, saying, "Thus speaketh the LORD of hosts, saying, 'Execute true judgment, and shew mercy and compassions every man to his brother, and oppress not the widow, nor the fatherless, the stranger, nor the poor; and let none of you imagine evil against his brother in your heart.'"

But they refused to hearken, and pulled away the shoulder, and stopped their ears, that they should not hear. Yea, they made their hearts as an adamant stone, lest they should hear the law, and the words which the

Lord of hosts hath sent in his spirit by the former prophets: therefore came a great wrath from the Lord of hosts.

"Therefore it is come to pass, that as he cried, and they would not hear; so they cried, and I would not hear," saith the Lord of hosts: "but I scattered them with a whirlwind among all the nations whom they knew not." Thus the land was desolate after them, that no man passed through nor returned: for they laid the pleasant land desolate. — Zechariah 7.

The Streets of the City Shall Be Full of Boys and Girls Playing

Again the word of the Lord of hosts came to me, saying, "Thus saith the Lord of hosts: 'I was jealous for Zion with great jealousy, and I was jealous for her with great fury.'

"Thus saith the Lord: 'I am returned unto Zion, and will dwell in the midst of Jerusalem: and Jerusalem shall be called a city of truth; and the mountain of the Lord of hosts the holy mountain.' Thus saith the Lord of hosts: 'There shall yet old men and old women dwell in the streets of Jerusalem, and every man with his staff in his hand for very age. And the streets of the city shall be full of boys and girls playing in the streets thereof.'

"Thus saith the Lord of hosts: 'If it be marvellous in the eyes of the remnant of this people in these days, should it also be marvellous in mine eyes?' saith the Lord of hosts.

Jerusalem Shall Be Restored

"Thus saith the Lord of hosts: 'Behold, I will save my people from the east country, and from the west country;

and I will bring them, and they shall dwell in the midst of Jerusalem: and they shall be my people, and I will be their God, in truth and in righteousness.'

"Thus saith the LORD of hosts: 'Let your hands be strong, ye that hear in these days these words by the mouth of the prophets, which were in the day that the foundation of the house of the LORD of hosts was laid, that the temple might be built. For before these days there was no hire for man, nor any hire for beast; neither was there any peace to him that went out or came in because of the affliction: for I set all men every one against his neighbour. But now I will not be unto the residue of this people as in the former days,' saith the LORD of hosts. 'For the seed shall be prosperous; the vine shall give her fruit, and the ground shall give her increase, and the heavens shall give their dew; and I will cause the remnant of this people to possess all these things. And it shall come to pass, that as ye were a curse among the heathen, O house of Judah, and house of Israel; so will I save you, and ye shall be a blessing: fear not, but let your hands be strong.' For thus saith the LORD of hosts: 'As I thought to punish you, when your fathers provoked me to wrath,' saith the LORD of hosts, 'and I repented not: so again have I thought in these days to do well unto Jerusalem and to the house of Judah: fear ye not.

"THESE THINGS YE SHALL DO"

"'These are the things that ye shall do: speak ye every man the truth to his neighbour; execute the judgment of truth and peace in your gates: and let none of you imagine evil in your hearts against his neighbour; and love no false oath: for all these are things that I hate,' saith the LORD."

And the word of the LORD of hosts came unto me, saying, "Thus saith the LORD of hosts: 'The fast of the fourth month, and the fast of the fifth, and the fast of the seventh, and the fast of the tenth, shall be to the house of Judah joy and gladness, and cheerful feasts; therefore love the truth and peace.' Thus saith the LORD of hosts: 'It shall yet come to pass, that there shall come people, and the inhabitants of many cities: and the inhabitants of one city shall go to another, saying, "Let us go speedily to pray before the LORD, and to seek the LORD of hosts: I will go also." Yea, many people and strong nations shall come to seek the LORD of hosts in Jerusalem, and to pray before the LORD.' Thus saith the LORD of hosts: 'In those days it shall come to pass, that ten men shall take hold out of all languages of the nations, even shall take hold of the skirt of him that is a Jew, saying, "We will go with you: for we have heard that God is with you."'"

— Zechariah 8.

"BEHOLD THY KING COMETH TO THEE"

The burden of the word of the LORD in the land of Hadrach and Damascus shall be the rest thereof: when the eyes of man, as of all the tribes of Israel, shall be toward the LORD.

"And Hamath also shall border thereby: Tyrus, and Zidon, though it be very wise. And Tyrus did build herself a stronghold, and heaped up silver as the dust, and fine gold as the mire of the streets. Behold, the LORD will cast her out, and he will smite her power in the sea; and she shall be devoured with fire. Ashkelon shall see it, and fear; Gaza also shall see it, and be very sorrowful, and Ekron; for her expectation shall be ashamed; and the king shall perish from Gaza, and Ashkelon shall not be inhabited. And a bastard shall dwell in Ashdod, and

I will cut off the pride of the Philistines. And I will take away his blood out of his mouth, and his abominations from between his teeth: but he that remaineth, even he, shall be for our God, and he shall be as a governor in Judah, and Ekron as a Jebusite. And I will encamp about mine house because of the army, because of him that passeth by, and because of him that returneth: and no oppressor shall pass through them any more: for now have I seen with mine eyes.

"Rejoice greatly, O daughter of Zion; shout, O daughter of Jerusalem: behold, thy King cometh unto thee: he is just, and having salvation; lowly, and riding upon an ass, and upon a colt the foal of an ass. And I will cut off the chariot from Ephraim, and the horse from Jerusalem, and the battle bow shall be cut off: and he shall speak peace unto the heathen: and his dominion shall be from sea even to sea, and from the river even to the ends of the earth. As for thee also, by the blood of thy covenant I have sent forth thy prisoners out of the pit wherein is no water. Turn you to the stronghold, ye prisoners of hope: even to-day do I declare that I will render double unto thee; when I have bent Judah for me, filled the bow with Ephraim, and raised up thy sons, O Zion, against thy sons, O Greece, and made thee as the sword of a mighty man. And the LORD shall be seen over them, and his arrow shall go forth as the lightning: and the Lord GOD shall blow the trumpet, and shall go with whirlwinds of the south. The LORD of hosts shall defend them; and they shall devour, and subdue with sling stones; and they shall drink, and make a noise as through wine; and they shall be filled like bowls, and as the corners of the altar. And the LORD their God shall save them in that day as the flock of his people: for they shall be as the stones of a crown, lifted up as an ensign upon his land.

For how great is his goodness and how great is his beauty!
Corn shall make the young men cheerful, and new wine
the maids.   — Zechariah 9.

The Lord Shall Bring Back the Captives

"Ask ye of the LORD rain in the time of the latter rain;
so the LORD shall make bright clouds, and give them
showers of rain, to every one grass in the field. For the
idols have spoken vanity, and the diviners have seen
a lie, and have told false dreams; they comfort in vain:
therefore they went their way as a flock, they were
troubled, because there was no shepherd. Mine anger was
kindled against the shepherds, and I punished the goats:
for the LORD of hosts hath visited his flock, the house of
Judah, and hath made them as his goodly horse in the
battle. Out of him came forth the corner, out of him the
nail, out of him the battle bow, out of him every oppressor
together.

"And they shall be as mighty men, which tread down
their enemies in the mire of the streets in the battle: and
they shall fight, because the LORD is with them, and the
riders on horses shall be confounded. And I will strengthen
the house of Judah, and I will save the house of Joseph,
and I will bring them again to place them; for I have
mercy upon them: and they shall be as though I had not
cast them off: for I am the LORD their God, and will
hear them. And they of Ephraim shall be like a mighty
man, and their heart shall rejoice as through wine: yea,
their children shall see it, and be glad; their heart shall
rejoice in the LORD. I will hiss for them, and gather
them; for I have redeemed them: and they shall increase
as they have increased. And I will sow them among the
people: and they shall remember me in far countries;
and they shall live with their children, and turn again.

I will bring them again also out of the land of Egypt, and gather them out of Assyria; and I will bring them into the land of Gilead and Lebanon; and place shall not be found for them. And he shall pass through the sea with affliction, and shall smite the waves in the sea, and all the deeps of the river shall dry up: and the pride of Assyria shall be brought down, and the sceptre of Egypt shall depart away. And I will strengthen them in the LORD; and they shall walk up and down in his name," saith the LORD.   — Zechariah 10.

THE LESSON OF THE TWO BROKEN STAVES

Open thy doors, O Lebanon, that the fire may devour thy cedars. Howl, fir-tree; for the cedar is fallen; because the mighty are spoiled: howl, O ye oaks of Bashan; for the forest of the vintage is come down. There is a voice of the howling of the shepherds; for their glory is spoiled: a voice of the roaring of young lions; for the pride of Jordan is spoiled. Thus saith the LORD thy God: "Feed the flock of the slaughter, whose possessors slay them, and hold themselves not guilty: and they that sell them say, 'Blessed be the LORD; for I am rich': and their own shepherds pity them not. For I will no more pity the inhabitants of the land," saith the LORD: "but, lo, I will deliver the men every one into his neighbour's hand, and into the hand of his king: and they shall smite the land, and out of their hand I will not deliver them. And I will feed the flock of slaughter, even you, O poor of the flock."

And I took unto me two staves; the one I called Beauty, and the other I called Bands; and I fed the flock. Three shepherds also I cut off in one month; and my soul loathed them, and their soul also abhorred me. Then said I, "I will not feed you: that that dieth, let it die; and that that is to be cut off, let it be cut off; and let the rest eat every one the flesh of another."

And I took my staff, even Beauty, and cut it asunder, that I might break my covenant which I had made with all the people. And it was broken in that day: and so the poor of the flock that waited upon me knew that it was the word of the LORD. And I said unto them, "If ye think good, give me my price; and if not, forbear." So they weighed for my price thirty pieces of silver.

And the LORD said unto me, "Cast it unto the potter": a goodly price that I was prised at of them.

And I took the thirty pieces of silver, and cast them to the potter in the house of the LORD. Then I cut asunder mine other staff, even Bands, that I might break the brotherhood between Judah and Israel.

And the LORD said unto me, "Take unto thee yet the instruments of a foolish shepherd. For, lo, I will raise up a shepherd in the land, which shall not visit those that be cut off, neither shall seek the young one, nor heal that that is broken, nor feed that that standeth still: but he shall eat the flesh of the fat, and tear their claws in pieces. Woe to the idle shepherd that leaveth the flock! The sword shall be upon his arm, and upon his right eye: his arm shall be clean dried up, and his right eye shall be utterly darkened."   — Zechariah 11.

THE LORD WILL SAVE THE HOUSE OF DAVID

"The burden of the word of the LORD for Israel," saith the LORD, which stretcheth forth the heavens, and layeth the foundation of the earth, and formeth the spirit of man within him.

"Behold, I will make Jerusalem a cup of trembling unto all the people round about, when they shall be in the siege both against Judah and against Jerusalem. And in that day will I make Jerusalem a burdensome stone for all people: all that burden themselves with it shall be cut in pieces, though all the people of the earth be gathered together against it.

"In that day," saith the LORD, "I will smite every horse with astonishment, and his rider with madness: and I will open mine eyes upon the house of Judah, and will smite every horse of the people with blindness. And the governors of Judah shall say in their heart, 'The inhabitants of Jerusalem shall be my strength in the LORD of hosts their God.'

"In that day will I make the governors of Judah like an hearth of fire among the wood, and like a torch of fire in a sheaf; and they shall devour all the people round about, on the right hand and on the left: and Jerusalem shall be inhabited again in her own place, even in Jerusalem. The LORD also shall save the tents of Judah first, that the glory of the house of David and the glory of the inhabitants of Jerusalem do not magnify themselves against Judah. In that day shall the LORD defend the inhabitants of Jerusalem; and he that is feeble among them at that day shall be as David; and the house of David shall be as God, as the angel of the LORD before them.

"And it shall come to pass in that day, that I will seek to destroy all the nations that come against Jerusalem. And I will pour upon the house of David, and upon the inhabitants of Jerusalem, the spirit of grace and of supplications: and they shall look upon me whom they have pierced, and they shall mourn for him, as one mourneth for his only son, and shall be in bitterness for him, as one that is in bitterness for his firstborn. In that day shall there be a great mourning in Jerusalem, as the mourning

of Hadadrimmon in the valley of Megiddon. And the
land shall mourn, every family apart; the family of the
house of David apart, and their wives apart; the family
of the house of Nathan apart, and their wives apart; the
family of the house of Levi apart, and their wives apart;
the family of Shimei apart, and their wives apart; all
the families that remain, every family apart, and their
wives apart.' — Zechariah 12.

"They Shall Be Refined as Silver and Tried as Gold"

"In that day there shall be a fountain opened to the
house of David and to the inhabitants of Jerusalem for
sin and for uncleanness.

"And it shall come to pass in that day," saith the
LORD of hosts, "that I will cut off the names of the idols
out of the land, and they shall no more be remembered:
and also I will cause the prophets and the unclean spirit
to pass out of the land. And it shall come to pass, that
when any shall yet prophesy, then his father and his
mother that begat him shall say unto him, 'Thou shalt
not live; for thou speakest lies in the name of the LORD':
and his father and his mother that begat him shall thrust
him through when he prophesieth. And it shall come
to pass in that day, that the prophets shall be ashamed
every one of his vision, when he hath prophesied; neither
shall they wear a rough garment to deceive: but he shall
say, 'I am no prophet, I am an husbandman; for man
taught me to keep cattle from my youth.'

"And one shall say unto him, 'What are these wounds
in thine hands?' Then he shall answer, 'Those with
which I was wounded in the house of my friends.'

"Awake, O sword, against my shepherd, and against
the man that is my fellow," saith the LORD of hosts:

"smite the shepherd, and the sheep shall be scattered: and I will turn mine hand upon the little ones. And it shall come to pass, that in all the land," saith the LORD, "two parts therein shall be cut off and die; but the third shall be left therein. And I will bring the third part through the fire, and will refine them as silver is refined, and will try them as gold is tried: they shall call on my name, and I will hear them: I will say, 'It is my people': and they shall say, 'The LORD is my God.'"

— Zechariah 13.

"Living Waters Shall Go Out from Jerusalem"

Behold, the day of the LORD cometh, and thy spoil shall be divided in the midst of thee. For I will gather all nations against Jerusalem to battle; and the city shall be taken, and the houses rifled, and the women ravished; and half of the city shall go forth into captivity, and the residue of the people shall not be cut off from the city. Then shall the LORD go forth, and fight against those nations, as when he fought in the day of battle.

And his feet shall stand in that day upon the Mount of Olives, which is before Jerusalem on the east, and the Mount of Olives shall cleave in the midst thereof toward the east and toward the west, and there shall be a very great valley; and half of the mountain shall remove toward the north, and half of it toward the south. And ye shall flee to the valley of the mountains; for the valley of the mountains shall reach unto Azal: yea, ye shall flee, like as ye fled from before the earthquake in the days of Uzziah, King of Judah: and the LORD my God shall come, and all the saints with thee. And it shall come to pass in that day, that the light shall not be clear, nor dark: but it shall be one day which shall be known to the LORD, not day, nor night: but it shall come to pass, that at evening time it shall be light.

And it shall be in that day, that living waters shall
go out from Jerusalem; half of them toward the former
sea, and half of them toward the hinder sea: in summer
and in winter shall it be. And the LORD shall be king
over all the earth: in that day shall there be one LORD,
and his name one. All the land shall be turned as a
plain from Geba to Rimmon south of Jerusalem: and it
shall be lifted up, and inhabited in her place, from
Benjamin's gate unto the place of the first gate, unto the
corner gate, and from the tower of Hananeel unto the
king's wine-presses. And men shall dwell in it, and there
shall be no more utter destruction; but Jerusalem shall
be safely inhabited.

And this shall be the plague wherewith the LORD will
smite all the people that have fought against Jerusalem:
their flesh shall consume away while they stand upon
their feet, and their eyes shall consume away in their
holes, and their tongue shall consume away in their
mouth. And it shall come to pass in that day, that a great
tumult from the LORD shall be among them; and they
shall lay hold every one on the hand of his neighbour, and
his hand shall rise up against the hand of his neighbour.
And Judah also shall fight at Jerusalem; and the wealth
of all the heathen round about shall be gathered together,
gold, and silver, and apparel, in great abundance. And
so shall be the plague of the horse, of the mule, of the
camel, and of the ass, and of all the beasts that shall be
in these tents, as this plague.   — Zechariah 14:1-15.

"THE POTS OF THE LORD'S HOUSE SHALL BE AS THE BOWLS BEFORE THE ALTAR"

And it shall come to pass, that every one that is left
of all the nations which came against Jerusalem shall
even go up from year to year to worship the king, the

LORD of hosts, and to keep the feast of tabernacles. And it shall be, that whoso will not come up of all the families of the earth unto Jerusalem to worship the King, the LORD of hosts, even upon them shall be no rain. And if the family of Egypt go not up, and come not, that have no rain; there shall be the plague, wherewith the LORD will smite the heathen that come not up to keep the feast of tabernacles. This shall be the punishment of Egypt, and the punishment of all nations that come not up to keep the feast of tabernacles.

In that day shall there be upon the bells of the horses, HOLINESS UNTO THE LORD; and the pots in the LORD's house shall be like the bowls before the altar. Yea, every pot in Jerusalem and in Judah shall be holiness unto the LORD of hosts: and all they that sacrifice shall come and take of them, and seethe therein: and in that day there shall be no more the Canaanite in the house of the LORD of hosts.   — Zechariah 14:16-21.

Obadiah

There is no way of knowing when this little prophecy, the shortest book of the Old Testament, was written. Obadiah is but a name; we know nothing of his home, his station. His prophecy is spoken against Edom, the ancient enemy of Israel, a nation whose bitter hatred survived until the last century before Christ, when the territory of Edom was incorporated with that of the Jewish kingdom, and out of it came that race of Herods which cursed the people in the days of Jesus.

The Prophecy of Obadiah

Thus saith the Lord GOD concerning Edom: "We have heard a rumour from the LORD, and an ambassador is sent among the heathen, 'Arise ye, and let us rise up against her in battle.'

HIS VISION

"BEHOLD, I have made thee small among the heathen: thou art greatly despised. The pride of thine heart hath deceived thee, thou that dwellest in the clefts of the rock, whose habitation is high; that saith in his heart, 'Who shall bring me down to the ground?' Though thou exalt thyself as the eagle, and though thou set thy nest among the stars, thence will I bring thee down," saith the LORD.

"If thieves came to thee, if robbers by night, (how art thou cut off!) would they not have stolen till they had enough? If the grapegatherers came to thee, would they not leave some grapes? How are the things of Esau searched out! How are his hidden things sought up! All the men of thy confederacy have brought thee even to the border: the men that were at peace with thee have deceived thee, and prevailed against thee; they that eat thy bread have laid a wound under thee: there is none understanding in him. Shall I not in that day," saith the LORD, "even destroy the wise men out of Edom, and understanding out of the Mount of Esau? And thy mighty men, O Teman, shall be dismayed, to the end that every one of the Mount of Esau may be cut off by slaughter.

"For thy violence against thy brother Jacob shame shall cover thee, and thou shalt be cut off forever. In the day that thou stoodest on the other side, in the day that the strangers carried away captive his forces, and foreigners entered into his gates, and cast lots upon Jerusalem, even thou wast as one of them. But thou shouldest not have looked on the day of thy brother in the day that he became a stranger; neither shouldest thou have rejoiced over the children of Judah in the day of their destruction; neither shouldest thou have spoken proudly in the day of distress. Thou shouldest not have entered into the gate of my people in the day of their calamity; yea, thou shouldest not have looked on their affliction in the day of their calamity, nor have laid hands on their substance in the day of their calamity; neither shouldest thou have stood in the crossway, to cut off those of his that did escape; neither shouldest thou have delivered up those of his that did remain in the day of distress. For the day of the LORD is near upon all the heathen: as thou hast done, it shall be done unto thee: thy reward shall return upon thine own head. For as ye have drunk upon my holy mountain, so shall all the heathen drink continually, yea, they shall drink, and they shall swallow down, and they shall be as though they had not been.

"But upon Mount Zion shall be deliverance, and there shall be holiness; and the house of Jacob shall possess their possessions. And the house of Jacob shall be a fire, and the house of Joseph a flame, and the house of Esau for stubble, and they shall kindle in them, and devour them; and there shall not be any remaining of the house of Esau; for the LORD hath spoken it. And they of the south shall possess the Mount of Esau; and they of the plain the Philistines: and they shall possess the fields of Ephraim, and the fields of Samaria: and Benjamin shall possess Gilead. And the captivity of this host of the children of Israel shall possess that of the Canaanites, even unto Zarephath; and the captivity of Jerusalem, which is in Sepharad, shall possess the cities of the south. And saviours shall come up on Mount Zion to judge the Mount of Esau; and the kingdom shall be the LORD's."

— Obadiah.

MODERN SCHOOL ON MOUNT ZION
Photograph by the Reverend Frederick J. Moore

This modern school for boys is built on Mt. Zion, within the walls of Jerusalem.

Malachi, My Messenger

At first, there was great enthusiasm over the building of The Temple, but that did not last long. The care of The Temple, the tithes, the provision for sacrifice,—all these were a very heavy burden upon people who were living under such hard conditions. They grew discouraged and neglected The Temple and The Temple worship.

The Prophecy of Malachi is directed against these conditions. He urges the keeping of the law, the maintenance of worship, in order that larger spiritual blessings may follow. " 'Bring ye all the tithes into the storehouse,' " he cries, " 'that there may be meat in mine house and prove me now,' saith the LORD of Hosts, 'if I will not open you the windows of heaven and pour you out such a blessing that there will not be room enough to receive it.' "

The prophecy uses the method of question and answer very effectively. There are noble and sustained passages such as,—"Then they that feared the LORD spake often one to another; and the LORD hearkened, and heard it, and a book of remembrance was written before him for them that feared the LORD, and that thought upon his name. 'And they shall be mine,' saith the LORD of hosts, 'in that day when I make up my jewels; and I will spare them, as a man spareth his own son that serveth him.' "

The name Malachi means "My Messenger"; nothing is known of the personality of the prophet.

The Prophecy of Malachi

The burden of the word of the LORD to Israel by Malachi.

GOD LOVES ISRAEL. "MY NAME SHALL BE GREAT AMONG THE GENTILES"

"I HAVE loved you," saith the LORD.

Yet ye say, "Wherein hast thou loved us?"

"Was not Esau Jacob's brother?" saith the LORD: "Yet I loved Jacob, and I hated Esau, and laid his mountains and his heritage waste for the dragons of the wilderness."

Whereas Edom saith, "We are impoverished, but we will return and build the desolate places"; thus saith the LORD of hosts, "They shall build, but I will throw down; and they shall call them, 'The border of wickedness,' and, 'The people against whom the LORD hath indignation forever.' And your eyes shall see, and ye shall say, 'The LORD will be magnified from the border of Israel.'"

— Malachi 1:1-5.

UNGRATEFUL ISRAEL

"A son honoureth his father, and a servant his master: if then I be a father, where is mine honour? And if I be a master, where is my fear?" saith the LORD of hosts unto you, O priests, that despise my name.

And ye say, "Wherein have we despised thy name?"

"Ye offer polluted bread upon mine altar; and ye say, 'Wherein have we polluted thee?' in that ye say, 'The table of the LORD is contemptible.' And if ye offer the blind for sacrifice. is it not evil? and if ye offer the

A FULLER AT WORK

Photograph by Professor Lewis Bayles Paton

The fuller has made the skeins of yarn as white as snow.

"But who may abide the day of his coming? and who shall stand when he appeareth? For he is like a refiner's fire, and like fullers' soap—*Malachi 3:2*.

"And his raiment became shining, exceeding white as snow; so as no fuller on earth can white them."—*Mark 9:3*.

lame and sick, is it not evil? Offer it now unto thy governor; will he be pleased with thee, or accept thy person?" saith the LORD of hosts.

"And now, I pray you, beseech God that he will be gracious unto us."

"This hath been by your means: will he regard your persons?" saith the LORD of hosts. "Who is there even among you that would shut the doors for naught? Neither do ye kindle fire on mine altar for naught. I have no pleasure in you," saith the LORD of hosts, "neither will I accept an offering at your hand. For from the rising of the sun even unto the going down of the same my name shall be great among the Gentiles; and in every place incense shall be offered unto my name, and a pure offering: for my name shall be great among the heathen,"

saith the LORD of hosts. "But ye have profaned it, in
that ye say, 'The table of the LORD is polluted; and the
fruit thereof, even his meat, is contemptible.' Ye said
also, 'Behold, what a weariness is it!' and ye have snuffed
at it," saith the LORD of hosts; "and ye brought that
which was torn, and the lame, and the sick; thus ye
brought an offering: should I accept this of your hand?"
saith the LORD. "But cursed be the deceiver, which hath
in his flock a male, and voweth, and sacrificeth unto the
LORD a corrupt thing: for I am a great King," saith the
LORD of hosts," and my name is dreadful among the
heathen.   — Malachi 1:6-14.

"THIS COMMANDMENT IS FOR YOU, O PRIESTS"

And now, O ye priests, this commandment is for
you.

"If ye will not hear, and if ye will not lay it to heart,
to give glory unto my name," saith the LORD of hosts,
"I will even send a curse upon you, and I will curse
your blessings: yea, I have cursed them already, because
ye do not lay it to heart. Behold, I will corrupt your
seed, and spread dung upon your faces, even the dung
of your solemn feasts; and one shall take you away with
it. And ye shall know that I have sent this commandment unto you, that my covenant might be with Levi,"
saith the LORD of hosts.

"My covenant was with him of life and peace; and
I gave them to him for the fear wherewith he feared me,
and was afraid before my name. The law of truth was
in his mouth, and iniquity was not found in his lips: he
walked with me in peace and equity, and did turn many
away from iniquity. For the priest's lips should keep
knowledge, and they should seek the law at his mouth:
for he is the messenger of the LORD of hosts. But ye are

departed out of the way; ye have caused many to stumble at the law; ye have corrupted the covenant of Levi," saith the LORD of hosts. "Therefore have I also made you contemptible and base before all the people, according as ye have not kept my ways, but have been partial in the law."

Have we not all one father? Hath not one God created us? Why do we deal treacherously every man against his brother, by profaning the covenant of our fathers?

— Malachi 2:1-10.

THE EVIL OF FOREIGN MARRIAGES

Judah hath dealt treacherously, and an abomination is committed in Israel and in Jerusalem; for Judah hath profaned the holiness of the LORD which he loved, and hath married the daughter of a strange god. The LORD will cut off the man that doeth this, the master and the scholar, out of the tabernacles of Jacob, and him that offereth an offering unto the LORD of hosts. And this have ye done again, covering the altar of the LORD with tears, with weeping, and with crying out, insomuch that he regardeth not the offering any more, or receiveth it with good will at your hand.

Yet ye say, "Wherefore?"

"Because the LORD hath been witness between thee and the wife of thy youth, against whom thou hast dealt treacherously: yet is she thy companion, and the wife of thy covenant. And did not he make one? Yet had he the residue of the spirit. And wherefore one? That he might seek a godly seed. Therefore take heed to your spirit, and let none deal treacherously against the wife of his youth. For the LORD, the God of Israel, saith that he hateth putting away: 'for one covereth violence with his garment,' saith the LORD of hosts: 'therefore take heed to your spirit, that ye deal not treacherously.' Ye have

wearied the LORD with your words. Yet ye say, 'Wherein
have we wearied him?'

"When ye say, 'Every one that doeth evil is good in
the sight of the LORD, and he delighteth in them'; or,
'Where is the God of judgment?'"   — Malachi 2:11-17.

"BEHOLD I WILL SEND MY MESSENGER:" JUSTICE WILL BE DONE

"Behold, I will send my messenger, and he shall
prepare the way before me: and the LORD, whom ye
seek, shall suddenly come to his temple, even the messenger of the covenant, whom ye delight in: behold, he
shall come," saith the LORD of hosts.

"But who may abide the day of his coming and
who shall stand when he appeareth? For he is like a
refiner's fire, and like fuller's soap: and he shall sit as a
refiner and purifier of silver: and he shall purify the
sons of Levi, and purge them as gold and silver, that
they may offer unto the LORD an offering in righteousness.
Then shall the offering of Judah and Jerusalem be pleasant unto the LORD, as in the days of old, and as in
former years. And I will come near to you to judgment;
and I will be a swift witness against the sorcerers, and
against the adulterers, and against false swearers, and
against those that oppress the hireling in his wages, the
widow, and the fatherless, and that turn aside the
stranger from his right, and fear not me," saith the LORD
of hosts. "For I am the LORD, I change not; therefore
ye sons of Jacob are not consumed. Even from the days
of your fathers ye are gone away from mine ordinances,
and have not kept them. Return unto me, and I will
return unto you," saith the LORD of hosts.

"But ye said, 'Wherein shall we return?'

"Will a man rob God? Yet ye have robbed me.

"But ye say, 'Wherein have we robbed thee?'

"In tithes and offerings.

"Ye are cursed with a curse: for ye have robbed me, even this whole nation. Bring ye all the tithes into the storehouse, that there may be meat in mine house, and prove me now herewith," saith the LORD of hosts, "if I will not open you the windows of heaven, and pour you out a blessing, that there shall not be room enough to receive it. And I will rebuke the devourer for your sakes, and he shall not destroy the fruits of your ground; neither shall your vine cast her fruit before the time in the field," saith the LORD of hosts. "And all nations shall call you blessed: for ye shall be a delightsome land," saith the LORD of hosts.

"Your words have been stout against me," saith the LORD.

"Yet ye say, 'What have we spoken so much against thee?'

"Ye have said, 'It is vain to serve God: and what profit is it that we have kept his ordinance, and that we have walked mournfully before the LORD of hosts? And now we call the proud happy; yea, they that work wickedness are set up; yea, they that tempt God are even delivered.'"

Then they that feared the LORD spake often one to another: and the LORD hearkened, and heard it, and a book of remembrance was written before him for them that feared the LORD, and that thought upon his name.

"And they shall be mine," saith the LORD of hosts, "in that day when I make up my jewels; and I will spare them, as a man spareth his own son that serveth him. Then shall ye return, and discern between the righteous and the wicked, between him that serveth God and him that serveth him not.

"For, behold, the day cometh, that shall burn as an oven; and all the proud, yea, and all that do wickedly, shall be stubble: and the day that cometh shall burn them up," saith the LORD of hosts, "that it shall leave them neither root nor branch. But unto you that fear my name shall the Sun of righteousness arise with healing in his wings; and ye shall go forth, and grow up as calves of the stall. And ye shall tread down the wicked; for they shall be ashes under the soles of your feet in the day that I shall do this," saith the LORD of hosts.

"Remember ye the law of Moses, my servant, which I commanded unto him in Horeb for all Israel, with the statutes and judgments. Behold, I will send you Elijah, the prophet, before the coming of the great and dreadful day of the LORD: and he shall turn the heart of the fathers to the children, and the heart of the children to their fathers, lest I come and smite the earth with a curse."   — Malachi 3; 4.

Joel

The Book of Joel is one of the most vigorous and eloquent of all the prophetic utterances. It has the strong, direct qualities of the Books of Amos and Micah. It abounds in quotable, poetic sayings. There is much doubt, however, with respect to the date of the prophecy. Because of its resemblance to the earlier prophets and because Assyria and Babylon are not mentioned by name, some have placed it very early; others, because it contains quotations from the early prophets, place it very late.

In the East, the swarms of locusts are a terrible visitation. They come like an army, darkening the sky and destroying every particle of vegetation, leaving the ground black and desolate as though a fire had swept over it. Joel makes such a visitation, in which the locust in the various stages of its growth rendered the land utterly barren, the basis of his vigorous appeals for repentance. The people do repent, and God forgives their transgressions.

Joel—Detail of the Sistine Chapel Ceiling

By Michelangelo Buonarroti (1475-1564)
In the Sistine Chapel of the Vatican, Rome
Photograph by Anderson, Rome

HERE is another of those majestic presences representing the prophets from the Sistine Chapel. Joel, with furrowed brow, studies a manuscript roll absorbed in deep reflection. What titantic strength of mind and body is here implied!

The Sistine ceiling frescoes were painted by Michelangelo at the request of Pope Julius II. The surface covered is estimated to be 10,000 square feet. Painting such a vast expanse of curved ceiling was impossible for any but a genius of tremendous energy and unfailing inspiration. Michelangelo, who always considered himself a sculptor, undertook this painting commission unwillingly. Soon finding that his assistants were unequal to the task, he dismissed all but a few laborers and attacked single-handed the great scheme of decoration which we see today.

When we realize what fatiguing work fresco painting was, and what rapidity and sureness of stroke was needed, the sheer wonder of the Sistine Chapel will forever amaze us. We are told that the touch of the fresco painter had to be sure, for a misstroke meant scraping off the wet plaster, relaying it, and starting all over again. A whole day's work could be spoiled by a single slip of the hand in the tired evening hour. Before Michelangelo's time a single head was a day's work for a good "frescante" (fresco painter). But Michelangelo completed the Sistine frescoes, containing some three hundred and forty figures of majestic proportions, in the incredibly short period of four years.

Michelangelo was of a melancholy temperament. He had at the same time a deeply poetic and religious mind. In the Sistine paintings we can visualize him working alone, brooding upon the mighty story of the Creation and the Fall of Man, filled with the spirit of the ancient prophets he was portraying. The result was the highest expression of sublimity in all pictorial art.

The Prophecy of Joel

The word of the LORD that came to Joel, the son of Pethuel.

THE DESOLATION OF THE LAND

HEAR this, ye old men, and give ear, all ye inhabitants of the land. Hath this been in your days, or even in the days of your fathers? Tell ye your children of it, and let your children tell their children, and their children another generation. That which the palmerworm hath left hath the locust eaten; and that which the locust hath left hath the cankerworm eaten; and that which the cankerworm hath left hath the caterpiller eaten. Awake, ye drunkards, and weep; and howl, all ye drinkers of wine, because of the new wine; for it is cut off from your mouth. For a nation is come up upon my land, strong, and without number, whose teeth are the teeth of a lion, and he hath the teeth of a great lion. He hath laid my vine waste, and barked my fig-tree: he hath made it clean bare, and cast it away; the branches thereof are made white.

Lament like a virgin, girded with sackcloth, for the husband of her youth. The meat offering and the drink offering is cut off from the house of the LORD; the priests, the LORD's ministers, mourn. The field is wasted, the land mourneth; for the corn is wasted: the new wine is dried up, the oil languisheth. Be ye ashamed, O ye husbandmen; howl, O ye vinedressers, for the wheat and for the barley; because the harvest of the field is perished.

The vine is dried up, and the fig-tree languisheth; the pomegranate-tree, the palm-tree also, and the apple-tree, even all the trees of the field, are withered: because joy is withered away from the sons of men. Gird yourselves, and lament, ye priests: howl, ye ministers of the altar: come, lie all night in sackcloth, ye ministers of my God: for the meat offering and the drink offering is withholden from the house of your God. — Joel 1:1-13.

The Call for a Fast

Sanctify ye a fast, call a solemn assembly, gather the elders and all the inhabitants of the land into the house of the LORD your God, and cry unto the LORD, "Alas for the day! for the day of the LORD is at hand, and as a destruction from the Almighty shall it come." Is not the meat cut off before our eyes, yea, joy and gladness from the house of our God? The seed is rotten under their clods, the garners are laid desolate, the barns are broken down; for the corn is withered. How do the beasts groan! The herds of cattle are perplexed, because they have no pasture; yea, the flocks of sheep are made desolate. O LORD, to thee will I cry: for the fire hath devoured the pastures of the wilderness, and the flame hath burned all the trees of the field. The beasts of the field cry also unto thee: for the rivers of waters are dried up, and the fire hath devoured the pastures of the wilderness. — Joel 1:14-20.

The March of the Locust-Swarm Like the March of a Terrible Army

Blow ye the trumpet in Zion, and sound an alarm in my holy mountain: let all the inhabitants of the land tremble: for the day of the LORD cometh, for it is nigh at hand; a day of darkness and of gloominess, a day of clouds and of

Assyrian Charioteers Attacking the Enemy

By courtesy of the British Museum, London

THE KING in the chariot shoots at the enemy
while the horses are driven by an attendant. On the right-hand side of the picture,
the enemy is retreating, and personal com-
bats are shown. The eagle of victory flies
overhead. This picture is of the time of
Ahab, King of Israel. The Assyrian chariots
were no less dreaded than the terrible cav-
alry. "Like the noise of chariots on the
tops of mountains shall they leap "

Many other Assyrian pictures may be
found in Volume 3.

thick darkness, as the morning spread upon the mountains: a great people and a strong; there hath not been ever the like, neither shall be any more after it, even to the years of many generations. A fire devoureth before them; and behind them a flame burneth: the land is as the garden of Eden before them, and behind them a desolate wilderness; yea, and nothing shall escape them. The appearance of them is as the appearance of horses; and as horsemen, so shall they run. Like the noise of chariots on the tops of mountains shall they leap, like the noise of a flame of fire that devoureth the stubble, as a strong people set in battle array. Before their face the people shall be much pained: all faces shall gather blackness. They shall run like mighty men; they shall climb the wall like men of war; and they shall march every one on his ways, and they shall not break their ranks: neither shall one thrust another; they shall walk every one in his path: and when they fall upon the sword, they shall not be wounded. They shall run to and fro in the city; they shall run upon the wall, they shall climb up upon the houses; they shall enter in at the windows like a thief. The earth shall quake before them; the heavens shall tremble: the sun and the moon shall be dark, and the stars shall withdraw their shining: and the LORD shall utter his voice before his army: for his camp is very great: for he is strong that executeth his word: for the day of the LORD is great and very terrible; and who can abide it?   — Joel 2:1-11.

"REND YOUR HEART AND NOT YOUR GARMENTS"

"Therefore also now," saith the LORD, "turn ye even to me with all your heart, and with fasting, and with weeping, and with mourning: and rend your heart, and not your garments, and turn unto the LORD your God:

for he is gracious and merciful, slow to anger, and of great kindness, and repenteth him of the evil. Who knoweth if he will return and repent, and leave a blessing behind him; even a meat offering and a drink offering unto the LORD your God?"

Blow the trumpet in Zion, sanctify a fast, call a solemn assembly: gather the people, sanctify the congregation, assemble the elders, gather the children, and those that suck the breasts: let the bridegroom go forth of his chamber and the bride out of her closet. Let the priests, the ministers of the LORD, weep between the porch and the altar, and let them say, "Spare thy people, O LORD, and give not thine heritage to reproach, that the heathen should rule over them: wherefore should they say among the people, 'Where is their God?'" — Joel 2:12-17.

THE PEOPLE HAVE HEARD THE CALL AND THE PROPHET GIVES A PROPHECY OF HOPE

Then will the LORD be jealous for his land, and pity his people. Yea, the LORD will answer and say unto his people, "Behold, I will send you corn, and wine, and oil, and ye shall be satisfied therewith: and I will no more make you a reproach among the heathen: but I will remove far off from you the northern army, and will drive him into a land barren and desolate, with his face toward the east sea, and his hinder part toward the utmost sea, and his stink shall come up, and his ill savour shall come up, because he hath done great things.

"Fear not, O land; be glad and rejoice: for the LORD will do great things. Be not afraid, ye beasts of the field: for the pastures of the wilderness do spring, for the tree beareth her fruit, the fig-tree and the vine do yield their strength. Be glad then, ye children of Zion, and rejoice

in the LORD your God: for he hath given you the former
rain moderately, and he will cause to come down for you
the rain, the former rain, and the latter rain in the first
month. And the floors shall be full of wheat, and the
fats shall overflow with wine and oil. And I will restore
to you the years that the locust hath eaten, the cankerworm, and the caterpiller, and the palmerworm, my
great army which I sent among you. And ye shall eat in
plenty, and be satisfied, and praise the name of the LORD
your God, that hath dealt wondrously with you: and my
people shall never be ashamed. And he shall know that
I am in the midst of Israel, and that I am the LORD
your God, and none else: and my people shall never be
ashamed.

"YOUR OLD MEN SHALL DREAM DREAMS: YOUR YOUNG MEN SHALL SEE VISIONS"

"And it shall come to pass afterward, that I will pour
out my spirit upon all flesh; and your sons and your
daughters shall prophesy, your old men shall dream
dreams, your young men shall see visions: and also upon
the servants and upon the handmaids in those days will
I pour out my spirit. And I will shew wonders in the
heavens and in the earth, blood, and fire, and pillars of
smoke. The sun shall be turned into darkness, and the
moon into blood, before the great and the terrible day
of the LORD come. And it shall come to pass, that
whosoever shall call on the name of the LORD shall be
delivered: for in Mount Zion and in Jerusalem shall be
deliverance, as the LORD hath said, and in the remnant
whom the LORD shall call.

"For, behold, in those days, and in that time, when
I shall bring again the captivity of Judah and Jerusalem,
I will also gather all nations, and will bring them down

into the valley of Jehoshaphat, and will plead with them there for my people and for my heritage Israel, whom they have scattered among the nations, and parted my land. And they have cast lots for my people; and have given a boy for an harlot, and sold a girl for wine, that they might drink.

PUNISHMENT TO JUDAH'S ENEMIES

"Yea, and what have ye to do with me, O Tyre, and Zidon, and all the coasts of Palestine? Will ye render me a recompence? And if ye recompense me, swiftly and speedily will I return your recompence upon your own head; because ye have taken my silver and my gold, and have carried into your temples my goodly pleasant things: the children also of Judah and the children of Jerusalem have ye sold unto the Grecians, that ye might remove them far from their border. Behold, I will raise them out of the place whither ye have sold them, and will return your recompence upon your own head: and I will sell your sons and your daughters into the hand of the children of Judah, and they shall sell them to the Sabeans, to a people far off: for the LORD hath spoken it.

"Proclaim ye this among the Gentiles; prepare war, wake up the mighty men, let all the men of war draw near; let them come up: beat your plowshares into swords, and your pruninghooks into spears: let the weak say, 'I am strong.' Assemble yourselves, and come, all ye heathen, and gather yourselves together round about: thither cause thy mighty ones to come down, O LORD. Let the heathen be wakened, and come up to the valley of Jehoshaphat: for there will I sit to judge all the heathen round about. Put ye in the sickle, for the harvest is ripe: come, get you down; for the press is full, the fats overflow; for their wickedness is great.

THE PROPHETS

AMOS   NAHUM   EZEKIEL   DANIEL

From the Frieze in the Boston Public Library,
Boston, Massachusetts
By John S. Sargent. From a Copley Print
Copyrighted by Curtis and Cameron, Inc.,
Boston, Massachusetts

OTHER sections of this great frieze are
reproduced on pages 30, 56 and 186 of this
volume.

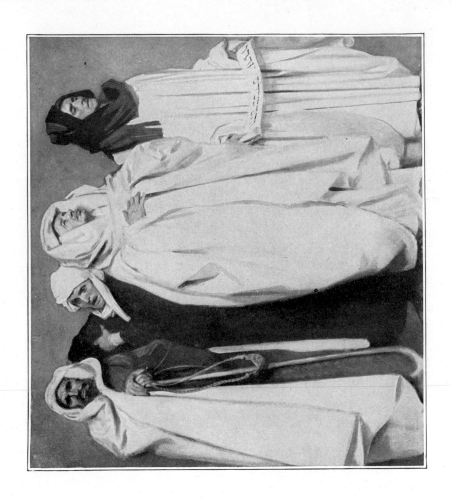

"MULTITUDES IN THE VALLEY OF DECISION"

"Multitudes, multitudes in the valley of decision: for the day of the LORD is near in the valley of decision. The sun and the moon shall be darkened, and the stars shall withdraw their shining. The LORD also shall roar out of Zion, and utter his voice from Jerusalem; and the heavens and the earth shall shake: but the LORD will be the hope of his people, and the strength of the children of Israel. So shall ye know that I am the LORD your God dwelling in Zion, my holy mountain: then shall Jerusalem be holy, and there shall no strangers pass through her any more.

"And it shall come to pass in that day, that the mountains shall drop down new wine, and the hills shall flow with milk, and all the rivers of Judah shall flow with waters, and a fountain shall come forth of the house of the LORD, and shall water the valley of Shittim. Egypt shall be a desolation, and Edom shall be a desolate wilderness, for the violence against the children of Judah, because they have shed innocent blood in their land. But Judah shall dwell forever, and Jerusalem from generation to generation. For I will cleanse their blood that I have not cleansed: for the LORD dwelleth in Zion."

— Joel 2:18–3:21.

Jonah

The First Foreign Missionary

There are those who regard the narrative portion of the Book of Jonah as historically true and there are others who regard the book as a poem or allegory. It is most unfortunate that discussions concerning the great sea animal have called the attention of readers away from the spiritual significance of one of the noblest and most inspired utterances of the human soul. It is a beautiful, poetic story; if it is also symbolical, like the "Pilgrim's Progress," it is none the less true.

It is a story which children should know by heart. The pictures are drawn by the hand of a master. The reluctant prophet who is ordered to Nineveh but who tries to escape from the commands of the Lord is introduced without any preliminary statement. He goes down to Joppa, and finds a Phoenician ship about to sail for the port of Tarshish. He pays his fare and goes below to sleep. He is a good sailor and does not awaken when the ship leaves port and encounters a terrific storm in the Mediterranean,— "The LORD hurled a great wind into the sea." All the sailors pray to their gods and cast the cargo overboard to lighten the ship. At last the captain wakens Jonah and bids him pray to his God, if he has one, for all the other gods fail. The sailors cast lots, to find who is the guilty person, and the lot falls upon Jonah. They are very courteous, loath to blame the stranger, and they ask him who his people are and what he has done. Still the storm rages and they ask him what they must do. He bids them cast him overboard. They try to save him and make a desperate effort to row to a haven. When the efforts fail, they cast him overboard and the sea becomes calm. Jonah is received into the belly of a great fish and after three days and nights he is cast ashore. He obeys the command of God and goes to Nineveh.

He is the first foreign missionary. For the first time in the Old Testament a prophet is sent to the Gentile world. All the other prophets speak for Israel. They warn their own land. They predict salvation for the chosen people. Jonah goes to Nineveh, "that great city," and brings the message of the Lord to its multitudes.

414

And the city did repent, from the king to the commoner, and repented in sackcloth and ashes. So God in his infinite compassion forgave Nineveh and forbore to destroy it. Whereupon Jonah was exceedingly angry and sulky. He went out in the country and made himself a booth from which he might watch, still hoping that something would happen to the city. A gourd, with its thick green foliage, sheltered him from the sun, but the vine was attacked by a worm and withered away. Thus God gave him the last great lesson of the book, which ends abruptly when we wish it might go on. "Thou hast had pity on the gourd, for the which thou hast not laboured, neither madest it grow; which came up in a night, and perished in a night: and should not I spare Nineveh, that great city, wherein are more than sixscore thousand persons that cannot discern between their right hand and their left hand; and also much cattle?"

This is the gospel in the Old Testament, the everlasting mercy of God for all his people, his care for them, even for the "much cattle." This is the same God as He of the New Testament, who cares for His children and for the sparrows that do not fall without His notice. This is what makes the little Book of Jonah one of the most precious in literature.

Jonah

JONAH IS TAUGHT A LESSON BY THE LORD

JONAH REFUSES TO OBEY THE COMMAND OF THE LORD AND SAILS FOR TARSHISH

NOW the word of the LORD came unto Jonah, the son of Amittai, saying, "Arise, go to Nineveh, that great city, and cry against it; for their wickedness is come up before me."

But Jonah rose up to flee unto Tarshish from the presence of the LORD, and went down to Joppa; and he found a ship going to Tarshish: so he paid the fare thereof, and went down into it, to go with them unto Tarshish from the presence of the LORD.

THE GREAT STORM ON THE MEDITERRANEAN

But the LORD sent out a great wind into the sea, and there was a mighty tempest in the sea, so that the ship was like to be broken. Then the mariners were afraid, and cried every man unto his god, and cast forth the wares that were in the ship into the sea, to lighten it of them. But Jonah was gone down into the sides of the ship; and he lay, and was fast asleep.

So the shipmaster came to him, and said unto him, "What meanest thou, O sleeper? Arise, call upon thy God, if so be that God will think upon us, that we perish not."

And they said every one to his fellow, "Come, and let us cast lots, that we may know for whose cause this evil is upon us." So they cast lots, and the lot fell upon Jonah.

Then said they unto him, "Tell us, we pray thee, for whose cause this evil is upon us: what is thine occupation and whence comest thou? What is thy country? And of what people art thou?"

And he said unto them, "I am an Hebrew; and I fear the LORD, the God of heaven, which hath made the sea and the dry land."

Then were the men exceedingly afraid, and said unto him, "Why hast thou done this?" For the men knew that he fled from the presence of the LORD, because he had told them.

Then said they unto him, "What shall we do unto thee, that the sea may be calm unto us?" for the sea wrought, and was tempestuous.

And he said unto them, "Take me up, and cast me forth into the sea; so shall the sea be calm unto you: for I know that for my sake this great tempest is upon

STREET IN OLD JOPPA
Photograph by Mrs. W. A. Pottenger expressly for The Book of Life

To this port came Jonah when he took passage on the Phoenician ship to escape going to Nineveh and here Peter lodged in the house of "Simon the tanner." The modern name of the city is Jaffa and it is the port entry for travelers going to Jerusalem.

you." Nevertheless the men rowed hard to bring it to the land; but they could not: for the sea wrought, and was tempestuous against them.

Wherefore they cried unto the LORD, and said, "We beseech thee, O LORD, we beseech thee, let us not perish for this man's life, and lay not upon us innocent blood: for thou, O LORD, hast done as it pleased thee." So they took up Jonah, and cast him forth into the sea: and the sea ceased from her raging. Then the men feared the

LORD exceedingly, and offered a sacrifice unto the LORD, and made vows.

A GREAT FISH SWALLOWS JONAH

Now the LORD had prepared a great fish to swallow up Jonah. And Jonah was in the belly of the fish three days and three nights.

JONAH'S PRAYER

Then Jonah prayed unto the LORD his God out of the fish's belly, and said, "I cried by reason of mine affliction unto the LORD, and he heard me; out of the belly of hell cried I, and thou heardest my voice. For thou hadst cast me into the deep, in the midst of the seas; and the floods compassed me about: all thy billows and thy waves passed over me. Then I said, 'I am cast out of thy sight; yet I will look again toward thy holy temple.'

"The waters compassed me about, even to the soul: the depth closed me round about, the weeds were wrapped about my head. I went down to the bottoms of the mountains; the earth with her bars was about me forever: yet hast thou brought up my life from corruption, O LORD my God. When my soul fainted within me I remembered the LORD: and my prayer came in unto thee, into thine holy temple. They that observe lying vanities forsake their own mercy. But I will sacrifice unto thee with the voice of thanksgiving; I will pay that that I have vowed. Salvation is of the LORD." And the LORD spake unto the fish, and it vomited out Jonah upon the dry land.

— Jonah 1; 2.

THE SECOND LESSON OF JONAH

THE MESSAGE OF THE LORD TO HIS CITY OF NINEVEH

And the word of the LORD came unto Jonah the second time, saying, "Arise, go unto Nineveh, that great city, and preach unto it the preaching that I bid thee."

So Jonah arose, and went unto Nineveh, according to the word of the LORD. Now Nineveh was an exceeding great city of three days' journey. And Jonah began to enter into the city a day's journey, and he cried, and said, "Yet forty days, and Nineveh shall be overthrown."

THE REPENTANCE OF THE PEOPLE

So the people of Nineveh believed God, and proclaimed a fast, and put on sackcloth, from the greatest of them even to the least of them. For word came unto the king of Nineveh, and he arose from his throne, and he laid his robe from him, and covered him with sackcloth, and sat in ashes. And he caused it to be proclaimed and published through Nineveh by the decree of the king and his nobles, saying, "Let neither man nor beast, herd nor flock, taste anything: let them not feed, nor drink water: but let man and beast be covered with sackcloth, and cry mightily unto God: yea, let them turn every one from his evil way, and from the violence that is in their hands. Who can tell if God will turn and repent, and turn away from his fierce anger, that we perish not?"

And God saw their works, that they turned from their evil ways; and God repented of the evil, that he had said that he would do unto them; and he did it not.

JONAH'S DISPLEASURE AT THE LORD'S COMPASSION

But it displeased Jonah exceedingly, and he was very angry. And he prayed unto the LORD, and said, "I pray thee, O LORD, was not this my saying, when I was yet in my country? Therefore I fled before unto Tarshish: for I knew that thou art a gracious God, and merciful, slow to anger, and of great kindness, and repentest thee of the evil. Therefore now, O LORD, take, I beseech thee, my life from me; for it is better for me to die than to live."

Then said the LORD, "Doest thou well to be angry?"

So Jonah went out of the city, and sat on the east side of the city, and there made him a booth, and sat under it in the shadow, till he might see what would become of the city.

GOD'S LESSON TO JONAH

And the LORD God prepared a gourd, and made it to come up over Jonah, that it might be a shadow over his head, to deliver him from his grief. So Jonah was exceeding glad of the gourd. But God prepared a worm when the morning rose the next day, and it smote the gourd that it withered. And it came to pass, when the sun did arise, that God prepared a vehement east wind; and the sun beat upon the head of Jonah, that he fainted, and wished in himself to die, and said, "It is better for me to die than to live."

And God said to Jonah, "Doest thou well to be angry for the gourd?"

And he said, "I do well to be angry, even unto death."

Then said the LORD, "Thou hast had pity on the gourd, for the which thou hast not laboured, neither madest it grow; which came up in a night, and perished in a night: and should not I spare Nineveh, that great city, wherein are more than sixscore thousand persons that cannot discern between their right hand and their left hand; and also much cattle?"   — Jonah 3; 4.

Daniel—Detail of Sistine Chapel Ceiling

By Michelangelo Buonarroti (1475-1564)
In the Sistine Chapel of the Vatican, Rome
Photograph by Anderson, Rome

THIS beautiful figure of the youthful Daniel writing is another of Michelangelo's incomparable portrayals of the prophets in the Sistine Chapel. For others see pages 66, 308, 358 and 402. In this figure of Daniel we are given the very expression of prophetic contemplation conceived as a state of active inspiration based upon eager study. Here, as in the others, we could never exhaust the full content of beauty or meaning.

Michelangelo Buonarroti was born March 6, 1475 at Caprese, near Florence. At thirteen he was apprenticed to Domenico Ghirlandaio, the painter, but soon discovered that he preferred the art of sculpture. He became one of the protegés of Lorenzo de' Medici, and under the guidance of Lorenzo's sculptor Bertholdo, mastered anatomy and modeling. When Michelangelo completed his statue of David in 1504, (see Volume III, page 28), his fame as a sculptor was established. In 1505 Pope Julius II summoned him to his employ at Rome. From this time until his death, Michelangelo's career under the patronage of four successive Popes was one long series of colossal undertakings in Rome and Florence in sculpture, painting and architecture. Although all of these projects except the Sistine ceiling (begun in 1508 and finished in 1512) were doomed to inadequate support, the artist achieved a life work of unexampled greatness.

Michelangelo had few interests outside of his profession and few friendships. His reserved nature, his nervous and melancholy temperament, his titanic capacity to feel and to work, made him a solitary man. Yet he was admired like a god and was recognized as the Nestor of all the arts without a rival. When he died, February 17, 1564 in Rome, the whole city was stirred. He was buried in Florence in the Church of Santa Croce, home of illustrious Florentine dead.

DANIEL

Daniel

The Book of Daniel was written to help and encourage people in time of trial and persecution. One purpose of this great book was to influence the people to stand fast by their religion, to show them that God would surely save them if they did, and to make plain that God is more powerful than the mightiest kings of the earth.

The six stories of Daniel and the captive Hebrew boys are told with such vividness and power that they have become universal favorites. The historical details and names in the book may not always be clear, but this does not alter the value of the stories, which lies in their "plea for courage and faith in God. Right will finally triumph and wrong be overthrown. The man who believes this will 'stand in his lot to the end of his days.' That is the heroism of faith which this book presents. 'Daniel' is a trumpet-call to courage in the moral battle of life. It sounds a note to which the higher spirits of humanity have always responded."

The latter part of the book contains symbolism which it is difficult now to understand, but which appeals strongly to the people for whom it is written. It also gives once again in the Old Testament a clearly expressed hope of a future life. The writer has urged his readers to stand firm for the faith, but this, in many cases, means death. No reward can come to such in this life, but they will receive a reward in the life to come. "The problem of God's justice, which is argued in 'Job,' has in 'Daniel' its final Hebrew answer in the hope of a future life."

THE YOUNG PRINCES IN CAPTIVITY

IN the third year of the reign of Jehoiakim, King of Judah, came Nebuchadnezzar, King of Babylon, unto Jerusalem, and besieged it. And the LORD gave Jehoiakim, King of Judah, into his hand, with part of the vessels of the house of God; and he carried them into the land of Shinar to the house of his god: and he brought the vessels into the treasure house of his god. And the king spake unto Ashpenaz, the master of his eunuchs, that he should bring in certain of the children of Israel, even of the seed royal and of the nobles, youths in whom was no blemish, but well favoured, and skilful in all wisdom, and cunning in knowledge, and understanding science, and such as had ability to stand in the king's palace; and that he should teach them the learning and the tongue of the Chaldeans. And the king appointed for them a daily portion of the king's meat, and of the wine which he drank, and that they should be nourished three years; that at the end thereof they might stand before the king. Now among these were, of the children of Judah, Daniel, Hananiah, Mishael, and Azariah. And the prince of the eunuchs gave names unto them: unto Daniel he gave the name of Belteshazzar; and to Hananiah, of Shadrach; and to Mishael, of Meshach; and to Azariah, of Abed-nego. But Daniel purposed in his heart that he would not defile himself with the king's meat, nor with the wine which he drank: therefore he requested of the prince of the eunuchs that he might not defile himself.

THE HEBREW BOYS THRIVE ON PULSE AND WATER

Now God made Daniel to find favour and compassion in the sight of the prince of the eunuchs. And the prince of the eunuchs said unto Daniel, "I fear my lord the king, who hath appointed your meat and your drink: for why should he see your faces worse liking than the youths which are of your own age? So should ye endanger my head with the king."

Then said Daniel to the steward, whom the prince of the eunuchs had appointed over Daniel, Hananiah, Mishael, and Azariah: "Prove thy servants, I beseech thee, ten days; and let them give us pulse to eat, and water to drink. Then let our countenances be looked upon before thee, and the countenance of the youths that eat of the king's meat; and as thou seest, deal with thy servants." So he hearkened unto them in this matter, and proved them ten days. And at the end of ten days their countenances appeared fairer, and they were fatter in flesh, than all the youths which did eat of the king's meat. So the steward took away their meat, and the wine that they should drink, and gave them pulse. Now as for these four youths, God gave them knowledge and skill in all learning and wisdom: and Daniel had understanding in all visions and dreams. And at the end of the days which the king had appointed for bringing them in, the prince of the eunuchs brought them in before Nebuchadnezzar. And the king communed with them; and among them all was found none like Daniel, Hananiah, Mishael, and Azariah: therefore stood they before the king. And in every matter of wisdom and understanding concerning which the king inquired of them, he found them ten times better than all the magicians and enchanters that were in all his realm. And Daniel continued even unto the first year of King Cyrus.   — Daniel 1.

Nebuchadnezzar Dreams and Daniel Acts as Interpreter

And in the second year of the reign of Nebuchadnezzar Nebuchadnezzar dreamed dreams, wherewith his spirit was troubled, and his sleep brake from him. Then the king commanded to call the magicians, and the astrologers, and the sorcerers, and the Chaldeans, for to shew the king his dreams. So they came and stood before the king.

And the king said unto them, "I have dreamed a dream, and my spirit was troubled to know the dream."

Then spake the Chaldeans to the king in Syriac, "O king, live forever: tell thy servants the dream, and we will shew the interpretation."

The king answered and said to the Chaldeans, "The thing is gone from me: if ye will not make known unto me the dream, with the interpretation thereof, ye shall be cut in pieces, and your houses shall be made a dunghill. But if ye shew the dream, and the interpretation thereof, ye shall receive of me gifts and rewards and great honour: therefore shew me the dream, and the interpretation thereof."

They answered again and said, "Let the king tell his servants the dream, and we will shew the interpretation of it."

The king answered and said, "I know of certainty that ye would gain the time, because ye see the thing is gone from me. But if ye will not make known unto me the dream, there is but one decree for you: for ye have prepared lying and corrupt words to speak before me, till the time be changed: therefore tell me the dream, and I shall know that ye can shew me the interpretation thereof."

The Chaldeans answered before the king, and said, "There is not a man upon the earth that can shew the king's matter: therefore there is no king, lord, nor ruler, that asked such things at any magician, or astrologer, or Chaldean. And it is a rare thing that the king requireth, and there is none other that can shew it before the king, except the gods, whose dwelling is not with flesh."

For this cause the king was angry and very furious, and commanded to destroy all the wise men of Babylon. And the decree went forth that the wise men should be slain: and they sought Daniel and his fellows to be slain.

Then Daniel answered with counsel and wisdom to Arioch, the captain of the king's guard, which was gone forth to slay the wise men of Babylon: he answered and said to Arioch, the king's captain, "Why is the decree so hasty from the king?"

Then Arioch made the thing known to Daniel.

Then Daniel went in, and desired of the king that he would give him time, and that he would shew the king the interpretation. Then Daniel went to his house, and made the thing known to Hananiah, Mishael, and Azariah, his companions: that they would desire mercies of the God of heaven concerning this secret; that Daniel and his fellows should not perish with the rest of the wise men of Babylon.

Then was the secret revealed unto Daniel in a night vision. Then Daniel blessed the God of heaven.

Daniel answered and said, "Blessed be the name of God forever and ever: for wisdom and might are his: and he changeth the times and the seasons: he removeth kings, and setteth up kings: he giveth wisdom unto the wise, and knowledge to them that know understanding: he revealeth the deep and secret things: he knoweth what is in the darkness, and the light dwelleth with him. I thank thee, and praise thee, O thou God of my fathers, who hast given me wisdom and might, and hast made known unto me now what we desired of thee: for thou hast now made known unto us the king's matter."

Therefore Daniel went in unto Arioch, whom the king had ordained to destroy the wise men of Babylon: he went and said thus unto him: "Destroy not the wise men of Babylon: bring me in before the king, and I will shew unto the king the interpretation."   —Daniel 2:1–24.

HOW DANIEL INTERPRETS THE KING'S DREAM AND GIVES GOD THE GLORY

Then Arioch brought in Daniel before the king in haste, and said thus unto him, "I have found a man of the captives of Judah, that will make known unto the king the interpretation."

The king answered and said to Daniel, whose name was Belteshazzar, "Art thou able to make known unto me the dream which I have seen, and the interpretation thereof?"

Daniel answered in the presence of the king, and said, "The secret which the king hath demanded cannot the wise men, the astrologers, the magicians, the soothsayers, shew unto the king; but there is a God in heaven that revealeth secrets, and maketh known to the king, Nebuchadnezzar, what shall be in the latter days. Thy dream, and the visions of thy head upon thy bed, are these; as for thee, O king, thy thoughts came into thy mind upon thy bed, what should come to pass hereafter: and he that revealeth secrets maketh known to thee what shall come to pass. But as for me, this secret is not revealed to me for any wisdom that I have more than any living, but for their sakes that shall make known the interpretation to the king, and that thou mightest know the thoughts of thy heart. —Daniel 2:25-30.

THE GREAT IMAGE WITH FEET OF IRON AND CLAY

"Thou, O king, sawest, and behold a great image. This great image, whose brightness was excellent, stood before thee; and the form thereof was terrible. This image's head was of fine gold, his breast and his arms of silver, his belly and his thighs of brass, his legs of iron, his feet part of iron and part of clay. Thou sawest till that a stone was cut out without hands, which smote the image upon his feet that were of iron and clay, and brake them to pieces. Then was the iron, the clay, the brass, the silver, and the gold, broken to pieces together, and became like the chaff of the summer threshing-floors;

and the wind carried them away, that no place was found
for them: and the stone that smote the image became a
great mountain, and filled the whole earth.

"This is the dream; and we will tell the interpretation
thereof before the king. Thou, O king, art a king of
kings: for the God of heaven hath given thee a kingdom,
power, and strength, and glory. And wheresoever the
children of men dwell, the beasts of the field and the fowls
of the heaven hath he given into thine hand, and hath
made thee ruler over them all. Thou art this head of
gold. And after thee shall arise another kingdom inferior
to thee, and another third kingdom of brass, which shall
bear rule over all the earth. And the fourth kingdom shall
be strong as iron: forasmuch as iron breaketh in pieces
and subdueth all things: and as iron that breaketh all
these, shall it break in pieces and bruise. And whereas
thou sawest the feet and toes, part of potters' clay, and
part of iron, the kingdom shall be divided; but there
shall be in it of the strength of the iron, forasmuch as
thou sawest the iron mixed with miry clay. And as the
toes of the feet were part of iron, and part of clay, so the
kingdom shall be partly strong, and partly broken. And
whereas thou sawest iron mixed with miry clay, they shall
mingle themselves with the seed of men: but they shall
not cleave one to another, even as iron is not mixed with
clay. And in the days of these kings shall the God of
heaven set up a kingdom, which shall never be destroyed:
and the kingdom shall not be left to other people, but
it shall break in pieces and consume all these kingdoms,
and it shall stand forever. Forasmuch as thou sawest
that the stone was cut out of the mountain without hands,
and that it brake in pieces the iron, the brass, the
clay, the silver, and the gold; the great God hath made
known to the king what shall come to pass hereafter:

and the dream is certain, and the interpretation thereof sure."

Then the king, Nebuchadnezzar, fell upon his face, and worshiped Daniel, and commanded that they should offer an oblation and sweet odours unto him.

The king answered unto Daniel, and said, "Of a truth it is, that your God is a God of gods, and a Lord of kings, and a revealer of secrets, seeing thou couldest reveal this secret."

DANIEL BECOMES A GREAT MAN

Then the king made Daniel a great man, and gave him many great gifts, and made him ruler over the whole province of Babylon, and chief of the governors over all the wise men of Babylon. Then Daniel requested of the king, and he set Shadrach, Meshach, and Abednego, over the affairs of the province of Babylon: but Daniel sat in the gate of the king. —Daniel 2:31–49.

The Hebrew Youths Refuse to Worship the Image of the King

Nebuchadnezzar, the king, made an image of gold, whose height was threescore cubits, and the breadth thereof six cubits: he set it up in the plain of Dura, in the province of Babylon. Then Nebuchadnezzar, the king, sent to gather together the princes, the governors, and the captains, the judges, the treasurers, the counsellors, the sheriffs, and all the rulers of the provinces, to come to the dedication of the image which Nebuchadnezzar, the king, had set up. Then the princes, the governors, and captains, the judges, the treasurers, the counsellors, the sheriffs, and all the rulers of the provinces, were gathered together unto the dedication of the image that Nebuchadnezzar, the king, had set up; and they stood before the image that Nebuchadnezzar had set up.

Then an herald cried aloud, "To you it is commanded, O people, nations, and languages, that at what time ye hear the sound of the cornet, flute, harp, sackbut, psaltery, dulcimer, and all kinds of music, ye fall down and worship the golden image that Nebuchadnezzar, the king, hath set up: and whoso falleth not down and worshipeth shall the same hour be cast into the midst of a burning fiery furnace."

Therefore at that time, when all the people heard the sound of the cornet, flute, harp, sackbut, psaltery, and all kinds of music, all the people, the nations, and the languages, fell down and worshiped the golden image that Nebuchadnezzar, the king, had set up.

Wherefore at that time certain Chaldeans came near, and accused the Jews.

They spake and said to the king, Nebuchadnezzar, "O king, live forever. Thou, O king, hast made a decree, that every man that shall hear the sound of the cornet, flute, harp, sackbut, psaltery, and dulcimer, and all kinds of music, shall fall down and worship the golden image: and whoso falleth not down and worshipeth, that he should be cast into the midst of a burning fiery furnace. There are certain Jews whom thou hast set over the affairs of the province of Babylon, Shadrach, Meshach, and Abed-nego; these men, O king, have not regarded thee: they serve not thy gods, nor worship the golden image which thou hast set up."

Then Nebuchadnezzar in his rage and fury commanded to bring Shadrach, Meshach, and Abed-nego. Then they brought these men before the king. Nebuchadnezzar spake and said unto them, "Is it true, O Shadrach, Meshach, and Abed-nego, do not ye serve my gods, nor worship the golden image which I have set up? Now if ye be ready that at what time ye hear the sound of the cornet, flute, harp, sackbut, psaltery, and dulcimer, and all kinds of music, ye fall down and worship the image which I have made; well: but if ye worship not, ye shall be cast the same hour into the midst of a burning fiery furnace; and who is that God that shall deliver you out of my hands?"

Shadrach, Meshach, and Abed-nego, answered and said to the king, "O Nebuchadnezzar, we are not careful to answer thee in this matter. If it be so, our God whom we serve is able to deliver us from the burning fiery furnace, and he will deliver us out of thine hand, O king. But if not, be it known unto thee, O king, that we will not serve thy gods, nor worship the golden image which thou hast set up."   — Daniel 3:1-18.

THE YOUTHS IN THE FIERY FURNACE

Then was Nebuchadnezzar full of fury, and the form of his visage was changed against Shadrach, Meshach, and Abed-nego: therefore he spake, and commanded that they should heat the furnace one seven times more than it was wont to be heated. And he commanded the most mighty men that were in his army to bind Shadrach, Meshach, and Abed-nego, and to cast them into the burning fiery furnace. Then these men were bound in their coats, their hosen, and their hats, and their other garments, and were cast into the midst of the burning fiery furnace. Therefore because the king's commandment was urgent, and the furnace exceeding hot, the flame of the fire slew those men that took up Shadrach, Meshach, and Abed-nego. And these three men, Shadrach, Meshach, and Abed-nego, fell down bound into the midst of the burning fiery furnace.

Then Nebuchadnezzar, the king, was astonied, and rose up in haste, and spake, and said unto his counsellors, "Did not we cast three men bound into the midst of the fire?"

They answered and said unto the king, "True, O king."

He answered and said, "Lo, I see four men loose, walking in the midst of the fire, and they have no hurt; and the form of the fourth is like the Son of God."

Then Nebuchadnezzar came near to the mouth of the burning fiery furnace, and spake, and said, "Shadrach, Meshach, and Abed-nego, ye servants of the most high God, come forth, and come hither."

Then Shadrach, Meshach, and Abed-nego, came forth of the midst of the fire. And the princes, governors, and captains, and the king's counsellors, being gathered together, saw these men, upon whose bodies the fire had no power, nor was an hair of their head singed, neither were their coats changed, nor the smell of fire had passed on them.

Then Nebuchadnezzar spake, and said, "Blessed be the God of Shadrach, Meshach, and Abed-nego, who hath sent his angel, and delivered his servants that trusted in him, and have changed the king's word, and yielded their bodies, that they might not serve nor worship any god, except their own God. Therefore I make a decree: that every people, nation, and language, which speak anything amiss against the God of Shadrach, Meshach, and Abed-nego, shall be cut in pieces, and their houses shall be made a dunghill: because there is no other God that can deliver after this sort." Then the king promoted Shadrach, Meshach, and Abed-nego, in the province of Babylon.　　　　— Daniel 3:19-30.

NEBUCHADNEZZAR'S PROCLAMATION

Nebuchadnezzar, the king, unto all people, nations, and languages, that dwell in all the earth:

"Peace be multiplied unto you. I thought it good to shew the signs and wonders that the high God hath wrought toward me. How great are his signs! And how mighty are his wonders! His kingdom is an everlasting kingdom, and his dominion is from generation to generation.

THE KING'S SECOND DREAM

"I, Nebuchadnezzar, was at rest in mine house, and flourishing in my palace: I saw a dream which made me afraid, and the thoughts upon my bed and the visions of my head troubled me. Therefore made I a decree to bring in all the wise men of Babylon before me, that they might make known unto me the interpretation of the dream. Then came in the magicians, the astrologers, the Chaldeans, and the soothsayers: and I told the dream before them; but they did not make known unto me the interpretation thereof.

"But at the last Daniel came in before me, whose name was Belteshazzar, according to the name of my god, and in whom is the spirit of the holy gods: and before him I told the dream, saying, 'O Belteshazzar, master of the magicians, because I know that the spirit of the holy gods is in thee, and no secret troubleth thee, tell me the visions of my dream that I have seen, and the interpretation thereof. Thus were the visions of mine head in my bed: I saw, and behold a tree in the midst of the earth, and the height thereof was great. The tree grew, and was strong, and the height thereof reached unto heaven, and the sight thereof to the end of all the earth: the leaves thereof were fair, and the fruit thereof much, and in it was meat for all: the beasts of the field had shadow under it, and the fowls of the heaven dwelt in the boughs thereof, and all flesh was fed of it. I saw in the visions of my head upon my bed, and, behold, a watcher and an holy one came down from heaven; he cried aloud, and said thus, 'Hew down the tree, and cut off his branches, shake off his leaves, and scatter his fruit: let the beasts get away from under it, and the fowls from his branches: nevertheless leave the stump of his roots in the earth, even with a band of iron and brass, in the tender grass of the field; and let it be wet with the dew of heaven, and let his portion be with the beasts in the grass of the earth: let his heart be changed from man's and let a beast's heart be given unto him; and let seven times pass over him. This matter is by the decree of the watchers, and the demand by the word of the holy ones: to the intent that the living may know that the most High ruleth in the kingdom of men, and giveth it to whomsoever he will, and setteth up over it the basest of men.

"'This dream I, King Nebuchadnezzar, have seen. Now thou, O Belteshazzar, declare the interpretation thereof, forasmuch as all the wise men of my kingdom are not able to make known unto me the interpretation: but thou art able; for the spirit of the holy god is in thee.'

"Then Daniel, whose name was Belteshazzar, was astonied for one hour, and his thoughts troubled him. The king spake, and said, 'Belteshazzar, let not the dream, or the interpretation thereof, trouble thee.'

"Belteshazzar answered and said, 'My lord, the dream be to them that hate thee, and the interpretation thereof to thine enemies. The tree that thou sawest, which grew, and was strong, whose height reached unto the heaven, and the sight thereof to all the earth; whose leaves were fair, and the fruit thereof much, and in it was meat for all; under which the beasts of the field dwelt, and upon whose branches the fowls of the heaven had their habitation: it is thou, O king, that art grown and become strong: for thy greatness is grown, and reacheth unto heaven, and thy dominion to the end of the earth.

"'And whereas the king saw a watcher and an holy one coming down from heaven, and saying, "Hew the tree down, and destroy it; yet leave the stump of the roots thereof in the earth, even with a band of iron and brass, in the tender grass of the field; and let it be wet with the dew of heaven, and let his portion be with the beasts of the field, till seven times pass over him"; this is the interpretation, O king, and this is the decree of the most High, which is come upon my lord the king: that they shall drive thee from men, and thy dwelling shall be with the beasts of the field, and they shall make thee to eat grass as oxen, and they shall wet thee with the dew of heaven, and seven times shall pass over thee, till thou know that the most High ruleth in the kingdom of men, and giveth it to whomsoever he will. And whereas they commanded to leave the stump of the tree roots; thy kingdom shall be sure unto thee, after that thou shalt have known that the heavens do rule. Wherefore, O king, let my counsel be acceptable unto thee, and break off thy sins by righteousness, and thine iniquities by shewing mercy to the poor; if it may be a lengthening of thy tranquillity.'

"All this came upon the king, Nebuchadnezzar. At the end of twelve months he walked in the palace of the kingdom of Babylon. The king spake, and said, 'Is not this great Babylon that I have built for the house of the kingdom by the might of my power, and for the honour of my majesty?'

"While the word was in the king's mouth, there fell a voice from heaven, saying, 'O King Nebuchadnezzar, to thee it is spoken: The kingdom is departed from thee. And they shall drive thee from men, and thy dwelling shall be with the beasts of the field: they shall make thee to eat grass as oxen, and seven times shall pass over thee, until thou know that the most High ruleth in the kingdom of men, and giveth it to whomsoever he will.'"

NEBUCHADNEZZAR IS DRIVEN FROM MEN TO EAT GRASS AS OXEN

"The same hour was the thing fulfilled upon Nebuchadnezzar: and he was driven from men, and did eat grass as oxen, and his body was wet with the dew of heaven, till his hairs were grown like eagles' feathers, and his nails like birds' claws. And at the end of the days I, Nebuchadnezzar, lifted up mine eyes unto heaven, and mine understanding returned unto me, and I blessed the most High, and I praised and honoured him that liveth forever, whose dominion is an everlasting dominion, and his kingdom is from generation to generation: and all the inhabitants of the earth are reputed as nothing: and he doeth according to his will in the army of heaven, and among the inhabitants of the earth: and none can stay his hand, or say unto him, 'What doest thou?'

"At the same time my reason returned unto me; and for the glory of my kingdom, mine honour and brightness returned unto me; and my counsellors and my lords sought unto me; and I was established in my kingdom, and excellent majesty was added unto me. Now I, Nebuchadnezzar, praise and extol and honour the King of heaven, all whose works are truth, and his ways judgment: and those that walk in pride he is able to abase."   — Daniel 4.

Belshazzar's Feast

Belshazzar, the king, made a great feast to a thousand of his lords, and drank wine before the thousand. Belshazzar, whiles he tasted the wine, commanded to bring the golden and silver vessels which his father, Nebuchadnezzar, had taken out of the temple which was in Jerusalem; that the king, and his princes, his wives, and his concubines, might drink therein. Then they brought the golden vessels that were taken out of the temple of the house of God which was at Jerusalem; and the king, and his princes, his wives, and his concubines, drank in them. They drank wine, and praised the gods of gold, and of silver, of brass, of iron, of wood, and of stone.

In the same hour came forth fingers of a man's hand, and wrote over against the candlestick upon the plaster of the wall of the king's palace: and the king saw the part of the hand that wrote. Then the king's countenance was changed, and his thoughts troubled him, so that the joints of his loins were loosed, and his knees smote one against another. The king cried aloud to bring in the astrologers, the Chaldeans, and the soothsayers. And the king spake, and said to the wise men of Babylon, "Whosoever shall read this writing, and shew me the interpretation thereof, shall be clothed with scarlet, and have a chain of gold about his neck, and shall be the third ruler in the kingdom."

Then came in all the king's wise men: but they could not read the writing, nor make known to the king the interpretation thereof. Then was King Belshazzar greatly troubled, and his countenance was changed in him, and his lords were astonied.

Now the queen by reason of the words of the king and his lords came into the banquet house: and the queen spake and said, "O king, live forever. let not thy thoughts trouble thee, nor let thy countenance be changed: there is a man in thy kingdom, in whom is the spirit of the holy gods; and in the days of thy father light and understanding and wisdom, like the wisdom of the gods, was found in him; whom the king, Nebuchadnezzar, thy father, the king, I say, thy father, made master of the magicians, astrologers, Chaldeans, and soothsayers; forasmuch as an excellent spirit, and knowledge, and understanding, interpreting of dreams, and shewing of hard sentences, and dissolving of doubts, were found in the same Daniel, whom the king named Belteshazzar: now let Daniel be called, and he will shew the interpretation."

Then was Daniel brought in before the king. And the king spake and said unto Daniel, "Art thou that Daniel, which art of the children of the captivity of Judah, whom the king my father brought out of Jewry? I have even heard of thee, that the spirit of the gods is in thee, and that light and understanding and excellent wisdom is found in thee. And now the wise men, the astrologers, have been brought in before me, that they should read this writing, and make known unto me the interpretation thereof: but they could not shew the interpretation of the thing: and I have heard of thee, that thou canst make interpretations, and dissolve doubts: now if thou canst read the writing, and make known to me the interpretation thereof, thou shalt be clothed with scarlet, and have a chain of gold about thy neck, and shalt be the third ruler in the kingdom."

Then Daniel answered and said before the king, "Let thy gifts be to thyself, and give thy rewards to another; yet I will read the writing unto the king, and make known to him the interpretation. O thou king, the most high God gave Nebuchadnezzar, thy father, a kingdom, and majesty, and glory, and honour: and for the majesty that he gave him, all people, nations, and languages, trembled and feared before him: whom he would he slew; and whom he would he kept alive; and whom he would he set up; and whom he would he put down. But when his heart was lifted up, and his mind hardened in pride, he was deposed from his kingly throne, and they took his glory from him: and he was driven from the sons of men; and his heart was made like the beasts, and his dwelling was with the wild asses: they fed him with grass like oxen, and his body was wet with the dew of heaven; till he knew that the most high God ruled in the kingdom of men, and that he appointeth over it whomsoever he will. And thou his son, O Belshazzar, hast not humbled thine heart, though thou knewest all this; but hast lifted up thyself against the Lord of heaven; and they have brought the vessels of his house before thee, and thou, and thy lords, thy wives, and thy concubines, have drunk wine in them; and thou hast praised the gods of silver, and gold, of brass, iron, wood, and stone, which see not, nor hear, nor know: and the God in whose hand thy breath is, and whose are all thy ways, hast thou not glorified: then was the part of the hand sent from him· and this writing was written.

"And this is the writing that was written, 'MENE, MENE, TEKEL, UPHARSIN.'

"This is the interpretation of the thing: 'MENE'; God hath numbered thy kingdom, and finished it.

"'TEKEL'; Thou art weighed in the balances, and art found wanting.

"'PERES'; Thy kingdom is divided, and given to the Medes and Persians."

DANIEL IS CLOTHED WITH SCARLET

Then commanded Belshazzar, and they clothed Daniel with scarlet, and put a chain of gold about his neck, and made a proclamation concerning him, that he should be the third ruler in the kingdom.

In that night was Belshazzar, the king of the Chaldeans, slain. And Darius, the Median, took the kingdom, being about threescore and two years old. — Daniel 5.

HOW JEALOUS RIVALS FORMED A PLOT AGAINST DANIEL

It pleased Darius to set over the kingdom an hundred and twenty princes, which should be over the whole kingdom; and over these three presidents, of whom Daniel was first: that the princes might give accounts unto them, and the king should have no damage. Then this Daniel was preferred above the presidents and princes, because an excellent spirit was in him; and the king thought to set him over the whole realm.

Then the presidents and princes sought to find occasion against Daniel concerning the kingdom; but they could find none occasion nor fault; forasmuch as he was faithful, neither was there any error or fault found in him.

Then said these men, "We shall not find any occasion against this Daniel, except we find it against him concerning the law of his God."

Then these presidents and princes assembled together to the king, and said thus unto him, "King Darius, live forever. All the presidents of the kingdom, the governors, and the princes, the counsellors, and the captains, have consulted together to establish a royal statute, and to make a firm decree, that whosoever shall ask a petition of any God or man for thirty days, save of thee, O king, he shall be cast into the den of lions. Now, O king, establish the decree, and sign the writing, that it be not changed, according to the law of the Medes and Persians, which altereth not." Whereupon King Darius signed the writing and the decree.

DANIEL KNEELS TOWARD JERUSALEM

Now when Daniel knew that the writing was signed, he went into his house; and his windows being open in his chamber toward Jerusalem, he kneeled upon his knees three times a day, and prayed, and gave thanks before his God, as he did aforetime. Then these men assembled, and found Daniel praying and making supplication before his God.

Then they came near, and spake before the king concerning the king's decree: "Hast thou not signed a decree, that every man that shall ask a petition of any God or man within thirty days, save of thee, O king, shall be cast into the den of lions?"

The king answered and said, "The thing is true, according to the law of the Medes and Persians, which altereth not."

Then answered they and said before the king, "That Daniel, which is of the children of the captivity of Judah, regardeth not thee, O king, nor the decree that thou hast signed, but maketh his petition three times a day."

Then the king, when he heard these words, was sore displeased with himself, and set his heart on Daniel to deliver him: and he laboured till the going down of the sun to deliver him.

Then these men assembled unto the king, and said unto the king, "Know, O king, that the law of the Medes and Persians is, that no decree nor statute which the king establisheth may be changed."

Daniel's Answer to the King

By Briton Rivière (1840-1920)
Painting in the Liverpool Gallery, Liverpool, England

YOU will like the vivid stories about Daniel. The one portrayed here begins on page 441.

This picture of Daniel was painted by the modern English artist, Briton Rivière. Rivière's father was of French descent and a famous artist. His mother was both an artist and a musician. His father believed that one should train the "eye to see and the hand to obey" before filling the mind with "book learning." Thus, Briton's early years in London and Cheltenham were spent in an atmosphere of dreaming and doing, and painting was always combined with schooling. Rivière loved animals. When he was no more than seven years of age, he began drawing them. Years later, when he wished to paint a Bible theme, it was natural that he chose one with animals in it.

Rivière painted two pictures on the subject of Daniel. The first, DANIEL IN THE LION'S DEN, was painted in 1872. In that Daniel stands bound facing the lions, just after being cast into the den. The beasts, ready to seize their prey, are held back by some unseen force. It is a moving portrayal of that tense moment (page 447-G.)

In 1890, the artist painted this sequel to the first Daniel picture and called it DANIEL'S ANSWER TO THE KING. This time he chose the morning hour, when, Daniel, still bound and still unharmed, makes answer to the waiting king. Daniel speaks thus: "My God hath sent his angel, and hath shut the lions' mouths, that they have not hurt me." Notice the lions milling about the den, their mouths indeed shut.

Rivière's two pictures show us how Daniel proved that faith in God brings assurance and protection in a time of great danger. It is a wonderful story feelingly portrayed. These pictures are among the best works of Rivière.

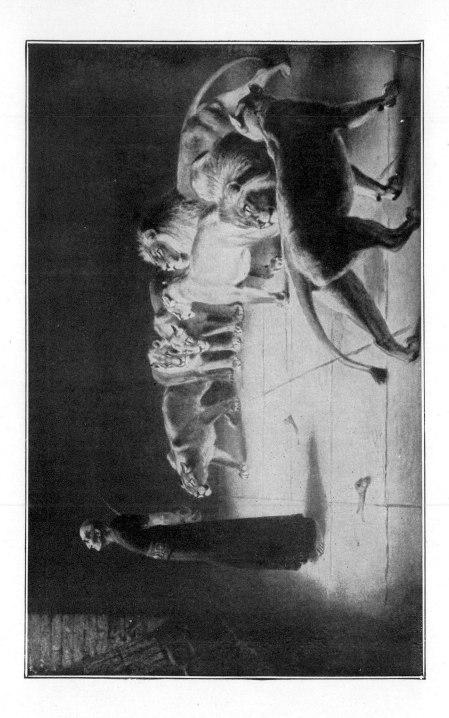

DANIEL IN THE LIONS' DEN

Then the king commanded, and they brought Daniel, and cast him into the den of lions.

Now the king spake and said unto Daniel, "Thy God whom thou servest continually, he will deliver thee."

And a stone was brought, and laid upon the mouth of the den; and the king sealed it with his own signet, and with the signet of his lords; that the purpose might not be changed concerning Daniel.

Then the king went to his palace, and passed the night fasting: neither were instruments of music brought before him: and his sleep went from him. Then the king arose very early in the morning, and went in haste unto the den of lions. And when he came to the den, he cried with a lamentable voice unto Daniel: and the king spake and said to Daniel, "O Daniel, servant of the living God, is thy God, whom thou servest continually, able to deliver thee from the lions?"

Then said Daniel unto the king, "O king, live forever. My God hath sent his angel, and hath shut the lions' mouths, that they have not hurt me: forasmuch as before him innocency was found in me; and also before thee, O king, have I done no hurt."

Then was the king exceeding glad for him, and commanded that they should take Daniel up out of the den. So Daniel was taken up out of the den, and no manner of hurt was found upon him, because be believed in his God.

HOW DANIEL'S BRAVERY WAS REWARDED

And the king commanded, and they brought those men which had accused Daniel, and they cast them into the den of lions, them, their children, and their wives, and the lions had the mastery of them; and brake all their bones in pieces or ever they came at the bottom of the den.

Then King Darius wrote unto all people, nations, and languages, that dwell in all the earth: "Peace be multiplied unto you. I make a decree, that in every dominion of my kingdom men tremble and fear before the God of Daniel: for he is the living God, and stedfast forever, and his kingdom that which shall not be destroyed, and his dominion shall be even unto the end. He delivereth and rescueth, and he worketh signs and wonders in heaven and in earth, who hath delivered Daniel from the power of the lions."

So this Daniel prospered in the reign of Darius, and in the reign of Cyrus, the Persian. —Daniel 6.

THE VISION OF THE FOUR BEASTS

In the first year of Belshazzar, King of Babylon, Daniel had a dream and visions of his head upon his bed: then he wrote the dream, and told the sum of the matters. Daniel spake and said, "I saw in my vision by night, and, behold, the four winds of the heaven strove upon the great sea. And four great beasts came up from the sea, diverse one from another. The first was like a lion, and had eagle's wings: I beheld till the wings thereof were plucked, and it was lifted up from the earth, and made stand upon the feet as a man, and a man's heart was given to it.

"And behold another beast, a second, like to a bear, and it raised up itself on one side, and it had three ribs in the mouth of it between the teeth of it: and they said thus unto it, 'Arise, devour much flesh.'

"After this I beheld, and lo another, like a leopard, which had upon the back of it four wings of a fowl; the beast had also four heads; and dominion was given to it.

"After this I saw in the night visions, and behold a fourth beast, dreadful and terrible, and strong exceedingly; and it had great iron teeth: it devoured and brake in pieces, and stamped the residue with the feet of it: and it was diverse from all the beasts that were before it; and it had ten horns. I considered the horns, and, behold, there came up among them another little horn, before whom there were three of the first horns plucked up by the roots: and, behold, in this horn were eyes like the eyes of man, and a mouth speaking great things. —Daniel 7:1-8

THE ANCIENT OF DAYS

"I beheld till the thrones were cast down, and the Ancient of days did sit, whose garment was white as snow, and the hair of his head like the pure wool: his throne was like the fiery flame, and his wheels as burning fire. A fiery stream issued and came forth from before him: thousand thousands ministered unto him, and ten thousand times ten thousand stood before him: the judgment was set, and the books were opened. I beheld then, because of the voice of the great words which the horn spake: I beheld even till the beast was slain, and his body destroyed, and given to the burning flame. As concerning the rest of the beasts, they had their dominion taken away: yet their lives were prolonged for a season and time.

"I saw in the night visions, and, behold, one like the Son of man came with the clouds of heaven, and came to the Ancient of days, and they brought him near before him. And there was given him dominion, and glory, and a kingdom, that all people, nations, and languages, should serve him: his dominion is an everlasting dominion, which shall not pass away, and his kingdom that which shall not be destroyed.   —Daniel 7:9-14

THE VISION INTERPRETED

"I, Daniel, was grieved in my spirit in the midst of my body, and the visions of my head troubled me. I came near unto one of them that stood by, and asked him the truth of all this. So he told me, and made me know the interpretation of the things. These great beasts, which are four, are four kings, which shall arise out of the earth. But the saints of the Most High shall take the kingdom, and possess the kingdom for ever, even for ever and ever.

"Then I would know the truth of the fourth beast, which was diverse from all the others, exceeding dreadful, whose teeth were of iron, and his nails of brass; which devoured, brake in pieces, and stamped the residue with his feet; and of the ten horns that were in his head, and of the other which came up, and before whom three fell; even of that horn that had eyes, and a mouth that spake very great things, whose look was more stout than his fellows. I beheld, and the same horn made war with the saints, and prevailed against them; until the Ancient of days came, and judgment was given to the saints of the Most High; and the time came that the saints possessed the kingdom.

"Thus he said, 'The fourth beast shall be the fourth kingdom upon earth, which shall be diverse from all kingdoms, and shall devour the whole earth, and shall tread it down, and break it in pieces. And the ten horns out of this kingdom are ten kings that shall arise: and another shall rise after them; and he shall be diverse from the first, and he shall subdue three kings. And he shall speak great words against the Most High, and shall wear out the saints of the Most High, and think to change times and laws: and they shall be given into his hand until a time and times and the dividing of time. But the judgment shall sit, and they shall take away his dominion, to consume and to destroy it unto the end. And the kingdom and dominion, and the greatness of the kingdom under the whole heaven, shall be given to the people of the saints of the Most High, whose kingdom is an everlasting kingdom, and all dominions shall serve and obey him. Hitherto is the end of the matter.'

"As for me, Daniel, my cogitations much troubled me, and my countenance changed in me: but I kept the matter in my heart." —Daniel 7:15-28

DANIEL HAS A SECOND VISION

"In the third year of the reign of King Belshazzar a vision appeared unto me, even unto me, Daniel, after that which appeared unto me at the first. And I saw in a vision; and it came to pass, when I saw, that I was at Shushan in the palace, which is in the province of Elam; and I saw in a vision, and I was by the river of Ulai. Then I lifted up mine eyes, and saw, and, behold, there stood before the river a ram which had two horns: and the two horns were high; but one was higher than the other, and the higher came up last. I saw the ram pushing westward, and northward, and southward; so that no beasts might stand before him, neither was there any that could deliver out of his hand; but he did according to his will, and became great.

"And as I was considering, behold, a he goat came from the west on the face of the whole earth, and touched not the ground: and the goat had a notable horn between his eyes. And he came to the ram that had two horns, which I had seen standing before the river, and ran unto him in the fury of his power. And I saw him come close unto the ram, and he was moved with choler against him, and smote the ram, and brake his two horns: and there was no power in the ram to stand before him, but he cast him down to the ground, and stamped upon him: and there was none that could deliver the ram out of his hand. Therefore the he goat waxed very great: and when he was strong, the great horn was broken; and for it came up four notable ones toward the four winds of heaven. And out of one of them came forth a little horn, which waxed exceeding great, toward the south, and toward the east, and toward the pleasant land. And it waxed great, even to the host of heaven; and it cast down some of the host and of the stars to the ground, and stamped upon them. Yea, he magnified himself even to the prince of the host, and by him the daily sacrifice was taken away, and the place of his sanctuary was cast down. And a host was given him against the daily sacrifice by reason of transgression, and it cast down the truth to the ground; and it practised, and prospered.

"Then I heard one saint speaking, and another saint said unto that certain saint which spake, 'How long shall be the vision concerning the daily sacrifice, and the transgression of desolation, to give both the sanctuary and the host to be trodden under foot?'

"And he said unto me, 'Unto two thousand and three hundred days; then shall the sanctuary be cleansed.'
—Daniel 8:1-14

DANIEL RECEIVES THE INTERPRETATION

"And it came to pass, when I, even I, Daniel, had seen the vision, and sought for the meaning, then, behold, there stood before me as the appearance of a man.

And I heard a man's voice between the banks of Ulai, which called, and said, 'Gabriel, make this man to understand the vision.'

"So he came near where I stood: and when he came, I was afraid, and fell upon my face: but he said unto me, 'Understand, O son of man: for at the time of the end shall be the vision.'

"Now as he was speaking with me, I was in a deep sleep on my face toward the ground: but he touched me, and set me upright. And he said, 'Behold, I will make thee know what shall be in the last end of the indignation: for at the time appointed the end shall be. The ram which thou sawest having two horns are the kings of Media and Persia. And the rough goat is the king of Grecia: and the great horn that is between his eyes is the first king. Now that being broken, whereas four stood up for it, four kingdoms shall stand up out of the nation, but not in his power. And in the latter time of their kingdom, when the transgressors are come to the full, a king of fierce countenance, and understanding dark sentences, shall stand up. And his power shall be mighty, but not by his own power: and he shall destroy wonderfully, and shall prosper, and practise, and shall destroy the mighty and the holy people. And through his policy also he shall cause craft to prosper in his hand; and he shall magnify himself in his heart, and by peace shall destroy many: he shall also stand up against the Prince of princes; but he shall be broken without hand. And the vision of the evening and the morning which was told is true: wherefore shut thou up the visions; for it shall be for many days.'

"And I, Daniel, fainted, and was sick certain days; afterward I rose up, and did the king's business; and I was astonished at the vision, but none understood it."

—Daniel 8:15-27

The Prayer of Daniel for His People

THE CONFESSION

"In the first year of Darius, the son of Ahasuerus, of the seed of the Medes, which was made king over the realm of the Chaldeans; in the first year of his reign, I, Daniel, understood by books the number of the years, whereof the word of the Lord came to Jeremiah, the prophet, that he would accomplish seventy years in the desolations of Jerusalem.

"And I set my face unto the Lord God, to seek by prayer and supplications, with fasting, and sackcloth, and ashes: and I prayed unto the Lord my God, and made my confession, and said, 'O Lord, the great and dreadful God, keeping the covenant and mercy to them that love him, and to them that keep his commandments; we have sinned, and have committed iniquity, and have done wickedly, and have rebelled, even by departing from thy precepts and from thy judgments: neither have we hearkened unto thy servants, the prophets, which spake in thy name to our kings, our princes, and our fathers, and to all the people of the land.

" 'O Lord, righteousness belongeth unto thee, but unto us confusion of faces, as at this day; to the men of Judah, and to the inhabitants of Jerusalem, and unto all Israel, that are near, and that are far off, through all the countries whither thou hast driven them, because of their trespass that they have trespassed against thee. O Lord, to us belongeth confusion of face, to our kings, to our princes, and to our fathers, because we have sinned against thee. To the Lord our God belong mercies and forgivenesses, though we have rebelled against him: neither have we obeyed the voice of the Lord our God, to walk in his laws, which he set before us by his servants the prophets. Yea, all Israel have transgressed thy law, even by departing, that they might not obey thy voice; therefore the curse is poured upon us, and the oath that is written in the law of Moses the servant of God, because we have sinned against him.

" 'And he hath confirmed his words, which he spake against us, and against our judges that judged us, by bringing upon us a great evil: for under the whole heaven hath not been done as hath been done upon Jerusalem. As it is written in the law of Moses, all this evil is come upon us: yet made we not our prayer before the LORD our God, that we might turn from our iniquities, and understand thy truth. Therefore hath the LORD watched upon the evil, and brought it upon us: for the LORD our God is righteous in all his works which he doeth: for we obeyed not his voice. And now, O Lord our God, that hast brought thy people forth out of the land of Egypt with a mighty hand, and hast gotten thee renown, as at this day; we have sinned, we have done wickedly.

—Daniel 9: 1-15

THE PLEA FOR FORGIVENESS

" 'O Lord, according to all thy righteousness, I beseech thee, let thine anger and thy fury be turned away from thy city, Jerusalem, thy holy mountain: because for our sins, and for the iniquities of our fathers, Jerusalem and thy people are become a reproach to all that are about us. Now therefore, O our God, hear the prayer of thy servant, and his supplications, and cause thy face to shine upon thy sanctuary that is desolate, for the Lord's sake. O my God, incline thine ear, and hear; open thine eyes, and behold our desolations, and the city which is called by thy name: for we do not present our supplications before thee for our righteousness, but for thy great mercies.

DANIEL IN THE LIONS' DEN by RIVIÈRE

" 'O Lord, hear; O Lord, forgive; O Lord, hearken and do; defer not, for thine own sake, O my God: for thy city and thy people are called by thy name.'

—Daniel 9: 16-19

THE WORDS OF THE MAN GABRIEL

"And while I was speaking, and praying, and confessing my sin and the sin of my people Israel, and presenting my supplication before the LORD my God for the holy mountain of my God; yea, while I was speaking in prayer, even the man Gabriel, whom I had seen in the vision at the beginning, being caused to fly swiftly, touched me about the time of the evening oblation. And he informed me, and talked with me, and said, 'O Daniel, I am now come forth to give thee skill and understanding. At the beginning of thy supplications the commandment came forth, and I am come to shew thee; for thou art greatly beloved: therefore understand the matter, and consider the vision.

" 'Seventy weeks are determined upon thy people and upon thy holy city, to finish the transgression, and to make an end of sins, and to make reconciliation for iniquity, and to bring in everlasting righteousness, and to seal up the vision and prophecy, and to anoint the Most Holy. Know therefore and understand, that from the going forth of the commandment to restore and to build Jerusalem, unto the Messiah the Prince, shall be seven weeks, and threescore and two weeks: the street shall be built again, and the wall, even in troublous times. And after threescore and two weeks shall Messiah be cut off, but not for himself: and the people of the prince that shall come shall destroy the city and the sanctuary; and the end thereof shall be with a flood, and unto the end of the war desolations are determined. And he shall confirm the covenant with many for one week: and in the midst of the week he shall cause the sacrifice and the oblation to cease, and for the overspreading of abominations he shall make it desolate, even until the consummation, and that determined shall be poured upon the desolate.' "

—Daniel 9:20-27

THE VISION OF THE MAN CLOTHED IN LINEN

"In the third year of Cyrus King of Persia a thing was revealed unto Daniel, whose name was called Belteshazzar; and the thing was true, but the time appointed was long: and he understood the thing, and had understanding of the vision.

"In those days I, Daniel, was mourning three full weeks. I ate no pleasant bread, neither came flesh nor wine in my mouth, neither did I anoint myself at all, till three whole weeks were fulfilled. And in the four and twentieth day of the first month, as I was by the side of the great river, which is Hiddekel; then I lifted up mine eyes, and looked, and behold a certain man clothed in linen, whose loins were girded with fine gold of Uphaz: his body also was like the beryl, and his face as the appearance of lightning, and his eyes as lamps of fire, and his arms and his feet like in colour to polished brass, and the voice of his words like the voice of a multitude.

"And I, Daniel, alone saw the vision: for the men that were with me saw not the vision; but a great quaking fell upon them, so that they fled to hide themselves. Therefore I was left alone, and saw this great vision, and there remained no strength in me: for my comeliness was turned in me into corruption, and I retained no strength. Yet heard I the voice of his words: and when I heard the voice of his words, then was I in a deep sleep on my face, and my face toward the ground.

—Daniel 10: 1-9

WHAT SHALL BEFALL IN THE LATTER DAYS?

"And, behold, a hand touched me, which set me upon my knees and upon the palms of my hands. And he said unto me, 'O Daniel, a man greatly beloved, understand the words that I speak unto thee, and stand upright: for unto thee am I now sent.' And when he had spoken this word unto me, I stood trembling.

"Then said he unto me, 'Fear not, Daniel: for from the first day that thou didst set thine heart to understand, and to chasten thyself before thy God, thy words were heard, and I am come for thy words. But the prince of the kingdom of Persia withstood me one and twenty days: but, lo, Michael, one of the chief princes, came to help me; and I remained there with the kings of Persia. Now I am come to make thee understand what shall befall thy people in the latter days: for yet the vision is for many days.'

"And when he had spoken such words unto me, I set my face toward the ground, and I became dumb. And, behold, one like the similitude of the sons of men touched my lips: then I opened my mouth, and spake, and said unto him that stood before me, 'O my lord, by the vision my sorrows are turned upon me, and I have retained no strength. For how can the servant of this my lord talk with this my lord?' For as for me, straightway there remained no strength in me, neither is there breath left in me.

"Then there came again and touched me one like the appearance of a man, and he strengthened me, and said, 'O man greatly beloved, fear not; peace be unto thee; be strong, yea, be strong.'

"And when he had spoken unto me, I was strengthened, and said, 'Let my lord speak; for thou has strengthened me.'

"Then said he, 'Knowest thou wherefore I come unto thee? And now will I return to fight with the prince of Persia: and when I am gone forth, lo, the prince of Grecia shall come. But I will shew thee that which is noted in the Scripture of truth: and there is none that holdeth with me in these things, but Michael, your prince.

—Daniel 10: 10-21

THE KINGS OF THE NORTH AND OF THE SOUTH

" 'Also I in the first year of Darius the Mede, even I, stood to confirm and to strengthen him. And now will I shew thee the truth. Behold, there shall stand up yet three kings in Persia; and the fourth shall be far richer than they all: and by his strength through his riches he shall stir up all against the realm of Grecia. And a mighty king shall stand up, that shall rule with great dominion, and do according to his will. And when he shall stand up, his kingdom shall be broken, and shall be divided toward the four winds of heaven; and not to his posterity, nor according to his dominion which he ruled: for his kingdom shall be plucked up, even for others besides those.

" 'And the king of the south shall be strong, and one of his princes; and he shall be strong above him, and have dominion; his dominion shall be a great dominion. And in the end of years they shall join themselves together; for the king's daughter of the south shall come to the king of the north to make an agreement: but she shall not retain the power of the arm; neither shall he stand, nor his arm: but she shall be given up, and they that brought her, and he that begat her, and he that strengthened her in these times. But out of a branch of her roots shall one stand up in his estate, which shall come with an army, and shall enter into the fortress of the king of the north, and shall deal against them, and shall prevail: and shall also carry captives into Egypt their gods, with their princes, and with their precious vessels of silver and of gold; and he shall continue more years than the king of the north. So the king of the south shall come into his kingdom, and shall return into his own land.

" 'But his sons shall be stirred up, and shall assemble a multitude of great forces: and one shall certainly come, and overflow, and pass through: then shall he return, and be stirred up, even to his fortress. And the king of the south shall be moved with choler, and shall come forth and fight with him, even with the king of the north: and he shall set forth a great multitude; but the multitude shall be given into his hand. And when he hath taken away the multitude, his heart shall be lifted up; and he shall cast down many ten thousands: but he shall not be strengthened by it. For the king of the north shall return, and shall set forth a multitude greater than the former, and shall certainly come after certain years with a great army and with much riches.

" 'And in those times there shall many stand up against the king of the south: also the robbers of thy people shall exalt themselves to establish the vision; but they shall fall. So the king of the north shall come, and cast up a mount, and take the most fenced cities: and the arms of the south shall not withstand, neither his chosen people, neither shall there be any strength to withstand.

" 'But he that cometh against him shall do according to his own will, and none shall stand before him: and he shall stand in the glorious land, which by his hand shall be consumed. He shall also set his face to enter with the strength of his whole kingdom, and upright ones with him; thus shall he do: and he shall give him the daughter of women, corrupting her: but she shall not stand on his side, neither be for him.

" 'After this shall he turn his face unto the isles, and shall take many: but a prince for his own behalf shall cause the reproach offered by him to cease; without his own reproach he shall cause it to turn upon him. Then he shall turn his face toward the fort of his own land: but he shall stumble and fall, and not be found. Then shall stand up in his estate a raiser of taxes in the glory of the kingdom: but within few days he shall be destroyed, neither in anger, nor in battle. And in his estate shall stand up a vile person, to whom they shall not give the honour of the kingdom: but he shall come in peaceably, and obtain the kingdom by flatteries. And with the arms of a flood shall they be overflown from before him, and shall be broken; yea, also the prince of the covenant.

" 'And after the league made with him he shall work deceitfully: for he shall come up, and shall become strong with a small people. He shall enter peaceably even upon the fattest places of the province; and he shall do that which his fathers have not done, nor his fathers' fathers; he shall scatter among them the prey, and spoil, and riches: yea, and he shall forecast his devices against the strong holds, even for a time. And he shall stir up his power and his courage against the king of the south with a great army; and the king of the south shall be stirred up to battle with a very great and mighty army; but he shall not stand: for they shall forecast devices against him. Yea, they that feed of the portion of his meat shall destroy him, and his army shall overflow: and many shall fall down slain. And both these kings' hearts shall be to do mischief, and they shall speak lies at one table; but it shall not prosper: for yet the end shall be at the time appointed.

" 'Then shall he return into his land with great riches; and his heart shall be against the holy covenant; and he shall do exploits, and return to his own land. At the time appointed he shall return, and come toward the south; but it shall not be as the former, or as the latter. For the ships of Chittim shall come against him: therefore he shall be grieved, and return, and have indignation against the holy covenant: so shall he do; he shall even return, and have intelligence with them that forsake the holy covenant. And arms shall stand on his part, and they shall pollute the sanctuary of strength, and shall take away the daily sacrifice, and they shall place the abomination that maketh desolate.   —Daniel 11:1-31

THE PEOPLE THAT KNOW THEIR GOD SHALL BE STRONG, AND DO EXPLOITS

" 'And such as do wickedly against the covenant shall he corrupt by flatteries: but the people that do know their God shall be strong, and do exploits. And they that understand among the people shall instruct many: yet they shall fall by the sword, and by flame, by captivity, and by spoil, many days. Now when they shall fall, they shall be holpen with a little help: but many shall cleave to them with flatteries. And some of them of understanding shall fall, to try them, and to purge, and to make them white, even to the time of the end: because it is yet for a time appointed.

" 'And the king shall do according to his will; and he shall exalt himself, and magnify himself above every god, and shall speak marvelous things against the God of gods, and shall prosper till the indignation be accomplished: for that that is determined shall be done. Neither shall he regard the God of his fathers, nor the desire of women, nor regard any god: for he shall magnify himself above all. But in his estate shall he honour the God of forces: and a god whom his fathers knew not shall he honour with gold, and silver, and with precious stones, and pleasant things. Thus shall he do in the most strong holds with a strange god, whom he shall acknowledge and increase with glory: and he shall cause them to rule over many, and shall divide the land for gain.

" 'And at the time of the end shall the king of the south push at him: and the king of the north shall come against him like a whirlwind, with chariots, and with horsemen, and with many ships; and he shall enter into the countries, and shall overflow and pass over. He shall enter also into the glorious land, and many countries shall be overthrown: but these shall escape out of his hand, even Edom, and Moab, and the chief of the children of Ammon. He shall stretch forth his hand also upon the countries: and the land of Egypt shall not escape. But he shall have power over the treasures of gold and of silver, and over all the precious things of Egypt: and the Libyans and the Ethiopians shall be at his steps. But tidings out of the east and out of the north shall trouble him: therefore he shall go forth with great fury to destroy, and utterly to make away many. And he shall plant the tabernacles of his palace between the seas in the glorious holy mountain; yet he shall come to his end, and none shall help him.   —Daniel 11:32-45

THEY THAT BE WISE SHALL SHINE AS THE BRIGHTNESS OF THE FIRMAMENT

" 'And at that time shall Michael stand up, the great prince which standeth for the children of thy people: and there shall be a time of trouble, such as never was since there was a nation even to that same time: and at that time thy people shall be delivered, every one that shall be found written in the book. And many of them that sleep in the dust of the earth shall awake, some to everlasting life, and some to shame and everlasting contempt. And they that be wise shall shine as the brightness of the firmament; and they that turn many to righteousness, as the stars for ever and ever. But thou, O Daniel, shut up the words, and seal the book, even to the time of the end: many shall run to and fro, and knowledge shall be increased.' —Daniel 12:1-4

GO THY WAY, DANIEL, FOR THOU SHALT REST AND STAND IN THY LOT AT THE END OF DAYS

"Then I, Daniel, looked, and, behold, there stood other two, the one on this side of the bank of the river, and the other on that side of the bank of the river. And one said to the man clothed in linen, which was upon the waters of the river, 'How long shall it be to the end of these wonders?'

"And I heard the man clothed in linen, which was upon the waters of the river, when he held up his right hand and his left hand unto heaven, and sware by him that liveth for ever, that it shall be for a time, times, and a half; and when he shall have accomplished to scatter the power of the holy people, all these things shall be finished.

"And I heard, but I understood not: then said I, 'O my Lord, what shall be the end of these things?'

"And he said, 'Go thy way, Daniel: for the words are closed up and sealed till the time of the end. Many shall be purified, and made white, and tried; but the wicked shall do wickedly: and none of the wicked shall understand; but the wise shall understand. And from the time that the daily sacrifice shall be taken away, and the

abomination that maketh desolate set up, there shall be
a thousand two hundred and ninety days. Blessed is he
that waiteth, and cometh to the thousand three hundred
and five and thirty days. But go thou thy way till the
end be: for thou shalt rest, and stand in thy lot at the
end of the days.' "   —Daniel: 12: 5-13

QUESTIONS

In the case of each of the prophets give his time, his surroundings,
the purpose of his message. Under which king or kings did each
prophesy? Look in each prophecy for these elements: statesmanship;
patriotism; poetry; exhortation; religious faith; religious experience;
denunciation; prediction; Messianic prophecy. Of what other countries did the prophets write? What were the Assyrian and the Anti-
Assyrian party in Jerusalem? What was Amos' attitude toward
wealth? Micah's? What likeness and difference between our social
problems and those of Amos' day do you find? Compare the style of
Amos and Isaiah; of Hosea and Isaiah. Point out the oratorical passages. Compare with Demosthenes in his efforts to save Greece;
Patrick Henry; Adams and Jefferson. What was Isaiah's political
policy? Was it wise? Would you have belonged to the peace-party
or the war-party? What was Isaiah's great ideal and teaching upon
God? worship? ethics? sin and suffering? the future of Israel? of
the world?

Compare Jeremiah's work with that of Isaiah. Which was the
more successful? Which would you call the greater prophet? Was
Jeremiah a sincere patriot? Why did his townsmen distrust him?
Was his attitude wise? What hardships did he suffer? What happened
to the first edition of his addresses? Who were his friends? What
symbols did he use? What were his ideas of God? of religion? of
morality? of the place and destiny of his country? What were his
elements of strength? Is he as easy to read and understand as Isaiah?
If not, why?

What was Micah's mission? Of what great American statesman
was Micah a favorite? Why? Compare Amos and Micah. Make a
list of the problems of the "social prophets." What was the solution
or suggestion for reform?

How did Hosea use his personal experience in his teaching? What was his great lesson? Contrast the emphasis of Hosea's teaching about God with that of Amos.

Compare the social and religious conditions as given in Zephaniah with those of Amos and Micah.

What nation is prominent in Nahum's prophecy? What does he mean by the "Lion of the North"? What is the spirit of the book?

What is Habakkuk's treatment of the problem of suffering?

What was Ezekiel's time and his work? What figure does Ezekiel use of Tyre?

What was the mission of Haggai? Was it successful? What was his exact date?

What were the visions of Zechariah? What did they probably mean?

What was Obadiah's message?

What was the occasion of the prophecy of Malachi? What were the conditions of his times? Is his style as lofty and inspiring as that of Isaiah and Amos?

What figures are used by Joel? Is his prophecy pessimistic? Has it the same spirit of social reform which we find in the earlier prophets?

Whom do you consider modern prophets?

Tell the story of Jonah. What effect had his message upon Nineveh? Why was he sorry? What lesson did God teach him?

What stories does the Book of Daniel contain? Why were they written? Compare the stories of Joseph and those of Daniel. What qualities did each show? Why were they so helpful to the people?

THE EMPIRE OF PERSIA

The Exile

THIS important period is perhaps less studied and appreciated than any other period of Jewish history. Yet out of it comes some of the very finest literature of the Old Testament: poems, stories, prophecies. For the second time in its history, Israel passed under the yoke of bondage. We are almost as familiar with the scenes of the first captivity as we are with the countries of modern Europe; for Egypt still lives. Recent discoveries bring the ancient days even of the great empire very close to us. There are still cities and towns on the Nile, mighty pyramids, temples, and colossal sculptures going back to the time when Israel was in bondage, when Hebrew slaves helped to build those memorials of the past.

The case of Assyria and Babylon, those great city empires, is far different. These great civilizations, the greatest, perhaps, in point of outward magnificence of all times, have completely vanished from the earth. Not a wall, not a temple, is standing. There is hardly any portion of the earth poorer, more forlorn, than the region which was the cradle of civilization, the site of the richest, most powerful city of the earth. Many records, however, we have, from the "books" of the time, written upon clay tablets which were burned into bricks, far more enduring than the papyrus of Egypt. Moreover, the great traveler of ancient times, Herodotus, visited Babylon, not indeed at the height of its glory, but while it was still intact, only one hundred years after the captivity of the Hebrews.

The following description by Dean Stanley is based upon Herodotus: "Far as the horizon itself, extended the circuit of the vast capital of the then known world. If the imperceptible circumference of our modern capitals has exceeded the limits of Babylon, yet none in ancient times or modern can be compared with its definite enclosure, which was on the lowest computation forty, on the highest sixty, miles round. Like Nineveh or Ecbatana, it was, but on a still larger scale, a country or empire enclosed in a city. Forests, parks, gardens were intermingled with the houses so as to present rather the appearance of the suburbs of a great metropolis than the metropolis itself. Yet still the regularity and order of a city were preserved. The streets, according to a fashion rare in Europe, whether ancient or modern, but common in ancient Asia — and adopted by the Greek and Roman conquerors when they penetrated into Asia, perhaps in imitation of Babylon — were straight, and at right angles to each other. The houses, unlike those of most ancient cities, except at Tyre, and afterwards in Rome, were three or four stories high.

"But the prodigious scale of the place appeared chiefly in the enormous size, unparalleled before or since, of its public buildings, and rendered more conspicuous by the flatness of the country from which they rose. Even in their decay, 'their colossal piles, domineering over the monotonous plain, produce an effect of grandeur and magnificence which cannot be imagined in any other situation.'

"The walls by which this Imperial city, or, as it might be called, this Civic Empire, rising out of a deep and wide moat, was screened and protected from the wandering tribes of the Desert, as the Celestial Empire by the Great Wall of China, as the extremities of the Roman Empire by the wall of Trajan in Dacia, . . . were not, like those famous bulwarks, mere mounds or ramparts, but lines as of towering hills, which must have met the distant gaze at the close of every vista, like the Alban range at Rome. They appeared, at least to Herodotus, who saw them whilst in their unbroken magnificence, not less than 300 feet high; and along the summit ran a vast terrace which admitted of the turning of chariots with four horses, and which may therefore well have been more than eighty feet broad.

"If to the inhabitants of Jerusalem, who were accustomed to the precipitous descent of the walls overhanging the valley of the Kedron, the mere height of the Babylonian enclosure may not have seemed so startling as to us, yet to the size of the other buildings the puny dimensions whether of the Palace or Temple of Solomon bore no comparison. The Great Palace of the Kings was itself a city within the city — seven miles round; and its gardens, expressly built to convey to a Median princess some reminiscence of her native mountains, rose one above another, to a height of more than seventy feet, on which stood forest trees of vast diameter side by side with flowering shrubs. On the walls of the Palace the Israelites might see painted those vast hunting-scenes which were still traceable two centuries later — of which one characteristic fragment remains in sculpture, a lion trampling on a man — which would recall to them the description in their own early annals of 'Nimrod the mighty hunter.'

"But the most prodigious and unique of all was the Temple of Bel. It was the most remarkable of all those artificial mountains or beacons, which, towering over the plains of Mesopotamia, 'guide the traveler's eye like giant pillars.' It rose like the Great Pyramid, square upon square; and was believed to have reached the height of 600 feet. Its base was a square of 200 yards. No other edifice consecrated to worship, no Carnac in Egyptian Thebes, nor Byzantine St. Sophia, nor Gothic Clugny, nor St. Peter's of Rome, has reached the grandeur of this primeval sanctuary, casting its shadow far and wide, over city and plain. Thither, as to the most sacred and impregnable fortress, were believed to have been transported the huge brazen laver, the precious brazen pillars, and all the lesser vessels of The Temple of Jerusalem together doubtless with all the other like sacred spoils which Babylonian conquest had swept from Egypt, Tyre, Damascus, or Nineveh. And when from the silver shrine at the summit of this building, the whole mass of mingled verdure and habitation for miles and miles was overlooked, what was wanting in grace or proportion must have been compensated by the extraordinary richness of colour. Some faint conception of this may be given by the view of Moscow from the Kremlin over the blue, green, and gilded domes and towers springing from the gardens which fill up the vacant intervals of that most Oriental of European capitals. But neither that view nor any other can give a notion of the vastness of the variegated landscape of Babylon as seen from any of its elevated points."

It was to such surroundings as these that the captives of Judah were transported. As in Egypt during the first captivity, the Hebrews increased rapidly in numbers, but still they kept their love for the little barren country among the hills, and its city, small and poor in comparison with Babylon, but inexpressibly dear in their eyes. They were homesick for the old hills and pastures. They hung their harps on the willows and refused to join the festivities of the magnificent court:

"By the rivers of Babylon, there we sat down,
 Yea, we wept, when we remembered Zion.
 We hanged our harps upon the willows in the midst
    thereof.

For there they that carried us away captive required
    of us a song;
And they that wasted us required of us mirth, saying,
'Sing us one of the songs of Zion.'
How shall we sing the Lord's song in a strange land?
If I forget thee, O Jerusalem, let my right hand forget
    her cunning."

Some of them occupied positions of responsibility
in the court,— Nehemiah was the king's cupbearer, as
Joseph was prime minister in Egypt,— but the noblest
souls, those who occupied the highest positions, were
those who longed most earnestly for their native land.
And so they went back, across the desert to the forlorn
heap of rubbish which was once Jerusalem. Is there
any finer, more heroic story than that of Nehemiah,
who left the luxury of the court and his high position,
to build amid scorn and hostility the walls of his own
dear city? The names of the period: Nehemiah, Ezra,
Zerubbabel, Zechariah, Haggai, are not so well known
as those of the earlier heroes but they shine as brightly
on the roll of the nation's glorious sons.

CONE OF KING NABOPOLASSAR

By courtesy of the British Museum

Baked clay cone of Nabopolassar, King of Babylon from B.C. 625 to B.C. 604, inscribed with a text recording the restoration of the temple of Marduk at Babylon.

BOUNDARY STONE OF RITTI-MARDUK

By courtesy of the British Museum

Limestone boundary stone inscribed with a text recording the restoration and confirmation of certain rights and privileges to Ritti-Marduk, the warden of Bit-Karzi-yabku, a district which was apparently situated on the confines of Elam, by Nebuchadnezzar I, King of Babylon, about B.C. 1120. The document was drafted by the scribe, Enlil-tabni-bullit, and the text concludes with a series of curses in which the great gods are entreated to destroy every one who shall attempt to injure Ritti-Marduk or destroy this stone.

BABYLONIAN DEMON

Terra-cotta figure of a Babylonian Demon.

Ezra

Five hundred and thirty-six years before Christ a wonderful
new era began for the Hebrew race. They had been under the power
of the Empire of Babylon. The best part of the people had been
taken to Babylonia, where they had longed in vain for their lost
land. Ezekiel and Isaiah 40–66 and some psalms show us how
strong the longing was. At last, in 539, Babylon fell under the conquering armies of Cyrus, king of the newly formed Empire of Persia,
beyond the mountains to the east of Babylon. Cyrus was a wise king
and a great statesman. He knew that discontented groups of people
weakened an empire, and very soon he gave to the members of
various nations who had been brought to Babylon permission to
return home. Among these were the Hebrews. They received this
permission with great joy; but when it came to making up an expedition, many of the best of the people could not go. They were
tied to their homes in Babylon by bonds that could not be broken,
and for hundreds of years the Jewish colony in Babylon was nearly
as important as the community in Jerusalem. These Jews of Babylon
became famous students of the Law, and from this colony came
Ezra and Nehemiah, and many others who tried to help the homeland.

Those who came to Jerusalem at first found there a small and
weak community of their own people, who had never been taken to
Babylon, surrounded and almost swamped by foreigners. They found
it hard to earn a living on the rocky hills of Palestine, so different
from the rich, fertile plains of Babylonia. It is not surprising that
they lost some of the first enthusiasm of the return. Yet they never
gave up their religion or their love for their nation, and, by stead-
fastness even when discouraged, they became the founders of the
new Jewish nation, which occupied Palestine in the New Testament
times. We may well honor them. Heroism consists, not in never
being discouraged, but in never giving up, no matter how discouraged
we may be.

These Jews brought back with them one thing which was of
great importance for the future. They brought a very strong love
for their nation, a spirit which would now be called "Nationalism."

The citizens of no modern country have a stronger national feeling than had the Jews of this period. It resulted, first, in a growing reverence for the books of the nation,—the writings of the prophets and the books of stories of olden time that they brought with them from the exile; second, in a great reverence for the laws of the nation; third, in a deep love for the worship of the God of their Fathers; fourth, in a strong desire to keep the blood of their race pure, lest they should be swallowed up and lost in the other more numerous races about them.

THE NEW NATION: THE DAYS OF THE RETURN

The king's decree reads as though he were a worshiper of Israel's God. He was not; but perhaps his decree to each captive people was sent to them in terms of their own religion.

Some psalms show the great joy with which the Jews saw this fulfillment of all their long hopes:

"When the Lord turned again the captivity of Zion,
We were like them that dreamed.
Then was our mouth filled with laughter
And our tongue with singing."   —Psalm 126:1, 2

Their joy was the greater that not only were the people allowed to return if they wished, but that the government sent back treasures of the temple, the loot of the conquest of Jerusalem fifty years before. The expedition was headed by Sheshbazzar, the appointed governor of the new nation.

THE KING GIVES PERMISSION TO RETURN

NOW in the first year of Cyrus, King of Persia, that the word of the LORD by the mouth of Jeremiah might be fulfilled, the LORD stirred up the spirit of Cyrus, King of Persia, that he made a proclamation throughout all his kingdom, and put it also in writing, saying, "Thus saith Cyrus, King of Persia, The LORD God of heaven hath given me all the kingdoms of the earth; and he hath charged me to build him an house at Jerusalem, which is in Judah. Who

is there among you of all his people? His God be with him,
and let him go up to Jerusalem, which is in Judah, and
build the house of the LORD God of Israel (he is the God),
which is in Jerusalem. And whosoever remaineth in any
place where he sojourneth, let the men of his place help
him with silver, and with gold, and with goods, and with
beasts, besides the free-will offering for the house of God
that is in Jerusalem.

THE EXPEDITION PREPARES

Then rose up the chief of the fathers of Judah and
Benjamin, and the priests, and the Levites, with all them
whose spirit God had raised, to go up to build the house
of the LORD which is in Jerusalem. And all they that
were about them strengthened their hands with vessels
of silver, with gold, with goods, and with beasts, and with
precious things, besides all that was willingly offered.

THE OLD TEMPLE TREASURES ARE RETURNED

Also Cyrus, the king, brought forth the vessels of the
house of the LORD, which Nebuchadnezzar had brought
forth out of Jerusalem, and had put them in the house of
his gods; even those did Cyrus, King of Persia, bring forth
by the hand of Mithredath the treasurer, and numbered
them unto Sheshbazzar, the prince of Judah.

And this is the number of them: thirty chargers of
gold, a thousand chargers of silver, nine and twenty
knives, thirty basins of gold, silver basins of a second
sort four hundred and ten, and other vessels a thousand.
All the vessels of gold and of silver were five thousand
and four hundred. All these did Sheshbazzar bring up
with them of the captivity that were brought up from
Babylon unto Jerusalem. —Ezra 1:1-11.

The whole congregation together was forty and two thousand three hundred and threescore, beside their servants and their maids, of whom there were seven thousand three hundred thirty and seven; and there were among them two hundred singing-men and singing-women. Their horses were seven hundred thirty and six; their mules, two hundred forty and five; their camels, four hundred thirty and five; their asses, six thousand seven hundred and twenty.

And some of the chief of the fathers, when they came to the house of the LORD which is at Jerusalem, offered freely for the house of God to set it up in his place. They gave after their ability unto the treasure of the work threescore and one thousand drams of gold, and five thousand pounds of silver, and one hundred priests' garments. So the priests and the Levites and some of the people and the singers and the porters and the Nethinim dwelt in their cities, and all Israel in their cities.

—Ezra 2:64-70.

PLANS FOR WORSHIP

In the ancient world sacrifice was the most important part of worship. The Jews of this time, however, had not been willing to sacrifice outside of Jerusalem; so all the years of their exile had been without this part of worship. Now that they were back, they hastened to build an altar. They planned to erect a temple as soon as possible; but the story shows how sadly this plan failed.

THEY BUILD AN ALTAR

And when the seventh month was come, and the children of Israel were in the cities, the people gathered themselves together as one man to Jerusalem. Then stood up Jeshua, the son of Jozadak, and his brethren, the priests, and Zerubbabel, the son of Shealtiel, and his brethren, and builded the altar of the God of Israel, to offer burnt-offerings thereon, as it is written in the law of Moses the man of God. And they set the altar upon his bases; for fear was upon them because of the people of those countries; and they offered burnt-offerings thereon unto the LORD, even burnt-offerings morning and evening.

THE FEAST OF TABERNACLES

They kept also the feast of tabernacles, as it is written, and offered the daily burnt-offerings by number, according to the custom, as the duty of every day required, and afterward offered the continual burnt-offering, both of the new-moons, and of all the set feasts of the LORD that were consecrated, and of every one that willingly offered a free-will offering unto the LORD. From the first day of the seventh month began they to offer burnt-offerings unto the LORD. But the foundation of the temple of the LORD was not yet laid.

PLANS TO BUILD THE TEMPLE

They gave money also unto the masons, and to the carpenters; and meat, and drink, and oil, unto them of

MOUNT MORIAH, SITE OF THE ANCIENT TEMPLE
Photograph by Professor Benjamin W. Robinson

Zidon, and to them of Tyre, to bring cedar-trees from
Lebanon to the sea of Joppa, according to the grant that
they had of Cyrus, King of Persia. Now in the second
year of their coming unto the house of God at Jerusalem,
in the second month, began Zerubbabel, the son of Shealtiel, and Jeshua, the son of Jozadak, and the remnant of
their brethren, the priests and the Levites, and all they
that were come out of the captivity unto Jerusalem; and
appointed the Levites, from twenty years old and upward, to set forward the work of the house of the LORD.

THE FOUNDATIONS ARE LAID

And when the builders laid the foundation of the
temple of the LORD, they set the priests in their apparel
with trumpets, and the Levites, the sons of Asaph, with
cymbals, to praise the LORD, after the ordinance of David,
King of Israel.

And they sang together by course in praising and
giving thanks unto the LORD:

Because he is good,
For his mercy endureth for ever toward Israel.

And all the people shouted with a great shout, when
they praised the LORD, because the foundation of the
house of the LORD was laid.

But many of the priests and Levites and chief of the
fathers, who were ancient men, that had seen the first house,
when the foundation of this house was laid before their eyes,
wept with a loud voice; and many shouted aloud for joy, so
that the people could not discern the noise of the shout of
joy from the noise of the weeping of the people; for the
people shouted with a loud shout, and the noise was
heard afar off.　　　　　—Ezra 3.

THE HOPES OF THE JEWS ARE THWARTED

The Samaritans, called "the adversaries" in Ezra, were the descendants of foreigners brought in after the fall of the Kingdom of Israel nearly two hundred years before. See page 356 and Volume III, pages 427–430. They had intermarried with the Israelites and adopted the worship of Jehovah. The Jews refused to acknowledge them as fellow members of the nation, and from this time there was enmity between Jews and Samaritans, as the Gospel of John shows. See Volume VI, page 262. The Samaritans soon built their own temple on Mount Gerizim, and kept their own worship of Jehovah.

Now when the adversaries of Judah and Benjamin heard that the children of the captivity builded the temple unto the LORD God of Israel, then they came to Zerubbabel, and to the chief of the fathers, and said unto them, "Let us build with you; for we seek your God, as ye do; and we do sacrifice unto him since the days of Esarhaddon, King of Assyria, which brought us up hither."

But Zerubbabel, and Jeshua, and the rest of the chief of the fathers of Israel, said unto them, "Ye have nothing to do with us to build an house unto our God; but we ourselves together will build unto the LORD God of Israel, as King Cyrus, the king of Persia, hath commanded us."

Then the people of the land weakened the hands of the people of Judah, and troubled them in building, and hired counsellors against them, to frustrate their purpose, all the days of Cyrus, King of Persia, even until the reign of Darius, King of Persia.

Then ceased the work of the house of God which is at Jerusalem. So it ceased unto the second year of the reign of Darius, King of Persia.　　　　—Ezra 4:1–5, 24.

THE TEMPLE AT LAST IS BUILT

For sixteen years discouragement followed the Jewish colony at Jerusalem. Then a new king, Darius, came to the throne, and the prophets, Haggai and Zechariah, urged the people to make another effort to build the temple. In this volume, beginning with page 356, will be found the stirring words of these prophets. How opposition arose and was overcome, and how the work of the people was at last successful, are told in this story.

THE JEWS AGAIN BEGIN THE GREAT ENTERPRISE

Then the prophets, Haggai the prophet and Zechariah the son of Iddo, prophesied unto the Jews that were in Judah and Jerusalem in the name of the God of Israel, even unto them. Then rose up Zerubbabel, the son of Shealtiel, and Jeshua, the son of Jozadak, and began to build the house of God which is at Jerusalem; and with them were the prophets of God helping them.

THE GOVERNOR QUESTIONS THEIR AUTHORITY

At the same time came to them Tatnai, governor on this side the river, and Shethar-boznai, and their companions, and said thus unto them, "Who hath commanded you to build this house and to make up this wall?"

They said unto them after this manner, "What are the names of the men that make this building?"

But the eye of their God was upon the elders of the Jews, that they could not cause them to cease, till the matter came to Darius; and then they returned answer by letter concerning this matter.

A LETTER OF INQUIRY: HAVE THE JEWS PERMISSION TO BUILD THE TEMPLE?

The copy of the letter that Tatnai, governor on this side the river, and Shethar-boznai, and his companions the Apharsachites, which were on this side the river, sent unto Darius, the king: they sent a letter unto him, wherein was written thus: "Unto Darius, the king, all peace.

EAST WALL OF JERUSALEM
Photograph by Professor Benjamin W. Robinson
The Golden Gate (Double Gate) which led into Temple Area may be seen
at the right, forming part of the city wall.

"Be it known unto the king, that we went into the
province of Judea, to the house of the great God, which
is builded with great stones, and timber is laid in the walls,
and this work goeth fast on, and prospereth in their
hands. Then asked we those elders, and said unto them
thus, 'Who commanded you to build this house, and
to make up these walls?' We asked their names also, to
certify thee, that we might write the names of the men
that were the chief of them.

"And thus they returned us answer, saying, 'We are
the servants of the God of heaven and earth, and build the
house that was builded these many years ago, which a
great king of Israel builded and set up. But after that our
fathers had provoked the God of heaven unto wrath, he
gave them into the hand of Nebuchadnezzar, the king of
Babylon, the Chaldean, who destroyed this house, and
carried the people away into Babylon. But in the first

year of Cyrus, the king of Babylon, the same King Cyrus made a decree to build this house of God. And the vessels also of gold and silver of the house of God, which Nebuchadnezzar took out of the temple that was in Jerusalem, and brought them into the temple of Babylon, those did Cyrus, the king, take out of the temple of Babylon, and they were delivered unto one, whose name was Sheshbazzar, whom he had made governor; and said unto him, "Take these vessels, go, carry them into the temple that is in Jerusalem, and let the house of God be builded in his place." Then came the same Sheshbazzar, and laid the foundation of the house of God which is in Jerusalem; and since that time even until now hath it been in building, and yet it is not finished.'

"Now therefore, if it seem good to the king, let there be search made in the king's treasure-house, which is there at Babylon, whether it be so, that a decree was

THE SINGLE GATE

Photograph by Professor Benjamin W. Robinson

This gate, long since closed, forms a part of the wall about Temple Area.

THE TRIPLE GATE

Photograph by Professor Benjamin W. Robinson

The Triple Gate, now sealed, forms part of the old wall on Mount Moriah where the Temple once stood.

made of Cyrus, the king, to build this house of God at Jerusalem, and let the king send his pleasure to us concerning this matter." —Ezra 5.

THE ANSWER: PERMISSION IS GRANTED

Then Darius, the king, made a decree, and search was made in the house of the rolls, where the treasures were laid up in Babylon. And there was found at Achmetha, in the palace that is in the province of the Medes, a roll, and therein was a record thus written:

"In the first year of Cyrus, the king, the same Cyrus, the king, made a decree concerning the house of God at Jerusalem: 'Let the house be builded, the place where they offered sacrifices, and let the foundations thereof be strongly laid; the height thereof threescore cubits, and the breadth thereof threescore cubits, with three rows of great stones, and a row of new timber; and let the expenses be given out of the king's house; and also let the golden and silver vessels of the house of God, which Nebuchadnezzar took forth out of the temple which is at Jerusalem, and brought unto Babylon, be restored, and brought again unto the temple which is at Jerusalem, every one to his place, and place them in the house of God.'"

"Now therefore, Tatnai, governor beyond the river, Shethar-boznai, and your companions the Apharsachites, which are beyond the river, be ye far from thence. Let the work of this house of God alone; let the governor of the Jews, and the elders of the Jews, build this house of God in his place. Moreover, I make a decree what ye shall do to the elders of these Jews for the building of this house of God: that of the king's goods, even of the tribute beyond the river, forthwith expenses be given unto these men, that they be not hindered. And that which they have need of, both young bullocks, and rams, and lambs, for the burnt-offerings of the God of heaven, wheat, salt, wine, and oil, according to the appointment of the priests which are at Jerusalem, let it be given them day by day without fail, that they may offer sacrifices of sweet savour unto the God of heaven, and pray for the life of the king, and of his sons.

"Also I have made a decree, that whosoever shall alter this word, let timber be pulled down from his house, and being set up, let him be hanged thereon; and let his house be made a dunghill for this. And the God that hath caused his name to dwell there destroy all kings and people, that shall put to their hand to alter and to destroy this house of God which is at Jerusalem. I, Darius, have made a decree; let it be done with speed."

THE TEMPLE IS COMPLETED

Then Tatnai, governor on this side the river, Shethar-boznai, and their companions, according to that which

Darius, the king, had sent, so they did speedily. And the elders of the Jews builded, and they prospered through the prophesying of Haggai, the prophet, and Zechariah, the son of Iddo. And they builded, and finished it, according to the commandment of the God of Israel, and according to the commandment of Cyrus, and Darius and Artaxerxes, King of Persia. And this house was finished on the third day of the month Adar, which was in the sixth year of the reign of Darius, the king.

THE GREAT CEREMONY OF DEDICATION

And the children of Israel, the priests, and the Levites, and the rest of the children of the captivity, kept the dedication of this house of God with joy, and offered at the dedication of this house of God an hundred bullocks, two hundred rams, four hundred lambs; and for a sin-offering for all Israel, twelve he-goats, according to the number of the tribes of Israel. And they set the priests in their divisions, and the Levites in their courses, for the service of God, which is at Jerusalem; as it is written in the book of Moses.

SAMARITAN PRIEST AND THE SACRED ROLL OF THE LAW

Photograph contributed by Professor Julius Seelye Bixler, Ph.D.

The Samaritan Bible consists of the first five books of the Bible, the laws of which they followed with great strictness. When, shortly after the time of Ezra, the Samaritans formed their own worship, the Jews themselves regarded the Law as so much more sacred than any of the other books that the Samaritans took only these books, and never added to them. Some description of the ancient rolls may be found in Volume viii, page 241.

THEY CELEBRATE A JOYFUL PASSOVER

And the children of the captivity kept the passover upon the fourteenth day of the first month. For the priests and the Levites were purified together, all of them were pure, and killed the passover for all the children of the captivity, and for their brethren, the priests, and for themselves. And the children of Israel, which were come again out of captivity, and all such as had separated themselves unto them from the filthiness of the heathen of the land, to seek the LORD God of Israel, did eat, and kept the feast of unleavened bread seven days with joy; for the LORD had made them joyful, and turned the heart of the king of Assyria unto them, to strengthen their hands in the work of the house of God, the God of Israel.

—Ezra 6.

THE STORY OF EZRA

At least fifty years and perhaps more had passed since the new temple had been dedicated with such joy. The struggles of the little nation with poverty and hard labor had quenched their enthusiasm. Perhaps Malachi had spoken before this time, chiding the people for their indifference to the temple. See page 392. Certain it is that the courage of the people was at a low ebb when Ezra came, and his reforms were made only with great difficulty.

Ezra was of the family of priests, but he was remembered chiefly as "the scribe"; that is, he was a teacher of the law of the nation. He was inflexibly honest, stern, rugged, uncompromising; shirking no labor; as rigid with himself as he was with others; holding at any cost to the right as he saw the right. The world does not usually love men who are so stern and rigid, but many a needed reform would never be carried through without such men as Ezra.

EZRA'S GREAT EXPEDITION TO JERUSALEM

Now after these things, in the reign of Artaxerxes, King of Persia, Ezra, the son of Seraiah, who was of the family of Aaron the chief priest, went up from Babylon;

and he was a ready scribe in the law of Moses, which the LORD God of Israel had given; and the king granted him all his request, according to the hand of the LORD his God upon him.

And there went up some of the children of Israel, and of the priests, and the Levites, and the singers, and the porters, and the Nethinim, unto Jerusalem, in the seventh year of Artaxerxes, the king. And he came to Jerusalem in the fifth month, which was in the seventh year of the king. For upon the first day of the first month began he to go up from Babylon, and on the first day of the fifth month came he to Jerusalem, according to the good hand of his God upon him. For Ezra had prepared his heart to seek the law of the LORD, and to do it, and to teach in Israel statutes and judgments.

THE KING'S COMMISSION

Now this is the copy of the letter that the king, Artaxerxes, gave unto Ezra, the priest, the scribe, even a scribe of the words of the commandments of the LORD, and of his statutes to Israel:

"Artaxerxes, king of kings: Unto Ezra the priest, a scribe of the law of the God of heaven, perfect peace, and at such a time.

"I make a decree, that all they of the people of Israel, and of his priests and Levites, in my realm, which are minded of their own free will to go up to Jerusalem, go with thee. Forasmuch as thou art sent of the king, and of his seven counsellors, to inquire concerning Judah and Jerusalem, according to the law of thy God which is in thine hand; and to carry the silver and gold, which the king and his counsellors have freely offered unto the God of Israel, whose habitation is in Jerusalem; and all the silver and gold that thou canst find in all the province of

Babylon, with the free-will offering of the people, and of the priests, offering willingly for the house of their God which is in Jerusalem; that thou mayest buy speedily with this money bullocks, rams, lambs, with their meat-offerings and their drink-offerings, and offer them upon the altar of the house of your God which is in Jerusalem. And whatsoever shall seem good to thee, and to thy brethren, to do with the rest of the silver and the gold, that do after the will of your God. The vessels also that are given thee for the service of the house of thy God, those deliver

ROBINSON'S ARCH

This picture shows the beginning of an arch which spanned a small valley and supported a road leading from the ancient Temple westward to the southwestern section of the city. The arch is named after its modern discoverer Edward Robinson. The picture was taken by Professor Benjamin W. Robinson, Ph.D., of Chicago Theological Seminary.

thou before the God of Jerusalem. And whatsoever more shall be needful for the house of thy God, which thou shalt have occasion to bestow, bestow it out of the king's treasure-house.

"And I, even I, Artaxerxes, the king, do make a decree to all the treasurers which are beyond the river, that whatsoever Ezra, the priest, the scribe of the law of the God of heaven, shall require of you, it be done speedily, unto an hundred talents of silver, and to an hundred measures of wheat, and to an hundred baths of wine, and to an hundred baths of oil, and salt without prescribing how much. Whatsoever is commanded by the God of heaven, let it be diligently done for the house of the God of heaven; for why should there be wrath against the realm of the king and his sons?

"Also we certify you, that touching any of the priests and Levites, singers, porters, Nethinim, or ministers of this house of God, it shall not be lawful to impose toll, tribute, or custom, upon them.

"And thou, Ezra, after the wisdom of thy God, that is in thine hand, set magistrates and judges, which may judge all the people that are beyond the river, all such as know the laws of thy God; and teach ye them that know them not. And whosoever will not do the law of thy God, and the law of the king, let judgment be executed speedily upon him, whether it be unto death, or to banishment, or to confiscation of goods, or to imprisonment." —Ezra 7:1, 6-26.

EZRA'S THANKSGIVING: "BLESSED BE GOD"

Blessed be the LORD God of our fathers, which hath put such a thing as this in the king's heart, to beautify the house of the LORD which is in Jerusalem, and hath extended mercy unto me before the king, and his counsellors, and before all the king's mighty princes.

THE EXPEDITION GATHERS—THE LEADER TELLS HIS OWN STORY

And I was strengthened as the hand of the LORD my God was upon me, and I gathered together out of Israel chief men to go up with me. And I gathered them together to the river that runneth to Ahava; and there abode we in tents three days; and I viewed the people, and the priests, and found there none of the sons of Levi. Then sent I for Eliezer, for Ariel, for Shemaiah, and for Elnathan, and for Jarib, and for Elnathan, and for Nathan, and for Zechariah, and for Meshullam, chief men;

SAMARITAN TENTS IN PREPARATION FOR THE PASSOVER

Photograph by Professor Julius Seelye Bixler

The Samaritans, who worshipped the God of Israel in a temple of their own on Mount Gerizim, still exist as a small community, and keep the passover on that mountain. Their temple has been destroyed long since, but they put up tents on the mountain, and stay in them during the feast. On the night of the passover they kill a sheep and make a feast, as did the Jews in old time.

also for Joiarib, and for Elnathan, men of understanding. And I sent them with commandment unto Iddo, the chief, at the place Casiphia, and I told them what they should say unto Iddo, and to his brethren the Nethinim, at the place Casiphia, that they should bring unto us ministers for the house of our God.

And by the good hand of our God upon us, they brought us a man of understanding, of the sons of Mahli, the son of Levi, the son of Israel; and Sherebiah, with his sons and his brethren, eighteen; and Hashabiah, and with him Jeshaiah of the sons of Merari, his brethren and their sons, twenty; also of the Nethinim, whom David and the princes had appointed for the service of the Levites, two hundred and twenty Nethinim; all of them were expressed by name.   —Ezra 7:27, 28; 8:15-20.

"COMMIT THY WAY UNTO THE LORD"

Then I proclaimed a fast there, at the river of Ahava, that we might afflict ourselves before our God, to seek of him a right way for us, and for our little ones, and for

all our substance. For I was ashamed to require of the
king a band of soldiers and horsemen to help us against
the enemy in the way; because we had spoken unto the
king, saying, "The hand of our God is upon all them for
good that seek him; but his power and his wrath is
against all them that forsake him." So we fasted and
besought our God for this; and he was entreated of us.

A GUARD FOR THE TREASURE

Then I separated twelve of the chief of the priests,
Sherebiah, Hashabiah, and ten of their brethren with
them, and weighed unto them the silver, and the gold,
and the vessels, even the offering of the house of our
God, which the king, and his counsellors, and his lords,
and all Israel there present, had offered. I even weighed
unto their hand six hundred and fifty talents of silver,
and silver vessels an hundred talents, and of gold an
hundred talents; also twenty basins of gold, of a thousand
drams, and two vessels of fine copper, precious as gold.
And I said unto them, "Ye are holy unto the LORD; the
vessels are holy also; and the silver and the gold are a
free-will offering unto the LORD God of your fathers.
Watch ye, and keep them, until ye weigh them before
the chief of the priests and the Levites, and chief of the
fathers of Israel, at Jerusalem, in the chambers of the
house of the LORD." So took the priests and the Levites
the weight of the silver, and the gold, and the vessels, to
bring them to Jerusalem unto the house of our God.

THE JOURNEY THROUGH THE DESERT

Then we departed from the river of Ahava on the
twelfth day of the first month, to go unto Jerusalem; and
the hand of our God was upon us, and he delivered us

from the hand of the enemy, and of such as lay in wait by the way.

THE JOURNEY'S END

And we came to Jerusalem, and abode there three days.

Now on the fourth day was the silver and the gold and the vessels weighed in the house of our God by the hand of Meremoth, the son of Uriah, the priest.

Also the children of those that had been carried away, which were come out of the captivity, offered burnt-offerings unto the God of Israel, twelve bullocks for all Israel, ninety and six rams, seventy and seven lambs, twelve he-goats for a sin-offering; all this was a burnt-offering unto the LORD.

And they delivered the king's commissions unto the king's lieutenants, and to the governors on this side the river; and they furthered the people, and the house of God.
—Ezra 8:21-36.

THE GREAT REFORM

The strong national feeling of the Jewish leaders after the exile led them to object to marriage with foreigners. At Jerusalem many mixed marriages had taken place. This seemed to Ezra a serious matter. If it went on there would soon be no Jewish nation. In principle he was right; the only way to preserve this small nation lay in purity of blood. So well did Ezra and others who thought like him do their work that the Jewish race lives to this day, while the other races of that land have disappeared. For other condemnations of foreign marriages see pages 396, 511. What Ezra did and how he won the people to his side are told in the following pages.

EZRA LEARNS THAT THE PEOPLE HAVE MARRIED FOREIGNERS

Now when these things were done, the princes came to me, saying, "The people of Israel, and the priests, and the Levites, have not separated themselves from the people of the lands, doing according to their abominations; for they have taken of their daughters for themselves, and for their sons; so that the holy seed have mingled themselves with the people of those lands; yea, the hand of the princes and rulers hath been chief in this trespass."

And when I heard this thing, I rent my garment and my mantle, and plucked off the hair of my head and of my beard, and sat down astonished. Then were assembled unto me every one that trembled at the words of the God of Israel, because of the transgression of those that had been carried away; and I sat astonished until the evening sacrifice.

EZRA IN PRAYER FOR THE NATION HE LOVES

And at the evening sacrifice I arose up from my heaviness; and having rent my garment and my mantle, I fell upon my knees, and spread out my hands unto the Lord my God, and said, "O my God, I am ashamed and blush to lift up my face to thee, my God; for our iniquities are increased over our head, and our trespass is grown up unto the heavens. Since the days of our fathers have we been in a great trespass unto this day; and for our iniquities have we, our kings, and our priests, been delivered into the hand of the kings of the lands, to the sword, to captivity, and to a spoil, and to confusion of face, as it is this day.

" And now for a little space grace hath been showed from the Lord our God, to leave us a remnant to escape, and to give us a nail in his holy place, that our God may lighten our eyes, and give us a little reviving in our bondage; for we were bond-men; yet our God hath not forsaken us in our bondage, but hath extended mercy unto us in the sight of the kings of Persia, to give us a reviving, to set up the house of our God, and to repair the desolations thereof, and to give us a wall in Judah and in Jerusalem.

"And now, O our God, what shall we say after this? For we have forsaken thy commandments, which thou hast commanded by thy servants the prophets, saying, 'The land unto which ye go to possess it, is an unclean land with the filthiness of the people of the lands, with their abominations, which have filled it from one end to another with their uncleanness. Now therefore give not your daughters unto their sons, neither take their daughters unto your sons, nor seek their peace or their wealth forever, that ye may be strong, and eat the good of the land, and leave it for an inheritance to your children forever.' And after all that is come upon us for our evil deeds, and for our great trespass, seeing that thou our God hast punished us less than our iniquities deserve, and hast given us such deliverance as this, should we again break thy commandments, and join in affinity with the people of these abominations? Wouldest not thou be angry with us till thou hadst consumed us, so that there should be no remnant nor escaping?

"O LORD God of Israel, thou art righteous: for we remain yet escaped, as it is this day. Behold, we are before thee in our trespasses; for we cannot stand before thee because of this."

—Ezra 9.

THE PENITENT ASSEMBLY: "WE HAVE TRESPASSED AGAINST OUR GOD"

Now when Ezra had prayed, and when he had confessed, weeping and casting himself down before the house of God, there assembled unto him out of Israel a very great congregation of men and women and children; for the people wept very sore.

And Shechaniah, the son of Jehiel, one of the sons of Elam, answered and said unto Ezra, "We have trespassed against our God, and have taken strange wives of the people of the land; yet now there is hope in Israel concerning this thing. Now therefore let us make a covenant with our God to put away all the wives, and such as are born of them, according to the counsel of my lord, and of those that tremble at the commandment of our God; and let it be done according to the law. Arise; for this matter belongeth unto thee; we also will be with thee; be of good courage, and do it."

Then arose Ezra, and made the chief priests, the Levites, and all Israel, to swear that they should do according to this word. And they sware.

Then Ezra rose up from before the house of God, and went into the chamber of Johanan, the son of Eliashib; and when he came thither, he did eat no bread, nor drink water; for he mourned because of the transgression of them that had been carried away. And they made proclamation throughout Judah and Jerusalem unto all the children of the captivity, that they should gather themselves together unto Jerusalem; and that whosoever would not come within three days, according to the counsel of the princes and the elders, all his substance should be forfeited, and himself separated from the congregation of those that had been carried away.

THE COVENANT OF REFORM

Then all the men of Judah and Benjamin gathered themselves together unto Jerusalem within three days. It was the ninth month, on the twentieth day of the month; and all the people sat in the street of the house of God, trembling because of this matter, and for the great rain.

And Ezra, the priest, stood up, and said unto them,

"Ye have transgressed, and have taken strange wives to increase the trespass of Israel. Now therefore make confession unto the LORD God of your fathers, and do his pleasure; and separate yourselves from the people of the land, and from the strange wives."

Then all the congregation answered and said with a loud voice, "As thou hast said, so must we do. But the people are many, and it is a time of much rain, and we are not able to stand without, neither is this a work of one day or two; for we are many that have transgressed in this thing. Let now our rulers of all the congregation stand, and let all them which have taken strange wives in our cities come at appointed times, and with them the elders of every city, and the judges thereof, until the fierce wrath of our God for this matter be turned from us."

And the children of the captivity did so. And Ezra, the priest, with certain chief of the fathers, after the house of their fathers, and all of them by their names, were separated, and sat down in the first day of the tenth month to examine the matter. And they made an end with all the men that had taken strange wives by the first day of the first month. —Ezra 10:1-17.

The Book of Ezra closes with the names of more than a hundred men, some of whom were priests and Levites and temple officials, who had married foreigners. The wives and their children were sent away. It must have been a heart-breaking time, for Ezra no less than for others; but it was done because they believed it was the right thing to do.

Nehemiah

After the rebuilding of the temple, there was a period of discouragement and apathy on the part of the returned exiles. The vigorous peoples on every side were pressing in, taking the best locations, preventing the independent development of the nation. While trade was beginning to revive, the walls of Jerusalem were broken down and the city was defenseless. At this crisis, there came a man who must be numbered among the great men of the history of the Hebrew people, Nehemiah, the builder.

Nehemiah was cupbearer to Artaxerxes. He heard from his relative, who had returned from Jerusalem, how desolate was the condition of the city. For four months he grieved, until the king noticed his sadness and made a kindly inquiry about it. Nehemiah poured out his heart in appeal to be permitted to return and rebuild the city of his fathers. Not only was the request freely granted but the king furnished an escort and building material.

The story of the rebuilding is simply but dramatically told:— the night survey of the walls, the resolute overcoming of difficulties, indifference within and opposition without. They came up from the neighboring villages and stood about and made fun of Nehemiah. "A great wall you're building!" they said. "A fox could knock it over." But still the walls on their massive foundations rose higher and higher. Hostility became more active and violent. Nehemiah ordered his laborers to work, sword in one hand, tools in the other. "So we built the wall." At last it was done and Jerusalem was again a city, a place of importance as no town could be without an enclosing defense. The walls were built and the future of the nation insured, because of the patient courage, the steadfast, indomitable will of one patient, simple-hearted, heroic man.

The words of Nehemiah, the son of Hachaliah.

NEHEMIAH RECEIVES A SAD REPORT FROM JERUSALEM

AND it came to pass in the month Chisleu, in the twentieth year, as I was in Shushan the palace, that Hanani, one of my brethren, came, he and certain men of Judah; and I asked them concerning the Jews that had escaped, which were left of the captivity, and concerning Jerusalem. And they said unto me, "The remnant that are left of the captivity there in the province are in great affliction and reproach: the wall of Jerusalem also is broken down, and the gates thereof are burned with fire."

NEHEMIAH'S PRAYER

And it came to pass, when I heard these words, that I sat down and wept, and mourned certain days, and fasted, and prayed before the God of heaven, and said, "I beseech thee, O LORD God of heaven, the great and terrible God, that keepeth covenant and mercy for them that love him and observe his commandments: let thine ear now be attentive, and thine eyes open, that thou mayest hear the prayer of thy servant, which I pray before thee now, day and night, for the children of Israel thy servants, and confess the sins of the children of Israel, which we have sinned against thee: both I and my father's house have sinned. We have dealt very corruptly against thee, and have not kept the commandments, nor the statutes, nor the judgments, which thou commandedst thy servant Moses. Remember, I beseech thee, the word that thou commandedst thy servant Moses, saying, 'If ye transgress, I will scatter you abroad among the nations: but if ye turn unto me, and keep

WOMEN WAILING FOR JERUSALEM

Photograph by W. A. Pottenger expressly for The Book of Life
This picture shows women at the wailing place of the Jews.

my commandments, and do them; though there were of you cast out unto the uttermost part of the heaven, yet will I gather them from thence and will bring them unto the place that I have chosen to set my name there.'

"Now these are thy servants and thy people, whom thou hast redeemed by thy great power, and by thy strong hand. O LORD, I beseech thee, let now thine ear be attentive to the prayer of thy servant, and to the prayer of thy servants, who desire to fear thy name: and prosper, I pray thee, thy servant this day, and grant him mercy in the sight of this man. For I was the king's cupbearer."

THE KING'S CUPBEARER MAKES A REQUEST

And it came to pass in the month Nisan, in the twentieth year of Artaxerxes, the king, that wine was before him: and I took up the wine, and gave it unto the king. Now I had not been beforetime sad in his presence.

Wherefore the king said unto me, "Why is thy countenance sad, seeing thou art not sick? This is nothing else but sorrow of heart."

Then I was very sore afraid, and said unto the king, "Let the king live forever: why should not my countenance be sad, when the city, the place of my fathers' sepulchers, lieth waste, and the gates thereof are consumed with fire?"

Then the king said unto me, "For what dost thou make request?" So I prayed to the God of heaven.

And I said unto the king, "If it please the king, and if thy servant have found favour in thy sight, that thou wouldest send me unto Judah, unto the city of my fathers' sepulchers, that I may build it."

And the king said unto me, (the queen also sitting by him,) "For how long shall thy journey be? And when wilt thou return?" So it pleased the king to send me; and I set him a time.

Moreover I said unto the king, "If it please the king, let letters be given me to the governors beyond the river, that they may convey me over till I come into Judah; and a letter unto Asaph, the keeper of the king's forest, that he may give me timber to make beams for the gates of the palace which appertained to the house, and for the wall of the city, and for the house that I shall enter into."

THE FAVOR OF THE KING

And the king granted me, according to the good hand of my God upon me.

Then I came to the governors beyond the river, and gave them the king's letters. Now the king had sent captains of the army and horsemen with me. When Sanballat, the Horonite, and Tobiah, the servant, the

Ammonite, heard of it, it grieved them exceedingly that there was come a man to seek the welfare of the children of Israel. — *Nehemiah 1; 2:1–10.*

Nehemiah's Work Begins

THE NIGHT SURVEY OF THE CITY

So I came to Jerusalem, and was there three days. And I arose in the night, I and some few men with me; neither told I any man what my God had put in my heart to do at Jerusalem: neither was there any beast with me, save the beast that I rode upon.

And I went out by night by the gate of the valley, even before the dragon well, and to the dung port, and viewed the walls of Jerusalem, which were broken down, and the gates thereof were consumed with fire. Then I went on to the gate of the fountain, and to the king's pool: but there was no place for the beast that was under me to pass. Then went I up in the night by the brook, and viewed the wall, and turned back, and entered by the gate of the valley, and so returned. And the rulers knew not whither I went, or what I did; neither had I as yet told it to the Jews, nor to the priests, nor to the nobles, nor to the rulers, nor to the rest that did the work.

Then said I unto them, "Ye see the distress that we are in, how Jerusalem lieth waste, and the gates thereof are burned with fire: come, and let us build up the wall of Jerusalem, that we be no more a reproach."

Then I told them of the hand of my God which was good upon me; as also the king's words that he had spoken unto me. And they said, "Let us rise up and build." So they strengthened their hands for this good work.

But when Sanballat, the Horonite, and Tobiah, the servant, the Ammonite, and Geshem, the Arabian, heard it, they laughed us to scorn, and despised us, and said, "What is this thing that ye do? Will ye rebel against the king?"

"WE WILL ARISE AND BUILD"

Then answered I them, and said unto them, "The God of heaven, he will prosper us; therefore we his servants will arise and build: but ye have no portion, nor right, nor memorial, in Jerusalem." —Nehemiah 2:11-20.

THE WALLS AND THE GATES OF THE CITY ARE REPAIRED

THE SHEEP GATE

Then Eliashib, the high priest, rose up with his brethren, the priests, and they builded the sheep gate; they sanctified it, and set up the doors of it; even unto the tower of Meah they sanctified it, unto the tower of Hananeel. And next unto him builded the men of Jericho. And next to them builded Zaccur, the son of Imri.

THE FISH GATE

But the fish gate did the sons of Hassenaah build, who also laid the beams thereof, and set up the doors thereof, the locks thereof, and the bars thereof. And next unto them repaired Meremoth, the son of Urijah, the son of Koz. And next unto them repaired Meshullam, the son of Berechiah, the son of Meshezabeel. And next unto them repaired Zadok, the son of Baana. And next unto them the Tekoites repaired; but their nobles put not their necks to the work of their LORD.

THE OLD GATE

Moreover the old gate repaired Jehoiada, the son of Paseah, and Meshullam, the son of Besodeiah; they laid the beams thereof, and set up the doors thereof, and the locks thereof, and the bars thereof. And next unto them repaired Melatiah, the Gibeonite, and Jadon, the Meronothite, the men of Gibeon, and of Mizpah, unto the throne of the governor on this side the river.

THE SONS OF THE GOLDSMITHS AND THE APOTHECARIES' GUILDS DO THEIR SHARE

Next unto him repaired Uzziel, the son of Harhaiah, of the goldsmiths. Next unto him also repaired Hananiah, the son of one of the apothecaries, and they fortified Jerusalem unto the broad wall. And next unto them repaired Rephaiah, the son of Hur, the ruler of the half part of Jerusalem. And next unto them repaired Jedaiah, the son of Harumaph, even over against his house. And next unto him repaired Hattush, the son of Hashabniah.

CYLINDER OF NABONIDUS, KING OF BABYLON

By courtesy of the British Museum, London

Inscribed with an account of the rebuilding of the temple of the Moon-god at Ur, on the site of an older temple which had been founded by the Kings Ur-Gur and Dungi about 2500 B.C. The text concludes with a prayer to the Moon-god on behalf of Nabonidus and of his eldest son Belshazzar.

THE TOWER OF THE FURNACES

Malchijah, the son of Harim, and Hashub, the son of Pahath-moab, repaired the other piece, and the tower of the furnaces. And next unto him repaired Shallum, the son of Halohesh, the ruler of the half part of Jerusalem, he and his daughters.

THE VALLEY GATE

The valley gate repaired Hanun, and the inhabitants of Zanoah; they built it, and set up the doors thereof, the locks thereof, and the bars thereof, and a thousand cubits on the wall unto the dung gate.

THE DUNG GATE

But the dung gate repaired Malchiah, the son of Rechab, the ruler of part of Beth-haccerem; he built it, and set up the doors thereof, the locks thereof, and the bars thereof.

THE GATE OF THE FOUNTAIN

But the gate of the fountain repaired Shallun, the son of Col-hozeh, the ruler of part of Mizpah; he built it, and covered it, and set up the doors thereof, the locks thereof, and the bars thereof, and the wall of the pool of Siloah by the king's garden, and unto the stairs that go down from the city of David.

THE WALL OVER AGAINST THE SEPULCHERS OF DAVID

After him repaired Nehemiah, the son of Azbuk, the ruler of the half part of Beth-zur, unto the place over against the sepulchers of David, and to the pool that was made, and unto the house of the mighty. After him repaired the Levites, Rehum, the son of Bani. Next unto him repaired Hashabiah, the ruler of the half part of Keilah, in his part. After him repaired their brethren, Bavai, the son of Henadad, the ruler of the half part of Keilah.

THE WALL GOING UP TO THE ARMORY

And next to him repaired Ezer, the son of Jeshua, the ruler of Mizpah, another piece over against the going up to the armoury at the turning of the wall. After him Baruch, the son of Zabbai, earnestly repaired the other piece, from the turning of the wall unto the door of the house of Eliashib, the high priest. After him repaired Meremoth, the son of Urijah, the son of Koz, another piece, from the door of the house of Eliashib even to the end of the house of Eliashib. And after him repaired the priests, the men of the plain.

EVERY MAN BUILDS THE WALL "AGAINST HIS OWN HOUSE"

After him repaired Benjamin and Hashub over against their house. After him repaired Azariah, the son of Maaseiah, the son of Ananiah, by his house. After him repaired Binnui, the son of Henadad, another piece, from the house of Azariah unto the turning of the wall, even unto the corner. Palal, the son of Uzai, over against the turning of the wall, and the tower which lieth out from the king's high house, that was by the court of the prison. After him Pedaiah, the son of Parosh. Moreover the Nethinims dwelt in Ophel, unto the place over against the water gate toward the east, and the tower that lieth out. After them the Tekoites repaired another piece, over against the great tower that lieth out, even unto the wall of Ophel.

THE HORSE GATE

From above the horse gate repaired the priests, every one over against his house. After them repaired

Zadok, the son of Immer, over against his house. After him repaired also Shemaiah, the son of Shechaniah, the keeper of the east gate. After him repaired Hananiah, the son of Shelemiah, and Hanun, the sixth son of Zalaph, another piece. After him repaired Meshullam, the son of Berechiah, over against his chamber. After him repaired Malchiah, the goldsmith's son, unto the place of the Nethinims, and of the merchants, over against the gate Miphkad, and to the going up of the corner.

THE SHEEP GATE

And between the going up of the corner unto the sheep gate repaired the goldsmiths and the merchants.

"A FOX WOULD BREAK DOWN THEIR STONE WALL"

But it came to pass, that when Sanballat heard that we builded the wall, he was wroth, and took great indignation, and mocked the Jews. And he spake before his brethren and the army of Samaria, and said, "What do these feeble Jews? Will they fortify themselves? Will they sacrifice? Will they make an end in a day? Will they revive the stones out of the heaps of the rubbish which are burned?"

Now Tobiah, the Ammonite, was by him, and he said, "Even that which they build, if a fox go up, he shall even break down their stone wall."

Hear, O our God; for we are despised: and turn their reproach upon their own head, and give them for a prey in the land of captivity: and cover not their iniquity, and let not their sin be blotted out from before thee: for they have provoked thee to anger before the builders.

"SO BUILT WE THE WALL, FOR THE PEOPLE HAD A MIND TO WORK"

So built we the wall; and all the wall was joined together unto the half thereof: for the people had a mind to work. —Nehemiah 3; 4:1-6.

THE ENEMY HINDERS THE WORK, BUT IT GOES ON

But it came to pass, that when Sanballat, and Tobiah, and the Arabians, and the Ammonites, and the Ashdodites, heard that the walls of Jerusalem were made up, and that the breaches began to be stopped, then they were very wroth, and conspired all of them together to come and to fight against Jerusalem, and to hinder it. Nevertheless we made our prayer unto our God, and set a watch against them day and night, because of them.

And Judah said, "The strength of the bearers of burdens is decayed, and there is much rubbish; so that we are not able to build the wall."

And our adversaries said, "They shall not know, neither see, till we come in the midst among them, and slay them, and cause the work to cease."

And it came to pass, that when the Jews which dwelt by them came, they said unto us ten times, "From all places whence ye shall return unto us they will be upon you."

THE PEOPLE WORK WITH THEIR WEAPONS AT HAND

Therefore set I in the lower places behind the wall, and on the higher places, I even set the people after their families with their swords, their spears, and their bows. And I looked, and rose up, and said unto the nobles, and to the rulers, and to the rest of the people, "Be not ye afraid of them: remember the LORD, which is great and terrible, and fight for your brethren, your sons, and your daughters, your wives, and your houses."

And it came to pass, when our enemies heard that it was known unto us, and God had brought their counsel to naught, that we returned all of us to the wall, every one unto his work. And it came to pass from that time forth, that the half of my servants wrought in the work, and the other half of them held both the spears, the shields, and the bows, and the habergeons; and the rulers were behind all the house of Judah. They which builded on the wall, and they that bare burdens, with those that laded, every one with one of his hands wrought in the work, and with the other hand held a weapon. For the builders, every one had his sword girded by his side, and so builded. And he that sounded the trumpet was by me.

And I said unto the nobles, and to the rulers, and to the rest of the people, "The work is great and large, and we are separated upon the wall, one far from another. In what place therefore ye hear the sound of the trumpet, resort ye thither unto us: our God shall fight for us."

NIGHT AND DAY THE WORK GOES ON

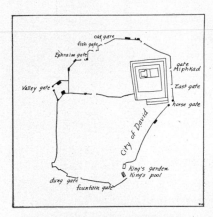

JERUSALEM OF NEHEMIAH

So we laboured in the work: and half of them held the spears from the rising of the morning till the stars appeared. Likewise at the same time said I unto the people, "Let every one with his servant lodge within Jerusalem, that in the night they may be a guard to us, and labour on the day." So neither I, nor my brethren, nor my servants, nor the men of the guard which followed me, none of us put off our clothes, saving that every one put them off for washing.   —Nehemiah 4:7-23.

THE PEOPLE ARE OPPRESSED

And there was a great cry of the people and of their wives against their brethren, the Jews. For there were

LIMESTONE SLAB

By courtesy of the British Museum, London

With votive inscription and a bearded figure which is probably that of Hammurabi, King of Babylon, sculptured in relief. It was dedicated to a goddess by a high official on behalf of the life of the king about 2200 B.C.

that said, "We, our sons, and our daughters, are many: therefore we take up corn for them, that we may eat, and live."

Some also there were that said, "We have mortgaged our lands, vineyards, and houses, that we might buy corn, because of the dearth."

There were also that said, "We have borrowed money for the king's tribute, and that upon our lands and vineyards. Yet now our flesh is as the flesh of our brethren, our children as their children: and, lo, we bring into bondage our sons and our daughters to be servants, and some of our daughters are brought unto bondage already: neither is it in our power to redeem them; for other men have our lands and vineyards."

NEHEMIAH CALLS A GREAT ASSEMBLY

And I was very angry when I heard their cry and these words. Then I consulted with myself, and I rebuked the nobles, and the rulers, and said unto them, "Ye exact usury, every one of his brother." And I set a great assembly against them.

And I said unto them, "We after our ability have redeemed our brethren, the Jews, which were sold unto the heathen; and will ye even sell your brethren or shall they be sold unto us?" Then held they their peace, and found nothing to answer.

Also I said, "It is not good that ye do: ought ye not to walk in the fear of our God because of the reproach of the heathen our enemies? I likewise, and my brethren, and my servants, might exact of them money and corn: I pray you, let us leave off this usury.

NEHEMIAH'S REFORM

"Restore, I pray you, to them, even this day, their lands, their vineyards, their oliveyards, and their houses, also the hundredth part of the money, and of the corn, the wine, and the oil, that ye exact of them."

Then said they, "We will restore them, and will require nothing of them; so will we do as thou sayest." Then I called the priests, and took an oath of them, that they should do according to this promise.

Also I shook my lap, and said, "So God shake out every man from his house, and from his labour, that performeth not this promise, even thus be he shaken out, and emptied."

And all the congregation said, "Amen," and praised the LORD. And the people did according to this promise.

NEHEMIAH WORKS WITHOUT THE PAY OF A GOVERNOR

Moreover from the time that I was appointed to be their governor in the land of Judah from the twentieth year even unto the two and thirtieth year of

THE GOLDEN GATE

Photograph by W. A. Pottenger expressly for The Book of Life

Artaxerxes, the king, that is, twelve years, I and my
brethren have not eaten the bread of the governor.
But the former governors that had been before me were
chargeable unto the people, and had taken of them bread
and wine, beside forty shekels of silver; yea, even their
servants bare rule over the people: but so did not I,
because of the fear of God. Yea, also I continued in the
work of this wall, neither bought we any land: and all
my servants were gathered thither unto the work. Moreover there were at my table an hundred and fifty of the
Jews and rulers, beside those that came unto us from
among the heathen that are about us. Now that which
was prepared for me daily was one ox and six choice
sheep; also fowls were prepared for me, and once in ten
days store of all sorts of wine: yet for all this required
not I the bread of the governor, because the bondage
was heavy upon this people.

Think upon me, my God, for good, according to all
that I have done for this people.   —Nehemiah 5.

THE ENMITY OF SANBALLAT AND GESHEM

Now it came to pass, when Sanballat, and Tobiah, and Geshem, the Arabian, and the rest of our enemies, heard that I had builded the wall, and that there was no breach left therein; (though at that time I had not set up the doors upon the gates;) that Sanballat and Geshem sent unto me, saying, "Come, let us meet together in some one of the villages in the plain of Ono." But they thought to do me mischief.

"I AM DOING A GREAT WORK; I CANNOT COME DOWN"

And I sent messengers unto them, saying, "I am doing a great work, so that I cannot come down: why should the work cease, whilst I leave it, and come down to you?" Yet they sent unto me four times after this sort; and I answered them after the same manner.

SANBALLAT'S THREAT

Then sent Sanballat his servant unto me in like manner the fifth time with an open letter in his hand; wherein was written, "It is reported among the heathen, and Gashmu saith it, that thou and the Jews think to rebel: for which cause thou buildest the wall, that thou mayest be their king, according to these words. And thou hast also appointed prophets to preach of thee at Jerusalem, saying, 'There is a king in Judah': and now shall it be reported to the king according to these words. Come now therefore, and let us take counsel together."

Then I sent unto him, saying, "There are no such things done as thou sayest, but thou feignest them out of thine own heart."

For they all made us afraid, saying, "Their hands shall be weakened from the work, that it be not done." Now therefore, O God, strengthen my hands.

OLD ARCHES IN THE TEMPLE AREA
Photograph by W. A. Pottenger expressly for The Book of Life

THE EXTERIOR OF THE
GOLDEN GATE

Photograph by W. A. Pottenger

STRATAGEMS OF THE ENEMY

Afterward I came unto the house of Shemaiah, the son of Delaiah, the son of Mehetabeel, who was shut up; and he said, "Let us meet together in the house of God, within the temple, and let us shut the doors of the temple: for they will come to slay thee; yea, in the night will they come to slay thee."

"SHOULD SUCH A MAN AS I FLEE?"

And I said, "Should such a man as I flee? And who is there, that, being as

I am, would go into the temple to save his life? I will not go in." And, lo, I perceived that God had not sent him; but that he pronounced this prophecy against me: for Tobiah and Sanballat had hired him. Therefore was he hired, that I should be afraid, and do so, and sin, and that they might have matter for an evil report, that they might reproach me.

My God, think thou upon Tobiah and Sanballat according to these their works, and on the prophetess, Noadiah, and the rest of the prophets, that would have put me in fear. —Nehemiah 6:1–14.

The Wall Is Finished and There Is a Great Meeting of All the People

So the wall was finished in the twenty and fifth day of the month Elul, in fifty and two days. And it came to pass, that when all our enemies heard thereof, and all the heathen that were about us saw these things, they were much cast down in their own eyes: for they perceived that this work was wrought of our God.

Moreover in those days the nobles of Judah sent many letters unto Tobiah, and the letters of Tobiah came unto them. For there were many in Judah sworn unto him, because he was the son-in-law of Shechaniah, the son of Arah; and his son, Johanan, had taken the daughter of Meshullam, the son of Berechiah. Also they reported his good deeds before me, and uttered my words to him. And Tobiah sent letters to put me in fear.

Now it came to pass, when the wall was built, and I had set up the doors, and the porters and the singers and the Levites were appointed, that I gave my brother Hanani, and Hananiah, the ruler of the palace, charge over Jerusalem: for he was a faithful man, and feared God above many.

And I said unto them, "Let not the gates of Jerusalem be opened until the sun be hot; and while they stand by, let them shut the doors and bar them: and appoint watches of the inhabitants of Jerusalem, every one in his watch, and every one to be over against his house."

Now the city was large and great: but the people were few therein, and the houses were not builded.

And my God put into mine heart to gather together the nobles and the rulers, and the people, that they might be reckoned by genealogy.

The whole congregation together was forty and two thousand three hundred and threescore, beside their manservants and their maidservants, of whom there were seven thousand three hundred thirty and seven: and they had two hundred forty and five singing men and singing women. Their horses numbered seven hundred thirty and six: their mules, two hundred forty and five:

WALL OF JERUSALEM
Photograph by Professor Lewis Bayles Paton
The great stones in the base of the wall are probably foundation stones of Herod's Temple.

their camels, four hundred thirty and five: six thousand seven hundred and twenty asses.

THE GIFTS OF THE PEOPLE

And some of the chief of the fathers gave unto the work. The Tirshatha gave to the treasure a thousand drams of gold, fifty basons, five hundred and thirty priests' garments. And some of the chief of the fathers gave to the treasure of the work twenty thousand drams of gold, and two thousand and two hundred pound of silver. And that which the rest of the people gave was twenty thousand drams of gold, and two thousand pound of silver, and threescore and seven priests' garments. So the priests, and the Levites, and the porters, and the singers, and some of the people, and the Nethinims, and all Israel, dwelt in their cities; and when the seventh month came, the children of Israel were in their cities.

EZRA, THE SCRIBE, STANDS IN A WOODEN PULPIT AND READS THE BOOK OF THE LAW

And all the people gathered themselves together as one man into the street that was before the water gate; and they spake unto Ezra, the scribe, to bring the book of the law of Moses, which the LORD had commanded to Israel. And Ezra, the priest, brought the law before the congregation both of men and women, and all that could hear with understanding, upon the first day of the seventh month. And he read therein before the street that was before the water gate from the morning until midday, before the men and the women, and those that could understand; and the ears of all the people were attentive unto the book of the law.

And Ezra, the scribe, stood upon a pulpit of wood, which they had made for the purpose; and beside him

THE GOLDEN GATE OF JERUSALEM
Photograph by W. A. Pottenger expressly for The Book of Life
This is an unusual view of the side of the Golden Gate.

stood Mattithiah, and Shema, and Anaiah, and Urijah, and Hilkiah, and Maaseiah, on his right hand; and on his left hand, Pedaiah, and Mishael, and Malchiah, and Hashum, and Hashbadana, Zechariah, and Meshullam. And Ezra opened the book in the sight of all the people; (for he was above all the people;) and when he opened it, all the people stood up: and Ezra blessed the LORD, the great God. And all the people answered, "Amen, Amen," with lifting up their hands: and they bowed their heads, and worshiped the LORD with their faces to the ground. Also Jeshua, and Bani, and Sherebiah, Jamin, Akkub, Shabbethai, Hodijah, Maaseiah, Kelita, Azariah, Jozabad, Hanan, Pelaiah, and the Levites, caused the people to understand the law: and the people stood in their place.

EZRA READS THE BOOK DISTINCTLY AND GIVES THE SENSE

So they read in the book in the law of God distinctly, and gave the sense, and caused them to understand the reading.

And Nehemiah, which is the Tirshatha, and Ezra, the priest, the scribe, and the Levites that taught the people, said unto all the people, "This day is holy unto the LORD your God; mourn not, nor weep." For all the people wept, when they heard the words of the law.

Then he said unto them, "Go your way, eat the fat, and drink the sweet, and send portions unto them for whom nothing is prepared: for this day is holy unto our LORD: neither be ye sorry; for the joy of the LORD is your strength."

"NEITHER BE YE SORRY"

So the Levites stilled all the people, saying, "Hold your peace, for the day is holy; neither be ye grieved." And all the people went their way to eat, and to drink, and to send portions, and to make great mirth, because they had understood the words that were declared unto them. —Nehemiah 6:15–7:5a and 7:66–8:12.

THE FEAST OF TABERNACLES

And on the second day were gathered together the chief of the fathers of all the people, the priests, and the Levites, unto Ezra, the scribe, even to understand the words of the law. And they found written in the law which the LORD commanded by Moses, that the children of Israel should dwell in booths in the feast of the seventh month: and that they should publish and proclaim in all their cities, and in Jerusalem, saying, "Go forth unto the mount, and fetch olive branches, and pine branches, and myrtle branches, and palm branches, and branches of thick trees, to make booths, as it is written."

So the people went forth, and brought them, and made themselves booths, every one upon the roof of his house, and in their courts, and in the courts of the house of God,

WEST WALLS OF JERUSALEM

Photograph by W. A. Pottenger expressly for The Book of Life

The modern walls of Jerusalem were built in 1542. They form an irregular quadrangle about two and one-half miles in circuit with seven gates and thirty-four towers.

"Besides the earthquakes, the city has endured nearly twenty sieges and assaults of the utmost severity—some involving considerable damage, others a total destruction of her walls and buildings; almost twenty more blockades or military occupations, with the wreck or dilapidation of prominent edifices; about eighteen reconstructions, embellishments and large extensions, the additions of suburbs, and the abandonment of parts of the habited area."

and in the street of the water gate, and in the street of the gate of Ephraim. And all the congregation of them that were come again out of the captivity made booths, and sat under the booths: for since the days of Joshua, the son of Nun, unto that day had not the children of Israel done so. And there was very great gladness. Also day by day, from the first day unto the last day, he read in the book of the law of God. And they kept the feast seven days; and on the eighth day was a solemn assembly according unto the manner.

THE CONFESSION OF THE ISRAELITES

Now in the twenty and fourth day of this month the children of Israel were assembled with fasting, and with sackclothes, and earth upon them. And the seed of Israel separated themselves from all strangers, and stood and confessed their sins, and the iniquities of their fathers. And they stood up in their place, and read in the book of the law of the LORD their God one fourth part of the day; and another fourth part they confessed, and worshiped the LORD their God.

Then stood up upon the stairs, of the Levites, Jeshua, and Bani, Kadmiel, Shebaniah, Bunni, Sherebiah, Bani, and Chenani, and cried with a loud voice unto the LORD their God.

THE STORY OF GOD'S DEALING WITH THE NATIONS IS REPEATED

Then the Levites, Jeshua, and Kadmiel, Bani, Hashabniah, Sherebiah, Hodijah, Shebaniah, and Pethahiah, said, "Stand up and bless the LORD your God forever and ever: and blessed be thy glorious name, which is exalted above all blessing and praise. Thou, even thou, art LORD alone; thou hast made heaven, the heaven of heavens, with all their host, the earth, and all things that are therein, the seas, and all that is therein, and thou preservest them all; and the host of heaven worshipeth thee. Thou art the LORD the God, who didst choose Abram, and broughtest him forth out of Ur of the Chaldees, and gavest him the name of Abraham; and foundest his heart faithful before thee, and madest a covenant with him to give the land of the Canaanites, the Hittites, the Amorites, and the Perizzites, and the Jebusites, and the Girgashites, to give it, I say, to his seed, and hast performed thy words; for thou art righteous: and didst see the affliction of our fathers in Egypt, and heardest their cry by the Red Sea; and shewedst signs and wonders upon Pharaoh, and on all his servants, and on all the people of his land: for thou knewest that they dealt proudly against them. So didst thou get thee a name, as it is this day.

"And thou didst divide the sea before them, so that they went through the midst of the sea on the dry land; and their persecutors thou threwest into the deeps, as a stone into the mighty waters. Moreover thou leddest them in the day by a cloudy pillar; and in the night by a pillar of fire, to give them light in the way wherein they should go. Thou camest down also upon Mount Sinai, and spakest with them from heaven, and gavest them right judgments, and true laws, good statutes and commandments: and madest known unto them thy holy Sabbath, and commandedst them precepts, statutes, and laws, by the hand of Moses, thy servant: and gavest them bread from heaven for their hunger, and broughtest forth water for them out of the rock for their thirst, and promisedst them that they should go in to possess the land which thou hadst sworn to give them.

"But they and our fathers dealt proudly, and hardened their necks, and hearkened not to thy commandments, and refused to obey, neither were mindful of thy wonders that thou didst among them; but hardened their necks, and in their rebellion appointed a captain to return to their bondage: but thou art a God ready to pardon, gracious and merciful, slow to anger, and of great kindness, and forsookest them not.

"Yea, when they had made them a molten calf, and said, 'This is thy God that brought thee up out of Egypt,' and had wrought great provocations; yet thou in thy manifold mercies forsookest them not in the wilderness: the pillar of the cloud departed not from them by day, to lead them in the way; neither the pillar of fire by night, to shew them light, and the way wherein they should go.

"Thou gavest also thy good spirit to instruct them, and withheldest not thy manna from their mouth, and gavest them water for their thirst. Yea, forty years didst thou sustain them in the wilderness, so that they lacked nothing; their clothes waxed not old, and their feet swelled not. Moreover thou gavest them kingdoms and nations, and didst divide them into corners: so they possessed the land of Sihon, and the land of the king of Heshbon, and the land of Og, King of Bashan.

"Their children also multipliedst thou as the stars of heaven, and broughtest them into the land, concerning which thou hadst promised to their fathers, that they should go in to possess it. So the children went in and possessed the land, and thou subduedst before them the inhabitants of the land, the Canaanites, and gavest them into their hands, with their kings, and the people of the land, that they might do with them as they would. And they took strong cities, and a fat land, and possessed houses full of all goods, wells digged, vineyards, and oliveyards, and fruit trees in abundance: so they did eat, and were filled, and became fat, and delighted themselves in thy great goodness. Nevertheless they were disobedient, and rebelled against thee, and cast thy law behind their backs, and slew thy prophets which testified against them to turn them to thee, and they wrought great provocations.

"Therefore thou deliveredst them into the hand of their enemies, who vexed them: and in the time of their trouble, when they cried unto thee, thou heardest them from heaven; and according to thy manifold mercies thou gavest them saviours, who saved them out of the hand of their enemies. But after they had rest, they did evil again before thee: therefore leftest thou them in the hand of their enemies, so that they had the dominion over them: yet when they returned, and cried unto thee, thou heardest them from heaven; and many times didst thou deliver them according to thy mercies; and testifiedst against them, that thou mightest bring them again unto thy law: yet they dealt proudly, and hearkened not unto thy commandments, but sinned against thy judgments, (which if a man do, he shall live in them;) and withdrew the shoulder, and hardened their neck, and would not hear.

"Yet many years didst thou forbear them, and testifiedst against them by thy spirit in thy prophets: yet would they not give ear: therefore gavest thou them into the hand of the people of the lands. Nevertheless for thy great mercies' sake thou didst not utterly consume them, nor forsake them; for thou art a gracious and merciful God.

"Now therefore, our God, the great, the mighty, and the terrible God, who keepest covenant and mercy, let not all the trouble seem little before thee, that hath come upon us, on our kings, on our princes, and on our priests, and on our prophets, and on our fathers, and on all thy people, since the time of the kings of Assyria unto this day. Howbeit thou art just in all that is brought upon us; for thou hast done right, but we have done wickedly: neither have our kings, our princes, our priests, nor our fathers, kept thy law, nor hearkened unto thy commandments and thy testimonies, wherewith thou didst testify against them. For they have not served thee in their kingdom, and in thy great goodness that thou gavest them, and in the large and fat land which thou gavest before them, neither turned they from their wicked works.

"Behold, we are servants this day, and for the land that thou gavest unto our fathers to eat the fruit thereof and the good thereof, behold, we are servants in it: and it yieldeth much increase unto the kings whom thou hast set over us because of our sins: also they have dominion over our bodies, and over our cattle, at their pleasure, and we are in great distress.

"And because of all this we make a sure covenant, and write it; and our princes, Levites, and priests seal unto it." — Nehemiah 8:13–9:38

The Covenant with the Lord:
Pledges of Offerings

And the people, the priests, the Levites, the porters, the singers, the Nethinims, and all they that had separated themselves from the people of the lands unto the law of God, their wives, their sons, and their daughters, every one having knowledge, and having understanding; they clave to their brethren, their nobles, and entered into a curse, and into an oath, to walk in God's law, which was given by Moses, the servant of God, and to observe and do all the commandments of the LORD our LORD, and his judgments and his statutes; and that we would not give our daughters unto the people of the land, nor take their daughters for our sons; and if the people of the land bring ware or any victuals on the Sabbath Day to sell, that we would not buy it of them on the Sabbath, or on the holy day: and that we would leave the seventh year, and the exaction of every debt.

THE OFFERINGS SHALL BE BROUGHT

Also we made ordinances for us, to charge ourselves yearly with the third part of a shekel for the service of the house of our God; for the shewbread, and for the continual meat offering, and for the continual burnt offering, of the Sabbaths, of the new moons, for the set feasts, and for the holy things, and for the sin offerings to make an atonement for Israel, and for all the work of the house of our God.

And we cast the lots among the priests, the Levites, and the people, for the wood offering, to bring it into the house of our God, after the houses of our fathers, at times appointed year by year, to burn upon the altar of the LORD our God, as it is written in the law: and to bring the firstfruits of our ground, and the firstfruits of all fruit of all trees, year by year, unto the house of the LORD: also the firstborn of our sons, and of our cattle, as it is written in the law, and the firstlings of our herds and of our flocks to bring to the house of our God, unto the priests that minister in the house of our God: and that we should bring the firstfruits of our dough, and our offerings, and the fruit of all manner of trees, of wine and of oil, unto the priests, to the chambers of the house of our God; and the tithes of our ground unto the Levites, that the same Levites might have the tithes in all the cities of our tillage. And the priest, the son of Aaron, shall be with the Levites, when the Levites take tithes: and the Levites shall bring up the tithe of the tithes unto the house of our God, to the chambers, into the treasure house. For the children of Israel and the children of Levi shall bring the offering of the corn, of the new wine, and the oil, unto the chambers, where are the vessels of the sanctuary, and the priests that minister, and the porters, and the singers: and we will not forsake the house of our God.

And the rulers of the people dwelt at Jerusalem: the rest of the people also cast lots, to bring one of ten to dwell in Jerusalem the holy city, and nine parts to dwell in other cities. And the people blessed all the men, that willingly offered themselves to dwell at Jerusalem.

— Nehemiah 10:28–11:2.

The Dedication of the Wall

And at the dedication of the wall of Jerusalem they sought the Levites out of all their places, to bring them to Jerusalem, to keep the dedication with gladness, both with thanksgivings, and with singing, with cymbals, psalteries, and with harps. And the sons of the singers gathered themselves together, both out of the plain country round about Jerusalem, and from the villages of Netophathi: also from the house of Gilgal, and out of the fields of Geba and Azmaveth: for the singers had builded them villages round about Jerusalem. And the priests and the Levites purified themselves, and purified the people, and the gates, and the wall. Then I brought up the princes of Judah upon the wall, and appointed two great companies of them that gave thanks, whereof one went on the right hand upon the wall toward the dung gate.

And the other company of them that gave thanks went over against them, and I after them, and the half of the people upon the wall, from beyond the tower of the furnaces even unto the broad wall; and from above the gate of Ephraim, and above the old gate, and above the fish gate, and the tower of Hananeel, and the tower of Meah, even unto the sheep gate: and they stood still in the prison gate. So stood the two companies of them that gave thanks in the house of God, and I, and the half of the rulers with me and the priests. And the singers sang loud, with Jezrahiah, their overseer. Also that day they offered great sacrifices, and rejoiced: for God had made them rejoice with great joy: the wives also and the children rejoiced: so that the joy of Jerusalem was heard even afar off.

And at that time were some appointed over the chambers for the treasures, for the offerings, for the firstfruits, and for the tithes, to gather into them out of the fields of the cities the portions of the law for the priests and Levites: for Judah rejoiced for the priests and for the Levites that waited. And both the singers and the porters kept the ward of their God, and the ward of the purification, according to the commandment of David, and of Solomon, his son. For in the days of David and Asaph of old there were chief of the singers, and songs of praise and thanksgiving unto God. And all Israel in the days of Zerubbabel, and in the days of Nehemiah, gave the portions of the singers and the porters, every day his portion: and they sanctified holy things unto the Levites; and the Levites sanctified them unto the children of Aaron. —Nehemiah 12:27-31; 12:38-47.

REFORMS

On that day they read in the book of Moses in the audience of the people; and therein was found written, that the Ammonite and the Moabite should not come into the congregation of God forever; because they met not the children of Israel with bread and with water, but hired Balaam against them, that he should curse them: howbeit our God turned the curse into a blessing. Now it came to pass, when they had heard the law, that they separated from Israel all the mixed multitude.

And before this, Eliashib, the priest, having the oversight of the chamber of the house of our God, was allied unto Tobiah: and he had prepared for him a great chamber, where aforetime they laid the meat offerings, the frankincense, and the vessels, and the tithes of the corn, the new wine, and the oil, which was commanded to be given to the Levites, and the singers, and the porters; and the offerings of the priests. But in all this time was not I at Jerusalem: for in the two and thirtieth

year of Artaxerxes, King of Babylon, came I unto the
king, and after certain days obtained I leave of the king.

THE HOUSEHOLD STUFF OF TOBIAH IS PUT OUT
OF THE CHAMBER

And I came to Jerusalem, and understood of the evil
that Eliashib did for Tobiah, in preparing him a chamber
in the courts of the house of God. And it grieved me sore:
therefore I cast forth all the household stuff of Tobiah
out of the chamber. Then I commanded, and they
cleansed the chambers: and thither brought I again the
vessels of the house of God, with the meat offering and
the frankincense.

And I perceived that the portions of the Levites had
not been given them: for the Levites and the singers,
that did the work, were fled every one to his field.

Then contended I with the rulers, and said, "Why
is the house of God forsaken?" And I gathered them
together, and set them in their place. Then brought
all Judah the tithe of the corn and the new wine and the
oil unto the treasuries. And I made treasurers over the
treasuries, Shelemiah, the priest, and Zadok, the scribe,
and of the Levites, Pedaiah: and next to them was
Hanan, the son of Zaccur, the son of Mattaniah: for
they were counted faithful, and their office was to dis-
tribute unto their brethren.

Remember me, O my God, concerning this, and wipe
not out my good deeds that I have done for the house of
my God, and for the offices thereof.

NEHEMIAH FORBIDS WORK AND TRADE ON THE SABBATH

In those days saw I in Judah some treading wine-
presses on the Sabbath, and bringing in sheaves, and
lading asses; as also wine, grapes, and figs, and all

manner of burdens, which they brought into Jerusalem on the Sabbath Day: and I testified against them in the day wherein they sold victuals. There dwelt men of Tyre also therein, which brought fish, and all manner of ware, and sold on the Sabbath unto the children of Judah, and in Jerusalem.

Then I contended with the nobles of Judah, and said unto them, "What evil thing is this that ye do, and profane the Sabbath Day? Did not your fathers thus, and did not our God bring all this evil upon us, and upon this city? Yet ye bring more wrath upon Israel by profaning the Sabbath."

And it came to pass, that when the gates of Jerusalem began to be dark before the Sabbath, I commanded that the gates should be shut, and charged that they should not be opened till after the Sabbath: and some of my servants set I at the gates, that there should no burden be brought in on the Sabbath Day. So the merchants and sellers of all kind of ware lodged without Jerusalem once or twice.

Then I testified against them, and said unto them, "Why lodge ye about the wall? If ye do so again, I will lay hands on you." From that time forth came they no more on the Sabbath.

And I commanded the Levites that they should cleanse themselves, and that they should come and keep the gates, to sanctify the Sabbath day.

Remember me, O my God, concerning this also, and spare me according to the greatness of thy mercy.

NEHEMIAH FORBIDS MIXED MARRIAGES

In those days also saw I Jews that had married wives of Ashdod, of Ammon, and of Moab: and their children spake half in the speech of Ashdod, and could not speak in the Jews' language, but according to the language of each people.

And I contended with them, and cursed them, and smote certain of them, and plucked off their hair, and made them swear by God, saying, "Ye shall not give your daughters unto their sons, nor take their daughters unto your sons, or for yourselves. Did not Solomon, King of Israel, sin by these things? Yet among many nations was there no king like him, who was beloved of his God, and God made him king over all Israel: nevertheless even him did outlandish women cause to sin. Shall we then hearken unto you to do all this great evil, to transgress against our God in marrying strange wives?"

And one of the sons of Joiada, the son of Eliashib, the high priest, was son-in-law to Sanballat, the Horonite: therefore I chased him from me.

Remember them, O my God, because they have defiled the priesthood, and the covenant of the priesthood, and of the Levites. Thus cleansed I them from all strangers, and appointed the wards of the priests and the Levites, every one in his business; and for the wood offering, at times appointed, and for the firstfruits.

Remember me, O my God, for good.   — Nehemiah 13.